# Critical Essays On Sherwood Anderson

# Critical Essays On Sherwood Anderson

## David D. Anderson

G. K. Hall & Company • Boston, Massachusetts

Library of Congress Cataloging in Publication Data
Main entry under title:
Critical essays on Sherwood Anderson

  (Critical essays on American literature)
  Includes index.
  1. Anderson, Sherwood, 1876-1941—Criticism and inter-
pretation—Addresses, essays, lectures. I. Anderson,
David D. II. Series.
PS3501.N4Z57          813'.52          81-6815
ISBN 0-8161-8421-6                     AACR2

*This publication is printed on permanent/durable acid-free paper*
MANUFACTURED IN THE UNITED STATES OF AMERICA

# CRITICAL ESSAYS ON AMERICAN LITERATURE

This series seeks to collect the most important previously published criticism on writers and topics in American literature along with, in various volumes, original essays, interviews, bibliographies, letters, manuscript sections, and other materials brought to public attention for the first time. David D. Anderson's volume on Sherwood Anderson admirably fulfills these expectations. In addition to reprinted essays by such notable writers and critics as F. Scott Fitzgerald, Carl Van Doren, Newton Arvin, and Norman Holmes Pearson, the volume contains a substantial introduction by David D. Anderson and original articles by Roger J. Bresnahan, Nancy Bunge, and Marilyn Judith Atlas. In addition, it contains three previously unpublished items by Sherwood Anderson, two letters to Sidney Hook and a brief piece entitled "Buckeye Blues." We are confident that this collection will make a permanent and significant contribution to American literary study.

JAMES NAGEL, GENERAL EDITOR

*Northeastern University*

*For Pat*
*and*
*For Eleanor*

# CONTENTS

# INTRODUCTION

## Sherwood Anderson
## and the Critics

When Sherwood Anderson died on March 8, 1941, his literary reputation was characterized by a curious dichotomy and a paradox, both of which were to continue for more than a quarter century after his death, and in some respects they are with us yet. The critical articles of faith in 1941 had relegated Anderson to a minor position in American literary history and had discounted the influence he had earlier presumably exerted, together with whatever promise he had presumably failed to fulfill. The critical books were closed on Anderson and the literary histories closed to him at that point, concluding that he had written earnestly if not well; he had written a handful of fine short stories, a number of mediocre or bad novels, some inept journalism, and that was all.

Such a collective critical judgement was not sudden, nor was it much different than Anderson had anticipated; he had lived with growing critical disfavor, particularly from the critics of the influential Eastern journals, since the mid-1920s, for more than half, in other words, of the creative life that had begun in 1914, when, at thirty-eight, he published his first short story in *Harper's Magazine* in July of that year. By 1919, with the publication of *Winesburg, Ohio*, Anderson had become a major, if controversial, contemporary literary figure. In 1921, after the publication of *Poor White*, he won the first *Dial* Prize, and in that year he was enshrined in the Eastern critics' favorite interpretation of the literature that was coming out of the Midwestern heartland. As Carl Van Doren insisted in the *Nation*[1] that year, Edgar Lee Masters, Sinclair Lewis, and Sherwood Anderson were, in effect, rejecting through revolt the Midwestern villages of their beginnings, as well as the culture and mores of their youth, as they sought a richer, more sophisticated urban fulfillment.

So attractive was this critical view to many who either had fled the Midwest, as had Van Doren, or had never known it, that "the revolt from the village" became the most widespread and most widely accepted literary metaphor of the Midwest. So pervasive was this view by the middle of the decade of the twenties that in his study of that period, published in 1955, the late Frederick Hoffman called it "a metaphor of abuse."[2] Both Van Doren's and Hoffman's interpretations have been so widely and uncritically accepted that they prevail even yet, unfortunately among people who should know better. In 1969, for example, Anthony Channell Hilfer essentially reinforced Van Doren's original misinterpretation.[3]

1

Both Hoffman and Hilfer should have seen, as others were indeed beginning to conclude at the time, that the phrase was an over-simplified generalization that was not supported by the facts. Not only had Van Doren and his contemporaries failed to see the affection and respect with which Anderson and his contemporaries regarded their people in Winesburg, in Spoon River, in Gopher Prairie, but those same critics did not perceive, in the decade that followed, what those or other Midwesterners were actually doing in their works or what they were actually saying about the people and the towns from whence they came. And too many academic critics have continued to follow that clearly-marked path to nowhere. This unnoticed reality has been discussed at length in respect to Anderson and Louis Bromfield in my "The Search for a Living Past" in *Sherwood Anderson: Centennial Studies* (1976).[4] That essay also reveals a great deal about the deteriorating relationship between Anderson and the critics as the decade of the 1920s advanced.

The years between 1922 and 1927 were for Anderson a period of intense emotional and psychological introspection as he sought to assess the meaning of his life and to determine the nature of his identity. Characterized by abandonment of Chicago, advertising, and his second wife, Tennessee Mitchell, by wandering South and East, with periods of residence in New York and New Orleans, these years were also characterized by literary work that was intensely personal and symbolically if not literally autobiographical. The period ended with his determination to settle permanently in the hill country of western Virginia.

These years were very productive for Anderson, as much because of his personal crisis as in spite of it; he published *Many Marriages* (1923), a long attempt to explain what was not yet clear to him; the first-rate collection of stories, *Horses and Men* (1923); his rejection of bohemia in *Dark Laughter* (1925); and his three volumes of pseudoautobiography: *A Story Teller's Story* (1924) and *Tar: A Midwest Childhood* and *Sherwood Anderson's Notebook* (both 1926).

This introspective, productive period affected Anderson in two ways: personally, it marked his coming to terms with his identity as a writer-craftsman and with the image of his father that had haunted him since his youth, and it marked his rediscovery and reaffirmation of the values and relationships of his Midwestern youth, still extant in the Virginia hill country. By 1927 he had determined to remain there, and he bought and for two years edited the two weekly papers in Marion.

As personally satisfying as this period turned out to be for Anderson, it marked the end of his romance, based on a misconception, with the Eastern critics, and the beginning of the deterioration of his literary reputation, a deterioration that continued almost without interruption until his death and after. The year 1927 also saw, in another way, Anderson's coming of age as a writer; it saw the publication of the first two books about him—and the last two until 1951, when two more appeared.

The first that appeared in 1927 was Bryllion N. Fagin's *Phenomenon of Sherwood Anderson*,[5] certainly not the "wildly ecstatic" work that Irving Howe has called it,[6] but rather reflective of the early twenties, the years during which Anderson appeared in the *Dial* more regularly than any other novelist and had reached his greatest level of acceptance among critics of the *Nation*, the *New Republic*, and other Eastern liberal journals. The other book, Cleveland B. Chase's *Sherwood Anderson*, in the Modern American Writers series,[7] serves as a summation and reiteration of the criticism that had been directed at Anderson since early 1923, echoing Lawrence S. Morris's devastating statement in the *New Republic* that same year:

A few years ago, when Sherwood Anderson was writing his short stories about life in Ohio towns and along the mud-flats of the Mississippi, his words appeared like shoots of new grass in a field of stubble. America was stale with novels which pictured men and women as everything except human beings. Anderson had then the genuine simplicity of the poet. He was sensitive to the taste and feel of life and he trembled at every sign he found of it, especially the shyest. . . . However wistful and frail his people were, they were individuals. In those days Anderson was writing from love, and the need to express certain outcast aspects of life. . . .

As we are all emotionally still more than half-adolescent, Anderson's world was recognized at once. . . . In his naïve pushing aside of dignity we found a truth we had needed. The words he used to express it were fresh words which had grown out of his own experience. He was minor and genuine.

But adolescence does not last. An emotion, whether in life or in the imagination, must mature, which means that it is concentrated on something definite; or else it grows more and more remote from its object and thins down into fancy. Fancy in its turn degenerates into sentimentality. In his growth as an artist, Anderson had reached this critical point. And there he stuck. . . .

In the meantime Anderson has been exposed to another temptation. At the beginning of his career as a writer he had used words to express what he had felt. They existed and had value only as they served him. But presently he discovered the thrill there was in the mere using of them. . . .

This posturing of pretty words, filled with vague emotion, is the double disease which has been consuming Anderson. . . . And in his sick state, Anderson prizes the eloquence above the principle. He has reached the place where he is content to put unreal emotion into unreal words. And as the words have grown more sumptuous, his spirit has grown more callous. He now saves sentimentality which might better have gone into the wastebasket. . . .

The author of "Winesburg, Ohio," is dying before our eyes.[8]

It seems unnecessary at this point to comment on the lapses in fact or in judgment that mark this summary statement, but it is necessary to point out the implications that were to govern much Anderson criticism for the next forty years. Central to Morris's comment is the suggestion that Anderson's publication of *Winesburg, Ohio* was essentially an aberration, a minor accomplishment in a career that had promised much but remained undistinguished.

During the next 24 years this critical assessment continued to dominate serious criticism of Anderson, just as it provided the underlying assumption in Irving Howe's *Sherwood Anderson*, published in 1951 as one of the American Men of Letters series.[9] In almost all of the studies in that period, Anderson was relegated to the role of a minor writer who had written one relatively successful book, but whose work was, as Lionel Trilling commented[10] and Howe echoed,[11] ultimately unsatisfactory.

It was during these years that the dichotomy grew between what became a majority view and a minority view, resulting in a literary paradox that is only now approaching resolution. The dichotomy resulted from continued critical attention to Anderson's works following *A Story Teller's Story*, the rejection of those works by Eastern critics, and by growing recognition of the solid worth of each as a contribution to the American literature of our time by a small minority of other critics.

The majority view was based on the conviction expressed by Morris and Chase that by the time of *A Story Teller's Story*, Anderson had exhausted his material and was forced to retell the old stories and reuse the same old material from his youth. Consequently, this view resulted in an article of critical faith concerning Anderson that found expression in a variety of ways, particularly in the early 1940s, as Anderson's life came to an end and the publishing industry began to revive with the end of the depression.

Significant at that time were three works with remarkably similar conclusions, all of them reminiscent of the view summarized and propagated by Chase in 1927. The three are Lionel Trilling's essay "Sherwood Anderson" in *Kenyon Review* for Summer, 1941, later reprinted in his *The Liberal Imagination* (1950);[12] and the observations and conclusions concerning Anderson in Oscar Cargill's *Intellectual America* (1941)[13] and Alfred Kazin's *On Native Grounds* (1942).[14] These conclusions are, not curiously, very much like Irving Howe's later, more detailed study as well as Chase's earlier assessment.

For Trilling, in spite of an oddly poignant sentimentalism, the critical jury has rendered its verdict on Anderson, and, in spite of his inclusion of a few errors of fact as well as uncritical acceptance of myth as reality, he records that verdict with the certainty of a man of faith:

> . . . Anderson should have been forever protected against artistic failure by the facts of his biography. At the age of forty-

five, as everyone knows, he found himself the manager of a small paint factory in Elyria, Ohio; one day, in the very middle of a sentence he was dictating, he walked out of the factory and gave himself to literature and truth. From the wonder of that escape he seems never to have recovered, and his continued pleasure in it did him harm. . . . Anderson was deeply concerned with the idea of justification; there was an odd, quickly, undisciplined religious strain in him that took this form; and he expected that although Philistia might condemn him, he would have an eventual justification in the way of art and truth. He was justified in some personal way, as I have tried to say, and no doubt his great escape had something to do with this, but it also has the effect of fatally fixing the character of his artistic life.[15]

In spite of (or perhaps because of) his sensitivity and compassion, Trilling accepts Anderson's mythical or symbolic truth of his escape from business as literally true, perhaps making inevitable his acceptance also of the myth created by the critics of the mid-1920s. In Trilling, as in Kazin, Cargill, and others of the time, the paradox inherent in critical appraisal of Anderson becomes especially evident. Trilling not only gives Anderson the kind of attention he insists Anderson does not deserve, but then, like Anderson in his autobiographical moments, he spends a good deal of time explaining why he does what he does. Perhaps an important reason for this sympathy and continued preoccupation lies in Oscar Cargill's simple explanation: "Later generations will appreciate the work of Dell, Anderson, Miss Millay, and others, but to no generation will any of these people mean as much as they do to ours. They set us free."[16] Inherent in this explanation is, I think, the continued attractiveness of Anderson's myth of escape—from the village, from business, from personal restraint—the preoccupation with which lies at the heart of each of these critical views.

Not only does Alfred Kazin accept uncritically the "revolt from the village" interpretation in spite of the fact that by the time of Anderson's death it should have been obviously misleading to one as perceptive as Kazin, but he accepts too, and equally uncritically, the fiction that Anderson's career had ended in the mid-1920s:

. . . No writer had written so much of liberation, no writer seemed less free. He was a Prospero who had charmed himself to sleep and lost his wand; and as the years went on Anderson seemed more and more bereft, a minor visionary whose perpetual air of wonder became a trance and whose prose distintegrated hopelessly from book to book. Yet knowing himself so well, he could smile over those who were so ready to tell him that it was his ignorance of "reality" and of "real people" that crippled his books. . . . It was not his vision that was at fault, no; it was that poignant human situation em-

> bodied in him, that story he told over and over again because it
> was his only story—of the groping that broke forth out of the
> prison house of life and . . . went on groping; of the search for
> freedom that made all its substance out of that search, and in
> the end left all the supplicators brooding, suffering, and
> overwhelmed. . . .[17]

At the end of this concluding summary it seems evident that Kazin, not
Anderson, is groping for an elusive underlying reality, that nearly within
his grasp is a metaphorical insight into one whose epitaph quotes his own
conviction that "Life, not death, is the great adventure," but that insight
eludes Kazin, and his conclusions are ultimately as incomplete and unsatisfactory as, he insisted, were Sherwood Anderson's own.

The two works not only tell us a good deal about the pervasiveness
of the view that Anderson was unsatisfactory as a writer and a failure as
an artist, his only redeeming work being *Winesburg, Ohio*, but they tell
us a great deal too about the critics—a matter discussed at length by
Welford Dunaway Taylor in a recent essay, "Anderson and the Problem
of Belonging," in *Sherwood Anderson: Dimensions of his Literary Art*
(1976)[18]—and they make clear the nature of the paradox underlying
almost all Anderson criticism until the recent past, a paradox that was
first noticed and defined in my own *Sherwood Anderson* (1967).[19]

The paradox was essentially this: that critical opinion between 1927
and the early 1960s had relegated Anderson to a minor role in American
literary history; it insisted that his only work of substance was *Winesburg,
Ohio* (1919); that shortly after its publication, in 1922 or 1923, his work
had begun a decline that continued to his death; and it maintained that
whatever influence Anderson had on the development of prose fiction in
this century was negligible. Nevertheless—and this is the essence of the
paradox—in spite of the fact that these critics relegate Anderson to a
minor position in American literary history, they are not only unable to
ignore him but give him more attention—in some cases much more attention—than many writers they consider to be more significant.

Some of the reasons for this paradox are, I think, obvious. Not only
was Anderson so very good at his best—and only Susan Sontag has ever
revealed critical shortcomings so blatantly as to remark that *Winesburg,
Ohio* (together with *For Whom the Bell Tolls*) is "bad to the point of being
laughable"[20]—particularly in *Winesburg* that the book, whatever one's
critical convictions, is recognized as a central work in the development of
fiction in this century. Another significant reason for the attention given
Anderson by hostile as well as sympathetic critics is the inherent sympathy
and fascination with which they regard the myth of the archetypical artistic journey that Anderson created in his search for the meaning of his
own life. In fact, many of the same critics of the late 1920s and 1930s, including Chase, Van Doren, Morris, and others, contributed to the pro-
pagation of that myth by accepting it as actual rather than metaphorical
truth and disseminating it widely in their essays, books, and lectures. By

the time of Anderson's death in 1941, in spite of the early work done by William Sutton, the myth seemed to be established permanently in American literary history as a factual chapter in the story of the American artist's struggle against Philistinism.

This critical acceptance of the Anderson myth as truth suggests what I think is the basic reason for the continuation of the paradox among Anderson critics. It is simply this: from the beginning of Anderson's literary career, and certainly by the time of *Winesburg, Ohio*'s critical reception, critics delighted in reading into Anderson many of the same hostilities and prejudices that they held against what they saw, rightly or wrongly, as a repressive and hostile American society, and Anderson, with his comments about industrialism, sexual repression, Puritanism, and materialism, seemed to be emerging as a spokesman against these anti-individual values and for a new liberation. Consequently, it was natural and perhaps inevitable that Van Doren and others saw *Winesburg* as a denunciation of village manners and morés, indeed a "revolt from the village."

With the acceptance of this quickly stereotyped view of the book and Anderson's attitude in it, it was inevitable that these same critics would misunderstand his use of nearly identical material in his works of the mid-1920's, particularly *A Story Teller's Story* and *Tar: A Midwest Childhood*; they would completely misinterpret his move to the Virginia hills and into journalism, and consequently fail to understand what he was doing in the last fifteen years of his life or what he was saying in his works written during that period. These misinterpretations are rooted in the fundamental failure of their assessments of *Winesburg, Ohio*. Not only did they fail to perceive that Anderson regarded his people not with revulsion but with love, but they failed to see that Anderson's attitude toward the town was not born of rejection but of regret at its passing. As George Willard departed from the town station for Chicago, the town did not become the symbol of the frustration and repression that Van Doren and others insisted it was; it became instead "a background on which to paint the dreams of his manhood."

With this fundamental misinterpretation of *Winesburg*, it was inevitable that other misinterpretations followed: the failure to see Anderson's rejection of liberation in *Dark Laughter*; the failure of escape in *Many Marriages*; the reassessment of his experience and the identification of himself with his father in *A Story Teller's Story*; the search for a meaningful past in *Tar* and for a living past in his move into the Virginia hills; the note of sympathetic awareness and celebration in *A New Testament*, *Hello Towns!* and *The American County Fair*; the social consciousness and clear faith in *Perhaps Women* and *Puzzled America*; the timely incisiveness in *Beyond Desire* and *Kit Brandon*; the solid accomplishment of *Death in the Woods*; the strong affirmative note in *Home Town* and the *Memoirs*.

Perhaps it was inevitable that when Irving Howe's *Sherwood Ander-*

*son* appeared in 1951, it not only overshadowed the solider and more sympathetic *Sherwood Anderson: His Life and Work* by James Schevill[21] in the same year, but unfortunately, and largely, I think, because of Howe's critical prominence, it is still too frequently used and cited. Particularly unfortunate is the fact that it perpetuates the fundamental misinterpretation that Chase and his colleagues had launched and made stylish a quarter-century before.

Particularly disturbing to me in Howe's critical survey is his tendency to dismiss without examination or support some of the key works in coming to terms with Anderson's creative and intellectual development. He writes, "What is *Many Marriages* but a stubborn and, as it were, principled refusal to think?"[22] and "Of the books written in these years only *Tar* makes a certain appeal to the imagination, but more than any of Anderson's works of fiction it justifies the critical commonplace that while he attracts sensitive adolescents he cannot satisfy the mature mind. . . . Despite its authentic moments *Tar* testifies to the weariness of an imagination aware that it is becoming a burden on its own past."[23]

Not only does Howe perpetuate the disturbingly short-sighted insistence that Anderson's creative imagination had failed at that point, but he perpetuates another, more serious accusation—that which appeared in a number of journal reviews and, in spite of Anderson's active social sympathy, took him to task for failing to commit himself fully and finally to doctrinaire social and economic panaceas. This criticism is the substance of what Oscar Cargill was talking about when he insisted that *Puzzled America* reflected a "puzzled Sherwood Anderson,"[24] and it is also reminiscent in kind but not in degree of the destruction of literary reputations as substantial as those of Louis Bromfield and James Branch Cabell by the reviewers in the liberal journals during the years between 1930 and 1936. Neither Bromfield's nor Cabell's reputation has ever rebounded from the decisiveness if not viciousness of those attacks. But Anderson's treatment was never vicious; instead, it took refuge in condescension. Howe, for example, concludes,

> But surely there is, there should be a place in our culture, even if only a minor one, for Sherwood Anderson. His faults, his failures and defeats can hardly be ignored: he was almost always limited in moral sensibility and social perspective. Yet there were a few moments when he spoke, as almost no one else among American writers, with the voice of love.[25]

Howe's conclusion is another key to understanding the paradoxical continued concern, including Howe's own, with this "minor" figure in American literary history. It is, I think, an unwillingness to abandon him, not merely for what are his allegedly few significant works, but because of a nagging suspicion that somewhere the critics rather than Anderson had taken a wrong turn, that perhaps there was more to his work than had indeed met the eye of the uncritical critic.

Recognition that this was indeed the case, that the critics rather than Anderson had indeed taken a wrong turn, was largely the point of the close critical assessment of all of Anderson's work that took place in the late 1950s and the decade of the 1960s. In a recent essay, "Anderson and Stieglitz: A Fellowship of Sayer and Seer," Robert E. Ned Haines sums up the activity of that decade in his concluding paragraph:

> The years 1923–1924 were indeed pivotal in Anderson's career. Some critics, notably Irving Howe, see those years as the beginning of a "downward curve," a slope toward personal crisis and creative disintegration. Later critics, led by David Anderson, see the same period as one in which the author began to regain his equilibrium, as evidenced by the rays of optimism and affirmation that began to brighten the inner landscape of his work. If the latter interpretation is correct—and I am convinced it is—then we should all remember Stieglitz in our orisons, for he was a fountainhead of Sherwood Anderson's faith in all that is clean and honest.[26]

From this point of departure, marked by my statement of nearly a decade ago that "as a man who approached life with reverence, who spoke of it with love, and who provided some of the most eloquent expressions of both in his time, his place is secure,"[27] Anderson's critical reputation has grown, and his stature and role are clearly defined.

It remains now to attempt to assess the direction and emphasis of Sherwood Anderson criticism in the future, a topic particularly interesting since the observance of Anderson's centennial year in 1976. As we enter his second century, begun by an observance spanning ten days in three locations, Michigan State University, Clyde, Ohio, and Marion, Virginia; as we note that virtually no anthology of American literature, of short fiction, or of expository prose is complete without a selection from Anderson's work; as we note that not only is *Winesburg, Ohio* still in print, as it has been continuously since 1919, but that more of Anderson's works are in print now than at any point during his lifetime, it is safe to observe that the critical myth perpetuated during the quarter-century between Chase and Howe and on into our own time, has finally been smashed, that Sherwood Anderson's later direction and later works are recognized as substantial, provocative works in their own right, that Anderson remained a profound, provocative, and perceptive writer to the end, and that he has much to say to those of us who live in the last quarter of the twentieth century.

Nevertheless, in spite of the accelerating rate at which Anderson studies are continuing, it is important to note that much is yet to be done and much must be redone or continued. Anderson was a far more prolific writer than most of his earlier critics, biographers, and bibliographers knew, and new discoveries of publications and letters occur frequently, to add to the list of those already known and to the extensive holdings readily available for scholarly use in the Newberry Library collection of more than 17,000 items, including letters and manuscripts.

No definitive biography of Anderson has yet appeared, although three important preliminary biographies exist. William A. Sutton's *The Road to Winesburg* (Metuchen, N.J.: Scarecrow Press, 1972) is based upon his doctoral dissertation, "Sherwood Anderson's Formative Years (1876–1913)," which contains much first-hand information for which Anderson scholars are indebted to Sutton. James Schevill's *Sherwood Anderson: His Life and Work* (Denver: University of Denver Press, 1951) is a detailed, reliable work that is now unfortunately out of print. Less satisfactory as biography—and in my view, as criticism—is Irving Howe's *Sherwood Anderson* (New York: William Sloan, 1951), now available in a paperback edition published by Stanford University Press. Schevill's and Howe's studies are critical biographies.

Numerous shorter studies of periods in Anderson's life have appeared, written by those who knew him as well as by scholars. Sutton's series of four essays in *Northwest Ohio Quarterly* (July, 1947; January, 1948; Winter, 1949–1950; Summer, 1950), much of which appears in *The Road to Winesburg*, his monograph *Exit to Elsinore* (Muncie, Indiana: Ball State University, 1967), also drawn from his dissertation; and his essay "Sherwood Anderson's Second Wife" (*Ball State University Forum*, Spring, 1966), are all important, particularly the latter. Among first-hand accounts generally less reliable than Sutton's meticulous works are Karl Anderson's "My Brother, Sherwood Anderson" (*Saturday Review of Literature*, September 4, 1948); George H. Daugherty's "Anderson, Advertising Man" (*Newberry Library Bulletin*, December, 1948), Waldo Frank's "Anderson: A Personal Note" (*Newberry Library Bulletin*, December, 1948); Roger Sergel's "The Man and the Memory" (*Newberry Library Bulletin*, December, 1948), and Paul Rosenfeld's "The Man of Good Will" (*Story*, September-October, 1941). Important but not entirely reliable is *Miss Elizabeth* (New York: Little, Brown, 1969) by Elizabeth Anderson, Sherwood's third wife, and Gerald R. Kelly.

Much biographical data appears in literary autobiographies, memoirs, and collections of letters by prominent writers, critics, and editors who were active in the twenty-five years of his literary life, a partial list of whom must include Gertrude Stein, H. L. Mencken, Edmund Wilson, Burton Rascoe, Harry Hansen, Edward Dahlberg, Waldo Frank, Van Wyck Brooks, William Faulkner, whose "Sherwood Anderson: An Appreciation" (*Atlantic Monthly*, June, 1953), is one of many such recognitions by writers. Two recent such acknowledgements are by William Saroyan (*New York Times*, August 15, 1976) and Saul Bellow (*New York Times*, November 21, 1976).

More recent book-length studies of Anderson contain varying amounts of biographical material that is limited but usually reliable: Brom Weber, *Sherwood Anderson* (Minneapolis, 1964); Rex Burbank,

*Sherwood Anderson* (New York: Twayne Publishers, 1964); my own *Sherwood Anderson: An Introduction and Interpretation* (New York: Holt, Rinehart & Winston, 1967), and Welford D. Taylor, *Sherwood Anderson* (New York: Frederick Unger, 1977). The biographical work which promises to be definitive, however, is that upon which Walter B. Rideout has been at work for more than a decade, brief portions of which have appeared in essays in periodicals and collections. William A. Sutton will soon publish his biography, *The Adventurous Desperation of Sherwood Anderson*; I am currently at work on *The Four Stages of a Man's Life: A Photo Biography of Sherwood Anderson*, and I anticipate early publication.

No critical edition of Anderson's books exists, and none is contemplated, although a collection adhering to the standards set by the Center for Editions of American Authors would be most useful to Anderson scholars. Critical editions and commentary upon the texts of a number of Anderson's published and previously unpublished works have appeared, beginning with William L. Phillips's "The First Printing of Sherwood Anderson's *Winesburg, Ohio*" (*Studies in Bibliography*, 1951–52), but few of the published editions have met the standards set by the Center for American Editions. Editions of Anderson's works extant include critical editions of *Marching Men* (Cleveland: Case Western Reserve University Press, 1972), edited by Ray Lewis White; *A Story Teller's Story* (Cleveland: Case Western Reserve University Press, 1968), edited by Ray Lewis White; *Tar: A Midwest Childhood* (Cleveland: Case Western Reserve University Press, 1969), edited by Ray Lewis White; *Sherwood Anderson's Memoirs* (Chapel Hill: University of North Carolina Press, 1969), edited by Ray Lewis White; *Many Marriages* (Metuchen, N.J.: Scarecrow Press, 1978), edited by Douglas G. Rogers; and two previously unpublished works, *The "Writer's Book"* (Metuchen, N.J.: Scarecrow Press, 1975), edited by Martha Mulroy Curry; and Anderson's notebook of his first trip to France in *France and Sherwood Anderson: Paris Notebook, 1921* (Baton Rouge: Louisiana State University Press, 1976), edited with an introductory essay by Michael Fanning. A projected series to be edited by Ray Lewis White and others, and published by Case Western Reserve Press, has been abandoned.

Other editions with useful introductions and other editorial material include *Windy McPherson's Son* (Chicago: University of Chicago Press, 1965), in Anderson's revised edition of 1922, with an introduction by Wright Morris; *Winesburg, Ohio* (New York: Viking Press, 1960), with an introduction and bibliographic essay by Malcolm Cowley; *Winesburg, Ohio: Text and Criticism* (New York: Viking Press, 1966), edited with an introduction by John H. Ferres; *Poor White* (New York: Viking Press, 1966), with an introduction by Walter B. Rideout; *A Story Teller's Story* (New York: Viking Press, 1969), with a preface by Walter B. Rideout; *Dark Laughter* (New York: Liveright Press, 1960), with an introduction by Howard Mumford Jones; *Beyond Desire* (New York: Liveright Press, 1961), with an introduction by Walter B. Rideout; and *Winesburg, Ohio* (New York: Viking Press, 1958, 1960, 1976), with an introduction by Malcolm Cowley.

Many of Anderson's other works have been reprinted in new editions in recent years, including much that was previously uncollected as well as Anderson's lesser or shorter works, the latter unfortunately often in handsome but limited and scarce editions. The three standard collections are *The Portable Sherwood Anderson* (New York: Viking Press, 1949, 1956, 1972), edited with an introduction by Horace Gregory; *The Sherwood Anderson Reader* (Boston: Houghton Mifflin Co., 1947), edited with an introduction by Paul Rosenfeld; and *Sherwood Anderson: Short Stories* (New York: Hill and Wang, 1962), edited with an introduction by Maxwell Geismar, all three of which contain previously unpublished or uncollected material. Useful too are three recent volumes of previously uncollected newspaper and magazine publications, introductions, and miscellaneous writings of varying quality: *Return to Winesburg: Selections from Four Years of Writing for a Country Newspaper* (Chapel Hill: University of North Carolina Press, 1967), edited by Ray Lewis White; *The Buck Fever Papers* (Charlottesville, Virginia: University of Virginia Press, 1971), edited by Welford D. Taylor; and *Sherwood Anderson: The Writer at His Craft* (Mamaroneck, N.Y.: Paul P. Appel, 1979), edited by Jack Salzman, David D. Anderson, and Kichinosuki Ohashi. The latter contains the text of Anderson's "A Writer's Conception of Realism" and the text of "Textiles," a radio play, both previously virtually unattainable.

Other recent editions of Anderson's works include a series of reproductions of original editions published by Paul P. Appel: (Mamaroneck, N.Y.): *Sherwood Anderson's Notebook* (1970); *Hello Towns!* (1970); *Perhaps Women* (1970); *No Swank* (1970); *Puzzled America* (1970); and *Home Town* (1975), with an introduction by David D. Anderson. *Homage to Sherwood Anderson* (1970), edited by Paul P. Appel, contains, in addition to the reprinted contents of *Story* 19 (September-October, 1941), devoted to tributes to Anderson, the texts of "The Triumph of the Egg" and *The Modern Writer* as well as previously unpublished letters. A complete collection of Anderson's short stories, edited by William V. Miller, is in progress.

Anderson's shorter works have always been favorites of small, fine-editions presses, and in the past decade a number have been republished: *Mid-American Chants* (Berkeley: Frontier Press, 1972), which is more useful although less attractive than the earlier *6 Mid-American Chants by Sherwood Anderson/11 Midwest Photographs by Art Sinsabaugh* (Highlands, N.C.: Jonathan Williams Publisher, 1964); *Alice and the Lost Novel* (Belfast, Maine: Porter Press, 1971); *Alice and the Lost Novel* (Folcroft, Pa.; Folcroft Press, 1971); and *Dreiser* (n.p. n.d.). These editions are scarce, and they command high prices in the rare book market.

Other useful sources readily available for research but also in need of continuation and/or re-editing are editions or publications of Anderson's letters and bibliographies of his writings and of biography and criticism. No complete collection of either his letters or his shorter writings is available, primarily because Anderson was so prolific, but also because previously unknown letters and periodical publications frequently turn up. The standard collection of letters is *The Letters of Sherwood Anderson* (Boston: Houghton Mifflin, 1953), edited by Howard Mumford Jones with Walter B. Rideout, with a valuable introduction by Jones, and it is soon to be supplemented by *Dear Bab: Letters of Sherwood Anderson to a Friend*, an important series of 308 letters written to Marietta D. Finley Hahn between September, 1916, and March, 1933. The latter volume is edited by the discoverer of the letters, William A. Sutton. *Sherwood Anderson/Gertrude Stein: Correspondence and Personal Essays* (Chapel Hill: University of North Carolina Press, 1972), edited by Ray Lewis White, is a useful collection, although much of the Anderson material has been reprinted elsewhere. Shorter collections of Anderson's letters have been published in periodicals and collections over the years, including those to V. F. Calverton in *Modern Quarterly* 2 (Fall, 1924); to Paul Rosenfeld in *Paul Rosenfeld, Voyager in the Arts* (New York: Creative Age Press, 1948), edited by Jerome Mellquist and Lucie Wiese; to Robert Morss Lovett and Ferdinand Schevill in *Berkeley* 1 (October, 1947); to his son John and to Theodore Dreiser in *Harper's Bazaar* 73 (February, 1949); to Gertrude Stein in *The Flowers of Friendship* (New York: Alfred A. Knopf, 1953), edited by Donald Gallup; and to a number of people in *Sherwood Anderson: Centennial Studies* (Troy, N.Y.: Whitson Publishing Co., 1976), edited by Hilbert H. Campbell and Charles E. Modlin. Only a fraction of the more than 6,000 known letters by Anderson have been published.

Anderson scholars are, however, fortunate in the ready availability of the Sherwood Anderson Collection in the Newberry Library. Initially the gift of Eleanor Copenhaver Anderson and supplemented by other gifts and purchases, it contains more than 17,000 items, including approximately 1,300 manuscripts, more than 6,000 letters by Anderson, approximately 8,000 letters written to Anderson, and hundreds of other documents, journals, photos, paintings, clippings, editions, and ancillary material.

Lesser collections are widespread, the more useful including those in the Library of Congress (131 letters, 2 manuscripts, and other holdings); University of Notre Dame (36 letters and other material); Smith College (30 letters); Cornell University (35 letters, 2 manuscripts, and other material); Columbia University (43 letters and other material); University of North Carolina (66 letters); Princeton University (163 letters, 4 manuscripts, and other material); University of Pennsylvania (220 letters, 3 manuscripts); University of Texas (94 letters and other material);

University of Virginia (72 letters, 8 manuscripts, and other material); the State Historical Society of Wisconsin (100 letters and other material). Other collections, including letters, manuscripts, photos, and paintings by Anderson, are in private hands.

Anderson bibliography has been well served in the past, with capable bibliographers building upon two pioneering works, both of which have shortcomings, as has each of their successors. The first, an M. A. thesis by Raymond D. Gozzi, "A Descriptive Bibliography of Sherwood Anderson's Contributions to Periodicals" (Columbia, 1947), has been published in abbreviated and somewhat different form in *The Newberry Library Bulletin*, Second Series, No. 2 (December, 1948). A skilled piece of research, it is incomplete and some errors occur, but it provides the basis for part of *Sherwood Anderson: A Bibliography* (Los Gatos, California: Talisman Press, 1960), by Eugene P. Sheehy and Kenneth A. Lohf. This more comprehensive work includes, in addition to the section drawn largely from Gozzi, two parts, "Works of Sherwood Anderson" and "Writings About Sherwood Anderson." In both sections works are omitted, some errors occur, and the work is for the most part nondescriptive. From this point, Anderson bibliographic research has attempted to correct errors, to expand listings, to incorporate new discoveries (one of the great pleasures of Anderson research is to discover previously-unknown periodical contributions or letters), to keep secondary materials up to date, to provide descriptive listings, and to identify foreign publications and translations, including new issues. Bibliographic research is the most exacting of the scholarly arts as well as one of the most important, and important contributions continue to be made.

Useful additions to Anderson bibliography include G. Thomas Tanselle's "Additional Reviews of Sherwood Anderson's Work" in *Papers of the Bibliographic Society of America*, 56 (Third Quarter, 1962), which filled in many of the gaps in Sheehy and Lohf; *Checklist of Sherwood Anderson* (Columbus: Charles E. Merrill, 1969), compiled by Ray Lewis White; *Sherwood Anderson: A Selective, Annotated Bibliography* (Metuchen, N.J.: Scarecrow Press, 1976), compiled by Douglas G. Rogers, which contains some errors in dates and page references; and *Sherwood Anderson: A Reference Guide* (Boston: G.K. Hall, 1977), compiled by Ray Lewis White. The latter is particularly useful, but it contains secondary material only. White has also compiled a checklist of foreign-language editions of *Winesburg, Ohio* in "*Winesburg* in Translation," which appeared in *Ohioana* 19 (Summer, 1976). Other brief, important new studies are "The Editions of *Winesburg, Ohio*" by William L. Phillips in *Sherwood Anderson: Centennial Studies* (Troy, N.Y.: Whitson Publishing Co., 1976); "Sherwood Anderson: Fugitive Pamphlets and Broadsides, 1918–1940," by Ray Lewis White, in *Studies in Bibliography* 31 (1978); and "*Winesburg, Ohio*: First-Impression Errors," in *Papers of the Bibliographic Society of America* 71 (April-June, 1977). No comprehensive, annotated Anderson bibliography has yet appeared.

The persistence of the interest in Anderson's works and the durability of his appeal for writers and critics as well as scholars is attested to by the regular appearance of special journal issues devoted to his life and work. The first, *Story* 19 (September-October, 1941), is a memorial issue that includes tributes and reminiscences as well as criticism. Two issues of the *Newberry Library Bulletin*, Second Series, No. 2 (December, 1948) and 6, No. 8 (July, 1971), commemorate, respectively, the opening of the Anderson collection to scholars and the accession by the Newberry of the manuscript of *Winesburg, Ohio* and the fiftieth anniversary of the book's publication. *Shenandoah* 13 (Spring, 1962), a special Sherwood Anderson Number, contains perceptive essays by Frederick J. Hoffman, Jon S. Lawry, Walter B. Rideout and Cratis D. Williams.

Two scholarly journals published special Anderson issues to mark his centennial year: *Twentieth Century Literature* 23 (February, 1977), guest-edited by Jack Salzman, and *American Notes and Queries* 15 (September, 1976), guest-edited by Hilbert H. Campbell and Charles E. Modlin. The former contains, in addition to "Being a Writer" by Anderson and a selection of photos from my forthcoming photo biography, six perceptive essays, for the most part by younger scholars, and overviews of "Sherwood Anderson in Japan: The Early Years" by Kichinosuki Ohashi and of "Sherwood Anderson in France: 1919–1939," by MarySue Schriber. The latter special issue contains brief, specialized essays by scholars who have long been part of the history of Anderson criticism.

A recently founded publication, *The Winesburg Eagle*, is now published twice a year. The publication of the Sherwood Anderson Society, the headquarters of which is at the University of Richmond, it is edited by Welford D. Taylor. It contains reviews, checklists, memoirs, and essays.

Five useful collections of Anderson criticism with remarkably little duplication among them have appeared. Three of them contain essays and excerpts drawn from past criticism: *The Achievement of Sherwood Anderson* (Chapel Hill: University of North Carolina Press, 1966), edited with an introduction by Ray Lewis White; *Winesburg, Ohio: Text and Criticism* (New York: Viking Press, 1966), edited with an introduction by John H. Ferres; and *Sherwood Anderson: A Collection of Critical Essays* (Englewood Cliffs, N.J.: Prentice-Hall, 1974), edited with an introduction by Walter B. Rideout. Two volumes published as part of the Anderson centennary observance contain criticism written for the collections, much of it by younger scholars who are becoming active in Anderson criticism. These are *Sherwood Anderson: Centennial Studies* (Troy, N.Y.: Whitson Publishing Co., 1976), edited by Hilbert H. Campbell and Charles E. Modlin; and *Sherwood Anderson: Dimensions of his Literary Art* (East Lansing: Michigan State University Press, 1976), edited with an introduction by David D. Anderson. The former contains important source material: letters, an interview of Anderson conducted by Eleanor Copenhaver late in 1931, prior to her marriage to Anderson, an interview

with Mrs. Anderson, a checklist of Anderson's library, and two essays on
the Anderson Collection in the Newberry, by Mrs. Amy Nyholm, the
former curator, and Ms. Diana Haskell, the present curator, as well as
eleven scholarly and critical essays. The latter contains eight essays.

The two centennary volumes combine to illustrate the direction that
Anderson criticism is currently taking: studies which compare or contrast
Anderson's works with those of other writers; criticism of individual
works, particularly those which have received inadequate study in the
past; thematic studies, of which Anderson's treatment of women
characters has become quite important; reassessment of earlier criticism;
bibliographic, manuscript, and textual studies; and the continued search
for previously unknown primary materials. In all of these areas, there is
much that remains to be done.

## Notes

1. Carl Van Doren, "Contemporary American Novelists—X. The Revolt from the Village: 1920." *The Nation*, 113 (12 October, 1921), 408–09, 410, 412.

2. Frederick J. Hoffman, *The 20's* (New York, 1962), p. 369.

3. Anthony Channell Hilfer, *The Revolt from the Village, 1915–1930* (Chapel Hill, 1969).

4. David D. Anderson, "The Search for a Living Past" in Hilbert H. Campbell and Charles E. Modlin, eds., *Sherwood Anderson: Centennial Studies* (Troy, 1976), pp. 212–23.

5. Bryllion N. Fagin, *The Phenomenon of Sherwood Anderson: A Study in American Life and Letters* (Baltimore, 1927).

6. Irving Howe, *Sherwood Anderson* (New York, 1951), p. 259.

7. Cleveland Chase, *Sherwood Anderson* (New York, 1927).

8. Lawrence S. Morris, "Sherwood Anderson: Sick of Words," *The New Republic* 51 (3 August 1927), pp. 277, 278, 279.

9. See "Preface," Howe, *Sherwood Anderson*, pp. xi–xii, for his summary thesis.

10. Lionel Trilling, "Sherwood Anderson," in *The Liberal Imagination* (New York, 1950), pp. 22–33.

11. Howe, *Sherwood Anderson*, pp. 254–56.

12. Trilling, "Sherwood Anderson," in both versions, insists that Anderson remained emotionally an adolescent while America moved into maturity.

13. Oscar Cargill, *Intellectual America: Ideas on the March* (New York, 1948), characterizes Anderson as a "gifted amateur" (p. 331) and agrees with Ernest Sutherland Bates that Anderson "enters a cloud-cuckoo land of bewildered musings" when he thinks. (p. 685)

14. Alfred Kazin, *On Native Grounds* (New York, 1942), explains Anderson's early success in simplistic terms: "he was clumsy and sentimental; he could even write at times as if he were finger-painting, but at the moment it seemed as if he had sounded the depths of common American experience as no man could." (p. 167)

15. Trilling, "Sherwood Anderson," pp. 23–24.

16. Cargill, *Intellectual America*, p. 763.

17. Kazin, *On Native Grounds*, pp. 172–73.

18. Welford D. Taylor, "Anderson and the Problem of Belonging" in David D. Ander-

son, ed., *Sherwood Anderson: Dimensions of his Literary Art* (East Lansing, Mich., 1976), pp. 61–74.

19. David D. Anderson, *Sherwood Anderson: An Introduction and Interpretation* (New York, 1967), pp. 163–73.

20. Susan Sontag, "Notes on 'Camp,' " in *Against Interpretation and Other Essays* (New York, 1966), p. 284.

21. James Schevill, *Sherwood Anderson: His Life and Work* (Denver, 1951).

22. Howe, *Sherwood Anderson*, pp. 193–94.

23. *Ibid.*, pp. 208–09.

24. Cargill, *Intellectual America*, p. 685.

25. Howe, *Sherwood Anderson*, p. 256.

26. Robert E. Ned Haines, "Anderson and Stieglitz: A Fellowship of Sayer and Seer," Campbell and Modlin, *Sherwood Anderson: Centennial Studies*, p. 210.

27. David D. Anderson, *Sherwood Anderson*, p. 173.

# REVIEWS

# "Emerging Greatness"

Waldo Frank*

We do not expect an Apocalypse, here in America. Out of our terrifying welter of steel and scarlet, a design must come. But it will come haltingly, laboriously. It will be warped by the steel, clotted with the scarlet. There have been pure and delicate visions among us. In art, there has been Whistler; and Henry James took it into his head to write novels. But the clear subtlety of these men was achieved by a rigorous avoidance of native stuff and native issues. Literally, they escaped America; and their followers have done the same, though in a more figurative meaning. Artist-senses have gone out, felt the raw of us, been repulsed by it, and so withdrawn to a magnificent introversion. So, when we found vision in America, we have found mostly an abstract art—an art that remained pure by remaining neuter. What would have happened to these artists, had they grappled with their country, is an academic question. But I suspect that the true reason for their *ivory tower* was lack of strength to venture forth and not be overwhelmed. This much is sure, however—and true particularly of the novel—that our artists have been of two extremes: those who gained an almost unbelievable purity of expression by the very violence of their self-isolation, and those who, plunging into the American maëlstrom, were submerged in it, lost their vision altogether, and gave forth a gross chronicle and a blind cult of the American Fact.

The significance of Sherwood Anderson whose first novel, "Windy McPherson's Son," has recently appeared (published by The John Lane Company), is simply that he has escaped these two extremes, that he suggests at last a presentation of life shot through with the searching color of truth, which is a signal for a native culture.

Mr. Anderson is no accident. The appearance of his book is a gesture of logic. Indeed, commentators of tomorrow might gauge the station at which America has arrived today by a study of the impulses—conscious and unconscious—which compose this novel. But it is not a prophetic work. Its author is simply a man who has felt the moving passions of his people, yet sustained himself against them just enough in a crude way to set them forth.

His story has its beginning in an Iowa town. His hero, with a naive unswervingness from type, is a newsboy. His passion is money and power.

*Originally published in *The Seven Arts*, 1 (November, 1916), pp. 73–78.

He goes to Chicago. He becomes rich. He marries the daughter of his employer. And then, he becomes powerful. There is nothing new in this; although the way of telling it is fresh and sensitive. This is the romance of inchoate America. Like the Greek fables, it is a generic wish fulfillment to be garbed by each poet in his own dress. It has been done in a folk way by Horatio Alger; with a classic might by Theodore Dreiser. But so far, it has been the entire story. With Mr. Anderson, it is only the story's introduction.

When Sam McPherson, by a succession of clumsy assaults, charges to the control of the Arms Trust of America, he does not find there, like his novelistic brothers, a romantic and sentimental and overweening satisfaction. He finds a great disgust, a great emptiness. And he becomes interested in his soul! He learns that what he has done is spiritually nothing; that it has left him as helpless before the commands of life, as in the old days when he amassed pennies in Caxton, Iowa. It dawns on him, that if man is a measurer of truth, he has paralyzed competition, enslaved wealth, disposed of power without really growing at all. So Sam McPherson puts aside his gains; and pilgrimages forth, searching for truth.

This is the second part of the novel; and in it lies the book's importance. McPherson's quest of the grail is an awkward Odyssey indeed. It has the improbability of certain passages of Dostoëvski—the improbability of truth poorly or clumsily materialized. Moreover, in it we find an unleashed and unsophisticated power that we have all along awaited in the American novel. The resemblance to the Russian is, I am convinced, a consequence of a like quality in the two men. It is a temperamental, not a literary thing.

The abdicated millionaire works as a bartender in Ohio, as a builder in Illinois; he joins a threshing crew in the West and a mining camp in the South. He knows prostitutes and working-girls. He tries to help and seeks truth. He learns that labor-unions are more concerned over the use of scab machinery than by the prospect of losing a righteous strike; that the men are more interested in a raise of wages than in preventing a private band of grafters from stealing the town's waterworks. He becomes very miserable over the lot of the street-walkers. He asks the drinkers in the saloon where he is employed why they get drunk, and is discharged with an oath. Puerile, fumbling stuff it is—its efficiency of presentment about on a level with McPherson's method of gaining the light. Yet through it all, is a radiant glow of the truth. Read the newspapers and the Congressional reports; read the platitudes of investigating commissions, of charity organizations, of revivalists and mushroom mysticisms—and you have the same helpless thing in extension. Sam McPherson, bewildered with his affluence and power, seeking the truth in the fair plains and the cancerous cities, ignorant and awkward and eager—is America today. And Sam McPherson, the boy, arrogant and keen and certain, hiding from himself his emptiness with the extent and occupation of the materials that his land floods upon him, is the America of our fathers.

For a feel of the America of tomorrow, do not look to this book. I am sure that Mr. Anderson will conduct himself better in subsequent works than he has in the conclusion of "Windy McPherson's Son." As we find the faint footprints of Horatio Alger at the book's beginning, so at the end is the smirch of Robert W. Chambers. (But after all, Balzac could not so wholeheartedly have swallowed France, had he not taken Pixérécourt and Madame de Scudéry along.) When Sam marries Sue Rainey, it is with the understanding that they are to have children and that they are to live gloriously for them. For a while, the magnate's money-madness slackens. But the pact fails, for the children can not come. Coolness between the two, with the goal of their creed denied them:—and at length, when Sam sacrifices his wife's father in his grapple toward dominion, she flees to New York. The man over whose fat body he has stepped to power shoots himself. And, sick of his tawdry, superficial kingdom, McPherson wanders off.

He gains nothing from his experiments, and this is well enough. He hunts in Africa, leisures in Paris, canoes in Canada and sentimentalizes in New York. All this we forgive him. But one day, he finds himself in St. Louis. He encounters a drunken mother, buys her three children, packs them into a train and drops them at the feet of his wife who, like some diluted Penelope, has been awaiting his return in a villa on the Hudson. "Not our children, but just *some* children is our need," he pronounces. And so, walks "across the lighted room to sit again with Sue at his own table, and to try to force himself back into the ranks of life." This is the last sentence of the book; the one episode that is *made* and insincere. I hope Mr. Anderson is ashamed of it. I hope he does not really believe that all man has to do, to find God, is to increase and multiply more helpless creatures like himself. This pretty surcease to trouble that comes from transferring the problems of life to the next generation is a biological fact. But it is not art. For with it is dimmed all the voluptuous speculation which flushes the novel as a sunrise transfigures a plain. Let life be happy, if it can. The sacred duty of art is to remain sorrowful, when it has challenged a consciousness of sorrow; to abide in the uncertain search of truth so long as the movement of mankind is hazardous. Let our heroes be joyous; but by conquering themselves, not by adopting children. The virtue of Mr. Anderson's book is that it is dynamic. His static ending is bad, because it breaks the rhythm. But it is worse since it slams the door on the vista of passionate inquiry which the book unfolds. Up to the end, we have a clear symbol of America's groping. At the end, we have nothing—in lieu of the suggested everything. But, of course, we may ignore the end. Or, in its fatuous simplicity, we may read still another symbol of America—a token of what might happen to us, if we sought at this stage to read our lives as a conclusion, rather than a commencement.

I was not certain that Theodore Dreiser was a classic, until I had read this novel of Mr. Anderson. Its first half is a portal from which emerges an American soul. This portal is the immediate past, and in the works of Mr. Dreiser we find its definite expression. Beside their magnificent mass-rhythms, the opening chapters of Mr. Anderson are paltry. One feels, indeed, that the uneasy spirit of Sam McPherson has come forth, not from his own youth, not from his own pages, but from the choking structures of Mr. Dreiser.

Mr. Dreiser may of course yet surprise us by the sudden discovery of a new spiritual light. He has not stopped writing. But I feel in his work the profound massiveness of a completed growth. Mr. Dreiser has caught the crass life of the American, armoring himself with luxury and wealth that he misunderstands, with power whose heritage of uses he ignores. The tragedy of his hero is that of a child suddenly in possession of a continent; too unknowing to know that he is ignorant; too dazzled to be amazed. His books are a dull, hard mosaic of materials beneath which one senses vaguely a grandiose movement—like the blind shifting of quicksands or the imperceptible breathing of a glacier. This is Mr. Dreiser, and this is enough. But with Mr. Anderson, the elemental movement begins to have form and direction; the force that causes it is being borne into the air.

Before Mr. Dreiser, there was "Huckleberry Finn"—there was, in other words, a formless delirium of color and of tangent. These are pre-cultural novels. And in the book of Mr. Anderson, I still find much of them. Indeed, the wandering of Sam McPherson has more than a superficial kinship with Huck Finn's passage down the Mississippi. The land that McPherson walks is still a land marred by men and women "who have not learned to be clean and noble like their forests and their plains." But Huck Finn is an animal boy, floating rudderless down a natural current, avid for food and play. And McPherson is a man, flung against his stream, avid for the Truth. . . .

In conclusion, let us not forget that this is Mr. Anderson's first book, and that a succession of them are already written and will appear in their turn. The fact that Mr. Anderson is no longer young is no hindrance to our hope of his growth. Genius in America, if it does not altogether escape America, rises slowly. For it has far to come. The European is born on a plateau. America is still at a sea-level. The blundering, blustering native was thirty-seven before he became Walt Whitman.

# "Discipline"

George Bernard Donlin*

It is a curious, mixed, provocative, and occasionally exasperating book, this second novel of Mr. Anderson's; but it is also interesting—chiefly, to my mind, as the exhibition of a temperament and the setting forth of a point of view that is highly idiosyncratic. Naturally all brief characterizations are unfair, but I suppose "Marching Men" might be described as a pæan to order and (quite incidentally, I hope) a naked and somewhat febrile celebration of force. It is, in fact, too insistently, too stridently and remorselessly dedicated to the main theme to make a wholly satisfactory novel. Nevertheless, it seems to me only natural that a book celebrating order, even a little shrilly, should have grown out of all the clutter and confusion of Chicago, and no doubt we should have had such a book even if Mr. Wells hadn't long since set the fashion.

In the days following the World's Fair Chicago began to accustom itself to criticism—none too tolerantly at first. Mr. Herrick was able to raise the dust by his mild animadversions on the architectural peculiarities of Cottage Grove Avenue. Such criticisms were easily dismissed as the morbidities of a sense refined, and possibly over-refined, by a prolonged familiarity with softer European surfaces, the vagaries, in short, of a delicate ego. Mr. Anderson, on the contrary, although he studies the Chicago of the same period, has little to say of our aesthetic lapses. No; what troubles him is our spiritual untidiness, our stupidity in the sphere of social integration, our vast welter of meaningless and frustrate lives. He is expressing, in other words, what has become the conventionality of the moment, but expressing it with a great deal of passion and in a way that is distinctive enough to excite interest. It is worth noting that neither our crudity nor our violence disturbs him. Force indeed, far from repelling him, fascinates him with what I can only call a slightly pathological fascination. His hero is a Berserker with a big fist, whose most potent argument is always a blow.

There is a corresponding violence in Mr. Anderson's own method. He sets his theme, for example, on the third page. "Standing in the doorway and looking up and down the bleak village street, some dim realization of the disorganized ineffectiveness of life as he knew it came into the mind of

*Originally published in *The Dial*, 63 (27 September, 1917), pp. 274–75.

the McGregor boy." And on the next page, the boy reflects: "If I could form the men of this place into an army I would lead them to the mouth of the old Shumway cut and push them in. . . ." McGregor is then a lad of fourteen or so, living in Coal Creek, Pennsylvania. I daresay there are bespectacled little monsters with a premature appetite for political philosophy who might muse so; but a boy simply bursting with vigor, a boy like "Cracked" McGregor's son; no, no! The love of order has always seemed to me to be distinctly a middle-aged virtue, associated with flagging vitality and the inability to absorb shocks. By this failure of the retrospective imagination, we are early warned to expect no nuances in Mr. Anderson's book, and so we are prepared for other reflections of this untaught miner's son.

> Men of Coal Creek . . . listen to the voice of McGregor. I hate you . . . I hate you because you are weak and disorganized like cattle. I would like to come among you teaching the power of force. I would like to slay you one by one, not with weapons but with my naked fists. If they have made you work like rats buried in a hole they are right. It is the man's right to do what he can. Get up and fight. Fight and I'll get on the other side and you can fight me. I'll help drive you back into your holes.

An adolescent Nietzsche might conceivably have heated his brain with such flights, but McGregor is throughout the foe of intellect. Why talk? Babbling makes a man loose-jawed and flabby. "On and on through life we go, socialists, dreamers, makers of laws, sellers of goods and believers in suffrage for women and we continuously say words, worn-out words, crooked words, words without power or pregnancy in them."

When McGregor arrives in Chicago, as a youth of eighteen or so, he is already filled with contempt for the talkers and there runs in his head the thought of marching men—a troop of soldiers that had put down a riot at Coal Creek. That vision is the nucleus of his whole philosophy—the "goose-step" is the way to solidarity. And so he sets the workers of Chicago to marching. Mr. Anderson's is surely the last word of anti-intellectualism; for the men who follow McGregor do not know why they are marching or whither. Mr. Anderson doubtless took his cue from the solidarity of the peoples at war, but he forgets that if the leaders of those men are quite as cynical as McGregor with regard to the thinking-powers of their men, they are still careful to supply substitutes. They manufacture public opinion and attach men to necessary purposes by holding forth the lure of ideals. So far as I am able to see, McGregor offers the marchers no end beyond the manifestation of power—the power of the workers. Marching satisfies a deep disposition. Very well, let them march, and trust to luck that the collectivist mind will emerge. To present a programme would be only to repeat the old intellectualist fallacy of the socialists and the organizers.

The habit of thinking in terms of groups and masses has rather blunted, I fancy, Mr. Anderson's sense of the intimate and the personal. There are fugitive glints of tenderness here and there, such as McGregor's attachment to the memory of his father or his yearning toward the once despised miners who follow his mother's coffin up the hillside; but on the whole his emotional life, even in the most intimate relations, as those with the tuberculous girl, the plow-manufacturer's daughter, and the little milliner whom he finally marries, is disturbingly arid. With a dim sense of his mission in life, McGregor instinctively fears love. Women are remorselessly possessive. And so McGregor sets himself the problem of loving without yielding to love. He rejects as contemptible the easy solution of the artistic barber, who prowls by night and ogles by day. He often poses the problem, but in the end he does not solve it: he marries the little milliner, who has become a habit and will not divert his attention, rather than the plow-manufacturer's daughter, who has awakened his passion. You are left to infer, if you like, that McGregor ends as he had begun by distrusting passion as the lure of the gods seeking to snare men for their own purposes. Take the scene in which the two women struggle for McGregor's love:

> "Stop," she cried. "I do not want you. I would never marry you now. You belong to her. You are Edith's."
> McGregor's voice became soft and quiet.
> "Oh, I know," he said; "I know! I know! But I want children. Look at Edith. Do you think she could bear children to me?"
> A change came over Edith Carson. Her eyes hardened and her shoulders straightened.
> "That's for me to say," she cried, springing forward and clutching his arm. "That is between me and God. If you intend to marry me come now and do it. I was not afraid to give you up and I'm not afraid that I shall die bearing children."

And after the decision is made McGregor says:

> One struggles to keep a thought in mind, to be impersonal, to see that life has a purpose outside his own purpose. You have perhaps made that struggle. You see I'm making it now. I'm going to take Edith and go back to work.

There is an insensitiveness here that reflects itself even in the words. Mr. Anderson's anti-intellectualism will allow him to leave nothing to the reader; he can't trust us to understand, and therefore he shouts instead of whispering. But I venture to doubt whether even a parishioner of the Reverend Bernard Shaw or a disciple of Professor Pearson really takes the great leap in quite that spirit.

To offset such deficiencies, Mr. Anderson has the skill to make you feel the thick press of life in great cities. The background of that cluttered, disorderly, and violent life of the old South Side, with its Red-Light district that was notorious from Shanghai to St. Petersburg, is effectively realized. Mr. Anderson knows how mixed was the whole network of influences that enmeshed the town, from highest to lowest, and he shows very well the kind of civilization Chicago had then achieved. His touch in the boulevards seems to me less sure, but then I should think the boulevards interest him very little, and he will not mind having such an impression recorded, especially since it is as far as possible from being an expert one. But when all is said Mr. Anderson's book interested me chiefly as the expression of a vigorous and sincere mind, a thoroughly individual mind, that stirs one to argument and tempts one to forget the author's own contempt for the chattering animal that is man.

# "Mid-America Awake"

A. C. Henderson*

Sherwood Anderson is a breaker of barriers, a builder of new bridges, a creator who, lacking the implements of song, will tear song from his bare breast, from the naked earth:

> Behold, I am one who has been building a house and driving nails with stones that break. The hammer of song has been given me. . . . I shall build my house with great hammers. New song is tearing the cords of my throat.

These songs represent a new plasticity in poetry. To quote from Mr. Anderson's brief preface: "Words run out beyond the power of words." And when the words run out thus, and they are given to us, the suggestions, the half utterances prove as forceful, as direct, as the more evolved crests of expression. Of course this method is one of shifting planes, of broken images, but the truth is in the final unity of the impression received. Many of the songs are moving as music is moving; we are emotionally stirred without knowing exactly why. Does the musician know the meaning of every note that comes to him? Mr. Anderson has been content to set down chords and phrases without troubling about context or sequence, letting the compelling emotion take care of that, letting the chain of associations work out in its own way. In a sense these songs are musical improvisations, with recurring themes and motives. In the *Song of Industrial America*, we have the opening theme, "They tell themselves so many little lies, beloved" . . . "They tell themselves so many little lies;" and then the recurrent, "I'm the broken end of a song myself" . . . "I'm a song myself, the broken end of a song myself." In the *Song of the Soul of Chicago*, it is "the bridges, always the bridges," and so on.

There is indeed much more design in the songs than Mr. Anderson would seem to indicate. Perhaps he wanted to forestall the critics by simply making them a present of what they might choose as their chief weapon—crudity! And they have taken the cue. But the crudity here is a knowing crudity, an expressive crudity. Mr. Anderson has a sure sense of what he wants to do. He is not fumbling. If there is apparent groping, a

*Originally published in *Poetry*, 12 (June, 1918), pp. 155–58, copyright © 1918 by the Modern Poetry Association. Reprinted by permission of the Editor of *Poetry* and Mrs. Edgar L. Rossin.

choked articulateness, it is because this is precisely the emotion to be conveyed. And what he conveys in this book is the groping, choked struggle of the soul in "Mid-America" towards song:

> I am a little thing, a tiny little thing on the vast prairies. I know nothing. My mouth is dirty. I cannot tell what I want. My feet are sunk in the black swampy land, but I am a lover. I love life. In the end love shall save me.

> First there are the broken things—myself and the others. I don't mind that—I'm gone, shot to pieces. I'm part of the scheme—I'm the broken end of a song myself. We are all that, here in the West, here in Chicago. Tongues clatter against teeth. There's nothing but shrill screams and a rattle. That had to be—it's part of the scheme.

> Little faint beginning of things—old things dead—sweet old things—a life lived in Chicago, in the West, in the whirl of industrial America.
> God knows you might have become something else—just like me. You might have made soft little tunes, written cynical little ditties, eh? Why the devil didn't you make some money and own an automobile?

It is the cry of the singer under the burden of industrialism, the dust of the cities against the clean green life of the corn-fields, the strident need for song above the clatter of the machines. And through it all is conveyed also a certain love of this thing that we call our civilization—the dust, the weariness, the undercurrent of remembrance of old sweet natural things; the factories, the engines, "the bridges, always the bridges"—with, somehow, a willingness to see the thing through, and the faith and the prayer that we may get back to the clean life of the growing corn at last.

Of course this "interpretation" really limits the book. It doesn't need any interpretation, any more than music does; it is to be felt. As Mr. John Butler Yeats says: "What can be explained is not poetry." It is significant, I think, that "Mid-America" is becoming self-conscious, is expressing itself in song in a fashion distinctive to itself. One has no wish to be partisan or sectional; but is it not through local consciousness that we shall achieve national expression? By local consciousness, of course, one does not mean anything so slight and superficial as "local color," which is only skin-deep. Mr. George Moore has said that cosmopolitanism kills art. But art was always cosmopolitan; the barriers which he assumed to be so absolute were always transcended, there was a tremendous amount of borrowing in the antique world. What really isolated art and produced that unique flavor which we call national or racial was the artist's attachment to place upon which his sense of identity depended; and this selection of place and atmosphere, this orientation of the spirit for the sake of the preservation of identity, will always operate—it will never be lacking to art, however much it may be lacking to all life outside art. What is significant, then, in the work of men like Vachel Lindsay, Carl Sandburg, Edgar Lee Masters and Sherwood Anderson, as well as other poets that one could name, is this sense of identity with their own country-side, their own city's streets, and with the past, present and future of "Mid-America." It is from this kind of thing that national art springs. Yet the work of these men is widely divergent—another hopeful sign of vitality and fertility. One may accept one and reject another; yet they are all, one must admit, expressively "Mid-American."

The reader will no doubt be repelled as well as attracted by many of these songs. That too is one source of their strength, of their expressiveness. No one poet will tell the whole story. Both Synge and Yeats reveal the soul of Ireland.

# "A Country Town"

Maxwell Anderson*

Every middle westerner will recognize Winesburg, Ohio, as the town in which he grew up. Devon, Iowa, would have furnished forth just such a book as this had an incisive historian made the community his own; so would Minnewaukan, North Dakota, or Wolf Point, Montana, or any one of ten thousand others. The story of a small town anywhere is the story of the revolt of youth against custom-morality; with youth winning only occasionally and in secret, losing often and publicly. In the middle west the dominant morality of the cross-roads is a puritan inheritance. Puritanism went over to Ohio from New England with the settlers, and has taken a firmer hold on the minds and lives of the inhabitants of the Mississippi valley than it ever had in the east. Hell-fire begins to look a trifle comical in Massachusetts. There is a wide-spread recognition of other inconveniences more direct and immediate. But in Kansas and Nebraska the most potent terror is still the anger of a deity.

The Winesburg of twenty years ago was like the Kansas of today, at least in philosophy. The known and accepted standards were those laid down some thousands of years ago by the leader of one of the nomadic tribes of Asia Minor, crudely adjusted to fit a more complex situation. In many ways the ancient laws could not be adjusted at all; they seem to have confused and darkened more often than they shed light. The wonder is that so few shins were broken on the ten tables of stone. Five hundred sensitive individuals isolated in a haphazard spot on the prairie and seeking to express themselves through the forms of a religion ill-understood, the methods of a business system inherently unjust, and the social customs of a more brutal and bitter era were fated to come upon tragic and pathetic difficulties. For that matter there has never been any truth in the notion of pensive hamlets and quiet little villages. Cranford may have dozed. There were no men in Cranford. But the dwellers in -villes and -burgs and -towns from Jamestown in Maine to Jamestown in California can tell you truths about their neighbors that will shatter forever what remains of the assumption that life seethes most treacherously in cities and that there are sylvan retreats where the days pass from harvest to harvest like an idyl of Theocritus. There is outward repose over Winesburg, a gar-

*Originally published in the *New Republic*, 19 (25 June, 1919), pp. 257, 260.

ment of respectable repose covering alike the infinite pain, the grief, the agony of futile groping, the momentary flare of beauty or passion of which the citizens are ashamed.

We are given our view of Winesburg through twenty-three sketches dealing with the crises in as many lives. The lives are inter-related, and a multitude of subsidiary figures drift through the incidents, appearing and disappearing, grouping and changing, in the manner of pedestrians along a by-street. The stories are homely and unemphatic. Crime and love and merry-making come casually into being; chance exalts and flatters, thwarts and subdues. The character that re-emerges oftenest is George Willard, reporter for the Winesburg Eagle. He is the ordinary, bumptious young man with dreams of getting "away from all this" and doing "something" huge and vague in distant cities. To him the town is dull and queer. Save when shocked or startled into a mood of insight he sees little but news values. It was old Parcival who first shocked him. He "began to plead with George Willard. 'You must pay attention to me,' he urged. 'If something happens to me perhaps you will be able to write the book that I may never get written. The idea is very simple, so simple that if you are not careful you will forget it. It is this—that everyone in the world is Christ, and they are all crucified. That's what I want to say. Don't you forget that. Whatever happens, don't you dare let yourself forget.' "

The most satisfactory of the sketches is the one called Paper Pills, a bit from the lives of Doctor Reefy and the tall dark girl who became his wife. There are only five pages of it, and it is told effortlessly, almost carelessly, yet it suggests better than any of the more conscious attempts the theme that engages Mr. Anderson throughout, the loneliness of human life, the baffled search of every personality for meanings and purposes deeper than anything that may be said or done, answers that will cut under the superficial axioms by which we are judged. "The girl and Doctor Reefy began their courtship on a summer afternoon. He was forty-five then, and already he had begun the practice of filling his pockets with the scraps of paper that became hard balls and were thrown away. The habit had been formed as he sat in his buggy behind the jaded grey horse and went slowly along country roads. On the papers were written thoughts, ends of thoughts, beginnings of thoughts. One by one the mind of Doctor Reefy had made the thoughts. Out of many of them he formed a truth that arose gigantic in his mind. The truth clouded the world. It became terrible and then faded away and the little thoughts began again." The girl had come to him because she was pregnant, and there was nobody else to confide in. We hear nothing of their talk together. "The condition that had brought her to him passed in an illness, but she was like one who has discovered the sweetness of the twisted apples, she could not get her mind fixed again on the round perfect fruit that is eaten in the city apartments. In the fall after the beginning of her acquaintanceship with him she married Doctor Reefy and in the following spring she died. During the winter he read to her all of the odds and ends of thoughts he had scribbled on the bits of paper. After he had read them he laughed and stuffed them away in his pockets to become round hard balls."

As a challenge to the snappy short story form, with its planned proportions of flippant philosophy, epigrammatic conversation, and sex danger, nothing better has come out of America than Winesburg, Ohio. Because we have so little in the field it is probably easy to over-estimate its excellence. In Chekhov's sketches simplicity is an artistic achievement. With Sherwood Anderson simplicity is both an art and a limitation. But the present book is well within his powers, and he has put into it the observation, the brooding "odds and ends of thoughts," of many years. It was set down by a patient and loving craftsman; it is in a new mood, and one not easily forgotten.

# "Mr. Sherwood Anderson's America"

Robert Morss Lovett*

Mr. Anderson, like Deukalion, creates his man from a clod of earth—"found in a little hole of a town stuck on a mud bank on the western shore of the Mississippi." Hugh McVey as a boy followed his father listlessly about the town, sweeping saloons, cleaning outhouses, or slept beside him on the river bank with the smell of the fish upon them and the flies about them. A New England woman, the wife of the station-agent, took Hugh and taught him "to keep his naturally indolent body moving and his clouded sleepy mind fixed on definite things." After her departure his awakened will forced him into activity. "He arose from his chair and walked up and down the station platform. Each time as he lifted one of his long feet and set it slowly down a special little effort had to be made. . . . 'If I do not move and keep moving I'll become like father, like all of the people about here' Hugh said to himself." His will carried his body to Bidwell, Ohio, and his mind through the laborious processes of inventing machines for planting cabbages and loading hay; the industrial expansion of the town bore him on to wealth and a kind of distinction. There Hugh sticks, and Mr. Anderson brings up his reserves in the person of Clara Butterworth, daughter of a magnate of the town who has made money out of Hugh's inventions. Clara's story is one of sexual awakening. Through her hoydenish girlhood on her father's farm, her course at a co-educational college, and her association with her masculine friend Kate Chanceller she remains dissatisfied. It is her will which forces Hugh into marriage and eventually into cohabitation with her. Mr. Anderson does not tie on a romantic conclusion as in Windy MacPherson's Son. He leaves Hugh and Clara incomplete and spiritually groping, part of

> "That life, whose dumb wish is not missed
> If birth proceeds, if things subsist;
> The life of plants, and stones, and rain."

In this severely elemental conception there is a certain grandeur. Hugh McVey is a distinct human type—a sort of sub-conscious Lincoln. Even when his individual story ceases to interest us he remains a symbol of

*Originally published in *The Dial*, 70 (January, 1921), pp. 77–79.

the country itself in its industrial progress and spiritual impotence. Hugh McVey, the physically overgrown, almost idiotic boy, is the microcosm of that Middle West in the early 'eighties which Mr. Anderson knows so well and sketches so laconically.

"In all the towns of mid-western America it was a time of waiting. The country having been cleared and the Indians driven away into a vast distant place spoken of vaguely as the West, the Civil War having been fought and won, the minds of men were turned in upon themselves. The soul and its destiny was spoken of openly on the streets. Robert Ingersoll came to Bidwell to speak in Terry's Hall, and after he had gone the question of the divinity of Christ for months occupied the minds of the citizens. The ministers preached sermons on the subject, and in the evening it was talked about in stores. Every one had something to say. Even Charley Mook, who dug ditches, and who stuttered so that not a half dozen people in town could understand him, expressed his opinion."

And Hugh McVey, harnessing his mind to problems of mechanical invention and solving them by a power he does not understand, typifies the spirit of industrial pioneering in all its crude force.

"A vast energy seemed to come out of the breast of earth and infect the people. Thousands of the most energetic men of the Middle States wore themselves out in forming companies, and when the companies failed, immediately formed others. In the fast-growing towns, men who were engaged in organizing companies representing a capital of millions lived in houses thrown hurriedly together by carpenters who, before the time of the great awakening, were engaged in building barns. Without music, without poetry, without beauty in their lives or impulses, a whole people, full of the native energy and strength of lives lived in a new land, rushed pell-mell into a new age."

The pattern of Mr. Anderson's book is determined even in its detail by this fundamental conception. He makes use of the abundant material which Winesburg, Ohio revealed without diminishing, and each minor character and episode contributes to the picture as a whole. Sarah Shephard with her school-mistressly formula: "Show them that you can do perfectly the task given you to do, and you will be given a chance at a larger task"—what is she but the spirit of New England, brooding on the vast abyss of the Middle West, and making it pregnant? Harley Parsons with his boast "I have been with a Chinese woman, and an Italian, and with one from South America—I'm going back and I'm going to make a record. Before I get through I'm going to be with a woman of every nationality on earth, that's what I'm going to do," what is he but an ironic incarnation of our national destiny? Joe Wainsworth, the harness maker who in warfare against machinery and machine-made goods kills his assistant—he is the ghost of the past attacking the present. Smoky Pete, the blacksmith who shouts out to the fields the scandal he dares not utter on Main Street—he is the true spirit of American prophecy, the Jeremiah of Ohio. These and countless other figures show Mr. Anderson's easy mastery of Middle Western life, and his power to touch it with significance. He has made his story a Pilgrim's Progress, peopled with characters as actual and as full of meaning as those of the immortal allegory.

Mr. Anderson's formula is realism, enlarged and made significant by symbolism. It is the formula of Frank Norris—but Mr. Anderson's realism is more seizing and his symbolism more sustained, while his emphasis is far less. It is in lack of emphasis that Mr. Anderson's novel falls below the effect of his short stories. Poor White does not end—it merely stops. Even so it may be regarded as an advance on Mr. Anderson's earlier novels. No ending is better than a false one, and perhaps any emphasis would be misplaced in Mr. Anderson's cosmos—or chaos.

# "An American Masterwork"

Lawrence Gilman*

Mr. Sherwood Anderson's extraordinary book, *The Triumph of the Egg*, labors under two handicaps. In the first place, it has won a prize—an actual hard-cash prize of $2,000 offered by *The Dial* for the best American book of the year, to be awarded in recognition of the service rendered to letters by some young American writer; and the usual quality of prize-winning novels, poems, plays, operas, symphonies, is known to all. In the second place, Mr. Anderson's book deals frankly and veraciously with the human scene—specifically, with the American scene. Under the double handicap thus indicated, is it any wonder that two varieties of readers are indisposed toward *The Triumph of the Egg?*—those who, being wary and experienced, cannot help shying at the kind of art that wins prizes; and those who are distressed by too sustained a display of intellectual and imaginative veracity.

We may dispose of the first matter—a serious potential prejudice—by the assurance that, according to the usual standards operative in the awarding of prizes for aesthetic endeavor, Mr. Anderson's book would not have had a chance in the world: for it flouts—or rather it quietly ignores—all of the conventionalized, institutionalized criteria that are influential in such cases. But it happens, wonderfully enough, that this particular contest was guided by sensitive, intelligent, and singularly courageous standards. The donors honored themselves in honoring Mr. Anderson. There remains the handicap imposed by the remorseless veracity of Mr. Anderson's book—a thing which cannot so easily or so quickly be condoned. Let us consider Mr. Anderson's achievement as leisurely and calmly as may be.

*The Triumph of the Egg* bears this sub-title: *A Book of Impressions from American Life in Tales and Poems*. The poems consist of a two-part prologue and an epilogue, and may be set aside for the moment. The "tales" are thirteen in number, and, with a single and negligible exception, they are precisely what the author calls them: "impressions from American life"—satirical, farcical, tragical, allegorical, idyllic; but all of them are profoundly grave and profoundly poignant. To the casual eye, the book is a collection of unrelated sketches and tales, with one novelette

*Originally published in *North American Review*, 216 (March, 1922), pp. 412–16.

filling about a third of the space. But this is not essentially their character. The parts form a unified whole; not through identity of characters or unity of place or continuity of action, but because, as Mr. Robert Morss Lovett has happily said of them, "they answer to each other like the movements of a *symphonie pathétique*, combining to give a single reading of life, a sense of its immense burden, its pain, its dreariness, its futile aspiration, its despair."

These impressions, tales, sketches, parables, fantasies—call them what you choose—conform to a certain kind of contemporary music rather than to the kind of writing that usually goes into American fiction. In certain of these pieces—for example, in *The Man in the Brown Coat*—the effect is curiously like that achieved by Stravinsky or Bloch or Schönberg or Ornstein in one of those haunting and intangible projections in tone which hold the quintessence of an experience. Mr. Anderson uses words with a strange and baffling magic. He uses them in such a way that they shed, slowly and almost imperceptibly, their familiar associations, and take on the unspecific, unshackled expressional quality of the tones of blended and complementary instrumental voices, weaving a musical pattern vaguely, delicately, but most potently evocative. And he does this by no elaborate and cunning effects of iridescence or the subtle interplay of rhythms and verbal tone-colors. The texture of his prose is as a rule curiously plain and humble, though sometimes it becomes piercingly lyrical, sometimes austere and almost processional. His words fly to their mark by the aid of a kind of elliptical speech more daring and subtle even than anything attempted by Meredith or Conrad or Henry James—an ellipsis that, again, has us back to the methods and achievements of a certain type of modern music, with its disuse of transitional framework and its concentration upon essentials.

It is by the aid of this plastic, sensitive, liberated order of verbal indication that he is able to accomplish the kind of revelatory utterance that distinguishes his art. It is a remarkable kind of legerdemain that he exerts—the legerdemain of a mystic, a symbolist, a fantaisiste. His prose is a genuine incantation. His words drift and sway before us, and we perceive hidden, disquieting images of reality. He is a naturalist doubled by a mystic: he is both seer and poet; and out of the drab, pitiful, terrible subject-matter of his tales—tales of trivial, gross, stunted, frustrated, joyless, ugly and twisted human lives—he is able to disclose to us, in revelation after revelation, the human actuality of these poor beings; the infinite pitifulness of these souls who are ourselves. Mr. Anderson is one of those profoundly understanding and clairvoyant artists who are able, by virtue of their sensibility and their compassion and their implacable candor, to tear away what Pater called that "veil of the familiar" which falls between man and his experiences, and which falls also between man and his fellows.

Mr. Anderson, like Maeterlinck, like Dostoievsky, like Tchehov, is determined to call us back to the contemplation of these mysteries. He holds—rationally or intuitively—that fundamental assumption of the mystic's creed: which is (said one of the most delicately perceptive of them) the assumption "of undercurrents in life, of lives within lives"; of, too, "the permanent, essential correspondence of life with life that must exist between the conception which emanates from man's spirit and the image of it which emanates from nature, animate or inanimate." The unspeakable loneliness of the soul, its immitigable detachment and yet its pathetic dependence, speak everywhere out of these intolerably poignant histories. "The spirit of the man who had killed his wife"—says the narrator in the tragic tale called *Brothers*—"came into the body of the little old man there by the roadside. It was striving to tell me the story it would never be able to tell in the court-room in the city, in the presence of the judge. The whole story of mankind's loneliness, of the effort to reach out to unattainable beauty, tried to get itself expressed from the lips of a mumbling old man, crazed with loneliness, who stood by the side of a country road on a foggy morning holding a little dog in his arms. . . . A sort of convulsion shook his body. The soul seemed striving to wrench itself out of the body, to fly away through the fog, down across the plain to the city, to the singer, the politician, the millionaire, the murderer, . . . down in the city. . . . 'We are brothers,' he said—'we have different names, but we are brothers.' " Like Rosalind Wescott in *Out of Nowhere into Nothing*, Mr. Anderson has ever before him that vision of the young girl, with swinging arms and shoulders, going down the stairway, "down into the hidden places in people, into the hall of the little voices. 'I shall understand after this; what shall I not understand?' she asked herself."

LeRoy, walking and talking beside the lake in *Seeds*, muses somberly. "I have seen under the shell of life, and I am afraid," he says. Mr. Anderson is afraid, too, but he is afraid only because of his dread lest he may not be able to make us see what he has seen—that these human histories may baffle him, elude him, address him in vain. He is afraid of his own limitations as communicant, as interpreter; and he makes this confession in his prologue:

Tales are people who sit on the doorstep of the house of my mind.
It is cold outside and they sit waiting.
I look out at a window.

The street before the door of the house of my mind is filled with tales.
They murmur and cry out, they are dying of cold and hunger.

I am a helpless man—my hands tremble.
I should be sitting on a bench like a tailor.
I should be weaving warm cloth out of the threads of thought.
The tales should be clothed.

They are freezing on the doorstep of the house of my mind.
I am a helpless man—my hands tremble.
I feel in the darkness but cannot find the doorknob.
I look out at a window.
Many tales are dying in the street before the house of my mind.

But he is only relatively "helpless". The tales, many of them, *are* clothed—wonderfully clothed. And they live for us unforgettably. Mr. Anderson has something of Maeterlinck's inestimable power of evocation, his ability to make us see, in a gesture or an inflection or a trivial act of recognition or refusal, the spiritual panorama of a whole life, an entire generation. These human Tales are observed, transfixed, set before us with a sobriety, a perfection of truth, a justness and tenderness of notation, an exquisite rectitude, for which it is not easy to find a parallel in fiction. A lesser, a grosser artist could not have touched such material without degrading it by sentimentalism or by travesty. Mr. Anderson is as austere as he is tender; he is, indeed, so fine, so scrupulous an artist that there is no degree of revelation, however bitter or devastating or terrible, which betrays him into a lapse of integrity.

This book—a great book, a very great book—is suffused with an almost unbearable poignancy. Some will not perhaps be ready to grant that it is also rich in beauty. In these transcriptions Mr. Anderson has achieved a beauty that irradiates his page. It is a beauty "wrought from within," wrought from a boundless compassion. For, viewing that importunate company of embodied Tales, he knows that they, that we, are travesties, distortions, anomalies. "To be sure she is a grotesque," says his LeRoy of the Iowa woman in the Chicago lodging-house; "but then all the people in the world are grotesques. We all need to be loved. What would cure her would cure the rest of us also. The disease she had is, you see, universal. We all want to be loved and the world has no plan for creating our lovers."

# "Sherwood Anderson on the Marraige Question"

F. Scott Fitzgerald*

In the last century literary reputations took some time to solidify. Not Tennyson's or Dickens's—despite their superficial radicalism such men flowed with the current of popular thought. Not Wilde's or De Musset's, whose personal scandals made them almost legendary figures in their own lifetimes. But the reputations of Hardy, Butler, Flaubert and Conrad were slow growths. These men swam up stream and were destined to have an almost intolerable influence upon succeeding generations.

First they were esoteric with a group of personal claqueurs. Later they came into a dim rippling vogue. Their contemporaries "tried to read *one* of their books" and were puzzled and suspicious. Finally some academic critic would learn from his betters that they were "the thing," and shout the news aloud with a profound air of discovery, arguing from interior evidence that the author in question was really in full accord with Florence Nightingale and Gen. Booth. And the author, old and battered and with a dozen imitators among the younger men was finally granted a period of wide recognition.

The cultural world is closer knit now. In the last five years we have seen solidify the reputations of two first class men—James Joyce and Sherwood Anderson.

"Many Marriages" seems to me the fullblown flower of Anderson's personality. It is good enough for Lee Wilson Dodd to write a kittenish parody for the Conning Tower. On the strength of "Many Marriages" you can decide whether Anderson is a neurotic or whether you are one and Anderson a man singularly free of all inhibitions. The noble fool who has dominated tragedy from Don Quixote to Lord Tim is not a character in "Many Marriages." If there is nobility in the book it is a nobility Anderson has created as surely as Rousseau created his own natural man. The genius conceives a cosmos with such transcendental force that it supersedes, in certain sensitive minds, the cosmos of which they have been previously aware. The new cosmos instantly approximates ultimate reality as closely as did the last. It is a bromide to say that the critic can only describe the force of his reaction to any specific work of art.

*Originally published in *The New York Herald*, March 4, 1923, section 9, p. 5. Reprinted by permission of Harold Ober Associates, Inc.

I read in the paper every day that, without the slightest warning, some apparently solid and settled business man has eloped with his stenographer. This is the central event of "Many Marriages." But in the glow of an unexhaustible ecstasy and wonder what is known as a "vulgar intrigue" becomes a transaction of profound and mystical importance.

The book is the story of two moments—two marriages. Between midnight and dawn a naked man walks up and down before a statue of the Virgin and speaks of his first marriage to his daughter. It was a marriage made in a moment of half mystical, half physical union and later destroyed in the moment of its consummation.

When the man has finished talking he goes away to his second marriage and the woman of his first marriage kills herself out of a little brown bottle.

The method is Anderson's accustomed transcendental naturalism. The writing is often tortuous. But then just as you begin to rail at the short steps of the truncated sentences (his prose walks with a rope around the ankle and a mischievous boy at the end of the rope) you reach an amazingly beautiful vista seen through a crack in the wall that long steps would have carried you hurriedly by. Again—Anderson feels too profoundly to have read widely or even well. What he takes to be only an empty tomato can whose beauty he has himself discovered may turn out to be a Greek vase wrought on the Ægean twenty centuries before. Again the significance of the little stone eludes me. I believe it to have no significance at all. In the book he has perhaps endowed lesser things with significance. In the case of the stone his power is not in evidence and the episode is marred.

There is a recent piece of trash entitled "Simon Called Peter," which seems to me utterly immoral, because the characters move in a continual labyrinth of mild sexual stimulation. Over this stimulation play the colored lights of romantic Christianity.

Now anything is immoral that consoles, stimulates or confirms a distortion. Anything that acts in place of the natural will to live is immoral. All cheap amusement becomes, at maturity, immoral—the heroin of the soul.

"Many Marriages" is not immoral—it is violently anti-social. But if its protagonist rested at a defiance of the fallible human institution of monogamy the book would be no more than propaganda. On the contrary, "Many Marriages" begins where "The New Machiavelli" left off. It does not so much justify the position of its protagonist as it casts a curious and startling light on the entire relation between man and woman. It is the reaction of a sensitive, highly civilized man to the phenomenon of lust—but it is distinguished from the work of Dreiser, Joyce and Wells (for example) by utter lack both of a concept of society as a whole and of the necessity of defying or denying such a concert. For the purpose of the book no such background as Dublin Catholicism, middle Western morality or London Fabianism could ever have existed. For all his washing machine factory the hero of "Many Marriages" comes closer than any character, not excepting Odysseus, Lucifer, Attila, Tarzan and, least of all, Conrad's Michaelis, to existing in an absolute vacuum. It seems to me a rather stupendous achievement.

I do not like the man in the book. The world in which I trust, on which I seem to set my feet, appears to me to exist through a series of illusions. These illusions need and occasionally get a thorough going over ten times or so during a century.

The man whose power of compression is great enough to review this book in a thousand words does not exist. If he does he is probably writing subtitles for the movies or working for a car card company.

# "Mr. Anderson's New Stories"

Newton Arvin*

> *Something there is that doesn't love a wall,*
> *That wants it down!*

Thus the quizzical farmer in Mr. Frost's best-known poem; and thus, if he spoke blank verse, almost any one of Mr. Sherwood Anderson's nostalgic, solitary personages. The one, I know, is a New Hampshire rebel; the others are farmers and small-town folk of the Middle West; but the difference is not a fundamental one. Mr. Anderson will tell you that his Middle Westerners are but a generation or two removed from New England; that the same frugal blood runs in their contracted veins; that, if they had stone walls to mend, they too would "keep the wall between them as they went." The recurrence throughout his fiction of this isolation-motive is no accident: Mr. Anderson could not be the authentic artist he is and not reflect, like a poet, the deep human truth of the milieu he has undertaken to interpret. One remembers Wing Biddlebaum in "Winesburg," who "did not think of himself as in any way a part of the life of the town where he had lived for twenty years." In the tale called "Unused," in his new volume, one recognizes the old predicament: of the girl May Edgely we are told that "if she was walled in, shut off from participation in the life of the Ohio town—hated, feared by the town—she could come out of the town." For the richness of their data, I repeat, these half-dozen stories are worth a library of sociological history, and no one who would know the heart of the Middle West can neglect them. Did such a task ever before or elsewhere force itself upon an artist like Mr. Anderson: the task of depicting a life so clumsily organized for human intercourse, so sterile in the values of personality, so poverty-stricken in what makes for humane conviviality, so hostile (as a consequence) to the integrity of the individual soul?

This, at any rate, is what I read into that singular spiritual delicacy of Mr. Anderson, into what I can only call his passionate puritanism. Only in regard to a life that in some sinister way threatened the purity of the individuals who capitulated to it, would an artist be so concerned for

*Originally published in *The Freeman*, 8 (5 December, 1923), pp. 307–08. Reprinted by permission of *The Freeman*.

the inviolability of the ego in its resistance to what philosophers call the "not-me." If this intense "idiocrasy" is not what puritanism always amounts to, it is characteristic of puritanism on its highest level: on the level on which Whitman defined the twin principle of democracy as "individuality, the pride and centripetal isolation of a human being in himself—identity—personalism."

The hero of Mr. Anderson's fable is the man who goes among his fellow-beings holding the cup of his "identity" as a kind of Grail, intangible by the profane. The special tragedy is that there are none but the profane to touch it; that the contacts which should be cleansing are for the most part smirching, and the experiences which should be joyously shared have to be joylessly withheld. The result can be only a kind of spiritual deformity. This, I suppose, is what the old man in the foreword to "Winesburg" means when he says "that the moment one of the people took one of the truths to himself, called it his truth, and tried to live his life by it, he became a grotesque and the truth he embraced became a falsehood." This is the perplexity of the young man in "A Chicago Hamlet," in this volume, bathing himself in cold water at night in the darkness of his room, obsessed with "this business of making oneself the keeper of the clean integrity of oneself." We are told that he had "a kind of almost holy inner modesty"; and we realize that the pathos of what happens at the end lies in the fugacity of an experience which momentarily offered a relationship not hostile to that modesty.

Like a certain sort of puritan, Mr. Anderson is more interested in the inner life than in anything else; indeed, "this vain show of things" seems to him but an aspect of the inner life, and he is not too curious about the line that divides material from spiritual. This is what gives his fiction its curiously poetic quality, and, in details, accounts for the seemingly unpremeditated beauty of many of his figures. ("My fruit shall not be my fruit until it drops from my arms, into the arms of others, over the top of the wall.") If the word had not too many dusty connotations, one would say that Mr. Anderson was a symbolist; he is at any rate a symbolist without the doctrine, a sort of congenital symbolist: to him the myth is not a theory but an irresistible mode of expression. It will not do to quarrel with him for not being a "realist." Mr. Edmund Wilson objects that none of the personages in "Many Marriages" has a persuasive reality; that they are consistently incredible as washing-machine manufacturers and housekeepers. But surely it should not need to be pointed out that reality exists on several planes; that the reality of "Babbitt," valid as it is, is but one kind of reality; that John Webster is not a washing-machine manufacturer, in any special literal sense, but the man who has walked part way down the road to death and has come back to walk the way of life. The employment of this mythopoetic reality is Mr. Anderson's special forte, and it can be vindicated on the solidest artistic grounds; it gives form and colour to fables of subtle subjective experience which would otherwise be too insubstantial for artistic treatment. The fiction of the inner life would hardly be possible on any other terms.

It is even doubtful whether we can with accuracy speak of Mr. Anderson as a novelist; at least if that name is to be reserved for writers in the tradition, for the followers of Flaubert (like Mr. Sinclair Lewis) or the followers of Henry James (like Mrs. Wharton). In any sense in which these people are novelists, Mr. Anderson must be denied the title; for their scrupulous account of the extrinsic truth, even for their manipulation of psychological drama, he has but mediocre capacities; he has little command over the cool irony which makes Mr. Lewis something of a satirist, and little skill in the handling of complex personal relationships such as Mrs. Wharton reports. He has almost nothing in common with those "erudite and elegant" writers whom Whitman inveighed against. This is indeed his artistic strength; the methods of the novelists I have mentioned would not begin to serve his special and difficult purpose; they are the fictional analogues of a highly organized, highly civilized, completely articulate social order, and the interpretation of such an order is not Mr. Anderson's task. Hitherto the novelist's rôle has not been much like that of the bard: he has attempted not so much to give utterance to confused communal emotions as to chronicle, either epically or dramatically, and with a certain detachment, the circumstances of the life about him. That he did not come, in the first place, until comparatively late, is a fact of some significance. Mr. Anderson is attempting—more or less unconsciously, no doubt—to fill the rôle of a kind of bardic poet: to put into simple and beautiful forms the vague and troubling pains of a bewildered people, to personalize a rather mechanical life, to give new values to a world that has discarded its old ones as invalid. And that, as the teller of "The Man's Story" says, "is I suppose what poetry is all about."

# "O Pioneers!"

Carl Van Doren*

There can never be too many such books as "A Story Teller's Story," and there will never be many. What Mr. Anderson has written he calls "the tale of an American writer's journey through his own imaginative world and through the world of facts." It is not, however, merely another literary biography. It is the record of a creative spirit making its way among a thousand obstacles, all of them trying to force it back into the obedient patterns of standardized America. There was little enough in Mr. Anderson's early circumstances to help make an artist of him. He drifted as aimlessly, if not as spectacularly, as Mark Twain through various undistinguished villages and towns, with only chance acquaintances and accidental reading to point a road away from the mediocrity which surrounded him. Strictly speaking, he was perhaps not aimless. His own discontent everlastingly drove him in the direction which his nature wanted him to take, but it could not furnish him with any detailed map of the route. All he knew was that he hated to live in a universe in which so many persons seemed contented to be dead. "To live," he held, "is to create constantly new forms: with the body in living children; in new and more beautiful forms carved out of materials; in the creation of a world of the fancy; in scholarship; in clear and lucid thought; and those who do not live die and decay and from decay always a stench arises." By such a conception Mr. Anderson steered his course. How long and how deviously he wandered in the wilderness his book reveals.

Yet the book wastes little time in blaming the conditions which postponed the historian's arrival at something like his goal. It is a rich, fullbodied history, bent upon the end, yet still delighting in the intermediate steps. Like another "Walden," "A Story Teller's Story" chronicles an unusual experience without vanity and with good humor. If it seems less systematic than "Walden," that is partly because Mr. Anderson is less a man of fact than Thoreau and because he was not so early aware of what he wanted. If it seems less exhaustive a commentary upon the times than "The Education of Henry Adams," that is partly because Mr. Anderson was less in contact with the great world than Henry Adams and had not so varied a culture to work with. But it may without serious

*Originally published in the *Century Magazine*, 109 (March, 1925), pp. 176–77.

48

danger from the comparison be mentioned with either of these books. It belongs with the few best American autobiographies.

In the development of Mr. Anderson's own art it marks a triumph which he has not hitherto achieved. Only a handful of his short stories have been so free and flexible and significant and harmonious. His novels are dimmed by his confessions. Hitherto he has, in his longer works, been not quite able to round his matter into form. In "A Story Teller's Story" he has achieved a large, bold outline and has sustained his narrative to its conclusion. This may be because the matter itself provided a form for him, but it could not have done so had he still lacked the artistic tact which he lacked when he wrote "Marching Men" or "Poor White." A delicate selection and a subtle emphasis have had a hand in the success with which he builds up the drama of his escape from the clutches of routine. One chapter follows another with the loose consecutiveness which men feel in their lives while they are looking at the immediate present, but with the steady unfolding which they see in them when they look back. Mr. Anderson's style is here at once beautiful and vernacular. He has at last fitted his art to his materials on a large scale.

# "From an Inner Fever"

It is very easy to be deceived by a book like this. "Testament" is in itself an imposing word, in whichever sense one reads it. In that title there is the insinuation of something definitive, of a new order, a new dispensation, set forth for all to see. And the suggestions of the title are pushed a step further by the format of the book. It looks as if it might be the "Little Flowers" of St. Francis or the "Garden of the Soul"—red and black title, correctly Gothic headings, a spattering of neat rubrics, blue silk marker. It looks as if it might become the tried companion of one's meditative or midnight moments. It looks as if every reading, year after year, would bring out deeper, richer meanings, as if—but one should look closer before taking a testament at its face value.

"A New Testament" is a book of fragments. A certain number of them are brought together from "The Triumph of the Egg," but most of them appear for the first time. The publishers of the book are slightly on the defensive when they remark that by calling these new forms poetry, they lay them open to "the microscope of the precisionist critic and the carping conservative." But this is a pure matter of labels, and has little real meaning. It should be granted at once that the fragments have all the character of spontaneous and rhythmic expression which would entitle them to the label of "poetry." But there is no need to be unduly impressed by that fact. Poetry and sincerity may both be here. But they are not keys that will open every door: truth lies hid sometimes in places where a man must have more than these bare attributes if he is to discover it. And it is here that Anderson's claim to be laying forth a "testament," a statement of order and doctrine, falls short. The book is one of fragments. They have beneath them the vague unity of one voice, one rhythm, one persistent questioning and struggle, but not the real unity of consistent discovery. And fragments they remain.

But they remain highly characteristic of Anderson.

One Who Looked Up at the Sky
It would be strange if, by a thought, a man could make
Illinois pregnant.

*Originally published in *The Saturday Review of Literature*, 4 (September 3, 1927), pp. 85–86. Reprinted by permission of *the Saturday Review*.

50

It would be strange if the man who just left my house and went tramping off in the darkness to take a train to a distant place came here from a far place, came over lands and seas, to impregnate me.

There is a testament out of life to the man who has just left my presence. There is a testament to be made to a woman who once held me in her arms and who got no child. There is a testament to be made to this house, to the sunshine that falls on me, to these legs of mine clad in torn trousers, to the sea and to a city sleeping on a prairie.

Diffuse and indeterminate, Anderson's ideas are never formulated to the satisfaction of a reader who is following him with *intelligence*, and not merely with an ear open to the filmy suggestions of a succession of loosely related images. Nor are they formulated to his own satisfaction. From first to last in these pieces, Anderson is a man groping in the thickets of his own words. For all the rhythmic beat of his phrases, the steady recurrence of these bare, stark images of pregnancy, of sex, of male and female, of cities and streets, the sense of Laocöon strivings—what happens? Does daylight flash suddenly through the forest? Does he ever rout his own phantoms? No: there is nothing but a rising tide of bewilderment. The bewilderment of this groping man is hidden at a first glance by the vivid sense of battling, sweating, physical effort which is conveyed by his spare, muscular words. But it is there, from first to last. The battle may be honorable, but it is without objective, undirected, baffled, protestant.

I have a passionate hunger to take a bit out of the now—the present. The now is a country to discover which, to be the pioneer in which I would give all thought, all memories, all hopes. . . . I would consume it quite. I would live my life in the present, in the now only.

For that purpose I would be ageless, impotent, potent, swift, a sluggish slow crawling worm, a singing rhythmical thing beating my wings, carried along for an instant in the flight of time. I would myself create a lull in the storm that is myself. If I am a stream gone dry, fill me with living waters. There is something stagnant in me. As I write, breathe, move back and forth in this room life is passing from me. Do you not see how I pass from one present into another unknowing? I would leave nothing unknown. To live in the presence of the unknown is death to me.

That passage is from one of the longer fragments, "A Thinker." It is difficult to isolate quotations from a work like this with fairness, but it is typical enough of the essential insipidness which is unexpectedly revealed by Anderson when he dispenses with the solid framework of his storytelling. In the case of a novelist so significant as the author of "The Triumph of the Egg" or "Many Marriages," it is worth while entering a caveat against this barren mysticism of "A New Testament." It contains no revelation. It is a long hammering against a closed door. It is a mysticism of mere struggle, and not of enlightenment. Its neurotic violence is a counterpart of that other false mysticism which finds its devotees amongst those who are ready to abandon the discipline of human reason and institutions, to sink into swooning resignation, "in tune with the infinite." Both are dangerous, but Sherwood Anderson's the less so because he is so seldom persuasive. It is enough to turn for a few minutes from "A New Testament" to almost any page of "Leaves of Grass:" at once one realizes which comes from an inner flame, which only from an inner fever.

# "Sherwood Anderson"

T. K. Whipple*

The publication, after seven years, of a new novel by Sherwood Anderson is a reminder, and a melancholy one, of the happy days from 1915 to 1925 when the movement in which he was conspicuous was in full swing. The reminder is melancholy, because that movement has vanished and has had as yet no adequate successor. Fifteen years ago the whole literary world was alive with the excitement of hope and expectation, but now, though good writers have recently appeared, they seem unrelated and sporadic, not a conquering, bannered host. To be sure, the movement which began in the flare-up over free verse and died in the flare-up over humanism failed to keep all its promises—too many of the luminaries we thought might be planets proved meteorites, burnt out as soon as ignited—but is not that because every genuine movement excites anticipations beyond any possible achievement?

We have merely witnessed again a common and recurrent phenomenon. Not only have meteorites always been the rule in the literary sky, planets the exception, but furthermore it is a law of literary history that "renaissances" and "movements," which look at the time novel and brave, as if in ushering in new eras, are regularly, on the contrary, ushering old eras out. I might illustrate this law with the Elizabethan Age and the Romantic Movement in England; but I will cite only the American period, our "Golden Day," which closed with "Leaves of Grass." Whitman undoubtedly thought he was announcing a quite fresh epoch, whereas he was actually terminating one that had begun some thirty-five years earlier. Similarly, the outburst of 1915–1925, instead of inaugurating anything, will probably be seen in retrospect to have ended a movement which had had its inception half a century before.

None of the galaxy of the Harding Era shone more brightly or went out more suddenly than Sherwood Anderson, and "Beyond Desire" helps explain both his own fate and that of his contemporaries. He and they were growing up, most of them in the midland, in the eighties and nineties, and the world of their youth, as Anderson's autobiographical writings show, was still in the main the older America—for convenience

*Originally published in *The Saturday Review of Literature*, 9 (December 10, 1932), p. 305.

let us call it Mark Twain's America: it was still in essentials the world of Tom Sawyer and Huck Finn. With this America, now blighted and moribund, Anderson dealt successfully, though in an appropriately bleak spirit, in all his best work from "Winesburg" on. That whole way of life was based upon free land and upon agriculture; it died with the disappearance of free land and the triumph of the machine. The United States entered upon a new phase of its history, and Anderson and his coevals found themselves precipitated into an alien day. His earlier work was all a sharp and bitter epitaph for the old world that was perishing, and a curse for the new world being born—and rightly so, since he belonged to his own times.

But now in "Beyond Desire" he has made an effort to catch up, to adapt both himself and his subject matter to the present. He has written a story of mill workers in Southern mill towns; his treatment reveals his new attitude towards communism. His hero, Red Oliver, a middle class boy, son of an unsuccessful doctor, and a college graduate, by going to work as a mill hand abandons his own social class without finding another, since he is not really accepted by the workers. With this boy Anderson contrasts on the one hand a group of girls who work in the mills, and on the other a woman of Oliver's class, the town librarian Ethel Long, discontented and unsatisfied, with whom Red has a sexual experience.

The jacket of the book says that the hero "must run the gamut of hungers, must satisfy all desires before he can himself be beyond desire"— a statement as misleading as any could be. For the point of the story, if there is one, must be that, so far from "satisfying all desires," nobody manages to satisfy any desire, however hard he tries. Red Oliver's social as well as his sexual longings are thwarted. Perhaps after he has attached himself to the Communists (with whom he has no sense of belonging) and has been shot for disobeying a militia captain's command, he may be said, being dead, to be beyond desire; but he arrives at that condition quite fortuitously, not by any design or ordered progress. When he disobeys, he feels himself as big a fool as the militia captain did after issuing the command. Both of them, like all the other people in the book, are caught in a situation they cannot understand or cope with. They are as puzzled, groping, and baffled as any of Anderson's previous characters.

Questioning and bewilderment, of course, have always been as conspicuous in the author as in his people, but in his better books, for all his perplexity, he was able as writer and artist to deal with his material. That ability seems to have deserted him. In part it is that in trying for a form more or less like Dos Passos's, he has fumbled it; even more it is that he has undertaken to handle people and situations which are not his own. At any rate, "Beyond Desire" lacks that amazing insight, that extraordinary power of "going beneath the surface of the lives of men and women," he displayed in treating the folk of his own generation. The modern young Americans in "Beyond Desire," though true enough as far as they go, are done from the outside, not with the inwardness of Anderson's earlier characters. That the material has not been creatively entered into, is shown by his taking refuge in annoying mannerisms, which have replaced honest, spontaneous writing, as well as by his failure to integrate the novel as a whole.

"Beyond Desire" is an account, by a man lost between two ages, of people likewise lost between two ages; he and they are in the same plight. If his account is unsatisfactory, it must be because he belongs chiefly to the last age, they to the next—he to the dead, they to the unborn. Hence comes the weakness of the novel: it is the product of an assumed attitude, of a point of view which the author thinks—no doubt correctly—he ought to have, but which is not natural and instinctive.

A comparison with Dos Passos is illuminating. "Beyond Desire" is just the book to have proved, in Dos Passos's hands, a brilliant triumph. But does not Dos Passos see the present social chaos so clearly and so truly because he sees it contrasted against a *prospective image of order* which is in his own mind? And that prospective image of order is the great lack in the birthright of Sherwood Anderson and in his contemporaries.

Just this lack accounts for the fate of the movement of 1915–1925— not for its failure, since it by no means failed—but for its disappearance. This lack justifies connecting the writers of that school rather with the American past than with the American future.

# "Anderson in America"

Hamilton Basso*

Reading this book was, for me, like reading the notebook of a traveler who has just returned from a country one knows very well. It had, therefore, the special, additional interest that comes from checking another person's observations against one's own. And many times during my reading, as some mountaineer or mill hand came suddenly to life, I found myself nodding in agreement: "Yes—that is true. That is the sort of man he is. That is what he would say."

Mr. Anderson, in this book, has put down the ideas and impressions gained from a tour of the country that took him from the mountains of southwestern Virginia, where he lives, down through the coal country into the cotton-raising and manufacturing districts of the Deep South and thence northwestward into Ohio, Kansas, South Dakota and Minnesota. A foreigner will learn nothing from this book about our geography. The immensity of America—the names of its states and mountains and rivers—does not affect Mr. Anderson as it does Mr. Thomas Wolfe. He has looked at the country in a different way, trying to see it through the eyes of mill workers, tenant farmers, the unemployed; the plain, simple people of the United States. What are they thinking? How do they feel? What will they do?

The final summing-up of Mr. Anderson's observations is that the people of America are deeply puzzled. They feel that something is happening, that the old established patterns of life and society are being rearranged, but they do not know what forms the new patterns will take or how they will fit their own lives into them. They do not know what they are going to do or just where they are going. All over America, like one of the dust storms that cover the Middle West, hangs a cloud of unrest and confusion.

By a simple device of rearrangement, Mr. Louis Adamic and Mr. Ernest Sutherland Bates have discovered the book to be no more than "Puzzled Sherwood Anderson." Both Mr. Adamic and Mr. Bates, in a way that is unworthy of either of them, have let their little obvious piece of wordjugglery carry the burden of their criticism. They have both implied, not without condescension, that Anderson is an all-right fellow when it

*Originally published in *The New Republic*, 82 (May 1, 1935), p. 348.

comes to telling a story, but when he ventures into the realm of thought he becomes like one of his own characters: fumbling, groping, lost.

It is not my purpose to argue that Mr. Anderson is a great thinker. I have never known him to pretend to be a great thinker and he would be the first one, I believe, to admit that in the field of economics and politics he plows a very ragged furrow. On the other hand, the fact remains that any person who goes out into America in this year of disgrace, seeing the country as it is and not as he wishes it to be, can hardly return without some mild puzzlement at least. The only persons immune to it are those who go equipped with a political philosophy that makes the future foreordained; and for each philosophy there is a different future. Mr. Anderson is no prophet. He does not pretend to know how we can get from one state of society into another. But he can see what lies under his nose (which is a kind of far-sightedness not to be discounted too lightly), and he can put down what he sees with accuracy and feeling. What he does, in effect, is to say, "Here is our contemporary America. Make of it what you can." It is a modest statement but, in making it, Mr. Anderson has written his best book since "A Story-Teller's Story."

# [*Kit Brandon*]

## Hamilton Basso*

Kit Brandon, by another name, is a living person. The daughter of a Great Smoky hill-farmer, born in that vast wilderness of space and sky that is just now being penetrated by highways and the T.V.A., she ran away from home as a child and, after many adventures, became a member of a gang of big-time bootleggers. In the mountains she grew into a sort of legend: one of the stories was that she had diamonds in her teeth. Eventually caught and imprisoned, her name and picture spread on the front pages of the newspapers, she was introduced by a mutual friend to Sherwood Anderson. Bit by bit, in long conversations, he got her story. He tells it in this book—a book that contains some of the very best, and some of the very worst, writing he has done: revealing, in an interesting way, the qualities that have made him, on one hand, our greatest genius of the short story and, on the other, our most confused social philosopher.

Let us say, to be brief, that when Anderson is telling the story of Kit Brandon—her childhood in the hills, her life as a mill-girl and a clerk in a five-and-ten—he is nothing short of superb. This book demolishes, if it does nothing else, the currently held opinion that a person of one class cannot enter into the life of a person of another. Sherwood Anderson is no mountaineer, but there has been nothing written in America that gets the feeling of our hill people with more sensitive understanding, more compassion and beauty, than Anderson gets it here. This part of the book is filled with sharp, wise, beautiful portraits—Kit's father and mother; old Tom Halsey, king of the moonshiners and his wife, Kate; the mill-girl radical, Agnes; little blond Sarah who likes to have a good time—these, and at least one of the finest stories Anderson has ever written: the tale of a boy who loves horses so much that, in moments of alcoholic exuberance, he becomes a horse himself.

If this book were simply the story of Kit Brandon, then it would be a magnificent job: ready to take its place with "Winesburg" and "A Story-Teller's Story." It is, however—and perhaps unfortunately—more than that. It is also the story of Sherwood Anderson's latest adventures in search of those two Holy Grails he has long been seeking: the essential truth of Woman and the essential truth of American Life. It would be im-

*Originally published in *The New Republic*, 88 (October 21, 1936), p. 318.

pertinent of me, who once sat at Sherwood Anderson's knee, to say that his searching has been in vain. Nor do I think it has: even if "Kit Brandon," in this respect, leaves me with the feeling that he is not any closer to his goal than he was in "Many Marriages" and "Poor White." Anderson, rejecting the scientific method, has used the method of the poet; and, if he has not given us any definite philosophy, he has, thanks to his poetic intuition, given us many important clues. When he says, for example, that what most Americans are seeking is something to which they can pledge their loyalties—not as members of any class but as human beings—he is saying something very important indeed.

"Kit Brandon," in the sense of Anderson's searching, gets worse as it goes along. It becomes incoherent in both form and language and there are various passages which I defy anybody (except God and Sherwood Anderson) to understand. And yet, even in such passages, we are reminded how much we owe this man and how deeply he has influenced our literature. Hemingway (who repudiated his master in "The Torrents of Spring"), Faulkner (whom Anderson discovered and whose first book was written under his immediate guidance), Caldwell, Thomas Wolfe, George Milburn—all these, among others, have been affected by him. There is a tendency, in our most advanced intellectual circles, to dismiss Anderson with a tolerant wave of the hand. He has been likened, by one critic, to a man who goes on talking on the radio after the current has been turned off. I do not think this is true. Anderson, for many years to come, will have something to say. And, meanwhile, I think it might be wise for us to remember that he was one of the headmasters at the school where so many of us learned our ABC's.

# [Plays: Winesburg and Others]

Anonymous*

A reading of Mr. Anderson's adaptation of some of his famous Winesburg stories into a long and loosely-constructed drama quickly reveals why no producer has yet offered it to Broadway audiences. About Mr. Anderson's short stories there was a strange, far-away atmosphere through which the characters moved in soft grey outlines as they went about their vague but poetic struggle between nostalgia and ambition. On the stage these characters have shed the qualities responsible for their charm, and rant and rave in a bold and frequently embarrassing manner. Crude photography has replaced painting, and the effect for Winesburg is not good.

Mr. Anderson has been troubled, too, by dramatic construction. He has fallen back on the makeshift device of using separate scenes, each a unit and joined to the others mainly by the recurrence of characters. The result is dislocated and bedraggled, though the author has attempted to achieve unity by the insertion of short but formidable interludes having to do mainly with bedroom chatter and throwing bottles at cats.

The success with which Mr. Jasper Deeter presented *Winesburg* at the Hedgerow Theatre, however, indicates that the play is not without possibilities. Part may have been due to Mr. Deeter's personal enthusiasm, and to the rustic setting. One surmises that its fate in a less intimate theatre would be otherwise.

Included in the volume are three one-act plays that somewhat reestablish Mr. Anderson as a dramatist. All are as tightly-woven and concise as *Winesburg* is sprawling, and deserve the attention of ambitious little theatres. *The Triumph of the Egg*, done by the Provincetown Theatre as a curtain raiser for O'Neill's *Different*, made quite a stir and ranks as a tour de force of Middle-Western humor and irony.

*Originally published in *Theater Arts Monthly*, 21 (October, 1937), pp. 824–25.

# Contemporary Social Problems

John C. Cort*

If this is just another item in the "God-Bless-America" campaign, it is still an item very much worth having. Or perhaps America is worth a blessing after all. "Home Town," at any rate, is a really beautiful book of pictures and essays on the American small town and the very interesting people who live there.

The pictures are by Farm Security Photographers (whatever they are) and are uniformly excellent throughout. The essays are by Sherwood Anderson, the famous rural editor and novelist, and discounting a little pantheism, are more than satisfactory and at times genuinely moving.

Anderson starts off by complaining about a young friend who "has a burning desire to remake life, the whole social scheme . . . he declares that the day of the individual has passed, that now we must think of people only in the mass." Anderson, however, thinks the young man should be "trying to get a little better understanding of the people in his own house, in the street on which his house stands; trying to get closer to the people of his own town."

Certainly this is a very Christian idea, and the young man's idea about submerging the individual in the mass is a very un-Christian one, however popular it may have become lately. Anything that can make us see the beauty and importance of life's little things, of life's little people, is a big help in any social scheme. At least we can be sure that no social scheme, however perfect, will be worth the paper on which it is blueprinted unless the men who set out to make it work have a strong feeling for that beauty and that importance. If not, they should read "Home Town" without delay.

*Originally published in *The Commonweal*, 33 (December 20, 1940), p. 233. Reprinted by permission of *The Commonweal*.

# ARTICLES

# "Sherwood Anderson, the Wistfully Faithful"

Nelson Antrim Crawford*

The first time I ever heard of Sherwood Anderson was in December, 1915, when in a copy of *The Little Review* I found a sketch of his entitled *Sister*. The story impressed me. It is not so significant a story as some of Anderson's later work, but that was seven years ago and in that particular seven years American fiction, with Anderson always among the leaders, has gone far.

*Sister* deals with a young woman artist. The author says: "She is my sister, but long ago she has forgotten that and I have forgotten." The only significant incident in the story is the whipping of the girl by her father because she had announced to the family that she was about to take a lover. The incident serves merely to focus the symbolism of the story, which is subsequently expressed thus:

"I am the world and my sister is the young artist in the world. I am afraid the world will destroy her. So furious is my love for her that the touch of her hand makes me tremble."

The entire sketch does not contain more than a thousand words. It shows, in embryo, however, the three factors that have made Anderson's work the most significant contribution to contemporary American literature. One of these factors is style. In this story, as in his later works, the reader feels as if the author were sitting across the table from him telling the story, not simply and directly as textbooks on story writing assume is the natural method, but with inversions, with steps to and fro, with divagations from the main tale, following up the associations of a person, a name, or a word. This is the way people actually think and feel. This is the natural way to tell a story. Anderson is one of the few living writers who can use this method.

In the second place there is manifest in this early work of his a keen feeling for the tragedy of current American life—a tragedy chiefly of frustration. This is a tragedy of youth, individual and national. In a recent book, *On English Poetry*, Robert Graves talks about the "temporary writing of poetry by normal single-track minds," which he says "is most common in youth when the sudden realization of sex, its powers and its

*Originally published in *The Midland*, 8 (November, 1922), pp. 297–308.

limited opportunities for satisfactory expression, turns the world upside down for any sensitive boy or girl." The artist has his art—poetry, or something else—for sublimation, but what of the great number of sensitive young men and women who, instead of talent, have inhibitions? In this our civilization, they are destined for repression and frustration, such as will destroy, or reduce to conventional debauchery, physical or spiritual, the possibilities of keen joy. It is with these folk that Anderson, from the beginning, has been concerned.

Finally, *Sister* shows the mystical symbolic quality which is destined to appear in all of Anderson's work, though subsequently it is much more closely blended with the other qualities of his work. *Sister* obviously goes beyond symbolism into emphatic allegory—an error which Anderson does not again make. Symbolism gives to his later work much of its distinctiveness.

But who is this Anderson who, in seven years, has moved from the pages of a small (though significant) literary magazine, to the position of certainly the most promising and original, if not the greatest, American writer of fiction? Whence comes he and what manner of man is he? Moreover, for what Lord is he a prophet in the wilderness of American industrialism? For whom would he make straight a highway in the desert?

Sherwood Anderson was born in a little town in southwestern Ohio—Camden by name—in 1876. He got no early education to speak of, but he had a heritage of talent, probably from his mother, to whom he dedicates *Winesburg, Ohio* with the statement that her "keen observations on life about her first awoke in me the hunger to see beneath the surface of lives." Two of his brothers became painters. Anderson worked at odd jobs and eventually drifted to Chicago. He was working in a warehouse there when the Spanish-American war broke out and he enlisted. He went to Cuba, but when he was demobilized he was not content to go back to his old way of life. He went to Springfield, Ohio, and entered Wittenberg College as a special student, doing odd jobs to support himself. He stayed there a year or two, then returned to Chicago and entered the advertising business. First he was an advertising solicitor, and later both a solicitor and a copy-writer. He has the reputation of being one of the best mail order copy-writers in America.

Anderson began writing for an advertising journal published by the firm with which he was connected. He prepared a series of short articles on types of business men. These articles, published years ago, attracted the attention of Cyrus Curtis, who was enough interested in them to call at the office of the agency for the purpose of meeting Mr. Anderson.

In 1906 Mr. Anderson became advertising manager of a mail order concern in Cleveland. The following year he went into business for himself in Elyria, Ohio, and divided his time between writing and trying to put a business on its feet. His health and his business both failed—his health only temporarily. He went back to the agency business in Chicago, and ever since that time has used advertising as a means of making a living. His practice has been to do advertising until he got a bit ahead financially, then to turn to writing and devote his sole attention to it for a time. Much of Anderson's writing, nevertheless, has been done in odd moments while he was waiting in hotels, railway stations, and offices in connection with his business.

It is obvious that there was a long period of preparation for the novels, tales, and poems, which most of us know as Sherwood Anderson's work. He himself says he burned a great quantity of writing even before he wrote *Sister*. His first book was published when he was 40 years of age—a striking contrast to many writers of the day, but an interesting confirmation of Carl Sandburg's theory that no writer does significant work before the age of forty. Mr. Anderson's explanation of the genesis of his writing is, as he himself comments, "outwardly at least, a simple matter." He says in a letter:

> "I was a business man and got sick of it, and went into writing, not to make a success, but to give myself an interest in life.
> "Probably I always was, in my outlook on life, an artist, loving the color of things, words, arrangements of words and ideas. I might, I suppose, have been a painter, as I can get excitement and interest out of that too."

Back of this there is, of course, a complexity which is not outward. There is Mr. Anderson's Mid-Western inheritance. There is his bringing up in Ohio, where modern industrialism had not quite overcome the older pride of trade and individual self-sufficiency and where the clouds of religious controversy between strange fanatical puritan sects still hung heavily over the country and the small towns. There was his own actual industrial and business experience. As a lad Anderson roved from job to job. As a man he was closely in touch with the executives of business of all sorts, for to such men no one gets closer than does the advertising agent. Add to these the mystical qualities which are to some extent found in every artist, but which are far more conspicuous in Anderson than in most, and you have some conception of the foundation on which his work rests. From these developed the complexes which betoken the artist and which appear in the writing as the realities of which the outward tendencies were merely symbols.

Anderson knows what he calls Mid-America, but he also knows humanity. Indeed, I am inclined to think that Mid-America is a symbol of the world. Probably something of this sort is true of any great writer, but it seems to me unusually evident in Anderson's work. One feels that the author himself is not an objective observer, but a subjective part of the life with which he deals. I am not sure but that he himself is Mid-America and the world. There is a pertinence to James Oppenheim's line, "He who bares self bares humanity."

Anderson's first two novels, *Windy McPherson's Son*, published in

1916, and *Marching Men*, published in 1917, do not impress me as much as that first little sketch of his that I read. They are scarcely authentic prophecies of his genius. They have understanding, tenderness, beauty, but they seem in a way to partake, unintentionally and not altogether artisitically, of the futility of the characters with which they deal.

*Marching Men* has a poetic, and to a certain extent, an apocalyptic quality. In it is the vision of revolution:

> "All over the city McGregor talked of old Labour and how he was to be built up and put before men's eyes by the movement of the Marching Men. How our legs tingled to fall in step and go marching away with him.
>
> "And all over the country men were getting the idea—the Marching Men—old Labour in one mass marching before the eyes of men—old Labour that was going to make the world see—see and feel its bigness at last. Men were to come to the end of strife—men united—Marching! Marching! Marching!"

Yet at the end of the book David says, "What if after all this McGregor and his woman knew both roads? What if they, after looking deliberately along the road toward success in life, went without regret along the road to failure? What if McGregor and not myself knew the road to beauty?"

The fact that these are not great novels has nothing much to do with Anderson's genius. It is simply a fact. We get to thinking that if one is to be a great writer one must achieve greatness in certain conventional forms. Here in America our main idea is that he must achieve it in the novel, and yet the novel is not a very old form of writing, and there is serious question whether it is by any means a permanent form. Certainly, if it is to last, it must take on a new meaning and power. In addition to giving the novel a new meaning and power, however, there is need for the creation of new forms. Anderson's novels are steps on the way to the creation of such forms. It is in that respect that they are particularly interesting.

These novels belong to Anderson's revolutionary period. In both *Windy McPherson's Son* and *Marching Men* the author seems to dream of some revolution—revolution for the sake of beauty—arising from the mass of men, starting here in the Middle West, where crudity and rawness prevail, but where there is nevertheless room for faith in humanity in the mass.

*Mid-American Chants*, his only volume of verse, marks a change in Anderson. He still writes:

> "Crush and trample, brother, brother—crush and trample 'til you die.
> Do not hold thy hand from strangling—crush and trample 'til you die."

But no longer does he look for a physical revolution even as a symbol. "Not the shouting and the waving of flags, but something else creeps into me," he writes. "You see, dear brothers of the world, I dream of new and more subtle loves for me and my men." Love, maturity, beauty, and song are the principal factors in the change toward which the author is looking. In the foreword of this book Mr. Anderson says:

> "I do not believe that we people of mid-western America, immersed as we are in affairs, hurried and harried through life by the terrible engine—industrialism—have come to the time of song. To me it seems that song belongs with and has its birth in the memory of older things than we know. In the beaten paths of life, when many generations of men have walked the streets of a city or wandered at night in the hills of an old land, the singer arises.
>
> "The singer is neither young nor old but within him always there is something that is very old. The flavor of many lives and of many gone weary to the end of life creeps into his voice. Words run out beyond the power of words. There is unworldly beauty in the song of him who sings out of the souls of peoples of old times and places but that beauty does not yet belong to us.
>
> "In Middle America men are awakening. Like awkward and untrained boys we begin to turn toward maturity and with our awakening we hunger for song. But in our towns and fields there are few memory-haunted places. Here we stand in roaring city streets, on steaming coal heaps, in the shadow of factories from which come only the grinding roar of machines. We do not sing but mutter in the darkness. Our lips are cracked with dust and with the heat of furnaces. We but mutter and feel our way toward the promise of song.
>
> "For this book of chants I ask only that it be allowed to stand stark against the background of my own place and generation. Honest Americans will not demand beauty—this is not yet native to our cities and fields. In secret a million men and women are trying, as I have tried here, to express the hunger within and I have dared to put these chants forth only because I hope and believe they may find an answering and clearer call in the hearts of other Mid-Americans."

The pathos of life in America, as Mr. Anderson sees it, is that so many men become embittered and ugly. The school teacher in the Ohio town, the farmer in his field, the stenographer in the city, and the 100 per cent American, the "go-getter," are alike childish and immature. They are ashamed to strive for life and beauty. They are constantly inhibited. They live in a place walled in by conventional business, social relations, economic conditions, and religion, and in many cases never see the light.

This point of view is clearly manifest in *Winesburg, Ohio*, between which and the *Spoon River Anthology* must lie, in my estimation, the honor of being the most significant book in American literature since *Leaves of Grass*. The characters in this book are of the sort one might meet every day in any small town, though they are essentially individuals rather than types. To the average observer, met casually they would seem normal people. Anderson sees beneath the surface, however, and brings to view the strange psychopathies of these people. They do not understand themselves and they are not understood by their neighbors. Most of them are, in fact, grotesques of the kind portrayed in the first tale in the book:

> "In the beginning when the world was young there were a great many thoughts but no such thing as a truth. Man made the truths himself and each truth was a composite of a great many vague thoughts. All about in the world were the truths and they were all beautiful.
> "The old man had listed hundreds of the truths in his book. I will not try to tell you of all of them. There was the truth of virginity and the truth of passion, the truth of wealth and of poverty, of thrift and of profligacy, of carelessness and abandon. Hundreds and hundreds of truths and they were all beautiful.
> "And then the people came along. Each as he appeared snatched up one of the truths and some who were quite strong snatched up a dozen of them.
> "It was the truths that made the people grotesque. The old man had quite an elaborate theory concerning the matter. It was his notion that the moment one of the people took one of the truths to himself, called it his truth, and tried to live his life by it, he became a grotesque and the truth he embraced became a falsehood."

*Winesburg, Ohio* is a spare and simple but deep-sighted picture of American life, showing its crudity and at the same time its ashamed, inhibited longing for beauty. Here and there, unfortunately, is a tendency to preach—the propagandist of Anderson's earlier work creeping through. In writing of Helen White, and George Willard, for instance, the author says: "For some reason that could not be explained they had both got from their silent evening together the thing needed. Man or boy, woman or girl, they had for a moment taken hold of the thing that makes the mature life of men and women in the modern world possible."

Anderson's most recently published novel, *Poor White*, is bigger than either of his previous novels. A larger theme is painted upon a larger canvas. At the same time, it is distinctively realistic. There is present an even keener longing for beauty—or, perhaps better, beauty and freedom, if the two can be separated. There is not a little propaganda in *Poor White*. Beauty and freedom, the author shows, are being steadily lost in the mechanics of industrial life, though at the end of the book there is no lack of hope. A rereading of the work reminds me strongly of a recent poem by J. E. Spingarn:

> I have loved freedom more than anything else;
> And freedom fades—I see her everywhere dying;
> Her troops are scattered and her army melts—
> On every hill-top the enemy's flag is flying.
>
> But still she does not die; insoluble man,
> Haunting her empty temples, hollow-eyed,
> Still hears the echo of her ancient ban;
> "Whoever thinks I am dead, himself has died."

In *The Triumph of the Egg*, Anderson's latest collection of tales, the author shows greater facility and greater variety in selection of material than in *Winesburg, Ohio*, but hardly greater poignancy. And yet when I read a tale like *I Want to Know Why* or *Out of Nowhere into Nothing*, I wonder if there is any greater poignancy utterly free from sentimental clap-trap, anywhere in American literature. There is even poignancy of humor in this book—a step in advance of *Winesburg, Ohio*. I was surprised at the effectiveness of this upon an audience of ordinary Middle Western folk when *The Egg* was read aloud to them.

In this book Anderson appears to feel the futility and inhibitions with which his characters are afflicted as parts of himself. He seems to himself to be futile and inhibited. It is this, for one thing, that makes his stories so effective. Perfect facility and fluency would never do in dealing with the characters and the themes with which he deals. What is to many writers a disadvantage is to Anderson a conspicuous advantage. He is both an observer of the life with which he deals and a part of it.

> I am a helpless man—my hands tremble.
> I feel in the darkness but cannot find the doorknob.
> I look out at a window.
> Many tales are dying in the street before the house of my mind.

No understanding of Sherwood Anderson would be complete without consideration of *A New Testament* which so far has had only the limited circulation of *The Little Review*. I know of nothing that is quite like it. It is Anderson himself, revealing himself as no American except Whitman has ever revealed himself before. The only way to describe *A New Testament* is to quote from it:

> "It would be absurd for me to try writing of myself and then solemnly to put my writings into print, I am too much occupied with myself to do the thing well. I am like you in that regard. Although I think of myself all the time I cannot bring myself to the conviction that there is anything of importance attached to the life led by my conscious self. What I want to

say is this:—men may talk to me until they are blind of the life force and of the soul that liveth beyond the passing away of the husk called the body—

"For me life centres in myself, in the hidden thing in myself. I am sorry my flesh is not more beautiful, that I cannot live happily in contemplation of myself and must of necessity turn inward to discover what is interesting in the marking of me. It would simplify things if I could love my outward self and it must be the same with you."

> "The female words have found no lovers.
> They are barren.
> It was not God's wish that it be so.
> I am one who would serve God.
> Have not my brothers the male words been castrated
>     and made into eunuchs?
> "I would be nurse to many distorted words.
> I would make my book a hospital for crippled words."

"In a plow factory, on the West Side in Chicago, there are great tanks in the floor. The tanks are kept filled with many colored fluids. By machinery plows are lifted from the factory floor and swung above the tanks. They are dipped and become instantly and completely black, red, brown, purple, grey, pink.

"Can a plow be pink? I have the trick of thinking too rapidly in color. I cannot remember the color of the eyes of my sister. The color of the cheeks of my mistress I cannot remember.

"An endless clanking goes on in my head. It is the machinery of the life in which I hang suspended. I and all the men and women in the streets are at this moment being dipped anew in the life of Chicago. There is no yesterday for any of us. We hang by the hook in the present. Whatever lies behind this second of conscious time is a lie and I have set myself to lie to the limit. By my lying and by that road only will I succeed in expressing something of the truth of the life into which I also have been flung.

"This is evidently true. Plows may not be pink but the prevailing color of the flesh of people is pink. We have all been dipped into a dawn."

"You are mistaken in thinking I will only exist for a certain number of years. I do not exist at all. I shall exist forever.

"Once I thought that by making love to women I could come at truth. Now I make love to women as the wings of an insect fleck the waters of a stream.

"Truth lies far out in the field of fancy, in the forest of doubt."

"I have conceived of life as a bowl into which I am cast. If the outer world is inhabited by gods, as I choose to believe it is, it is because I am minute and you minute.

"I cannot keep my footing on the side of the bowl of life. There is, however, no humbleness in me. I constantly strive to reach out. It is that makes me seem strange in your sight. If you have heard my voice, laughing at the bottom of the bowl, it is because I have an ambition to be a flea in God's ear. I have wished to set up a roaring in God's head. I have wished to roar of men, women, and children I have seen walking in the valley of a river. I have wished to remind God of my love of my fellows.

"That last statement I fear is a lie. I am not concerned with the fate of my fellows. If you think I am you are mistaken about me."

The incidents in *A New Testament* may or may not be actual experiences. Probably some of them are and some are not. But they are all psychological experiences, and the psychological experiences of a writer are more significant, more revealing, than his physical experiences.

One inevitably looks for greater achievements in the future than Anderson has yet made. Notwithstanding the point that he has now reached, it is impossible not to feel that his most significant contributions to American letters are yet to come. He is now the clearest sighted, deepest visioned interpreter of the Middle West, not merely to those outside the region, but to us within it, even to himself. There is in him utter faithfulness. Moreoever, it is a wistful faithfulness. From such a rock streams innumerable and immeasurable may flow.

# "Sherwood Anderson"

Paul Rosenfeld*

They pass us every day, a grey and driven throng, the common words that are the medium of Sherwood Anderson. In the thick ranks of the newspapers they go drab and indistinct as miners trooping by grim factory walls in latest dusk. Men's lips form them wherever in all the land talk is, but we mark their shapes no more than we mark those of the individual passengers in the subway press, the arm and overcoat jumble, each tired night at six. The objects symbolized by them lie in the range of vision of those who make each day the city trip to the office and workshop and back flatward again. They lie in the range of those who ride dully into country towns over dusty roadways, or work about their barns or in their fields or inside farm cottages. But the walls of the city thoroughfares do not impinge on us, or on the men who talk, or on the hacks who write. The earth and board sides and fences and plantations remain in a sullen murk. And the words that signify the things and their simple qualities remain in millions of voices dreary dead.

Story tellers have come with banner and hallo to lift them out of Malebolge, to burnish them, to write English, and have washed them to no more scintillance than has the tired crowd of Christmas shoppers in the Chicago loop. Dreiser himself sought to point and sharpen them, to set them together as squarely as dominoes are set together in the backrooms of German saloons. He merely succeeded in forming a surface like that of water-logged, splintery beams, unfit for any hardy service. It was only Brontosaurus rex lumbering through a mesozoic swamp. In American novels, the words remained the dreariest, most degraded of poor individuals. But out of these fallen creatures, Sherwood Anderson has made the pure poetry of his tales. He has taken the words surely, has set them firmly end to end, and underneath his hand there has come to be a surface as clean and fragrant as that of joyously made things in a fresh young country. The vocabulary of the simplest folk; words of a primer, a copybook quotidianness, form a surface as hard as that of pungent freshplaned boards of pine and oak. Into the ordered prose of Anderson the delicacy and sweetness of the growing corn, the grittiness and firmness of

*Originally published in *The Dial*, 72 (January, 1922, pp. 29–42; reprinted in Paul Rosenfeld, *The Port of New York* (New York: Harcourt, Brace & Co., 1924), pp. 175–98.

black earth sifted by the fingers, the broad-breasted power of great labouring horses, has wavered again. The writing pleases the eye. It pleases the nostrils. It is moist and adhesive to the touch, like milk.

No rare and precious and technical incrustations have stiffened it. The slang of the city proletariat has not whipped it into garish and raging colour. Even in his pictures of life on the farms and in the towns of Ohio, Anderson is not colloquial. Very rarely some turn of language lifted from the speech of the Ohio country folk, gives a curious twist to the ordinary English. The language remains homely sober and spare. The simplest constructions abound. Few adjectives arrest the course of the sentence. At intervals, the succession of simple periods is broken by a compound sprawling its loose length. Qualifying clauses are unusual. Very occasionally, some of the plain massive silver and gold of the King James version shines when biblical poetry is echoed in the balancing of phrases, in the full unhurried repetition of words in slightly varied order. But the words themselves are no longer those that daily sweep by us in dun and opaque stream. They no longer go bent and grimy in a fog. Contours are distinct as those of objects bathed in cool morning light. The words comport themselves with dignity. They are placed so quietly, so plumbly, so solidly, in order; they are arrayed so nakedly, so foursquarely; stand so completely for what they are; ring so fully, that one perceives them bearing themselves as erectly and proudly as simple healthy folk can bear themselves. Aprons and overalls they still wear, for they are working-words. But their garments became starched and fragrant again, when Anderson squared and edged his tools. They leave us freshened as gingham-clad country girls driving past in a buggy do. If they are a little old and a little weary, they hold themselves like certain old folk who wear threadbare shawls and shiny black trousers, and still make their self-regard felt by their port.

It is the voice of Anderson's mind that utters itself through the medium of words. It is the voice of his lean, sinewy mid-American mind that marshalls the phrases, compels them into patterns. In this dumb American shoot of the Ohio countryside, a miracle has begun to declare itself. The man is brother to all the inarticulate folk produced by a couple of centuries of pioneering in the raw new world. He is the human who has sacrificed, that he might take root in virgin land, what centuries warmed to life in his forbears across the Atlantic. He grew in a corn-shipping town of post-Civil-War Ohio; grew among people who had forgotten the beauty laboriously accumulated in Europe; grew ignorant of the fact that beauty made by human toil existed anywhere on the globe. Around him, too, everything was quantity, not quality; everything urged to personal ambition. He lived the days lived by countless other smart little boys in that meagre civilization; volunteered to fight Spain and typhoid in Cuba; spent the money gained in soldiering in acquiring a little education at a fresh-water college; worked in factories, in bicycle-foundries; set out, driven by the universal goad, to become a successful business man; did become a successful business man. And still, in Anderson, in this life, one from out the million of dumb unconscious lives, beauty is, as upspringingly as in any stone of Chartres. The hysterical American mouth with its fictitious tumult and assurance, its rhetorical trumpeting, is set aside in him, disdained. There is no evasion of the truth in him. There is no pink fog over the truth of the relationship of men and women in this country. There is no evasion of self-consciousness by means of an interest centred entirely in the children; no blinding dream that entrance into a house full of spick furniture and nickled faucets will suddenly make life flow sweet-coloured and deep; no thankfulness to God that He has made a universe in which every one, or every one's offspring may climb to the top of the heap and become rich or a leader of the bar, that murderer of nascent sympathy. Nor does he speak Main Street in denigrating Main Street. An element higher than all the land is at work. The great critical power of the race is articulate; the race is crying. Fear, tribal fear, in this man has been overcome. He hears what the other dumb Americans with their protesting voices dare not hear. At the rear of his brain there murmurs audibly the quivering liquid flow always in progress in every being. A quiet stream, a black deep brook of feeling with whispering trickle, faery-like starts and gushes, is louder in this drawling Yankee than is all the sentimental Niagara of dust with its bellowings of the high state of women in Minneapolis, the efficiency and hygienicness of the clothing factories in Cleveland, the invigorating struggle for existence in New York. What Anderson veritably lives in Chicago and suffers and desires, is known to him; what his muddy-streaming compatriots have done and still are doing to him; what his joys are, and what his pains. In the land where it is always dusk, and shapes are indistinct; in the land of the mind, where the most of us this side the water have with miserable fumbling to grope a wavering way, Anderson moves, with the sureness and calmness of a sleepwalker.

Wherever he goes, in Chicago, out on the sandy foggy plain without the monster town, in the tiresome burgs where he sells the ideas of the advertising man, the voice of his spare fledgling mind, the echo of the inner columnear movement of his being, is heard of him. It is ever near the surface, ready to spurt. The most ordinary objects glimpsed from an office-window high in the loop; the most ordinary sad bits of life seen in the endless avenues, a tree in a backyard, a layer of smoke, a man picking butts out of the gutter, can start it making gestures. A cake of cowdung rolled into balls by beetles, a flock of circling crows, milk turned sour by hot weather, give Anderson the clue of a thin grey string, and set him winding through his drab and his wild days to find the truth of some cardinal experience and fill himself. The premature decay of buildings in America, the doleful agedness of things that have never served well and have grown old without becoming beautiful, the brutality of the Chicago skyline, open to him through a furtive chink some truth of his own starved powerful life, his own buried Mississippi Valley, his own unused empire. Or, the health that is left in the fecund soil of the continent, in the great watered spread of land, the nourishing life of forests and plantations, is powerful to make known to him in mad drunken bursts, his own toughness and cleanness, and healthiness. Young corn growing like saplings makes rise and quiver deliciously and soar in him sense of his own resilient freshness, his crass newness on a new earth. Young corn makes chant in him delight in his own unbreakable ability to increase for ever in sensitivity, to transmute the coarse stuff of rough America into delicate spirit-strength, and become in the easy mid-Western shape ever a healthier, sweeter, finer creature. Horses trampling through the grain are to him certitude eternal of the ever-replenishment of the male gentle might that has descended to him intact through his muscled ancestry and makes sweet his breast; of the phallic daintiness that all the stupid tangle and vulgarity of life in the raw commercial centres cannot wear down in him, and brutalize. A thousand delicate and mighty forms of nature are there, to pledge and promise him, the man cut loose from Europe, life abundant.

For Anderson touches his fellows of the road and Chicago street. The *rigor mortis* of the sentimental Yank is relaxing. The man is sensitive indeed. His arms are stretching open to the world. Not alone to the world of the boy, the before-puberty world of Huck Finn. His arms stretch open to the days of the sex-hung man. Life begins to walk a little joyously, if a little crassly, on Michigan Boulevard; because of the smokiness, it wears socks and haberdashery a trifle exuberant. Walls are noiselessly a-crumble in Anderson. Of a sudden, he is breast to breast with people, with the strange grey American types, men and women he has seen the day previously; men and women, farmers, artisans, shopkeepers he has not glimpsed in the flesh these five and twenty years. What happens only rarely, instantaneously only, to the most of us, the stretching of a ligament between another creature's bosom and our own, that happens in Anderson swiftly, repeatedly, largely. A visage, strange, grey, dun, floats up out of the dark of his mind. A man is seen doing something, lying face downward in a field, or fluttering his hands like birdwings. A woman is seen making a gesture, or walking down the railway-track. The figure may have had its origin in someone long known, in someone seen but a furtive hour, in someone seen merely through hearsay. It may have its origin in the dullest, weariest creatures. But suddenly, the poet is become another person. He is someone who has never before existed, but now, even in a condition of relative colourlessness, has a life of his own as real as those of the straphanging men brushed every day in the streetcars. Anderson is suddenly become a labour leader. He is mad with eagerness to teach stupid labourers to synchronize their steps, to make them understand what it is to march in the daily life shoulder to shoulder as soldiers march, to fill them full with a common stepping god in whom all find their fulness of power. He is a "queer" man working in a shabby little store. The more he strives to explain himself, the more incomprehensible and queer he becomes to his neighbours. He is Melville Stoner, the little long-nosed bachelor of Out of Nowhere Into Nothing. And is ironically resigned to the futility of seeking to establish a permanent contact with another creature. He is tired to his marrow with the loneliness of existence. Or, he is a farm girl mortally stricken in her breast by the insensitiveness and cowardice of men to whom she turns for expression. Or, the face is that of the lanky, cold-footed inventor who cannot channel his passion into human beings. To overcome the profound inner inertia, he sets himself to doing little definite problems. Machinery is born of his impotence. And then the inventions break loose of his hands, and enslave into a drab world the creatures Hugh McVey wanted to love, and could not reach. Or, it is the face of The Man in the Brown Coat, who sits all day inside a book-lined room and knows minutely what Alexander the Great and Ulysses S. Grant did, that floats up before Anderson. Or, it is merely the figure of the officer of the law who strolled by swinging his billy as the author left his office. He is heard muttering to himself his feet ache; seen at night slowly pulling off his shoes and wriggling his stockinged toes.

Then, it is with Sherwood Anderson as it was with the two farmhands of The Untold Lie who suddenly hear themselves each in the other; hear in the other the voice telling that the assumption of responsibility to women and children is death, the voice telling that the assumption of the responsibility is life. In the people suddenly known to him through the imagination, Anderson recognizes the multiple pulls of his own will; hears speak in the men known the same pulls; hears in those bodies a voice, and in his own body the self-same murmur. Things long since heard in village stores, in factories and offices, spark with significance. Memories appear from nowhere, carry to him the life of a fellow forgotten long since; and the life against the childhood Ohio background is relieved and sharply drawn. Out of the murky, impenetrable limbo, a block, an idea, a shape, has been moved, and in the region of faint grey light stands outlined. What in himself he feared, what he, the fearful rebel in the Yankee flock, thought his own most special insanity, his own pariah marking, that is suddenly perceived an universal trait, present everywhere. His loneliness, that he thought a desolation all his own, is sensed in a million tight, apart bodies. His boastfulness, lust, self-infatuation, his great weariness, promptings of the messianic delusion, despair, they are suddenly perceived everywhere; they, and not the outer mask that men wear in each other's blind sight, are seen the truth. He knows people writhe; sees them, men and women, so hard and realistic, doing the things he does and then is frightened; he knows the many mad chanting voices in each fact-crowded skull. What he is beholding, what he holds in his hands before him, is himself. It is himself, Sherwood Anderson, the man who looks like a racing tout and a divine poet, like a movie-actor and a young priest, like a bartender, a business-man, a hayseed, a mama's boy, a satyr, and an old sit-by-the-stove. It is himself as his father and his mother, as the people who moved about him in Clyde, Ohio, in his childhood and moved away from him, the many thousand humble and garish lives he has touched, the men he has done business with, the women he has taken, have made him.

The floating faces insist he attend upon the voice of the mind, without, within. They will not let him talk big, and ignore it. His heart can no longer leap with the remainder of the country's at thought of the big beautiful business man creating with his strong mind lots of work for poor people. He can no longer turn from women in the dream of an irradiant companion, all mother, who takes the man to her bosom as the nurse the suckling, and gives with crowded hands, and wants for herself nothing but the privilege of serving in a great career. It is too late to avoid humankind with the sentimentalities of the popular authors, or the self-pitifulness of the Main Street men, the cohort of little haters. The heads will have nothing but full entry into lives, even though he perish in the effort of entering. They want the facts of the relationships of men. It is what he really knows of the truth, what he really knows of what has happened to him, what he really knows of what he has done to folk as well as what they have done to him, that is demanded of him now. Anderson has to face himself where Freud and Lawrence, Stieglitz and Picasso, and every other great artist of the time, have faced themselves: has had to add a "phallic Chekov" to the group of men who have been forced by something in an age to remind an age that it is in the nucleus of sex that all the lights and the confusions have their centre, and that to the nucleus of sex they all return to further illuminate or further tangle. New faces mount upward continually; sit, as he tells us, on the doorsill of his mind; are driven off by the helplessness of the American artist who has inherited no orientation in art; return and resist the cold and force him to make the effort to take them in. New faces mount up that contain more and more copiously the author, more and more copiously humanity, and demand ever finer eyes and ears.

Out of the unconscious the style arises, the words charged with the blood and essence of the man. For quite as Anderson hears his own inner flux through the persons of other men, through materials and constructions, so, too, he hears it in the language itself. Words, like corn, like horses themselves, and men, give Anderson pricking sensations. Strange and unusual words do not have to be summoned. He hears the thin vocabulary of his inarticulate fellows not only as concepts of concrete objects, but as independent shapes and colours. Words are bifurcated in his mind; while the one limb rests on the ground, and remains symbol of the common object by which generations of English speakers have managed to make themselves and their offspring survive materially, the other points into blue air, becomes symbol of the quality of inner life engendered by the material preoccupations. Corn is the support of the body on the American prairie; man and beast lean on it; Anderson, born and bred in corn-shipping villages, hears in the word that symbolizes the nourishing stalk the overtones of all the delicacies and refinements that bodily energy produces in him. So, too, with the words bowl and coat, that have a dark and grim resonance in his heart. The necessity of preoccupying themselves with the production of the simple tools of existence had a most definite result on life through the relationship of men and women; and Anderson knows his own life a thing at the base of a bowl, an immense feeding trough, withheld from contacting the living world, by the high rims. He knows that he has within him a brown coat, that in this conventionally tinted stuff he sits wrapped all his days, cannot wear bright colours of the mind, cannot get out of this felt garment. He knows that when in writing he searches for touch with his fellows, he feels his way blindly in the dark along a thick wall, the wall left in men when they broke from their own traditions, and came into the presence of other men who too had broken from their traditions, and found no way to contact.

All Anderson's artistry consists in the faithfulness with which he has laboured to make these overtones sound in his prose, to relate the simple words so that while remaining symbolic of the outer men, they give also their inner state. At first, in the two early novels, Windy McPherson's Son and Marching Men, the word quality was fairly thin. The author was forced to rely far more on a crude symbolism of action to manifest his inner music than on his medium itself. Still, particularly in the latter book, the inner voice was gathering strength. The language in which the mining town is described in the earlier chapters communicates something larger than the life of towns of the sort. It give powerfully a sense of a grimy, cold, messy state of passion into which what Waldo Frank has so brightly called the barbaric tam-tam measure of Beaut McGregor's dream breaks as breaks a march rhythm into a sluggish orchestra. In the next book, Winesburg, Ohio, however, form obtains fully. The deep within Anderson utters itself through the prose. The tiny stories of village life are like tinted slits of isinglass through which one glimpses vasty space. The man's feeling for words, present always in him, re-enforced one casual day when someone, expecting to produce a raw haha, showed him the numbers of Camera Work containing Gertrude Stein's essays on Matisse, Picasso, and Mable Dodge, is here mature. The visual images, the floating heads, have fleshed themselves, are automatically realized, by marriage with verbal images that had risen to meet them, and that contained, in their turn, the tough, spare, sprawling life in the poet. So this style, even more than the subject matter, is impregnated with the inarticulate American, the man whose inner dance is as the dance of a bag of meal. For in these words, the delicate inner column of Sherwood Anderson has risen to declare itself, to protest against the ugliness that lamed it down, to pour its life out into the unnumbered women and men. And, in his latest work, in the best of the stories in The Triumph of the Egg, and in the pieces of A New Testament, it works with always simpler means, begins to manifest itself through a literature that approaches the condition of poetry, that is more and more a play of word-timbres, a design of overtones, of verbal shapes and colours, a sort of absolute prose.

There has been no fiction in America like this. Small it is indeed by the mountainous side of the masses of Balzac, with their never-flagging volumnear swell, their circling wide contact on life, their beefy hotness. Anderson, to the present, has been most successful in the smaller forms. The short-stories show him the fine workman most. The novels, the *nouvelles*, Out of Nowhere Into Nothing, wander at times, are broken in sweep by evasions and holes. A many-sided contact with life is not revealed. The man is not an intellectual critic of society. His range is a fairly limited one. There is a gentle weariness through him. And still, his stories are the truest, the warmest, the most mature, that have sprung out of the Western soil. One has but to compare these fragile, delicate fictions with those of the classic novelists, Poe and Hawthorne, to perceive immediately the reality of his beginning. The two ante-bellum novelists give us in place of flesh, as Brooks so trenchantly showed, exquisite iridescent ghosts. They themselves were turned away from their day, and filled the vacuums in which they dwelt with sinister and rainbow-tinted beams. Their people satisfy no lust of life. Both have only fantasy of a fine quality to offer in its place. And Dreiser's characters? Golems, in whose breast the sacred word has not been thrust. Anderson, on the contrary, expresses us. He has had, from the first, the power to find through his prose style protagonists in whom every American could feel himself to pulse. Sam McPherson is the truest of all Ragged Dicks. The quaint little mushroom-like heads of Anderson's tales, the uneducated, undignified village dreamers, with their queer hops and springs, straggly speech, ineffectual large gestures, they are the little mis-shapen humans in this towering machine-noisy inhuman land, the aged infants grown a little screw-loose with inarticulateness. The sounds they make as they seek to explain themselves to one another, as they rave and denounce and pray, lie, boast, and weep, might come out of our own throats. They do come out of our own. The author may dub his heads Seth Richmond or Elsie Leander, George Willard or Wing Biddlebaum; they may be seen ever so fitfully; the stories by means of which Anderson has created them may set them out in mid-American farmland thirty years since. But they are flesh of our flesh and bone of our bone; and through them, we know ourselves in the roots of us, in the darkest chambers of the being. We know ourselves in Anderson as we know ourselves in Whitman. He is about the job of creating us, freeing us by giving us consciousness of selves.

For Sherwood Anderson is one in whom the power of feeling has not been broken. He is one in whom the love of the growing green in men, so mortally injured in the most of us, has found a way of healing itself of the wounds dealt it by the callous society in which he sprung. He came, most probably, to suffer from the universal wrong in the common way. A man and woman, perhaps, whom life had wounded, bruised in their sensibilities, hurt him in acting on each other. Or, the passive callousness of the world of outsiders did the deed, starved the nascent gentleness in the child. The society which sheltered the growing lad was one becoming rapidly industrialized. Handicraftsmen remain sensitive more readily than do mechanics. Their immediate relation to the material in which they work preserves some sort of nervous fluidity in them. But the factory was eating into rural Ohio during the 'eighties and the early 'nineties. And there was not, what there still is in rural Europe, the reliquary of the passionate past to buttress anything of fine feeling that remained in the injured boy. No Gothic vault, no painted glass, no soft stone and nourished earth, were there to thaw the thickening ice. There was about him only the shoddy work of men disabled as he had been disabled. Indeed, the world might have seemed in conspiracy to make permanent the wound. A gigantic machinery was in readiness to aid any and all to make themselves free of their fellows. The anarchical society, that had come into existence the world over as the growing differentiations of men made sympathy more difficult, and placed a price on narcissistic irresponsibility, was there in its extremest form to welcome another lord of misrule. Everything in raw America stimulated ugly ambitiousness, exploitations of human beings and of the soil, sense of rivalry with all men, devastating sense of god-manhood. The two images that fortify narcissism, the images of the marvellous mother-woman and of the semi-divine all-powerful general or business man, that prevent men from finding much in the woman save the whore, and keep their interests centred on their own persons, were in the very air given the lad to breathe.

During a period, Anderson seems to have acquiesced, to have gone the way of all mortified flesh, to have become a smart competing business man, and to have lived as alone as only a wounded lover can. Only a gift of telling stories, and Anderson was famous in Chicago for his Mama Geigen story long before he commenced to write, remained to prove the old power of sympathy that he had brought with him into the world not entirely broken. Some toughness, perhaps, present with all the extreme sensibility, had saved him, given him the power to recuperate. Or, perhaps, someone near him in his first years had guarded him for a while, had stood between him and the all-present evil sufficiently long to give him headstart. One of the stories in Winesburg, Ohio, called Mother, is the incorporation of a sense present in the author of an influence stilly goading him all his days to live his life and not settle down in cheap ambition, to grow and to learn; it is perhaps to this influence that the man owes his art. And Anderson showed he had the power within him to right himself. Towards his thirty-fifth year, he became sick of soul. He commenced to feel the state in which he was living as filthy. He began to perceive that his relations with men and with women, through his sunken state, were filthy. He began to perceive that he himself was giving out poison to others precisely in the same manner that poison had been given to him, was still being given to him by his contacts. Business began to become a bore. Business men, with their self-importance and gosling simplicity, began to become ludicrous. Suddenly, it appeared to him that Chicago, the mid-West, all America, was empty. There were no people. The census reports proclaimed tens upon tens of millions of inhabitants. But there were no people living human lives. There were automatons gyrating about, repeating sentences written by unconsciously lying reporters in the newspapers. No one knew the truth. No one knew what he felt, what the man reading the newspaper next him felt. No one felt, at all. In all the crowded streets and tenements of the titanic town, there was the unpeopled waste of the antarctic night.

Sickness of soul took Anderson away from business. Simultaneously a channel leading in an equally divergent direction opened itself for his energies. The gift of story telling began taking an intellectual route. At odd hours, after business, in railway trains, he began to write. And, lo, in the process of writing, the old wound began to close. He commenced to touch people again. He commenced to enter into lives. The people he met, the people he had rubbed against, were no longer adamant impenetrable surfaces to him. They began to open themselves. They began, when he met them casually, in all the ordinary ways of intercourse, to give him something nourishing to his sense of beauty, and to take from him something he needed to bestow. The sense of dirt, of whoring, of infinite degradation began to pass in his labour. For the business of seeing people without romanticizing them, of drawing them without putting himself below or above them, but merely by feeling their lives in all the dwarf-ishness and prodigious bloom, is to Anderson what it is to all men, an act of love, and, as love, subconsciously initiated. The old godhead that shines in the eyes of every new-born child, revives itself through that labour of art. The business of seeing folk clearly, steadily, wholly, is a mystical marriage with the neighbour. It is not love of one's image in the partner; it is the love of all men and women through the body of a spouse. For its motive is the preservation in another of an intact soul.

It was not a thing, this power of feeling truly, that sprang full armed in Anderson. It has rather been a gradual growth, a slow, patient learn-ing. The current of life in the country was against it. The current swept inside Anderson himself. We see him, at the close of Windy McPherson's Son, flinch from drawing the relentless line; loose his contact with life, and return into the fantasy world of the American imperviousness. Marching Men, in its later passages, demonstrates a faulty sense of women. Even in Poor White, the tendency to stop feeling delicately, to harangue and seek to influence his readers directly shows at moments its cloven foot. But the artist has been solidifying steadily in the man. In A New Testament he tells us how each night he "scrubbed the floor" of his upper room. There are miracles of tender, fragile sensibility in Winesburg, in Poor White, in the later stories and poems. For, in this second crisis in Anderson's moral life, there was help at hand. He was no longer entirely solitary in his struggle with the habits of the country. Creatures able to strengthen him were about. His mind, like the span of a Gothic arch, in springing upward, met another upspringing span and found support. It was in the guise of the most powerful outward bulwark of his mature life that the work of Van Wyck Brooks came to Sherwood Anderson. In it he encountered another conscious American who spoke his language. Here was a critic, a polished and erudite man, who brought him corroboration in his inmost feelings, and told him that nations had become great, and life burned high, because men had done what he was labouring to do; and that America had remained grey and terrible and oafish because men could not within her borders feel the truth. In that voice, Anderson recognized an American realler than the one that, outside and in, strove to deflect him and break his touch. What had happened to Whitman, decay for want of comprehension, was not to happen to him. He was afoot to so remain. Anderson's pledge to himself, the song to himself as he goes his rocky road, is recorded in Mid-American Chants. The little book is a sort of pilgrim's scrip for those who, in America, are trying to keep their faith in the work of the artist intact. And Anderson can begin writing A New Testament, assured that in setting down the voice of the mind murmurous in him, he is furthering some new religious life dawning in men.

The new feeling that is in America, it is only an infant. It is no more than a puny child born in the nadir of the year, a helpless, naked mite. In all the grey winter of the land, under the leaden immeasurable vault, it is a nigh invisible fleck. And still, somehow, it is there, born. You have but to read Anderson, to know it well. Something is different in us since these stories and novels have commenced to circulate. Something has changed in the scene outside the rooms, in the thoroughfares through which we tread, since he began telling us the railway conductor's daughter walked down the track, the policeman goes thinking how much his feet hurt him. The people in the street, the ever strange, the ever remote, the ever unyielding people in the street, they are come a little out of their drab mist, are become a little less repellent, less hostile, less remote. They have departed a little from their official forms, the forms that are imposed on them by the lie in the brain of all, the Roman lie, with its hierarchies, positions, offices, principles, duties, laws. You will perceive it the next time you pass by the Italian grocer on the corner, that formerly mealy and uninviting universe. You will perceive it when next the washerwoman comes with her basket of laundry to the door. You will perceive it when you pass the blue-coated, sallow-faced law swinging his club on the corner. They will not know that anything has happened between you and them. They may believe they see you with the old eyes. But they do not. In them as in yourself something has taken place. They have all opened a little, to let you see for a blinking instant into them. You, who have read Anderson, know it. They have all turned gentler for a second, and let you perceive inside their coats, a thing you well know. It is inside the rich fur-collared coat of the stock-gambler in Wall Street. It is inside the old army coat of the grey-faced job-hunting Third-Avenue walker. It is inside all men and women, that thing that you thought you own alone. It is you in diverse forms, you suffering and egoistic and lazy, you wanting to live and give life to others and exuding venom instead. It is you, dying always by your own hand, always miraculously producing again the power to live.

It seems as though the mysterious Third Person, the being who comes into existence at the moments walls fall between men and men, and dies when they rebuild themselves again, had been given another last chance.

# "In Retrospect"

Cleveland Chase*

Anderson has little reason to complain at the reception he has had at the hands of the American reading public. His books have been bought and read; the critics have treated him seriously and, for the most part, sympathetically; he is generally recognized to be one of the important contemporary writers; his books are recommended to foreigners who enquire about the present state of American literature, and they are beginning to be translated. His position and his reputation are such that it is no longer necessary to consider his works entirely tentatively.

It has been the habit of American critics in speaking of him to remark about succeeding volumes as they have appeared, "In this new work there are plain foreshadowings of the Anderson who is ahead." Anderson has published thirteen books. Perhaps it is not out of place to enquire just how much of a contribution to American literature these volumes seem to represent.

From this point of view, as we run again through the list of his works, we must strike off first of all his two volumes of poems. They show promise of a certain sort, but they most certainly fail to come up to a very high standard of accomplishment. With them, and for the same reason, must go *Tar* and four out of his five novels. In *The Triumph of the Egg* and *Horses and Men* perhaps half a dozen or eight short stories escape the blue pencil. We have left: *Dark Laughter*, *A Story Teller's Story* and *Winesburg, Ohio*. The first is a competent novel, but it is no better than many others that have appeared in America in the last fifteen years; it is well written, but not enough so to mark Anderson as an outstanding writer. It is a little more difficult to place *A Story Teller's Story*; one is never sure how much of its interest is due to the publicity the author has received and to a natural curiosity on the part of the reader to know about him. We can class it as an interesting book of reminiscences, but it is doubtful whether it warrants a very high literary rating. That leaves us with *Winesburg, Ohio*; and *Winesburg*, limited and incomplete as it is, seems, to my mind, a definite contribution to American literature. As a first volume of short stories it entirely justified the hopes, so often ex-

*From Cleveland Chase, *Sherwood Anderson* (New York: Robert M. McBride & Co., 1927), pp. 74–84.

pressed, that at last there had developed in America a "home-bred," un-Anglicized writer who would take his place beside the great writers. But Anderson has not progressed; on the contrary, each succeeding volume makes it seem less likely that he will fulfill the great things that were expected of him. From time to time since the publication of *Winesburg* he has shown evidence of his qualities of greatness, but seldom for more than fleeting moments.

To paraphrase the author, "something is wrong with Anderson's writing, and Anderson himself doesn't want to look at it." After nine years of constant writing and the publication of ten subsequent books, his reputation still rests upon his first volume of short stories, and not thus supported, it would be negligible. We can find no more suitable point from which to undertake a discussion of his shortcomings than his essay, *A Note on Realism*, in which he voices his literary philosophy.

"There is something," he writes, "very confusing to both readers and writers about the notion of realism in fiction. As generally understood it is akin to what is called 'representation' in painting. The fact is before you and you put it down, adding a high spot here and there to be sure. . . . No man can quite make himself a camera. Even the most realistic worker pays some tribute to what is called 'art.' Where does representation end and art begin? . . .

"Easy enough to get a thrill out of people by reality. A man struck by an automobile, a child falling out at the window of an office building. Such things stir the emotions. No one, however, confuses them with art.

"This confusion of the life of the imagination with the life of reality is a trap into which most of our critics seem to fall about a dozen times each year. Do the trick over and over and in they tumble. 'It is life,' they say. 'Another great artist has been discovered.'

"What never seems to come quite clear is the simple fact that art is art. It is not life.

"The life of the imagination will always remain separated from the life of reality. It feeds upon the life of reality, but it is not that life—cannot be. Mr. John Marin painting Brooklyn Bridge, Henry Fielding writing *Tom Jones*, are not trying in the novel and the painting to give us reality. They are striving for a realization in art of something out of their own imaginative experiences, fed to be sure upon the life immediately about. A quite different matter from making an actual picture of what they see before them.

"And here arises a confusion. For some reason—I myself have never exactly understood very clearly—the imagination must constantly feed upon reality or starve. Separate yourself too much from life and you may at moments be a lyrical poet, but you are not an artist. Something within dries up, starves for want of food. Upon the fact in nature the imagination must constantly feed in order that the imaginative life remain significant. The workman who lets his imagination drift off into some experience altogether disconnected with reality, the attempt of the American to depict life in Europe, the New Englander writing of cowboy life—all that sort of thing—in ninety-nine cases out of a hundred ends in the work of such a man becoming at once full of holes and bad spots. The intelligent reader, tricked often enough by the technical skill displayed in hiding the holes, never in the end accepts it as good work. The imagination of the workman has become confused. He has had to depend altogether upon tricks. The whole job is a fake."

Anderson has stated the case with sufficient clearness. "Art is art. It is not life." Neither is it imagination of the type displayed by the New Englander describing cowboys—and neither is it imagination of the type displayed by Anderson when he sentimentally remakes the world according to his own measurements. Anderson writing about women, Anderson writing about most sexual phenomena, Anderson writing about philosophies of life, Anderson writing about Beauty, Truth, Love, Purity and other abstractions is in the same category with the New Englander writing about cowboys. They are both projecting qualities that they miss in life into something they know little about.

Anderson realizes the danger of writing from a notebook, but he fails to realize that similar faults may spring out of writing from an undisciplined imagination. At the risk of being boring, I would repeat that there are two kinds of imagination. One is powerful enough to penetrate completely, sympathetically into the world, or into some part of the world, as it exists. It we might call the interpretive imagination. The other is forced to create a world of its own as it is unable to understand and sympathize with the one that exists. In his conception of the stories in *Winesburg, Ohio,* and for brief moments in some of his other books, Anderson shows that he possesses this interpretive imagination. But most of his work is the product of that lower order of imagination that must remake the world in accordance with its own limitations.

In discussing realism and "art," Anderson fails to realize that it is of slight importance whether or not a writer makes an "actual picture" of what he sees. It may be that what one man sees is so grouped and arranged that by portraying it as it is the writer expresses that which he desires; it may be that to achieve such a result he will be forced to combine, rearrange and reconstruct. In this same essay Anderson gives a concrete example of the confusion under which he labors. He remarks that he sees a man walking down the street and wants to use him in a story. But to use this man as he is is too "realistic." "A matter easy enough to correct. A stroke of my pen saves me from realism. The man I knew in life had red hair; he was tall and thin. With a few words I have changed him completely. He has black hair and a black mustache. He is short and has broad shoulders. And now he no longer lives in the world of reality. He is a denizen of my own imaginative world." In short he isn't the red-haired man at all but "two other fellows." It is not that it matters whether the man is short or tall, red or black haired. Anderson by taking him into his own "imaginative world" has begun to distort him. In almost all of his writing he continues the process. When the man would really do one thing, Anderson makes him do another. Because he is not reproducing facts, he feels that he is writing imaginatively. He is not. To lie about life is not to write with imagination, but without it.

Anderson has never needed to be "saved from realism." He needs to be saved from a cheap, soft sentimentality that distorts and castrates almost everything he writes. He has the comparatively rare gift of stating human problems validly; but once having stated them, he runs off, hysterically frightened at what he has done. He has sufficient insight into people, events, and emotions to broach a number of pertinent subjects, but not once, even in *Winesburg*, has he carried his investigations to the end without flinching.

It is hard and often grueling work to be a creative writer, and Anderson has shirked the task. He has done so because he has allowed himself to confuse the interpretive and the evasive types of imagination that he possesses. How far that confusion has gone is witnessed in the passage just quoted in which he notes with surprise and mystification that "art" is connected with and derived from life. Had Anderson been writing as he should and is able to write, he would be more conscious of the fact that what he calls "art" is a heightened and concentrated expression of the emotional factors of life.

As we glance back through Anderson's works it is striking to note what a large part of them is devoted to sexual questions and relations. It is even more striking to note that his only successful treatment of this theme is when he depicts sexual frustration. His other attempts to deal with it are ridiculously inadequate. Anderson would like to be a great historian of love but, to judge by his writings, his emotional experience is not great enough for the task. When he is not definitely dealing with sexual frustration, Anderson's attitude seems strangely akin to the one he attributes to Hugh McVey in *Poor White*: "It did not seem to him at the moment that it was worth while for him . . . to try to find a place . . . where such a wonderful thing as happened to the man in the barn (who kissed his fiancée) might happen to him."

And in a way complementary to this is Anderson's attitude toward women. Except for some of the studies in suppression in *Winesburg* he has never drawn a really convincing woman. He subconsciously places them on such a pedestal that he can't possibly treat them as human beings. Like David Ormsby in *Marching Men* we can hear him shout, "Women are not understandable. They do inexplicable things, have inexplicable fancies." One would say that he had indelibly stamped on his mind the traditional American and Victorian conception of marital virginity and purity which makes him write, as he does in *The Triumph of the Egg*, "The marriage night there was a brutal assault and after that the woman had to try to save herself as best she could." The nearest Anderson comes to acknowledging the fact that a woman can have normal emotions is when, in *Dark Laughter*, he writes stiltedly of Bruce Dudley that he could "be the man to her woman, for the moment at least."

Roughly, the subjects about which Anderson writes may be grouped as follows: He romantically rewrites his childhood and adolescence as it was or as it would have been pleasant had it been. He day-dreams on paper and tells himself fairy stories about "strong men" and "purposeful women" that make one wonder why the movies have never signed him up. He dramatizes, often sentimentally, stories or thoughts about the warped and deformed unfortunates whom modern life has left in its track. He tries to express the baffledness and mystification that he feels about ideals, sex, and the meaning of life—or else he tries to make some character solve these problems for him. He describes the physical background of contemporary America.

It is only when he is writing about frustration and in a few of his descriptions of the background of modern American that Anderson achieves any manner of success. The rest of the time one feels that he is writing for the pleasure of writing and not because he has anything to say. His dislike for modern life has dimmed his understanding of it and has left him in the unfortunate position of a reactionary who is trying to be and is often said to be a radical. His early experience left him bitter against commercialism, against the cheapness of quantity production, and convinced that no good can come of the present trend of life and that the only hope for the future is that the next generation may "reach down through all the broken surface distractions of modern life to that old love of craft out of which culture springs." (From *A Story Teller's Story*.) Anderson is a writer born out of his age.

It is doubtless noticeable that in this study little has been said of the other writers who seem to have influenced Anderson's work. This is largely because, although like almost all writers he has been influenced, he has absorbed and assimilated these influences until they have become indistinguishable from his ordinary views and reactions; and the process of searching out the sources of his methods and mannerisms throws little light on his writing itself. His early work owes a great deal to Dreiser's novels and to Whitman's feelings about America. The Old Testament has been very influential in the formation of his style, both in prose and poetry. There is a striking similarity between his theory of the history of life as a history of moments and the technique of Katherine Mansfield's short stories. The likeness of *Winesburg, Ohio* and some of his other writings to the work of the Russians, especially of Chekhov, has often been commented upon and, despite Anderson's repeated denials that he had read any Russian literature before the composition of *Winesburg*, it seems quite sure that, directly or indirectly, he was influenced by it. Be this as it may, the fact remains that Anderson is one of the most thoroughly and integrally American writers who has ever existed.

Sherwood Anderson, going into writing to escape from life, made one too-brief attempt to re-enter life and then dashed frightened back to his refuge. In *Winesburg, Ohio*, and in parts of *The Triumph of the Egg* he seemed on the verge of penetrating imaginatively beneath the surface of this ugly, blatant life of ours and of tapping that rich vein of human nature which, changeless throughout the ages, has provided the stuff of all significant writing. But Anderson was unequal to the task. To the pure metal of genuine inspiration he preferred cheap substitutes, and so returned to his world of thin romanticism and sentimentality. The chance was his; we can but regret that he has not yet made real use of it.

# "Sherwood Anderson: Some Entirely Arbitrary Reactions"

Rachel Smith*

The waning day of Sherwood Anderson invites inquiry. Having said his piece (several times in fact) the moment for "the fade-out" has just about arrived. This superior craftsman whose happily wrought cadences have often pleased us, this poet whose lyric music has charmed our ear every once in a while, this analytical psychologist whose "wistful idealizations of the male menopause" and other phenomena, alternately shocked and moved us—and occasionally convinced us—is undoubtedly passing into the dusk which precedes an obliterating darkness. Each year of the passing is marked with a new novel, written with the avowed intention of recording the intense or aware moments of human life, of righting the wrong of machine-made civilization, of covering clean white sheets of paper with combinations of "singing words," of sounding the true note as an individual ring above the meaningless outcryings of the rest of mankind—and so on, and so on.

Sherwood Anderson, skilled craftsman, passionately and wistfully pleading his incoherence, in getting across the message with which his mind and soul are supposed to be pregnant, and writing incomprehensible verse in the manner of a mystic, is distinctly annoying. One of the most potent reasons for his early literary demise will be his lack of message. One does not require, of course, that his message have social or moral import but it is essential that a novelist have something to say, and say it. Anderson's message, if any, was stated rather badly in his first works and is still being stated, much less badly, but with the repetition becoming more and more irksome. We must give him credit for telling us about the "wall." While not exactly a brand new idea, he has given this isolation of the individual an aura of pathos that wears well. He seems to be aware that something should be done about the deplorable condition which machine industry has created. He cogitates upon the immense possibilities of organized labor—and stops. Most of us have reached that far. He has also discovered that most people of imagination find life a bit flat if they have become successful before middle age, and long for an

*Originally published in *Sewanee Review*, 37 (April, 1929), pp. 159–63. Reprinted by permission of *Sewanee Review*.

escape from the monotony of money-getting and obligations of various sorts, into an El Dorado of freedom and self-expression. So far and very little further. No conclusions are reached, the characters never solve their problems, never even face them. There is a fundamental lack of structural thought. When his characters are faced with a problem involving their contact with society or industry or a spiritual confict of some sort, they think and talk about it extensively and say strange things. And presently decamp with, say, their stenographer. Some critic suggests that this over-working of the escape-motif is indicative of Anderson's whole attitude toward life and art. Instead of making his characters react in a realistic way to real conditions, he lets them wander away into the dim passages of fancy which, if one lacks interpretive imagination, must be much easier. Unfortunately, however, his characters suffer immeasurably. We recall but few that were convincing or memorable. A limited number of minor characters have enduring qualities and are more objectively and spontaneously done. His main characters are shadows of himself viewed from different angles. Fleeting visual images of them in impossible attitudes are about all that remain to the reader. "I know a tall man with red hair. I have made him short and squat with dark hair falling over his eyes," exclaims Sherwood Anderson delightedly. Exactly! His childish pleasure in meaningless distortion, explains partly his apparent inertia of imagination in dealing with real people. These queer animals move in a world of lurid fancy and seldom feel firm ground beneath their feet—indeed would be unable to cope with actual physical surroundings.

This lack of interpretive imagination which renders him incapable of using the material at hand, has an unpleasant offspring in a certain self-consciousness which is usually not found in the person who has a lot to say. He admits in a weak moment that it would gratify him exceedingly if people who saw him passing, said, "There goes Sherwood Anderson. He can be a bad man when he is aroused," or "There goes Sherwood Anderson. He can be a lustful male when he is aroused." Few can say that they have never experienced a similar feeling: but with Anderson the thing goes farther. While he disclaims any attempt to shock, wishing only, he says, to open up dark houses to the light, one feels strongly the bad-man swagger projecting itself onto the clean white sheets of paper which he covers. Despite a distaste for the Dreiserian form of prose, we do feel a sincerity which has little time for posturing of any sort. Dreiser at least thinks he has a message. We suspect that Sherwood Anderson doesn't even fool himself. We detect something a little panicky in his oft-repeated definitions of art, realism, mysticism, and so on. He protests too much.

At one time Sherwood Anderson said something very pertinent about the poison-plot and he has done a great deal to hasten its departure by his excellent short stories. Unfortunately he seems to forget his praiseworthy thesis when he takes up his pen to begin a novel. Never was a man more harassed for something for his characters to do. Driven to desperation, they indulge in unthinkable gestures, forced and foolish. Entirely lacking the beautiful spontaneity (except in notable spots) of his short stories, the grotesqueries seem to have lost any connection with the people whose identity they claim. Any long novel must have high spots but in a real work of art one seldom finds the bright places so surrounded by pages and pages of absolutely meaningless drivel. And the high spots themselves are so doubtful. This forcing of the action, with the interjection of a lot of pointless philosophizing helps to produce a deplorable lack of structure and form.

Anderson, his admirers contend, is "American," if nothing else, and so he is, if he would let himself be. But so concerned is he with his inner consciousness that only at the beginning of some of his novels and in a few minor characters does his vision of America break through the veil of "himself" that he has thrown over all his work. He stands bareheaded and awe-stricken before the enormous complexity of Sherwood Anderson, his mind and temperament. Books and books he has written about himself, but still he finds his ego interesting and unfathomable—and so continues. This immense preoccupation extends itself into his style. One hears that he has lifted American idiom from the status of mere slang and made it "art." He has, it is true, given a certain Homeric quality to the idiom of the factory, the race course, and the pool room; but unfortunately, it is no longer American slang. Vigorous still and ungrammatical, but Andersonized beyond recognition. He starts out promisingly to be an "American" but loses entirely the flavor by the time it has sifted through the devious paths of his mind and got onto paper.

An English critic gives as a reason for the unproductiveness of Americans in art the wealth of material which the geographical and racial variety of America offers. The enormous amount of local color makes it too easy for a writer to do "acceptable" things which are neither art nor truly American. The varied and colorful backgrounds draw the attention of the reader away from the deficiencies of the characters. For this reason few real characters exist in the modern American novel, nor are they more than superficially American. The English critic also points out our unfortunate concern over the social well-being of our fellow countrymen. This proclivity for reform has so far produced little of real artistic value in America. We feel that Anderson handles his local color rather well, subordinating it sufficiently and yet giving enough of it to form an interesting and explanatory background. He does, however, fall into the last category suggested by our English critic. Anderson feels the need of reforming a good many things and sets about his task to the great loss of his work—as art. Not being very clear in stating the evils which he would correct, he is not even a very good reformer.

As with his attempted Americanism, he falls short of mysticism; of course missing the mark pretty far. His vision of God is entirely obscured by the interesting figure of Sherwood Anderson. Now and then a rift in the clouds sheds a mystic light on a piece of his work but for the most part he mistakes himself for God. One does not find this intense subjectivity so objectionable in his verse. After reading pages of incomprehensible word combinations which lack notably the force and flow of the true mystic, one happens on three or four lines of lyric beauty usually concerned with the "wall," which are refreshingly lovely. This isolation is so keenly felt that its pathos is unforgettable and extremely convincing.

In his study of humanity as reflected in his own temperament he seldom ascends the heights but is forever plumbing the depths. This proclivity should not be deprecated unduly. It is necessary that the dark places be shown the light, but repetition becomes monotonous; these dark places once lighted lose interest and the switching on of the electric light in a room already bright with the noon-day sun is just a little foolish. Incidentally few could do it as successfully as Anderson does. He keeps us thinking he has done more than repeat the gesture, that he has shown us an impressive symbolism, which we would do well to think upon seriously—until the book is finished and we realize that he has done the same old thing—skilfully as usual.

The doctrine of dealing with aware moments in the lives of individuals, while apt to make his novels spotty, is an excellent one for the writing of short stories, and with these of course one can have no quarrel. *Winesburg, Ohio*, speaks for itself, and with it Anderson almost manages to bridge the gap which separates the craftsman from the artist. While the grotesque individuals of whom he writes are scarcely recognizable as our cousins from the corn belt, they are impressive as personifications of abnormalities, sexual and otherwise. Our "phallic Chekov" measures up handsomely to his Russian prototype and to Maupassant in craftsmanship, and more than equals them in vigor.

# "Sherwood Anderson"

Robert Morss Lovett*

A revaluation of Sherwood Anderson must necessarily take account of the extraordinary impact that he made upon American literature almost at his appearance. In spite of the crudity of his first novels the impression was general that an original and distinguished talent was to be reckoned with. This recognition extended to European critics, among whom M. Fay committed himself to the statement in the Revue de Paris: "I believe that Sherwood Anderson is one of the greatest writers of the contemporary world, and the best in America." This verdict may be accounted for by Anderson's possession, in truer balance than any other of his contemporaries, of three qualities marked by Maeterlinck as requisites for great literature: a sure touch upon the world of our senses; a profound intimation of the mystery that surrounds this island of our consciousness; and the literary technique comprehended in the term style.

I first met Sherwood Anderson in 1913 at Ernestine Evans' studio in Chicago, whither he came to read a manuscript. He was in house painter's clothes, and seemed the proletarian writer for whom we were already on the lookout. His writing suggested Dreiser. It was minutely naturalistic, but of anything beyond this present scene, anything of grace of style, I now recall no trace. Floyd Dell, then literary editor of The Chicago Post, who lent his august presence to the occasion, saw with his usual discernment the promise in this attempt, and, I understand, recommended "Windy McPherson's Son" to John Lane in London, where it was received as a genuine American document. This it undoubtedly is in its first part, its substance drawn from Anderson's early life in the Middle West, but as in more than one of his novels, the point at which realism gives way to badly conceived romance is easily marked. The same verdict falls upon Anderson's second novel, "Marching Men." In the latter, however, there is an imaginative effort to transcend the actual, to embody the significance of the great union, symbolized by the march of the toilers. Already Anderson was writing the poetry which appeared the next year in "Mid-American Chants," and infusing his prose with the soaring rhythms that carry his fiction at times into a realm in which realistic criticism is irrelevant.

*Originally published in The New Republic, 89 (November 25, 1936), pp. 103–05.

96

"Winesburg, Ohio," in 1919, marks an important date in American literary history, and in itself profiled by an obvious timeliness. It was the year after the War, and readers stupefied by tales of its abominations needed to be reassured that peace hath its horrors no less worthy of renown. D. H. Lawrence had discovered sex as a source of incongruity of character. Katherine Mansfield had developed after Chekhov the story in which nothing happens but a sudden moment of illumination and awareness. The stream-of-consciousness method was a recent invention. Edgar Lee Masters in "The Spoon River Anthology" had assembled a community of people whose confessions revealed the deep places of human experience hidden by their provincial lives.

In "Winesburg, Ohio" Anderson shows perfect command of the small-town stuff familiar to him from his youth. True, he protests:

> I myself remember with what a shock I heard people say that "Winesburg, Ohio" was an exact picture of Ohio village life. The book was written in a crowded tenement district of Chicago. The hint for almost every character was taken from my fellow lodgers in a crowded rooming house, many of whom had never lived in a village.

Nevertheless, they live there now. In the process of transference from the crowded rooming house into an environment which Anderson controlled so completely that the reader takes it for granted, they have assumed an actuality that is not dependent on realism. They move among the material furnishings of the world with the deftness and precision of sleep walkers. If Anderson had left them in their rooming house he might have written another "Pot-Bouille." Instead he has made a character sketch of the rotten little town which has become as much a part of the American scene as Gopher Prairie or Muncie, Indiana. As a literary form, a group of tales adding up to a unit greater than the sum of its parts, the book is a masterpiece. Mr. Cleveland B. Chase in his rather disparaging brochure on Anderson admits that it is "one of the most important products of the American literary renaissance, and has influenced writing in America more than any book published in the last decade."

"Winesburg, Ohio" represents the solution of the problem that Anderson consciously set himself. His own experience, unusually rich and varied, gave him his grip on the actual world in which he was to live so abundantly. He has borne testimony to this in his numerous autobiographical writings, but as an artist his aim was constantly to emerge from the chrysalis stage of realism into the winged career of imagination. "Imagination must feed upon reality or starve" is a sentence from his notes which in effect recurs again and again. Of the process of transubstantiation he has given explicit account in "A Story-Teller's Story." As a boy he listened to his father, a fantastic liar who had served in the Civil

War and on the basis of that fact made himself the hero of a dozen campaigns to the delight of his audience. Sherwood inherited or learned the knack. "When I was a lad," he tells us, "I played with such fanciful scenes as other boys played with brightly colored marbles. From the beginning there have been, as opposed to my actual life, these grotesque fancies. Later, to be sure, I did acquire more or less skill in bringing them more and more closely into the world of the actual."

In so doing he worked at this relation of material to imagination, and the projection of fact into fiction. Humble and sordid realities, the trivia of observed phenomena, bring to him an emotion which is the essence of poetry. In "A Story-Teller's Story" he recalls such a moment of inspiration. Looking from a window, he sees a man in the next yard picking bugs off potato vines. The man's wife comes to the door, scolding. He has forgotten to bring home the sugar. A quarrel follows. And for Anderson his own life and interests, his business, and his waiting dinner are forgotten. "A man and a woman in a garden have become the center of a universe about which it seemed to me I might think and feel in joy and wonder forever." It is in thus seizing on scraps of reality and projecting them beyond the small range controlled by the senses that Sherwood Anderson's imagination brings fiction to the enhancement of life, and enlarges his art beyond the limits of naturalism into expressionism. Not the fact, but the emotion with which the artist accepts it, is the essence of living.

"Winesburg, Ohio" is not only an instance of the evolution of a literary theory; it marks also Anderson's achievement of a craftsmanship which is an essential part of that theory. When, in his preface to "The Triumph of the Egg" he speaks of himself as a tailor, "weaving warm cloth out of the thread of thought" to clothe the tales which, born of experience and imagination, "are freezing on the doorstep of the house of my mind," he is using a figure that comes naturally to him. He was an artisan before he was an artist. His work as sign painter and mechanic gave him a sense of the relation of materials and tools. As a tailor of tales he finds excitement in pen or pencil and paper, thousands of sheets of it, waiting for his hand. The author's medium is words, which are to him what pigments are to the painter, or food stuffs to the cook. One of his happiest sketches is that of Gertrude Stein bustling genially about her kitchen choosing the ingredients of her pastry. From her, it may be conjectured, Anderson gained something of the assurance that words have qualities inherent in them other than meaning. "Words have color, smell; one may sometimes feel them with the fingers as one touches the cheek of a child." It is through words that the experience of men and women in the actual world is communicated and shared.

For the communication of the immediate scene Sherwood Anderson has mastered his instrument. But, as he repeatedly asserts, mere realism is bad art. His peculiar quality resides in his intuition of something behind the scene, something "far more deeply interfused" whose dwelling is not for him "the light of setting suns" but rather "the heart of man." As Mr. Boynton remarks: "Anderson did not hit on this true note of his own until he reached the point where he became more interested in what was happening in the minds of his individuals than in what was going on outside their bodies." It is in states of consciousness which eventuate in moments when the unconscious wells up and overwhelms personality with a sense of completion in the larger unity of life that his creative power resides, and it is with such moments that his characteristic stories deal. A recurring theme in them is the effort of the character to break down the wall which confines the individual in isolation from this general life which he shares with his fellows. Sometimes this theme comes to explicit utterance, as in "The Man in the Brown Coat":

> I'll tell you what—sometimes the whole life of this world floats in a human face in my mind. The unconscious face of the world stops and stands still before me.
> Why do I not say a word out of myself to the others? Why, in all our life together, have I never been able to reach through the wall to my wife? Already I have written three hundred, four hundred thousand words. Are there no words that lead into life? Some day I shall speak to myself. Some day I shall make a testament unto myself.

Naturally in this pursuit of unity, in this breaking down of separateness, Anderson is much concerned with human relations and especially with sex. Through sex is maintained the great flow of the race of which each individual is but a drop. Sexual intercourse seems the most hopeful point of assault upon the wall which keeps each individual a prisoner. "The Egg," in his second series of tales, is concerned with a desperate effort of a broken man to preserve some sort of human relationship through the performance of a trick, but the title gives an ironical significance to the volume—"The Triumph of the Egg." Nearly all the stories are concerned with sex, from the boy's view of its mystery in "I Want to Know Why," to the tragedies of frustration in "Seeds," "Unlighted Lamps," "The Door of the Trap," "Out of Nowhere into Nothing." It is worth while to mention them, for each is a triumph, a witness to Anderson's mastery of the short-story form. The next series, "Horses and Men," continues the theme in "Unused." It also reflects a love of horses, which in adolescence passes the love of women.

Anderson's later novels bear an increasingly definite relation to the social scene. For him, the Middle West reveals on a large scale the restless striving, the frustration of unfulfilled purpose, which is so often the theme of individual life treated in his short stories. "Poor White" is an ambitious attempt in which, as in the earlier novels, a firmly realized conception tends to lose its way in cloudy romance. Hugh McVey is a boy in "a little

hole of a town stuck on a mud bank on the western shore of the Mississippi," where he follows his father listlessly about, sweeping saloons,
cleaning outhouses, or sleeping on the river bank with the smell of fish
upon him. and the flies. A New England woman takes Hugh in hand and
trains him, so that after her departure his awakened will forces him into
sustained activity. He becomes an inventor, an industrial magnate. Like
Same McPherson and Beaut McGregor in "Marching Men" the hero loses
identity, but throughout the mass of the book the symbolism is closely
woven into the realism, as warp and woof.

Hugh McVey, the physically overgrown, almost idiotic boy, is the
Middle West in the last decade of the century. When by sheer strength of
will he harnesses his mind to problems of mechanical invention and solves
them by a power he does not understand, he typifies the spirit of industrial pioneering in all its crude force. Sarah Shepherd with her school-
mistressy formula, "Show them that you can do perfectly the task given
you to do, and you will be given a chance at a larger task," is the spirit of
New England brooding on the vast abyss of the Middle West and making
it pregnant. Harley Parsons with his boast: "I have been with a Chinese
woman, and an Italian, and with one from South America. I am going
back and I am going to make a record. Before I get through I am going to
be with a woman of every nationality on earth, that's what I'm going to
do"—what is he but an ironic incarnation of our national destiny? Joe
Wainsworth, the harness-maker who in his hatred of machinery or
machine-made goods kills his assistant, is the ghost of the horse-and-
buggy age attacking the present. Smokey Pete, the blacksmith who shouts
to the fields the scandal he dares not utter on Main Street, is the spirit of
American prophesy, a Jeremiah of Ohio. Anderson has made his story a
sort of Pilgrim's Progress of the Middle-Western state he knows so well.

The best of Anderson's novels is undoubtedly "Dark Laughter." It is
not only a good novel in structure and movement, but more subtly than
"Poor White" or "Many Marriages" it is of that thoughtful quality which
entitles it to rank among the novels of ideas. The two themes which are
woven together are leading ones with Anderson—boredom through
craftsmanship, and through love. The hero, Bruce Dudley, walks out of
his home and job as a reporter and finds work in an Ohio village in Grey's
carriage factory. There he meets Sponge Martin, who teaches him how to
paint carriage wheels and how to live. His philosophy is that of art as a
guide to life:

> Perhaps if you got the thoughts and fancies organized a
> little, made them work through your body, made thoughts and
> fancies part of yourself—they might be used then, perhaps as
> Sponge Martin used a brush. You might lay on them something
> as Sponge Martin would lay varnish on it. Suppose about one
> man in a million got things organized a little. What would that
> mean? What would such a man be? Would he be a Napoleon?
> A Caesar?

Bruce meets Aline Grey, the wife of his employer, and with her steps forth on the road to freedom. Meanwhile the Negro world which surrounds them, in its dark laughter, sounds an ironic chorus.

In his later novels Anderson has shifted his scene to the South. There the process of industrialization, going on more ruthlessly, fills him with horror. Scenes in the cotton mills recur with a kind of obsession. Rather timidly he puts forward his social remedy in "Perhaps Women," the result of "a growing conviction that modern man is losing his ability to retain his manhood, in the face of the modern way of utilizing the machine, and that what hope there is for him lies in women." "Beyond Desire" is an expression of the two elements—sex and industry—but it can scarcely be maintained that any essential relation between them is established. "Kit Brandon" is an example of that "assisted autobiography" in which the author enters into the experience of another person, in this case a bootlegger whose career is not without social implications. In form it is evidence of Anderson's ability to enforce his claim, "I write as I like"—but the reader finds himself sighing for the lucid simplicity of Moll Flanders.

Recently Anderson put forth a brief statement in Story Magazine which emphasizes what is true of his writing at its best, that in its fact and its imaginative penetration beyond fact, it is a phase of his experience:

> I think that writing or painting or making music . . . is merely a tool a man can sometimes use to get at this business of living. . . . It is all wrapped up in this other thing . . . a man's relationships . . . his handling of relationships, his striving, if you will, for the good life. Relationships, I should say, with the world of nature too, development of the eyes, ears, nose, fingers. It is even, I think, concerned with the way you touch things with your fingers.

Some years ago Anderson forsook the "solemn and perhaps even asinine business, this being what is called great, doing immortal work, influencing the younger generation, etc.," and engaged in the humble business of editing a small-town newspaper—two, in fact, for there were two in town, one Democratic and one Republican. In playing the parts appropriate to the several stock characters in the newspaper play, society reporter, sports reporter, editorial writer, etc., he found abundant opportunities for cultivating relationships and leading the good life. Whether we get masterpieces from him or not, he has given an indication of the sincerity of his profession that art is a part of experience, not something added thereto, and that an artist may be too interested in life to care overmuch about success in it.

# "Anderson and the New Puritanism"

Norman Holmes Pearson*

*Winesburg, Ohio* appeared in 1919, and gave Sherwood Anderson his reputation. It was symptomatic of many things in the development of American literature besides the further discovery of the village, for which it now seems to serve as an historical marker. It represented a good deal of the liberating excitement that was in the early twentieth-century air, but more essentially it was simply a new point in a sustained tradition of self-consciousness and self-examination which has been a characteristic of American literature from the publication of the first soul-searching sermons of the New Englanders, down through the essays of Emerson and Thoreau to the introspective novels and tales of Hawthorne and the critical fiction of Henry James. With all of them, Anderson has affinity.

American literature like American life has always been coming of age, and the characters of its fiction have been sad young men. It seems in a sense paradoxical for this to have been so in a milieu of constant expansion of wealth and power. But from the beginning the Puritan tradition of introspection has been dominant. There was always questioning. Materially we are growing toward the top. Where do we stand spiritually? It is possible that the very extremes and exaggerated possibilities of American life have fostered the American sensibility in suspecting the difference between the appearance of things and their true state of being. A national life which has been a constant adolescent growing has retained for us the personal apprehensions of adolescence, and if we have our moments of exuberant confidence they have been balanced by the uncertainties and doubts, the awkward sense of personal gaucheries, which are the torment of the young.

*Winesburg, Ohio*, is then, unmistakably American in much more than the middle-western scene which is its setting. As a protest against materialism and against the ritualized conventions of social behavior, it was greeted by the Nineteen-Twenties as a war-cry against what it liked to call Puritanism. By Puritanism was meant the almost complete subordination of the spirit of man to material considerations, and to an ethic

*Originally published in the *Newberry Library Bulletin*, Second Series, No. 2 (December, 1948), pp. 52–63. Reprinted by permission of the Newberry Library.

which had no basis of reality in terms of our own situation. Puritanism which originally had risen as a movement against conformity and deadening ritual had by now become itself conformity and ritual, an unthinking bourgeois morality without a vital core of feeling and belief.

Sherwood Anderson had grown up in such a milieu in Ohio. A child's life is an interplay of yearning for convention and acceptance within the mores, at the same time that he longs for the establishment of his individuality by revolting from them. Anderson's case was no exception. The pattern of his family life was vagrant and disorganized. There was no easy sense of belonging to the community or of being accepted by it. From the moment when Anderson first started to sell his newspapers, his boyhood idea seems to have been that of establishing a position and stature for himself within the conventions. He was, as his brother Karl, describes him, "the go-getter." "He wanted to get on in the world." And he began to get on, in a pattern of "rags to riches" which he was to describe over and over again in the novels and tales he was to write. There was a kind of desperation in the attempt to establish himself in normal citizenry.

If anything is evident about Anderson's biography it is the fact that he never "belonged." If there is anything that we have to be grateful for, it is that fact that he wanted to, even if he had to reshape himself and the world in order to achieve it. At thirty-six, in 1912, came the famous episode when he walked out from the small paint factory in Elyria, of which he was head, and, leaving his wife and children, headed ultimately for Chicago and the quest for a new spiritual order. It was a still youthful gesture.

"I have a story to tell, how should I tell it?" he later wrote. The story was already his; the way of telling it came to be his constant path of discovery. The story was always that of the individual who wanted to belong, but who was not sure of what he wanted to belong to. He was a go-getter. He took it for granted that men ought to march forward, but he wanted to march in company and in the right direction. The goal was from rags to riches, but the question grew as to where the essential richness lay.

*Windy McPherson's Son* (1916) was Anderson's first public attempt to express the search. "There was an upward and onward note in all the early pages of the book, a boy, coming out of an Iowa corn-shipping town to rise in the business world, that fitted into the American mood of the day." "I was trying to think and feel my way through a man's life. I wanted it to come to some satisfactory end for him as I would like my own life to come to some satisfactory end." So Anderson described the book in his *Memoirs*. If the book reminds one of immediate antecedents it is the progression of Dreiser's sympathetic studies of the aspirations and torments of the American man of potential power. *Marching Men* (1917) was much the same kind of book, marked by the same loneliness and doubts that accompanied comparative success. In both of them the powers of reasoning and shrewdness were manifest and manifold; the ability to feel one's way was more latent, though struggling to the surface in each case. They were studies of individual education in a disorganized curriculum of life.

*Winesburg, Ohio* was his first successful working out of this problem of self-education, knowledge and brotherhood. There are no plots in these tales, because the plot as a device in fiction had become a kind of deadening ritual, like the pattern of success itself. It was an orthodoxy to which the easy yearner might succumb, but against which the true seeker must struggle. And in the normal sense of the word there were to be no heroes in his stories, whose careers of success or failure could bring an aspect of formal distinction. What Anderson sought was an organic form which might arise out of a parade of minor characters, by which he might present them in their struggles, in their gropings, and in their inevitable conflicts with the society against which they stood in tension. The only seeming link is the growing awareness and understanding of George Willard, the young newspaper reporter, as he comes to know the grotesques of his village. It was the representation of Anderson's own consciousness and understanding.

It has sometimes been said that Anderson's fiction marks a step in the naturalistic presentation of American life. This is hardly true in any vital sense of the term. For naturalism, although it presents the facts of life in detail, supposes no order nor outcome of them. Anderson was fundamentally an exuberant optimist. The superficial crudity of American life existed as a fact which must be taken into consideration in the presentation of life. In a brief essay called "An Apology for Crudity," which he published in *The Dial* in 1917, he made this clear, but with such stress that academic criticism, keen on the classification of literature, seized the phrase and forgot the intent.

Anderson called his characters "grotesques," but they were "grotesques" because of their involvement with the disorder of society. His apology for crudity was not a plea for it. Anderson's plea was actually for a resolution of the grotesqueness into a conformity with a world which was truly ordered. *Marching Men* had looked to the leadership of a powerful man for the order of march and the destination. *Mid-American Chants* (1918), which followed between it and *Winesburg, Ohio*, found an almost religious outlet in the veneration of land and nature. In a series of free-versed lyrics, whose manner lay somewhere between the Song of Solomon and the poems of Sandburg, Anderson discovered the key to affirmation. This yearning note of love he never lost, guised though it was to be in a variety of settings. As poetry, *Mid-American Chants* is not successful; but Anderson's success dates from it.

The manner of Anderson's revelation was to be recapitulated in a later story which he called "Death in the Woods." It is, I think, both his masterpiece and the narration of his artistic fulfillment. In his "Apology for Crudity" Anderson had said to American writers: "New paths will have to be made. The subjective impulse is almost unknown in us. Because it is close to life it works out in crude and broken forms." But the discordance, agonizing as it is, is superficial rather than basic. The form of "Death in the Woods" is not crude and not really broken, nor are the stories of Winesburg, nor his novels. In all these stories, the expression of the tentative gestures of the characters, the blind gropings and beatings against the walls of personal inhibitions and social conventions, seems to have a violence of desperation. "Hands" has a frustrated impulse towards the achievement of form and beauty in life. The schoolteacher, in another tale, clutching her pillow to her, aches for the fully formed circle which sex might have completed. Always there is the same timid trembling of the hands towards the apple (a thing of beauty and a seed of knowledge), which Anderson describes in the foreword to *Horses and Men* (1923). When a man in writing tries to get beneath the skullbones, the problem of the characters becomes problems of form. Because these characters of Anderson grope toward a full life, which is the matter of form in life, the technique of expressing their search may be tentative. But the underlying form exists; it is the search which is naive and vagrant.

The problem is one of feeling and of understanding. "Death in the Woods" is a completely satisfying realization of form, both in its composition and in the ultimate comprehension of the chief character. This chief character is not the old woman who dies, but the boy who sees her dead. By the accretion of detail, as he comes to understand it through experience and maturity, the meaning of the old woman's life and the sudden, at the moment inexplicable, vision of the beauty of her dead body becomes clear. Clear, though the sense of the mystery in life remains. Bit by bit the story takes form. Not until all of these bits are fused is the story complete. Then there is achieved form. What would have appeared crude and broken had the boy's comprehension been stopped short in its education, would have been that only because the story was not complete. "A thing so complete has its own beauty," Anderson said in the conclusion of his story.

I said something like this about "Death in the Woods" to Anderson, and he said things in answer that I like to remember about his work. "I presume," he said, "that we all, who begin the practice of an art, begin out of a great hunger for order. We want brought into consciousness something that is always there but that gets so terribly lost. I am walking on a country road and there is a man on a hillside plowing. There is something nice, even beautiful, in the man striding at the plow handles, in the breasts of the horse pulling, in the earth rolling back from the plow, in the newly turned earth below and in the sky above. We want not only to know that beauty but to have him, at the plow handles, know. You see, I have the belief that, in this matter of form, it is largely a matter of depth of feeling. How deeply do you feel it? Feel it deeply enough and you will be torn inside and driven on until form comes.

"I think this whole thing must be in some way tied up with something I can find no other word to describe aside from the word morality. I suppose I think that the author who doesn't struggle all his life to achieve this form, let it be form, betrays this morality. It is terribly important because, to my way of thinking, this morality may be the only true morality there is in the world.

"For—and this particularly true of the story writer—there are always others involved. The story writer is not in the position of the painter who is seeking form in nature. He brings other people into his stories.

"And what is so little understood is that, in distorting the lives of these others—often imagined figures to be sure—to achieve some tricky effect, you are betraying not only this indefinable thing we call form but you are betraying all of life . . . in short that it is as dirty and unworthy a thing to betray these imagined figures as it would be to betray or sell out so-called real people in real life.

"And so, this whole matter of form involves, for the story writer, also this morality. And it may well be that, in some way, it is just this artist's point of view, this morality, always to be gone toward, and that occasionally forces him to bring his materials into real form, that is the only thing that may, in the end, pull mankind out of its mess."

At times Anderson would laugh at the didactic moralism of the New England gods whom he would so willingly discard, "trying to find honest, mid-western American gods." But he himself was the most moral of men and the most concerned with the lesson he could teach his time. He was not unique in this respect of course. The writers of his time, like the writers before them, were moralists. Dreiser, Masters, Mencken, Cabell, Stein, and the others, all shook fingers and pointed ways. But what marked Anderson and gave him his particular appeal to men younger than himself was his capacity for love and his sense of optimism. He restored the possibility of beginning again. He maintained the irrepressibility and vitality of youth. Brushed by the inadequacies of society, he was a reformer rather than a revolutionary, a revitalizer rather than a cynic. He could find again and again the joy of re-discovery and of crashing down the old barriers encrusting belief and the power of feeling. In the front ranks of the assault on Puritanism, Anderson was a leader among the New Puritans.

There was a strong religious flavor to Anderson as there was to Vachel Lindsay. In looking at the spiritual sterility of his time, Anderson sensed still alive beneath it an almost primitive mystic urgency, whose recapture was necessary to man. To his friend, Waldo Frank, in 1918, he wrote:

A curious notion comes often to me. It is not likely that when the country was new and men were often alone in the fields and forests they got a sense of bigness outside themselves that has now in some way been lost? I don't mean the conventional religious thing that is still prevalent and that is nowadays being retailed to the people by the most up-to-date commercial methods, but something else. The people I fancy had a savagery superior to our own. Mystery whispered in the grass, played in the branches of the trees overhead, was caught up and blown across the American line in clouds of dust at evening on the prairies.

I am old enough to remember tales that strengthen my belief in a deep semi-religious influence that was formerly at work among our people. The flavor of it hangs over the best work of Mark Twain. That's what makes it so moving and valuable. I can remember old fellows in my home town speaking feelingly of an evening spent on the big empty plains. . . . It made them significant.

One can say that the coming of industrialism has brought about the present day emptiness and shrillness of the arts, and there must be something in the saying, but, Lord, man, can art be superseded by the clatter of the machinery in a shoe factory? The prairies are still here. The Mississippi flows southward to the sea, it is but a step from the heart of the loop district in Chicago to the shores of Lake Michigan.

This was a matter of false gods and idols, with both the direction of man's power of feeling and his very capacity for feeling, lost. Though the power of reason to excite ecstasy or to penetrate to the mystery of the order of things had proved inadequate, there was no compensating trust in the power of the senses and of intuition as a way to knowledge. What was lacking was, as the elder James had understood in the training of his sons, "a better sensuous education than they are likely to get here." "It is largely a matter of depth of feeling," was Anderson's way of putting it. In a limited way, the conflict of the late eighteenth century was being repeated in our own time; and in an effort to get back to the essential instinctive man, Freud's noble savage was offered in substitution for Rousseau's. But if the New Puritans offered the sexual drive as a source of revitalization, it was for a man like Anderson only a useful symbol for which other symbols and means could be, and were, supplied.

Art was a means of devotion, and the poem or tale was a form of prayer. Words and rhetoric, formalized into clichés, were a barrier to communication, as liturgy had been. Anderson sensed this as others did, and as Emerson had done in his own efforts toward a renaissance. Gertrude Stein was a kind of modern Emerson, and Anderson found in her slim volume *Tender Buttons* (1914) a new azure *Nature*. James Joyce, too, gave his lessons. To a friend of later year, Burton Emmett, Anderson wrote in 1926:

> What, for example, have I not stolen from Joyce?
> Stein is something special. She is not a story-teller—perhaps not an artist. She has given me a lot. An artist in phrase making, sound combinations, something like that. She is a saintly tool maker.
> That's a lot.

But Sherwood Anderson could have gone farther back into his own history for the concern with words which he had as an artist. For some years before his first "literary" writing appeared in magazines like *The Dial*, *Seven Arts*, and *The Masses*, he had written a series of commercial sketches for house organs like the Chicago *Agricultural Advertising*. They are unknown, but they should not be if one is concerned with Anderson as a writer. In one of them, called "The Undeveloped Man" (1904), he tells of the "dense forest of untried oaths" through which an unseen brakeman made his way. It was an advertising man, like Anderson, who listened in awe and admiration.

> "Say, young feller, you're different. What you so interested in that feller for?"
> "Well, I'll tell you," said the advertising man. "I was just thinking what a good man he would be in the advertising business. He knows the value of words, that fellow does. Did you hear the way he made that conductor and that engineer look faded out like a scorched shirt front? He knows how to use words and that's why I think he'd make an advertising man. How to use words, and say, Mr. Cowman, that's what advertising is, just using words; just picking them out like that fellow picked out his swear words and then dropping them down in just the right place so they seem to mean something. I don't want you to be making fun of that brakeman. You'll find he's a long ways different man than that Arizona chap you tell of imitating a jewsharp. He's a word man, that brakeman is, and words are the greatest things ever invented."

It all "fitted into the American mood of the day," as Anderson was to say in another regard. "I had not got the slant on business I later got."

The slant on business, which was to shadow it, was above all its deadening effect upon the spirit. Anderson had begun to see this as early as 1904, before he had walked from the paint factory. In another of his commercial sketches, called "The Man of Affairs," he wrote:

> "It is common for us to say that the strong men don't care for the money; that it is the power they seek; but, for my part, I am not able to see the distinction. The result to the man is ex-

actly the same. . . . He has learned the weaknesses of humanity now and is busy playing upon these weaknesses, and the
blood that hurries through his brain draws warmth from his
once big heart. Because he despises and sees the weaknesses of
all men, all men hate and fear him, and he goes on his way, en-
vied by no man except it be Green, the assistant bookkeeper, or
the dentist on Madison street. Peter Macveagh is a product of
the times and the opportunities."

Anderson's shift in slant came as he grew to understand the fuller
significance of the loss of emotion and with it a path towards understanding. Much later, in 1933, he wrote to Burton Emmett:

I believe, Burt, that it is this universal thing, scattered about
in many people, a fragment of it here, a fragment there—this
thing we call love—that we have to keep on trying to tap . . .
You know, Burt, how I have always hit at money and positions. The whole subject isn't as important to me as you may
think, and the only reason I hit at it is because I think it often
gets in the way of understanding. . . . The only thing about
money or the lack of it is that it gets into our thoughts when it
shouldn't.

These fragments were what, so long as they were scattered, Anderson
saw as the crudity of disorder, but which could cohere as "this universal
thing." Words had been scattered, too, and it was only through their
emotional charging, the love of words and love in words, that their arrangement could coincide with the order of things. Nothing, if seen and
felt deeply enough, could remain outside of order or the truly organic
form of a work of art, for which one hungered as one hungered for order
in society. By a poet this would have been called a denial of the anti-
poetic in subject matter. Anderson was very close to the art of the poet in
his writing. That is, perhaps, why *Mid-American Chants* set him going,
as he himself acknowledged. In *Winesburg, Ohio*, which so successfully
followed, he was to say again and again that this was the subject for a
poet. "It is a job for a poet." It may explain, too, why on the whole
Anderson was more successful in the medium of the short story than that
of the novel, for the impulse of emotional affirmation suits the lyric better
than the long poem. The poets of our time, following in the same anti-
intellectual path of intuitive affirmation, have been great, but great as
lyric poets. Pound, Eliot, and Hart Crane, as examples, have even in their
most ambitious works never achieved more than a string of linked lyrics.
Anderson's strong emotional feeling could be sustained and formalized
within the short story as though it too were a lyric. His novels were often
linked tales.

The public did not always see the prose of Sherwood Anderson as an
optimistic affirmation of the possibilities of American life. They saw the

grotesques who figured the pages of his books, and saw them only as grotesques. But the writers and artists of his own time, and those younger than himself, learned to see as he saw, and learned partly by his example. Their comments to him in letters came firm in their fervor. Stieglitz wrote to him in 1923:

> You seemed to stand there in my forest like some wonderful tree that had no name—a large simple tree—with strong branches and tender leaves.

Hart Crane wrote to him in the warmth of fellow-craftsmanship, and Thomas Wolfe, before the publication of *Look Homeward, Angel*, could write:

> May I also say that I want to be your friend—as I am—and I want you to be mine, as I believe you are. When I told you how I felt about you and your work, I was not laying it on with a trowel. I don't think of you as a father, as an elderly influence, or anything of the kind. So far as I know, your work has not "influenced" me at all, save in the ways in which it has enriched my life, and my knowledge of my country. I think you are one of the most important writers of this century, that you have plowed another deep furrow in the American earth, revealed to us another beauty that we knew was there but that no one else had spoken. I think of you with Whitman and with Twain—that is, with men who have seen America with a poet's vision and with a poetic vision of life—which to my mind is the only way ultimately it can be seen.

This was a returning of the love which Anderson knew how to give, a love intense and ordering. It was there early in him and stayed to the end. In 1917 Waldo Frank wrote to him, rejoicing in his power. "I receive a sense of ecstasy from the best of your work which I can not find in the writers farther from home." It was this sense of ecstasy, above all, which informed Anderson's successful writing and was to be felt even in his moments of comparative failue. It redeems him as he hoped to have it redeem others. It is romantic in an age of American writing which neither could suppress romanticism nor tried to. Insofar as it has validity it is that of the youthful dream which still hopes to pass through purification to a permanent order of felt beauty and natural morality.

# "The Permanence of Sherwood Anderson"

John T. Flanagan*

The biographer or critic who has tried vainly to assemble the literary remains of long-dead authors or who has labored to get access to papers and manuscripts still in private possession must look with pleasure on the tendency of twentieth-century writers to place their material in college or institutional libraries. Sometimes, indeed, letters, proof sheets, and first editions are deposited by the authors themselves, often of course with temporal restrictions on their use. The Mark Twain papers, to cite an older example, have found an enviable final resting place in the Huntington Library. More recently the University of Pennsylvania has become the permanent custodian of the Theodore Dreiser collection, while the Yale Library is the depository for the papers of such authors as Stephen Vincent Benet, Sinclair Lewis, and Gertrude Stein. Through the courtesy of the novelist's widow, Mrs. Eleanor Copenhaver Anderson, the Newberry Library of Chicago has added to its other treasures the Sherwood Anderson manuscripts, a collection which may well stimulate a revaluation of the position of the author himself.

The Anderson material is particularly rich. It includes the manuscripts of unpublished stories, tentative sketches and fragments of unfinished work, and well over ten thousand letters, some seven thousand to Sherwood Anderson, some three thousand letters by him to a variety of persons. Hardly any major figure of twentieth-century American letters is unrepresented in the correspondence, and the letters which passed between Anderson and such writers as H. L. Mencken, Theodore Dreiser, Ernest Hemingway, Paul Rosenfeld, Waldo Frank, and Van Wyck Brooks have special salience. The majority of Anderson's letters are dated after his first celebrity as a writer and consequently shed little light on the factors that impelled him to leave a business career for authorship, yet on many occasions he glanced backward or talked freely about his craft and literary practitioners in general.

It is unlikely that a careful winnowing of these papers will produce anything of signal consequence, since Anderson's last published works

*Originally published in *The Southwest Review*, 35 (Summer, 1950), pp. 170–77. Reprinted by permission of *The Southwest Review* and John T. Flanagan.

were undeniably repetitious and trivial. But one recalls that various volumes of hitherto unpublished Mark Twain papers have revealed certain obscure aspects of Samuel Clemens, and it is more than probable that the numerous manuscripts will illuminate not only Anderson himself but the milieu in which he worked and the craftsmen with whom he labored. Certainly they will dissipate some of the shadows which have unaccountably gathered about the man who once described himself as the most talked-about, unread, and unbought author in America.

The republication of Sherwood Anderson's best work in inexpensive editions has brought to the writer a delayed and somewhat derivative popularity, but Anderson was never in any sense a best seller. He himself repeatedly remarked with chagrin that only *Dark Laughter* had made him any money. If one glances through Frank Luther Mott's volume on American literary successes, *Golden Multitudes*, one will look vainly for Anderson's name; not even in the index is there any reference to the creator of *Winesburg, Ohio*, to the author of what are conceivably the best short stories produced by an American writer of this century. But fortunately there is no close correlation between contemporary fame and permanent significance. Melville's *Moby Dick* was not a best seller, either in 1851 or later, nor was *Walden*, or *Leaves of Grass*, or *Sister Carrie*. If Thoreau's contention that to be great is to be obscure has validity, then Sherwood Anderson had small cause for complaint and critical esteem has corrected errors in popular taste. It is possible that his actual audience today is not significantly larger than it was when *Poor White* or *Tar* was a new book, but few indeed are the students of American culture who do not know and appreciate Anderson's work.

When Sherwood Anderson died of peritonitis in 1941 he was sixty-five years of age, yet all the work which brought him literary celebrity had appeared within the previous quarter of a century. Rarely does a writer wait until middle age to publish his first book, although that experience is commoner for a novelist than for a poet. Sherwood Anderson's first novel, *Windy McPherson's Son*, appeared when he was forty, an age which Keats and Shelley and Byron never reached. But the requirements of fiction are different from those of lyric poetry. Where the poet sings and feels, the novelist narrates, describes, judges, and above all interprets. The complexities of internal life fascinate him more than the beauties of the physical world, and the buried emotions of man transcend the momentary transfixion of a mood. The richness of experience and observation that infuses great fiction is not the product of youth. When Anderson in mid-channel turned to writing he had already lived variously, and the maturity of understanding thus gained he focused largely on the people of the rural Middle West.

For Anderson was as much the product of the midwestern small town as Sinclair Lewis or Edgar Lee Masters. His early years were passed in such small Ohio communities as Camden, where he was born in 1876,

Caledonia, Clyde, and Elyria. It was Clyde that saw him in adolescence, Clyde that introduced him to school and sex and racetracks and books, and Clyde that eventually furnished him the prototype for *Winesburg, Ohio* (although Anderson always insisted that he sketched the characters for that memorable volume while observing the roomers in his boardinghouse in Chicago). And it was Elyria that was the scene of his paint business, a business which one day he unceremoniously left never to return because deep in his soul he felt an ineluctable hatred for routine and drudgery against which his individualism rebelled. In between Clyde and Elyria he had served in Cuba during the Spanish-American War, had attended Wittenberg College very briefly, and had tried his hand at advertising writing in Chicago, a profession which he resumed when he finally left Ohio for good.

In one sense the Ohio countryside colored everything that Anderson wrote, even in his later days when he was living in Marion, Virginia, and publishing two weekly newspapers, one Democratic and one Republican. He himself once remarked that if *Main Street* were any criterion, Sinclair Lewis must have had a sorry life as a boy because he missed so much of the simple joys of rural existence. Anderson had played on the local baseball team, had roamed the fields and woods, fished the streams, idled in the cornfields or near the racetracks, met the trains that brought romance and strangers from the big cities to Clyde. His eagerness to be a newsboy, grocery boy, stable attendant, and farm laborer brought him the nickname of "Jobby," and while such jobs undoubtedly helped him financially and allowed him to contribute his mite to a family which was never comfortably well off, they were also invaluable later in teaching him something of human relationships and human frailties. More than one of his stories, for example, has the point of view of the newsboy watching life from the sidelines.

In his fiction Anderson preserved these memories and experiences. County fairs, fields planted to cabbages or corn, the stores, taverns, and stables of Main Street, farmhouses and village homes, these supplied the scenes of his stories, just as the itinerant housepainters, the drummers, the owners of race horses and the racetrack touts, farmers, clerks, housewives became the protagonists. As Anderson sold papers or helped to curry stallions he listened to the incomparable tales of rustic narrators who were both unhurried and long-memoried, narrators like his own father who was an unreliable provider but a charming raconteur. Not all his fiction reveals the flavor and character of rural Ohio, but in such stories as "Death in the Woods" and "I'm A Fool," in all of *Winesburg*, and in most of *Poor White*, the setting is his native state. Indeed, one might consider *Winesburg* as the third and greatest book in a kind of trilogy of Ohio small-town life which began with William Dean Howells' nostalgic picture of Hamilton in *A Boy's Town* (1890) and includes Clarence Darrow's charming and intelligent sketch of the community of his youth which he called *Farmington* (1904). Since Anderson was the greatest artist, his book is the most mature and the richest; he did imperishably in 1919 what the others had achieved only in part some decades before.

But fidelity to background is after all only a kind of photography, and photography is seldom art. It was Anderson's treatment of character, his intuitive perception and sympathy in portraiture, which won him quick recognition and which will ensure him permanent attention. Deliberately he wrote about what he called "grotesques," or possibly he singled out in usually normal people the basic motive or inhibition which served to distort their whole lives. The result is that the town of Winesburg has as many eccentrics and neurotics as Spoon River, as many banal materialists as Gopher Prairie; but where Masters and Lewis reviled and satirized, Anderson was persistently sympathetic. In his stories a minister's fondness for staring from his church study at a schoolteacher lying naked in her bed, the tactile sensitivity of a man which impels him to touch his students, the repressed intelligence of a doctor who writes his thoughts down on scraps of paper and then flings the paper pellets around his office, become human aberrations, neither perverted nor sinister. The buried life revealed itself to Anderson in many ways, and all of its manifestations were interesting.

Indeed he repudiated any direct obligation to Sigmund Freud and quite possibly had never read the Austrian psychologist's work when he began to produce his own stories. But the characters and themes he consistently selected suggest that his interest in frustration, inhibition, neurosis was almost professional. Of course it was not his understanding of psychology but rather his imaginative impulse to project himself into the minds and souls of others that explains his fiction. He recognized his own unreliability as a factual reporter, even of facts relating primarily to himself, so that his so-called autobiographical volumes are notoriously inconsistent and inaccurate. But people and their behavior fascinated him. One of the great tributes to him as a writer is that so many readers today consider him clean and honest despite the fact that his pages reveal details of homosexuality, prostitution, nympholepsy, adultery, and incest. The intrinsic sensationalism of such subjects did not appeal to him as they did to William Faulkner when he was writing *Sanctuary*; rather Anderson utilized them because he felt that their omission would prevent him from giving a rounded picture of human existence. No doubt the first audiences of *Hamlet* were occasionally disturbed by a play which included incest, insanity, a suicide, and five murders—and only afterward realized that the essential impact of the drama was not due to its sanguinary violence. Similarly Anderson deprecated certain aspects of human life but was reluctant to ignore or conceal them because to him they explained, if they did not justify, many actions of the animal named man.

For Sherwood Anderson was principally concerned with the individual and with that individual's relationship to society. He himself grew up in the days when the new industrialism was just reaching the Middle West. Oil and gas had been discovered in northern Ohio and had brought dreams of wealth to many. The old artisan saw his careful work duplicated cheaply and quickly by machines, exactly as the harness-maker in *Poor White* who was so proud of his craftsmanship observed the arrival on the market of harnesses which might not last as long as, but were gaudier and cheaper than, any he could produce. Everywhere the skilled workman's livelihood was being taken away from him, his pride and joy in achievement dissipated. To Anderson there was something tragic in this economic change. Industrialism might elevate the standard of living with its endless flow of cheap goods, but it also removed a certain sincerity and integrity from life. Surely the basic irony of *Poor White* is that after the inventive genius of Hugh McVey has produced a small boom in the town of Bidwell, it is followed by overcapitalization, technological unemployment, and extensive labor unrest, so that one can never be sure whether Hugh McVey has been an asset or a detriment to his adopted town.

Eleven years later the theme of *Poor White* became the thesis of *Perhaps Women*, in which Anderson expressed impressionistically, half in prose and half in verse, his conviction that men had lost their maleness in their struggle with the industrial age. Machinery had made them impotent, and the survival of the race and its civilization depended more and more upon women. Anderson never allowed his criticism of industrialism to degenerate into satire or revilement. He was even capable of praising with the words of a poet the clean lines and the cold efficiency of machines. But he always speculated as to whether the new economy was any genuine improvement over the old, whether physical progress was a fair equivalent for frustrated individualism. Like an earlier southern Democrat, Thomas Jefferson, Anderson would probably have found his utopia in an intelligent agrarianism stemming from a nation of cultivated and self-sustaining farmers.

He was even more sympathetic in depicting revolt against routine and social convention. The most crucial event in his own life was his decision to leave the Elyria paint factory for a life of writing, a decision which was sudden and unpredicted if not unmotivated. Similarly the fictional situation which he repeatedly employs presents a man in early middle age who all at once sees life as empty, futile, meaninglessly repetitive, and who without long premeditation flees in revolt. Anderson's autobiographical volumes shed little light on his own sense of obligation to family or society. And certainly his protagonists seldom consider either. Sam McPherson, John Webster, Bruce Dudley, all of them established figures in society, suddenly rebel against marriage, business, routine in general; they seek not only their individual freedom but the ultimate meaning of life. In *Many Marriages* and *Dark Laughter* Anderson offers no solution, since the circumstances of flight come at the end of the volumes; but Sam McPherson in *Windy McPherson's Son*, after trying such psychological sedatives as alcohol, big game hunting, and manual labor, creeps back to his wife (who has presumably been waiting patiently for just such a return) with some adopted children and the assumption that the final answer to the problems posed by life may be found at home. Like the Greenwich Village radicals of the 1920's Anderson sacrificed on the altar of liberty without realizing that, as William Dean Howells once shrewdly remarked, "To do whatever one likes is finally to do nothing that one likes, even though one continues to do what one will."

Anderson's characters, like himself, were more emotional than logical. It has been said that the people of *Winesburg, Ohio* feel but never think. Surely neither Sam McPherson nor Bruce Dudley, Anderson's best-known fugitives, ever analyzed their situation or did anything but yield to the impulse of the moment. And Hugh McVey, who fled from his wife on their marital night but who did not evade his social responsibilities, was troubled by the chaos which he had apparently brought to Bidwell, although he lacked the mental capacity either to understand or to solve his dilemma. A moralist might call Anderson's characters spineless and conscienceless; a satirist such as Jonathan Swift would probably deride them as a typical part of the asinine human race. To Anderson himself they were merely human; he found their doubts and frailties, their abhorrence of a stale routine, perfectly intelligible.

This antagonism against convention and stability Anderson carried into the very structure of his stories. His novels are vaguely biographical, with the chronology of the protagonist's life providing whatever focus or unity the plot has. What he strove to find was not a well-ordered plot built upon such Aristotelian principles as a beginning, a middle, and an end, but the flow and flavor of life. His stories lack suspense, dramatic acceleration, climax, but somehow in their very fidelity to life they hold the reader's attention. Their imaginative truth is unchallengeable. It is no longer startling to read of an academic critic like Stuart Pratt Sherman finding the opening pages of *Dark Laughter* comparable in their art and finish to the opening pages of Jane Austen's *Pride and Prejudice*, for in each case the writer captured the tone of a society. In the best work of both there are qualities which will endure. The "new looseness" which Anderson admittedly sought in constructing *Winesburg, Ohio* was firm enough to form the necessary matrix for his tales.

Yet one must admit that Anderson's novels were not artistic successes. However much one may admire such qualities as sensitivity and sympathy and a poetic understanding (and notwithstanding volumes like *Mid-American Chants*, Anderson was most often a poet when he was not writing in verse), the longer forms of fiction demand a tightness and a plan which Anderson was incapable of providing. His novels are rich in episodes but deficient in continuity, repetition replaces development in them, and the tangential becomes more important than the organic. *Poor White* is perhaps the most unified—and even here the protagonist is forgotten for almost one-fifth of the novel—and *Dark Laughter* is the most opulent in style and mood. When one says of them that they are best in fragments, in moments, one immediately puts one's finger on the underlying significance of Sherwood Anderson's work.

For his proper field was obviously the short story. Here with a few characters, often incompletely realized, a simple situation, usually a single setting, Anderson could draw upon all his richness as a storyteller and interpreter of people. Here he could picture a mood, as in "Brothers," or deal with an episode, as in "Death in the Woods," with the perfection of the miniaturist. The compression of a small canvas allowed him to taste a scene to the full, and his selection of uncomplex characters gave special value to such presentational methods as repetition and simplicity of language. Method and theme coalesce perfectly in "I Want To Know Why" and "I'm A Fool," both of them told autobiographically in the vernacular by adolescent and uncultivated boys who do not lack intelligence. In "The Triumph of the Egg" Anderson treated the discouraged chicken farmer who graduated to restaurant-keeping and in an attempt to attract customers strove to be entertainer as well as host. His futile effort to force a vinegar-treated egg through the neck of a bottle so infuriated him that he began to throw eggs at his solitary midnight customer—a curious example of impotent rage.

The people of these tales are naïve, simple, pathetic folk for the most part, fixed for a moment in their erratic lives by Anderson's observation and insight, projected suddenly against a screen in sight of all. There is nothing heroic or permanent about them; even as protagonists of stories they are feeble. But something about them temporarily captured Anderson's imagination. His narrative framework is the spotlight into which they suddenly wander and waver; shortly the incandescence dims and they slip back to their habitual obscurity.

Anderson's medium was the sketch, impressionistic, deceptively formless, personal, inconclusive. For a memorable impression, honest and perceptive, it sufficed. Anderson himself was conscious both of the inertness of much of his material and of his impoverished vocabulary. But to him language had other functions than simple communication. Like the nonobjective painter for whom raw pigments and geometrical figures or lines are superior to visual import, Anderson regarded words as having color, shape, and form over and above their simple denotation. A word not only meant something to him, it was something (his paraphrase of Archibald MacLeish's dictum that a poem should not mean but *be*)—possibly a notion derived from his friendship with Gertrude Stein. Just as the nuances of life were more important to him than the hard exterior facts, so language assumed values as symbol and connotation. As a consequence, qualities such as his repetition, his banality, his almost childish simplicity characterize a sincere and deliberate attempt to combine meaning with impression, to saddle words with more than their literal significance.

This interest in words as more than mere counters of meaning suggests a final aspect of Sherwood Anderson, his combination of the earthy and the gossamer, his fusion of objective fact which was harmonious if not accurate with the ineffable longings and fancies and projections of the self—the kind of singular mixture which once prompted Harry Hansen to call him a corn-fed mystic. For alone among the midwestern realists of the 1920's Anderson saw the invisible and heard the inaudible. The phenomenon by itself never satisfied him. He was familiar with the empathy of the psychologist, and his common method was a physical and psychic projection of himself into the world around him. Often in this activity both his technique and his language proved inadequate so that the impact of the projection was lost. But when the means of expression harmonized with the purpose of the expression, as was true in many of the short stories and in parts of the novels, Sherwood Anderson was memorably successful.

It may seem gratuitous indeed to find a parallel between Anderson and a novelist whom time and geography in this connection make almost antipodal. But Anderson's treatment of character and his probings into the subconscious suggest an earlier writer whose single subject was the Yankee or at least the Puritan soul, and who was at least as indifferent to external fact as Anderson himself. Nathaniel Hawthorne was also a psychologist who wrote fiction, a storyteller who subordinated suspense and climax, an observer interested in the inhibitions and thwarted desires of man. The differences between the two are obvious, differences in heredity, education, professional preparation, even style. But both emerged slowly from obscurity into fame, both published their best work as mature men after a long apprenticeship, both shifted from the short story to the novel as a fictional medium, both treated character imaginatively and impressionistically, both explored the penumbral world and the world below the surface—Hawthorne owing a debt possibly to Cotton Mather and Jonathan Edwards, Sherwood Anderson somewhat circuitously to Sigmund Freud. In a sense too both men were moralists. Hawthorne continually investigated the effect of evil deeds upon the conscience and in his portrait of Donatello in *The Marble Faun* showed the educative effect of sin; Anderson laid bare the gropings and yearnings of men and revealed the frequently hidden causes of action with rare sympathy and perception. Neither man judged the sinner for his peccadilloes. For some offenses, no doubt, punishment is condign, but for all the grievances, angers, envies, and passions of which the human spirit is capable Hawthorne and Anderson had only a single emotion—compassion.

Sherwood Anderson was undisciplined in both his life and his writings. There was never any danger that his grasp might exceed his reach. The structural convention that he evaded and sometimes maligned might have worked to his advantage, could he have made intelligent use of it. But the honesty and integrity of his work are rare qualities at any time and probably greater in the long run than any inherent in mere discipline. The American short story is richer and freer because Sherwood Anderson once lived.

# "Sherwood Anderson: A Sweet Singer, 'A Smooth Son of a Bitch' "

Chandler Brossard*

The memory of Sherwood Anderson has just lately been evoked for me by the publication of a critical study of the man and his work, written by Irving Howe (published by Sloane Associates in their American Men of Letters Series).

When I read *Winesburg, Ohio*, for the first time I experienced a strange, intense pleasure that has been given to me by only two other American books, *Huckleberry Finn* and *The Sun Also Rises*. It was a pleasure that was quite literally sensual: my body suddenly unfroze, I experienced a sensation similar to goose pimples, I got an excited, hurried feeling as I read (the way you do when you are going out on a date), I spoke out loud a couple of times from sheer uncontrollable admiration and delight, and I could not put the book down until I had finished every last page of it.

This may sound a little hot and heavy, but that's actually the way it happened. The language in *Winesburg* (and the other two books mentioned) so exquisitely, so perfectly expressed the feeling and meaning of the material, the form and the content were so remarkably mated, that not for one moment did I disbelieve anything that went on. Nothing seemed hoked up. Beyond this, Anderson was using the American language in its purest form, its spoken form; the writing was not, as it was in almost everything else I had read by Americans, literary and superimposed, hit or miss, on the material at hand. This was my language—it could not have been written, or spoken, by an Englishman, a Frenchman, a German, or anybody else on the outside.

What Anderson was doing, of course, was solidifying the break away from the English and European influence in American writing, and at the same time helping to widen the split in literature between the spoken language and the written language, and returning to the original source of literature, the oral story teller. It had been done here to some extent before his time, Mark Twain being the first great proponent of these

*Originally published in *The American Mercury* 72 (May, 1951), pp. 611–16. Reprinted by permission of *The American Mercury*.

moves in American literature, with his masterpiece *Huckleberry Finn*, spoken in Mississippi River dialects, by a twelve-year-old boy. Then came Gertrude Stein, with *Three Lives* and *The Making of an American*, then Anderson, and finally Hemingway, who was actually an on-the-spot pupil and protégé of both Anderson and Stein.

Anderson, Twain, Stein, and Hemingway all wrote this spoken language, whether or not the particular work was written in the third person or in the first. If it was in the third, the presence of a narrator was always heavily felt throughout; there was not the feeling of a piece of fiction that had anonymously written itself. The idea was that the written language, or the literary language, was exhausted, just about dead, and there had to be a return to the continually moving, continually developing vigor of the spoken English.

While it may look and read easy, this spoken style is a most exacting and dangerous thing to fool around with. Where it is used, say, in Anderson's famous story, "I Want to Know Why," narrated by an ignorant young country boy, it must never for an instant fall out of character, never in any word say or think anything that would not be characteristic of the boy with all of his traits and limitations. Besides this primary requisite, the technique must be used with a careful eye toward all possible ironies and subtle tensions: there must be a counterpointing of the simple style with the complexity of the situation, there must be implied something going on in the story that seems beyond the narrator, and his occasional incomprehension, which is caught immediately by the aware reader, adds to the reader's possibility of participating more rewardingly in the story.

Today the technique of the first person is used most frequently because it is simply easier for a writer to write as though he were talking, instead of displacing himself into the third person. This of course merely results in a hybrid combination of journalism and fiction. Or if the narrator in the third person is used in the way I have mentioned above, it is done so with no respect for the subtle demands and possibilities therein.

To return to Sherwood Anderson, it was this careful respect for his material and his technique, his utter profound commitment to his craft, that made him, in his best work, a beautiful and illuminating writer to read. It was the disintegration of his control and his careful respect, in his worst work, that made him, in the eyes of his admirers, a frustrating, irritating, disappointing writer. At this point he became a derelict parody of himself.

Of all the important American writers of the last thirty years or so, Anderson probably had the most harrowing and obstacle-laden career of them all. His midwestern childhood was financially and emotionally as insecure as you can possibly imagine (his father was a wind bag and a drunk, often jobless, his mother strangely Puritanical and remote); far into his twenties his literacy was widely open to question (throughout his entire life it was always touch and go with his spelling and grammar) and his life ambitions were almost schizophrenically divergent. While he imagined himself, and actually was, an aggressive, sharp-witted, sly businessman, he also saw himself as a drifter, a bum, an emotional child in need of female domination, a poet with no poems, a seeker after the light of happiness, a constant brooder in the darkness.

It was only logical that these antipodal pulls would finally have their effect on Anderson. At the age of thirty-six or so, when he was at the peak of his business career (being the manager of a sizable paint factory) and at the same time just beginning his writing, he suddenly had a breakdown. He forgot his identity and wandered aimlessly through the open country and through various cities for four days, until he was finally identified by someone in a drugstore in a distant city. His vanity forced him, in later years, to claim that the breakdown was a hoax, self-induced so that he could gain new experiences not otherwise available to him, and that he knew all along what he was doing. This of course is the sheerest nonsense, and one wishes that Anderson had never tried to palm it off on the literary world, had had just a bit more courage than that.

It was after this that Anderson saw he must become a writer and nothing else, so he grimly set about it, at an age when most other people barely have enough adventure and self-assurance to change their brand of toothpaste, much less their whole way of life. He quit his business and worked hard at his new profession from that day on—in his spare time at night or full time in the day—until he died, some twenty odd years later, on a trip to South America.

His character and career were a composite of nearly all the things we associate with serious American writers: he could not make a living on his writing alone, so he had to hustle as a publicity man and advertising writer, which he loathed; he both hated and loved the things of his miserable childhood, including all the members of his family; he had an ineradicable mother, or Oedipus complex, which drove him from woman to woman (four wives), always marrying a mother type who would manage him but toward whom he never really felt physically attracted; he had a morbid fear of intellect and intellectuals, thinking that the one would corrupt his pure instinctiveness by too much examination of life, and that the other would try to con him into something or other, or just shake his faith in himself with their questions and traditional sneers. (This last fear is rather amusing when you consider the fact that he regarded himself as a sort of con man . . . "the truth is I was a smooth son of a bitch.") He finally lost control of himself and his talent and, either out of vanity or sheer lack of self-understanding, went on writing long after he should have stopped. ("I had a world and it slipped away from me. . . . Nothing I do has any meaning.")

But while he had all these things (shortcomings if you like) common to American writers, he had a couple of things they seldom have—he had passion, a longing for old style heroic emotions—sentiment (he wasn't afraid of being corny), generosity, love. ("In the end the real writer becomes a lover.") And he had vision, a point of view, a personal morality in his writing. It is this final thing that separates a real writer from one who is just making a kind of living at it. Almost none of the writers who at the moment are considered major, or just important, have this personal vision, this point of view that finally gives them distinction and meaning beyond their surface. I don't know what in God's name they are personally up to. But perhaps this is an age, unique I should say in history, when a point of view is not an attribute. It is a result (part of it anyway) of the high degree of mechanism and professionalism in our country: such a thing as a personal vision would seem to hinder one's slick professionalism, which should enable one to play well on several different ball teams in the same season without confusing oneself.

Another aspect of Anderson's life that seems to be a basic component of the American writer is the desperate need he had for friendship and guidance. These things were not only not taken for granted, as they are in a more traditional culture, but there was such a deep anxiety about them that his pursuit of them becomes almost maudlin and suspect. He seemed to lean on his friends Van Wyck Brooks, Paul Rosenfeld, and Waldo Frank almost as you would lean on your nurse or psychoanalyst.

> Do try to form the habit of writing me some of your thoughts occasionally, *he wrote to Brooks*. It is lonely out here. . . . When I talked to Waldo . . . I felt in him a sense of background I have never had. I wondered if he knew the (my?) utter lack of background. It means so very much that you know and of course he must know also.
>
> What friendship you give strengthens. It is a thing that cuts across the darkness and mist.
>
> Well if you see things in me give me your friendship as Waldo has done. Let me see your mind at work as often as you can.

And to Frank he wrote:

> I care not a damn what you are thinking. . . . What I do care is how are you brother? How blows the wind, how falls the morning light on the bed where you sleep?

And to Rosenfeld, when Rosenfeld was offering to pay his way to Europe:

> O Paul, I can't tell you what this chance and the opportunity it offers for companionship with you means to me.

This friendship-guidance anxiety appears to run through too many other American writers for it to be mere coincidence or a superficial characteristic. Hemingway continually let everybody know that the only thing that really counted in this life was friendship; one of F. Scott Fitzgerald's memorable statements was that another person, Edmund Wilson, "is my intellectual conscience;" and Thomas Wolfe's clinging studential friendship with his editor, Maxwell Perkins, is by this time legendary. It is a serious aspect of the American writer's adolescence and it is the very thing that makes it almost impossible for him to conceive, in his writing, and very frequently in his private life, anything approaching a detached, complex view of human relations; there is always something slightly distorted or childish or dreamy about his concepts.

As always in such neurotic relations, a bitterness and betrayal and rejection pattern set in after one person or the other has served his time and/or function. Anderson was forgotten and derided in his later years by the country that had so dearly loved him and called him its sweetest singer; his close friends and guides did not really guide him as they might have, almost pampered him it seems, then passively pitied him when he was through; he was bitched and savagely parodied by two of the people he had most vigorously helped get published and read, William Faulkner and Ernest Hemingway. It's the old primitive story of the prince having to kill his father the king in order to ascend the throne and live peacefully. Apparently they can't just let the old bastard live out his years and die naturally. Not in these parts at any rate.

I see that I've said nothing about Mr. Howe's work on Anderson. It's really quite a competent, convincing job, admiring, well documented. It is loaded with some very sharp insights into Anderson as well as American writers and writing, but unfortunately the best of these insights are the quoted writings of other critics.

The only statement in Mr. Howe's book that I must take sharp exception to is the major reason he gives for Anderson's becoming a writer—"because the abuse of language inevitable to advertising often arouses in sensitive copywriters (such as he was) a desire to use it honestly and creatively."

That's the silliest damn statement I've heard in years.

# "Anderson and 'The Essence of Things' "

Brom Weber*

Sherwood Anderson is one of the few American writers of the past half-century who, like Faulkner, demands the complete critic. Approaching him with a negligible critical apparatus, with a what-should-be! attitude instead of a what-is? sense of inquiry, militates against the likelihood of intelligent judgment. In Anderson's special case, the biographical legends and half-truths which stud his career tend to engender their own state of confusion in the careless. An awareness of the pitfalls to be encountered is probably reflected in the paucity of attention received by Anderson since his death in 1941.

Recent critical essays have been few and varied in quality. Only one, to my knowledge, focuses an intensive gaze on a specific work. Alwyn Berland's perspicacious essay on *Winesburg, Ohio* (*Western Review*, Winter 1951) would have gained in stature had he extended his conclusions to the corpus of Anderson's writing. Two articles by Lionel Trilling were combined into one in his *Liberal Imagination* (1950), but the summary nature of the examination and its failure to deeply probe Anderson's craftsmanship seriously reduce its weight. Of the two Anderson anthologies in existence, each has its own special merits. Paul Rosenfeld's *Sherwood Anderson Reader* holds a broad selection of Anderson writings, but is not discriminating enough in its choices. The introduction is keenly perceptive in its discussion of Anderson's prose style and personal ambiguity, but grows overly involved in Rosenfeld's brand of rhetoric. The *Portable Anderson* is more satisfactorily arranged; the excellently-balanced critical and biographical remarks of Horace Gregory form a valuable foreword to Anderson. It would have been a well-nigh perfect anthology were the body of writing done after 1924 drawn upon more freely.

Now two literary biographies appear to disturb the quietude which hovered over Anderson during his last fifteen years and enshrouded his memory. It will no longer be likely that the generations which came of age during the Thirties and Forties continue to think of Anderson only as the author of a classic volume titled *Winesburg, Ohio*, a mysterious figure

*Originally published in *Sewanee Review*, 59 (Autumn, 1951), 678–92. Reprinted by permission of *Sewanee Review* and Brom Weber.

who vanished in the Biercean manner after publication of his book in 1919.

Mr. Irving Howe's book[1] perversely interests me far more than Mr. James Schevill's,[2] though I must confess greater sympathy with the latter's tone. Mr. Schevill, however, is too often descriptive and chronological, when he might profitably lean over to the critical and analytical corner. He rarely evolves any crucial generalizations, though his book is enriched with a number of acute insights. Nor does he range far afield in reviewing Anderson's path through American life for six decades. In fact, the primary emphasis made by Mr. Schevill falls into the category of technique.

This consist of his reasonable stress upon Anderson's use of the impressionist method, and the degenerative hurts suffered by his craft after he fell under the domineering influence of Joyce. When supposedly least impressionistic, as in the *Winesburg* (1919) and *Horses and Men* (1923) stories, Mr. Schevill finds Anderson integrated, most successful in style, form, and meaning. From 1924 onward, Anderson is represented as heading toward looseness and disintegration, with only sporadic returns to the organized brilliance of his opening efforts. This is a plausible theory, yet Schevill should have convincingly buttressed it with a systematic exposition of literary impressionism's virtues and disadvantages. Furthermore, we are not told why impressionism did not damage the writing of the *Winesburg* period and the years immediately following.

Despite these cavils, Mr. Schevill's book, rather than Mr. Howe's, will be the major secondary source toward which those curious about the sequence of events, people, and publications in Anderson's life will turn. The main biographical outlines are much the same in both books. But Mr. Schevill offers a great number of valuable details, and he seems generally more reliable because of his nonpartisan arrangement of facts. Far from declining into vain eulogies, his appreciation of the best in Anderson has scrupulously set itself alongside an honest account of Anderson's flesh-and-blood reality. It is Mr. Schevill's distinctive contribution that he has furnished sufficient material to inspire a fresh return to Anderson.

Mr. Howe's book is worlds away from Mr. Schevill's, as far apart as the University of California halls in which the latter teaches are from the New York editorial offices of *Partisan Review* and *Time* to which the former has contributed extensively. Mr. Howe, on the basis of this book and his magazine pieces, seems to be that phenomenon of our age called forth by the increase in literates and periodicals: the highbrow journalist who must say something no matter what; who must take a position on anything, especially for symposia; whose income drops as he learns more, thinks more, writes less. Psychologists have taught us over the past thirty years that the citizen can be manipulated as easily as one of Pavlov's dogs. So long, that is, as solid rhetoric and the expert's poised assurance clothe the verbal message of advertiser, politician, and public relations expert.

Neither conscience nor inhibition has kept literary criticism from infection by the assumption that the positive manner is so persuasive that any assertions it palms off won't be questioned on the score of validity. The assumption is as life-preserving for its pragmatic believer as natural color camouflage is for the plant and animal kingdoms. Were this criticism limited to the mass-circulation periodicals and the publishers' auxiliary sales agents, it would be localized, identifiable, less insidious. But when it turns up in Mr. Howe's book with the pretentions of serious reasoning and learning blooming over a bed of fallacious evidence, shoddy demonstrations, and question-begging emotional appeals, then a straightforward consideration of the miscarriage becomes, no matter how unpleasant, an immediate critical necessity in the purposes of this review.

Mr. Howe's book is provocative. Its author seems to know a great deal about every relevant field of learning and revels in terminology and theory . . . he commands the arts of logic and persuasion . . . he has a large vocabulary under control . . . his self-confidence is immense. He believes that the critic-biographer's task resides primarily in the presentation of blinding analytic revelations which should lay bare the eternal significance of an artist's life and works. But he lacks the discriminating patience required for significant generalizations which gain their brilliance by virtue of their being unassailable. Perhaps he has been forced into this wet firecracker position by the editors of the American Men of Letters Series, the project being uneven in quality and aspiring for a lively and succinct production. Whatever the cause, the majesty of the performance dwindles as two salient aspects of the study gather momentum and overpower the reader. On the one hand, a strange single-mindedness lies over the pages like a pall, prohibiting the intrusion of items which might disturb Mr. Howe's thesis. For here there crouches a thesis which, like the party line of the Communists and other rigid entities, ruthlessly sacrifices deviations in the greater interests of uniformity and dynamics. The other disturbing element consists of the excessive personal animus directed against Anderson by Howe. This bias manifests itself in an irascible nasty impatience which automatically relegates every positive achievement of Anderson's to the realm of unavoidable and regrettable accidents. Meanwhile, every seeming error of judgment, craft, personality, and taste is meticulously highlighted and totted up like a headmaster's report on a wayward delinquent. If we were to engage in psychography as Mr. Howe so vividly does, we would ascribe his petulance to exasperation at having to write the book at all. This reviewer wonders why he did, for as recently as April 1948 Mr. Howe had neatly sewed up and dumped overboard "this bumbling writer," so he called Anderson in a *Partisan Review* sketch which revealed that Howe not only disliked Anderson and failed to understand him, but also that he had not read much of his published work.

The thesis dominating Mr. Howe's study demands that the artist be a thinker above all. By implication and statement, he must also be a good deal of a moralist, a social scientist, a systematic psychologist, a cultural historian, a responsible participant in the social ferment of his day, etc., etc. Finally, dependent upon the degree to which he adheres to the initial prescription, he will be an artist of a certain kind and caliber. This thesis permeates the critical thinking of what has been termed the naturalistic left. Perhaps the designation of neo-liberal rationalism would be more appropriate, for it is no accident that its doctrine receives its most enlightened and mannerly presentation of Lionel Trilling's *The Liberal Imagination*. If one wanted to sum up its tone and method concisely, he could do no better than quote Ortega y Gasset's patronizing description of those who do not enjoy the "virtues of the head": "Of limited intelligence, sentimental, instinctive, intuitive."

The neo-liberal rationalists are unimpressed with that which merely is. They pin their faith on that which can be *proved* to deserve being. Thus arises a dependence upon philosophy, logic, morality, psychoanalysis, scientific knowledge, on everything human which is considered to be intellectual and systematic . . . an abhorrence of the mere experience, the wish, the emotional, the dream, the biological, all that which partakes of animality, "irrationality," and impulse. This modernized version of nineteenth-century English liberalism is valuable for its inclusions. It fails dismally insofar as art is concerned, because of its dislikes and its imaginative timidity and sterility.

That which cannot be seen directly is slighted by the new rationalists. The overt communicability of language is stressed, leading to an inevitable disparagement and neglect of its ambiguity of meaning and tone. The realistic groundwork of fiction must always maintain a fixed position, regardless of the contextual significance of suggestive elements like symbolism and emotiveness. The distinction between the artist as a systematic thinker and the artist as a *creative thinker* is not in evidence. There is no understanding of the rational impulses inherent in the artist's effort to impose a creative order on existence, and the foretold scientific inadequacy of the artistic result precludes any sensible evaluation. It was the liberal rationalist Morris Raphael Cohen who wrote that "Scientific method thus minimizes the shock of novelty and the uncertainty of life. It enables us to frame policies of action and of moral judgement fit for a wider outlook than those of immediate physical stimulus or organic response." D. H. Lawrence revolted from such an attitude when he declared "The certain moral scheme is what I object to." And Sherwood Anderson ranged himself beside Lawrence and other artists when he reached out for "the sense of mystery in life," when he said that "Dim pathways do sometimes open before the eyes of the man who has not killed the possibilities of beauty in himself by being too sure."

Certainty and mystery represent the extremes. Yet it would seem that the artist must hover closer to one end of the spectrum if he would encompass what Ortega y Gasset has described as the "metaphysical hesitancy which gives to everything living its unmistakable character of tremulous vibration." The critic, rationalist or not, should be capable of covering the whole front.

Unfortunately for their effectiveness, some neo-liberal critics do not always possess the scope necessary for their jobs, especially when a non-conformist artist like Anderson becomes the center of attention. Smarting under the practical and intellectual failures alleged to have been undergone by American equalitarianism and Marxist revolutionary theory and practice, currents of thought to which many neo-liberals previously adhered, they reject with Jacobin ferocity and without qualification almost all which they or their predecessors once upheld. Because Anderson wrote tenderly about ordinary people, he is foolishly accused of the "populist heresy," as though he were a political demagogue who had unwarrantably ennobled the common man. Neo-liberal deprecation of American nativism and Eastern European collectivism is accompanied by an exaltation of Western Europe and a slighting of the small town which was Anderson's origin and fertile field of operation. Life in this milieu, as anywhere in the United States west of the Hudson, south of New York Harbor, and north of Riverdale (to the East lies Europe), is beaten down as arid, stultifying, crude, materialistic, isolated (Spender is the authority for this point), and Anderson swept out in the excitement. Anderson's memory of Clyde, Ohio as the "fair and sweet town" of his boyhood shocks Mr. Howe unless of course Anderson spoke with "visible irony or malice." As well cite Faulkner for a fool because he finds beauty and meaning in his Mississippi country. Tradition: Anderson's father fell down on the job of bringing up a literary son by not providing, in the manner of Howells' father, a library with the latest literature from Boston and London . . . nor did the elder Anderson engage in profound arguments with the customers who purchased harness and painting jobs from him. Howe's faith in the virtues of tradition is so great that he makes no effort to untangle the special features of Anderson's achievement which developed *despite* or *because of* his inadequate cultural background.

This reviewer finds himself in general agreement with many of the tenets of neo-liberal rationalism. But *a priori* agreement with particulars should not blind one to the limitations inherent in any grouping of them. Mr. Trilling and Mr. Howe, whose book is virtually an expansion of the former's earlier writing on Anderson, do not reckon with antitheses as serious matters. They employ the methodology of a rigid modern science which knows what it wishes to prove and selects data which will facilitate its procedure. But, as Whitehead aptly remarked, "The true rationalism must always transcend itself by recurrence to the concrete in search of inspiration. A self-satisfied rationalism is in effect a form of anti-rationalism." This last condition is the paradoxical outcome of Mr. Howe's labors, despite the many sensible premises with which he opens and the many cogent conclusions stated by him.

Descending to the concrete, we find that Mr. Howe's dogmatic zeal has given us a sizable number of minor distortions, misinterpretations, and inconsistencies which dubiously light up his balance and credibility. They are strikingly out of place in the pages of a writer impatient with human defects and bitingly sharp in writing of them. Just a few at random can be cited here. (1) Hart Crane turns up as one of Anderson's "close literary friends" in the Twenties, when the fact is that the slight relationship was a negligible one for Anderson, based on the exchange of a few letters and one unpleasant meeting in Cleveland, and limited to Anderson as master and Crane as apprentice. (2) "*A Story Teller's Story* is false in its feeling, its thought, and its composition . . . neither record nor fiction, loyal neither to fact nor to imagination." Yet Mr. Howe readily quotes from the book to document Anderson's motive in volunteering for the Spanish-American War. (3) Mr. Howe uses Anderson's admission in the same work to the effect that it is a product of "the fancy," rather than the "particularized recollection or imaginative creation" which Mr. Howe says it ought to have been, in order to bolster his indictment. But Mr. Howe neglects to indicate that Anderson employs "imagination" and "fancy" interchangeably in the book. Anderson may thus be shown to lack critical acumen, but he does not admit failure as Mr. Howe implies. (4) Mr. Howe ridicules Anderson's composition of "what passes for elegant language among businessmen," citing "His *sang froid* had returned to him." A few pages later, critical judgment is suspended as Mr. Howe writes: "she arranged that Cornelia, the three children, Anderson, and she go, one might almost say *en famille*. . . ." Almost, but not really. (5) The so-called mindlessness of Anderson's *Marching Men* (1917) is laid at the door of Populism's "programmatic mindlessness." However, Mr. Howe asserts, the socialists to whom "Anderson contemptuously refers . . . as people who merely wag their jaws" at least "profess to base their views on reason." This review should demonstrate, if it was not known earlier, that the distance between abstention from reason and a mistaken claim to it is quite narrow. Actually there was little difference between the Populists' specific aims at the last century's close and the immediate demands of the various socialist programs in the early 1900's. The hundred thousand protesters who belonged to the Socialist Party in 1912, the 900,000 who voted for Socialist presidential candidate Debs in that year, had many of them given their allegiance in prior years to the Populists. They switched to the Socialists when the Populist movement disintegrated, because they recognized the heirdom of the Socialists. That surely does not imply or prove that Socialist Party members and supporters were more reasonable than their opponents. With hindsight, there is considerable justification for believing that socialists in the United States, as elsewhere, did not exercise enough reason nor own a monopoly of it. Nor were the socialists of the *Marching Men* period exempt from their quota of grotesque delusions, of sadistic idealists and messiahs, and the arrogance and hysteria which Mr. Howe isolates in Populism. No political movement ever has been, despite the plethora of manifestoes, polemical articles, pamphlets, and intellectual clamors with which it festoons its daily affairs. On this basis to slight the planks of Populism's program is to confuse goals with organization and action, to distort history in the same manner that Anderson's novel has been misconstrued. (6) For the story "Death in the Woods" Mr. Howe is full of praise; he comments enthusiastically on its achievement of a thematic success similar to that of Tolstoi's "Death of Ivan Ilyitch." Later, in discussing *Tar* (1926), he hastily generalizes that "more than any of Anderson's work it justifies the critical commonplace that while he attracts sensitive adolescents he cannot satisfy the mature mind." As it happens, "Death in the Woods" appeared in *Tar* almost exactly as it finally came out in 1933, the only difference being that Anderson added two short concluding paragraphs and substituted pronouns for the family name used in the novel. Mr. Howe thinks it unimportant to comment on the coincidence, or to qualify his sweeping generalization because of it.

The strange love of intellectual beauty churning about in Mr. Howe's breast smothers his discriminating response to aesthetic beauty. One of his paragraphs typifies his insensitivity to the texture of prose, and in fairness to him I shall quote it:

> Like Mark Twain before him, Anderson uses the Mississippi as a symbolic presence to suggest the strength, contentment, and silence for which his central character yearns. Twain: "When it was dark I set by my campfire smoking and feeling pretty satisfied, but by and by it got sort of lonesome, *and so I went and set on the bank and listened to the current swashing along and counted the stars and drift-logs and rafts that came down* and then went to bed; there ain't no better way to put in time when you are lonesome. . . ." Anderson: "Above his head a breeze played through the branches of the trees, and insects sang in the grass. Everything about him was clean. A lovely stillness pervaded the river and the woods. He lay on his belly and gazed down over the river out of sleep-heavy eyes into hazy distances." Admittedly, the Twain passage, if only because it is so much less "literary," is the better of the two—but then there have been few American writers who could match the beauty of such passages in *Huckleberry Finn*. What is important, however, in this comparison is the continuity of feeling between the two writers, a continuity based as much on similarity of response as on literary adaptation.

First of all, only the clause italicized by this reviewer is comparable with the *Poor White* passage in terms of substance. The Anderson lines, furthermore, have been torn out of a larger context of several pages. Twenty-year-old Hugh McVey, slowly attaining maturity after a childhood during which longing for a significant ordered existence struggled against an overwhelming tendency to indolence and inarticulateness, returns to the riverbanks on which he dozed as a boy. Anderson fuses visions of the past into the present, and the entire section renders a mystical moment in which McVey's consciousness apparently leaves his body and pantheistically becomes one with sky and earth. The dynamic narrative of the Twain lines is not a relevant apposition to the few physically-passive Anderson sentences from which, at best, we derive only a wrenched minimal representation of a larger entity.

On the other hand, assuming that it is permissible to match Twain's reaction to the river with the Anderson passage, still another incongruity exists. A fundamental difference between the two extracts resides in their varying points of view. Twain gives the first-person recitation of a quick-witted, nervous, imaginative, articulate boy, whereas Anderson is using a third-person approach keyed to a sluggish adult personality.

Far more urgent as a base for consideration of the two passages, though passed over by Mr. Howe as well, is the reticent tone of Twain and Anderson's contrasting emotiveness. One sees Twain as determined not to express directly the psychological details of Huck's experience. Here is the American frontier type who uses words to communicate only those bits of physical information which move him along in the material world, which movement must implicitly convey his states of mind and all too often does not, leaving him an unfeeling husk. In the Anderson section, however, as in most of his better writing, there functions a realized intention to place into tangible expression the most subtle, evanescent, psychological conditions. Where Twain is therefore evasive and only indirectly suggestive, Anderson is more thoroughly expressive as the shaper of an art should be. It was Mr. Howe's critical responsibility to inform his reader that Anderson was as successful as Twain on *another* front.

But apparently Mr. Howe cannot respond to the poetic qualities and the refinements of fictional composition. His commentary stamps him as favoring the denotative aspects of writing rather than the connotative. He is evidently unsuited to say much of genuine value about a prose writer like Anderson whose achievements, such as they were, lie precisely in that area distinguished by allusion, symbolism, a verbal texture as active as that in poetry, who encompasses aspects of life easier to experience and reflect on than to create in language. Mr. Howe's imaginative weakness graphically reveals itself when we examine his treatment of more than a single passage from Anderson.

Eager to tie up loose ends as usual and disdaining their heterogeneity, Mr. Howe sums up his chapter on "The Short Stories" with the following: "One is struck by how remarkably devoid they are of any account of external experience, how vague in background and hazy in evocation of place and thing." Though this is true in part of some of the stories, it involves an utter misreading of "The New Englander," which Mr. Howe has considered in the chapter.

This story will remain one of the finest embodiments of the merits potentially contained in Anderson's lyrical-symbolic method. It can be found in the *Sherwood Anderson Reader* or in *Triumph of the Egg*, in case someone is ambitious enough, as this reviewer was, to have a first-hand look at Mr. Howe's victim. Such curious souls will be amazed to learn that Anderson's description of the Vermont countryside in which the story opens is remarkably, though selectively, rich in poetic details which evoke the cramped barren fields: "The fields were like cups filled with a green liquid that turned gray in the fall and white in the winter. The mountains, far off but apparently near at hand, were like giants ready at any moment to reach out their hands and take the cups one by one and drink off the green liquid. The large rocks in the field were like the thumbs of the giants." The story moves on to the "gray empty Iowa fields," and we read that "All of the fences in all of the fields that stretched away out of sight to the north, south, east, and west were made of wire and looked like spider webs against the blackness of the ground when it had been freshly plowed."

In Iowa, Elsie Leander, the New Englander who was for Anderson what Thoreau had earlier defined as "a pagan suckled in a creed outworn," bursts from her chrysalis and emerges onto the hot sensual prairie. She is bewildered by the phallic imagery which sears her eyes, by corn tassels which murmur in the breezes. But she is unable to achieve the physical fruition grasped so firmly by Elizabeth, her sixteen-year-old cousin, who engages in sex play as naturally as any animal on the farm. Elsie's heritage permits her only a short step toward fulfillment, as she lies between the corn rows with the yellow pollen falling from the cornstalks forming "a golden crown about her head." Her repressed body and mind find release in vivid sexual ecstasy, but the experience assumes a pathological connotation for her as she witnesses Elizabeth in a farmhand's arms. The story closes with a bitter symbolic rejection of the New England past—Elsie weeping in the fields as a rainstorm drenches her, sitting "on the earthen floor inside the house of corn," refusing to take shelter in her father's house.

To complain that "The New Englander" doesn't have "external experience" is to miss the absolute heart of artistic form, namely, that elements of art do not exist in fixed proportions. The extent to which they are developed in a given piece of work is determined by contextual relationships. Anderson didn't provide a full sequence of physical events. However, the main action is psychological. Thus sufficient external experience exists for the story's forward movement. The symbolism of rock, rabbit, bird, and corn is denigrated by Mr. Howe because "there is nothing viable in relation to which the symbols can act." The answer to this is, as D. H. Lawrence wrote, that symbols are "organic units of consciousness with a life of their own, and you can never explain them away. . . ." Mr. Schevill's sensitivity to this phase of Anderson's craft should be noted, for he conclusively links Anderson with preceding American symbolists like Hawthorne and Melville on the basis of style as well as content.

Setting aside the questionable nature of Mr. Howe's contributions on the whole, there is little doubt that some of the difficulties he experienced are the fault of Sherwood Anderson. Anderson was one of his own most interesting and baffling creations. The impulse of the artist was beset with uneasy self-doubt, and yet the age in which he was formed called for a romantic self-assertion; between these poles Anderson struggled, never at rest with a stable picture of himself. This ambivalence affected him as artist as well as person; it brought about a fluidity, a hesitation, an uncertainty which blurred the line between illusion and reality, which softened his artistic conscience when he needed most to be harsh with it, which aroused extremes of emotional and critical reaction from onlookers. It has evoked an unjust accusation of "mindlessness" from Wyndham Lewis, Trilling, and Howe, the latter's book an attempt to document the charge.

Unquestionably Anderson was careless with facts. As early as 1924, he openly acknowledged in A Story Teller's Story that "these notes make no pretence of being a record of fact. . . . It is likely that I have not, and will not, put into them one truth, measuring by the ordinary standards of truth. It is my aim to be true to the essence of things." In the Winesburg pieces and later writings, he argued against the formal reasoning of man which reduces facts to order and adjusts man's existence to them. His personal behavior was egotistical, chaotic, emotional, not a human life plotted in accordance with the precepts of a system constructed after trial and error and thought. Anderson was not an intellectual, and he never pretended to be one.

Not mindlessness, but literary anarchism, is a proper description of Anderson's condition. The strain of individualism in revolt against all shackles, personal and social, grew powerfully within him. It marks his life and work from the moment in the 1910's when he could no longer continue as a young business man and model husband, when he was writing Marching Men with its criticism of the democratic process and its glorification of a dedicated Nietzschean elite. It remained within him when he wrote with horror in 1924, that democracy had lost its vitality, and he prophesied of the period when "the real commoners shall come—and that shall be the worst time of all." In the 1930's when the expected collapse of democracy seemed imminent and the need for collectivism undeniable, Anderson supported the Communist Party. But he never joined it and was not under its control; his major concern throughout these years was for the survival of culture, even though he had a poignant sympathy for the wretched people suffering from the economic collapse. He recognized, in a realistic manner, that the existence of art and artists was dependent upon the generosity of a moneyed aristocracy which, charged with the destruction of democracy, was now in turn to be dynamited by the proletarian revolution.

Above all else, Anderson was an artist. His thinking, whatever it was, took place at those moments when he was creating fictional actors, himself among them. Frankly (witness his 1926 statement in *Tar* that he was unconcerned that his brothers objected to his "recreating them" and their parents "to suit my fancy"), with no intention of concealing the process by which he "falsified" reality and narrated what it should have been or what he thought it was, he demonstrated rational desires and purposes as vital as those of any intellectual. One of the contributions of Mr. Schevill's book is the attention it gives to Anderson's myth-making propensity, and he suggests that in this connection Anderson may have influenced Faulkner's later construction of a regional myth. There is evidence in Anderson's work, not only in *Winesburg* but in such works as "An Ohio Pagan," *Poor White*, and "Unused" where the town of Bidwell and recurring characters figure prominently, that he was undertaking prior to 1923 to construct an imaginative world-picture. In following years, one observes his search for meaningful ritual in *Many Marriages*, the organic rhythm delineated in *Dark Laughter*, his deliberate assumption of a fictitious origin and experience in order to introduce tradition, status, choice, and pattern into the history of his life. These are all symptoms of a profound rationality, even if they don't depend upon logic and the scientific method.

Anderson did much to damage his reputation as a significant writer. Like many another literary man, he wrote too much about himself in autobiographical works which were unusually revelatory. *A Story Teller's Story* may have distorted Anderson's real childhood and family group, but it gave an accurate picture of the mature man's personality and problems. How uncomfortable it makes one now to read his protestations of inability to achieve classical literary excellence:

> The result of the scribbling, the tale of perfect balance, all the elements of the tale understood, an infinite number of minute adjustments perfectly made, the power of self-criticism fully at work, the shifting surface of word values and color in full play, form and the rhythmic flow of thought and mood marching forward with the sentences—these are things of a dream, of a far dim day toward which one goes knowing one can never arrive but infinitely glad to be on the road.

This humility and self-consciousness, coupled with more explicit confessions ("I have never been one who can correct, fill in, rework his stories. I must try, and when I fail must throw away. Some of my best stories have been written ten or twelve times." *Memoirs*, 1941), aroused horror in the writers and critics formed in the 1920's. This unromantic generation's contacts with European refinement and tradition disposed them against the aura of self-admitted crudity of style, form, and substance which hung about Anderson's work and stamped him as a pure American.

Anderson's apparent abandonment of fiction during the late Twenties was regarded as another admission of failure. This led to the disregarding of his work, and was vindicated by the uneven quality of his later fiction and the extensiveness of his journalistic commitments. Actually, of course, Anderson's earlier work had also ranged from very good to very bad, but the serious criticism given him then was more interested in his spirit and subject than in his technical mastery. By the early Twenties it began to be noted that Anderson repeated certain themes, situations, and characters without increased depth or varied surface, and that a steady redundancy was the effect. An insatiable narcissism seemed to weaken his imaginative powers—he didn't invent sufficiently, and himself lost interest in what he was doing. In *Kit Brandon* (1936), for example, Anderson placed much of the material which had appeared earlier in magazine pieces during the early Thirties. The posthumous *Memoirs*, in turn, contains material which first saw daylight in *Kit Brandon*. Anderson's literary gift was inspirational, lyrical rather than dramatic. But he insisted upon writing poorly-constructed novels rather than the short stories and sketches which his intuition and emotional vitality could successfully manage.

All that has been said should nonetheless not blind a critic-biographer to the enduring values in Anderson's life and works. Mr. Howe errs greatly in damning the final fifteen years of Anderson's production so as to be able to prove a thesis which prohibits any development and attainment. Mr. Schevill is more objective. He grants flashes of success to sections of novels and to some of the post-1926 stories. As one ought to. "Brother Death" was written in 1933. Its consistent tone and controlled flow of psychological and physical action render it superior in artistry to almost any one of his earlier short pieces. In the sketches and notices which he wrote for his Virginia papers under the pseudonym of "Buck Fever," Anderson re-established and deepened the vein of tragi-comedy which had been displayed in "The Egg" a decade earlier. The story of the poor man who wanted to own a fine horse, but to whom realization came only when he learned to walk on all fours like a paced thoroughbred, is a muted masterpiece to be found in *Kit Brandon*. In almost every one of Anderson's large failures, sufficient pages of great quality will be found worthy of preservation to make a sizeable anthology. In fact, although Mr. Howe completely disregards the *Memoirs*, Mr. Schevill makes us recognize the serious merits of the volume. He underscores the need for a new edition critically taking into account the manuscripts which were assembled to create the posthumously-published book.

Mr. Schevill's responsible attention to Anderson's writing suggests the direction which any future work on Anderson must take before we are to have a definite statement of his place in American culture. It is in order, therefore, to remark that little will be gained by continuing to analyze Anderson's books in accordance with their chronological sequence of publication. Many of these books were compilations of scattered pieces written between intervals of several years. Mr. Schevill implicitly acknowledges this by separately considering Anderson's first published story, as well as two other early stories, in order to make the point that Anderson was anti-naturalistic from the beginning. He has also gone to the trouble of reading the manuscripts in the Newberry Library collection of Anderson papers for accurate information on the *Memoirs*. What is needed is further study of all the manuscripts and the published works to establish their dates and Anderson's method of composition, to ascertain that which was published in unfinished condition like "An Ohio Pagan." Anderson's participation in the anti-naturalistic trend of our times must be seen in relationship to such matters as his diction, his prose rhythm, and other stylistic elements. We have not yet had the last word on this controversial artist.

Notes

1. *Sherwood Anderson.* American Men of Letters Series. William Sloane. 271 pp.
2. *Sherwood Anderson: His Life and Work.* University of Denver Press. 360 pp.

# "The Purity and Cunning of Sherwood Anderson"

Herbert Gold*

## 1. "A Little Worm in the Fair Apple of Progress."

He said it of himself. He saw himself curled up, busily feeding on midwestern America, sheltered, destructive, loving his host, and needed by this age and place in order that they could get some sense of buoyancy and carry within them the richness of growth. He recognized his own childish self-absorption, great even for an artist, a breed accused by everyone of being childishly self-absorbed. Therefore he wrote about death with praise because "it will in any case give us escape from this disease of self." Self-love is surely the beginning of the love of others, but it is only the beginning. Sherwood Anderson, an old child, suffered a merely erratic love of himself, therefore writhed with a tormented love of others. All his stories are bound up in this sense of the self's isolation, seen as glory and sickness, as sickness and glory. He is one of the purest, most intense poets of loneliness—the loneliness of being an individual and of being buffeted in the current, the loneliness of isolation and that of being swallowed. One type represents the traditional retreat into the self for self-possession; the other, and its adversary at times, arises out of the angry resentment of a sensible man in an assemblyline civilization. Anderson's work is a manual of the ways in which loneliness can be used. It was his nourishment and sometimes his poison.

"I pour a dream over it. . . . I want to write beautifully, create beautifully, not outside but in this thing in which I am born, in this place where, in the midst of ugly towns, cities, Fords, moving pictures, I have always lived, must always live." Yet he fled it always. He fled in order to find himself, then prayed to flee that disease of self, to become "beautiful and clear . . . plangent and radiant." He felt that he loved only the midwestern land and people, but was still fleeing when he died—in the Panama Canal Zone.

In his photographs he often showed his hair hanging over his eyes. The affectation means a great deal: first mere arty affectation (how he loved the "free spirits" of Greenwich Village and New Orleans!), then

*Originally published in *Hudson Review*, 10 (Winter, 1957–58), pp. 548–59. Reprinted by permission of Herbert Gold.

something feminine and wanting to be pretty and lovable for prettiness, and then of course the blurring of sight when you try to see through your own hair. What do you see? A world organized by your hair. "I must snap my finger at the world. . . . I have thought of everyone and everything." His sympathy and his oceanic feelings alternate with arrogant despair in which the arrogance can deceive no one. So desperately hurt he is, trying so hard to convince the "word-fellows" he wanted to admire him. But then his nostalgia gives us the mood he sought to force: ". . . old fellows in my home town speaking feelingly of an evening spent on the big, empty plains. It has taken the shrillness out of them. They had learned the trick of quiet. It affected their whole lives. It made them significant."

We understand him at last!

And then again the helpless bombast: "At my best, brother, I am like a great mother bird. . . ." He exuded through his pores the ferocious longing of a giant of loneliness. The typical chords from his letters sound under the changing heroes of the stories:

Youth not given a break—youth licked before it starts.

Filled with sadness that you weren't there.

I have a lot I want to tell you if I can. . . . Anyway you know what I mean when we talked of a man working in the small, trying to save a little of the feeling of man for man.

The romantic sentimentalist held up his mirror to look at his world, peered deeply, saw himself instead, of course; wrote painfully about what he saw; and it turned out that he was writing about the world after all, squeezing it by this palpitating midwestern honesty out of his grandiose sorrows and longings. Sometimes, anyway. He was not a pure man; he had a kind of farmer cunning, plus his groaning artiness and pretense, with which he hoped to convince the "word-fellows" and the pretty girls that he was a Poet although not a young one. What he really wanted was to be alone in that succession of gray furnished rooms he talked about so eloquently, making immortal the quiet noise and gentle terror of his childhood. "I try to believe in beauty and innocence in the midst of the most terrible clutter." But clutter too was the truth of his life; he fed on it; how else does a poet take the measure of his need for "beauty and innocence"? He must have remained an optimist, too, amidst all his disillusion. He married four times. To the end of his life he went on believing, and marrying.

Anderson the writer arouses a poking curiosity about Anderson the man even in the most resolutely detached critic. The note of confession is always with us: Here I am, it's good that you know! he seems to be saying.

His very paragraphs are soaked in his own groping speech. He repeats, he cries out, he harangues, he pleads. All his work, the abysmal

failures and the successes which have helped to construct the vision
Americans have of themselves, represents an innocent, factitious, im-
provised, schemed reflection and elaboration of the elements of his own
life. He turns the private into the public and then back into the private
again. His mystery as a man remains despite his childish longing to reveal
himself—the mystery of a man who looks at a man with a beard and a
scar in a conference room and sees, instead, a lover fleeing his girl's
brothers through the fields. (They had knives and slashed—could this be
the same man? he asks himself.) Anderson confounds us with bombast and
wit, tenderness and softheadedness, rant and exquisite delicacy.

The best of his work is what matters.

Let us now look more closely at what the worm made of his apple.

## 2. "My Feet Are Cold and Wet."

He loved to create, he loved his fantasy as the lonely boy does. In his
best work, as in some of the stories of *Winesburg, Ohio*, the fantasy is
most controlled, or if not exactly controlled, simplified, given a single
lyrical line. The novels had trouble passing the test of the adult imagination, being wild proliferations of daydream. The simple stories of Kate
Swift ("The Teacher") or Wing Biddlebaum ("Hands") join Sherwood
Anderson with the reader's sense of wonder and despair at the pathetic in
his own past—childish hope of love, failed ambition, weakness and
loneliness. As music can do, such stories liberate the fantasies of our secret
lives. However, musicians will agree that music is for listening, not to be
used as a stimulus for fantasy. We must attend to the song itself, not take
advantage of it and make it the passive instrument of our dreaming. In
the same way, the great writers hope to arouse and lead the reader's
imagination toward a strong individual perspective on experience. Sherwood Anderson, however, was not of that vividly individualistic company, despite his personal hobby of eccentric Bohemianism. Rather, he
was the dreamy, sad, romantic within each of us, evoking with nostalgia
and grief the bitter moments of recognition which have formed
him—formed all of us in our lonely America.

James Joyce used the word "epiphany," which he took from Catholic
ritual, to name that moment of revelation when words and acts come
together to manifest something new, familiar, timeless, the deep summation of meaning. The experience of epiphany is characteristic of great
literature, and the lyric tales of Anderson give this wonderful rapt
coming-forth, time and time again.

In "The Untold Lie," for example, two men tenderly meet in order to
talk about whether one, the younger, should marry the girl he has made
pregnant. The older man, unhappy in his own marriage, wants to see the
young man's life free and charged with powerful action as his own has
never been. But it is revealed to him—revelation is almost always the

climax of Anderson's stories—that life without wife and children is impossible and that one man's sorrows cannot be used by him to prevent another man from choosing the same sorrows. It would be a lie to say that the life of conjugal sorrows is merely a life of conjugal sorrows: the story finally breathes the sadness, the beauty, the necessary risks of growr up desire. "Whatever I told him would have been a lie," he decides. Each man has to make his own decisions and live out his chosen failures of ideal freedom.

Many of Anderson's stories take for their realization objective circumstances which have a grandiose folkish quality, and many of both the most impressive and the most mawkish are concerned with an archtypical experience of civilization: the test which, successfully passed, commands manhood. Such a story as "The Man Who Became a Woman" objectifies even in its title the boy's wondering and fearful dream. The end sought is manliness, that new clean and free life; failure is seen as a process of being made effeminate, or falling into old patterns of feeling and action. At his best in these stories, there is a physical joy in triumph which is fresh, clean, genial—we think of Mark Twain, although a Twain without the robust humor; at his weak moments, we may also think of the sentimental sick Twain, and we find also the maundering moping of a prettified Thomas Wolfe.

The line between the subjects of Anderson's stories and Sherwood Anderson himself is barely drawn. His relation as artist to his material, as shaper of his material, is as intense and personal as that of any modern writer. Unlike most writing dealing with unhappy and frustrated people, Anderson's work is absolutely authentic in the double sense—not merely in communicating the feeling of these people as people, but also in giving us the conviction that the author shares both their bitter frustration and their evanescent occasional triumphs. By comparison with Sherwood Anderson, Dostoevsky is a monument of cool detachment. His identification is perfect, sometimes verging on the morbid: "Everyone in the world is Christ and they are all crucified." He has a primitive idealism, a spoiled romanticism like that of Rousseau: we could be all innocent and pure in our crafts if the machines of America and the fates that bring machines did not cripple us.

This romantic idealism can be illustrated again by his treatment of another theme, marriage, in the story "Loneliness," in which he writes of Enoch Robinson: "Two children were born to the woman he married,"—just as if they did not happen to Robinson at all, which is indeed the truth about the self-isolated personality he describes. "He dismissed the essence of things," Anderson can write, "and played with realities." Again the romantic Platonist sees a conflict between the deepest meaning and the fact of our lives, between what we do and what we "really" are. With a kind of purity and cunning, Anderson seems to thrive on this curiously boyish notion the limitations of which most of us quickly learn. We work and love because we know that there is no other way to be ourselves than in relation to the rest of the world. The kind man is the man who performs kind acts; the generous man is a man who behaves generously; we distrust the "essential" generosity which is sometimes claimed for the soul of a man who selfishly watches out only for himself. And yet we can be reminded with a strange force by Anderson's conviction in his boyish dream of isolated personality that there is something totally private, untouchable, beyond appearance and action, in all of us. The observation is a familiar one, but the experience can be emotionally crucial. Cunningly Anderson makes us turn to ourselves again with some of his own purity.

The last sentence of "Departure" says of George Willard: "Winesburg had disappeared and his life there had become but a background on which to paint the dreams of his manhood." Abstracted people, playing out their time in the fragmentary society of Winesburg, these "heroes" are isolated, as Anderson himself was isolated, by art or unfulfilled love or religion—by the unsurmounted challenge of finding the self within relationship with others. It was the deep trouble of Anderson's own life that he saw his self, which could be realized only by that monstrous thing, the Life of Art, as flourishing in opposition to decent connections with others in society. Marriage, work, friendship were beautiful things; but the gray series of furnished slum rooms, in which he wrote, enough rooms to fill a city, were his real home. Writing letters and brooding behind his locked door, he idealized love, he idealized friendship. He withdrew to the company of phantom creatures. He hoped to guard his integrity. He kept himself the sort of child-man he described with such comprehending sympathy in the character of Enoch Robinson.

In many writers dealing with the grim facts of our lives, the personal sense of triumph at encompassing the material adds a note of confidence which is at variance with the story itself. Hemingway is a good example; his heroes go down to defeat, but Papa Hemingway the chronicler springs eternal. In Anderson this external note of confidence and pride in craft is lacking, except in some of the specious, overwilled novels which he wrote under political influences. Generally he does not import his poetry into the work—he allows only the poetry that is *there*—nor does his independent life as a creator come to change the tone of these sad tales. The stories of Winesberg are unselfconsciously committed to him as he is sworn true to them; the identification—a variety of loyalty—is torturingly complete; he is related to his material with a love that lacks esthetic detachment and often lacks the control which comes with that detachment. They are practically unique in this among modern storytelling, and it is partially this that gives them their sometimes embarrassing, often tormenting and unforgettable folk quality. Still they are not folktales but, rather, pseudofolktales. The romantic longing and grieving is not characteristic of the folktale, despite the other elements, a direct matter-of-fact storytelling, colloquial American language (complicated by chivalry and the Bible, but at its best not "literary"), and the authority of Anderson's priestly devotion to his lives and people. Later, of course, the romantic judgment culminated in rebellion, sometimes in a kind of esthetic rant against the way things are.

In "The Strength of God," the Reverend Curtis Hartman (as in a parable, Heart-man) "wondered if the flame of the spirit really burned in him and dreamed of a day when a strong sweet current of power would come like a great wind into his voice and his soul and the people would tremble before the spirit of God made manifest in him. 'I am a poor stick and that will never really happen to me,' he mused dejectedly, and then a patient smile lit up his features. 'Oh well, I suppose I'm doing well enough,' he added philosophically."

These, as *The New Yorker* would put it, are musings that never got mused and philosophic additions that never got philosophically added. They have a curious archaic directness that amounts to a kind of stylization. The unanalytic simplicity itself is a sophisticated manner. As the officer of the Pharisees said, "Never man spake like this man." It recalls to us the day of the storyteller who suggested the broad line of an action, and allowed us to give our imaginations to it. Nowadays we demand detail upon detail, and the phrase "I am a poor stick" would require a whole book of exposition in the hands of most contemporary novelists.

The pathos of the pious man's temptation by the flesh has a flavor beautifully evocative of adolescence. We no longer think of "carnal temptation" as Anderson did. But we remember our fears and guilts, and are reminded of ourselves as great literature always reminds us. Hartman's silent, secret battle with himself over Kate Swift is given part of its bite by her own story—this pimply, passionate young school teacher who strikes beauty without knowing it and can find no one to speak to her. Her story is told with a brilliant delicacy that reflects Anderson's own strange reticence about women. Enoch Robinson, he says, "tried to have an affair with a woman of the town met on the sidewalk before his lodging house." To have an affair is his strange idiom for a pickup! (The boy got frightened, and ran away; the woman roared with laughter and picked up someone else.)

Except for the poetic schoolteacher and a very few others, women are not women in Anderson's stories. There are the girls who suffer under the kind of sensitivity, passion, and lonely burning which was Anderson's own lot; and then there are the Women. For Anderson women have a strange holy power; they are earth-mothers, ectoplasmic spirits, sometimes succubi, rarely individual living creatures. In "Hands" they are not girls but "maidens," where the word gives a quaint archaic charm to the creature who taunts poor, damned, lonely Wing Biddlebaum. The berry-picking "maidens" gambol while the boys are "boisterous," and the hero flutters in his tormented realm between the sexes.

In somewhere like Wing Biddlebaum's tormented realm, Sherwood Anderson also abode. American cities, as he wrote, are "noisy and terrible," and they fascinated him. He got much of the noise and terror into his writing about big cities, and the quiet noise and gentle terror of little towns into his stories about them. And among the fright of materialistic life, he continually rediscovered the minor beauties which made life possible for him—the moment of love, of friendship, of self-realization. That they were but moments is not entirely the fault of Anderson's own character.

### 3. "The Air of a Creator."

Anderson is shrewd, sometimes just, and has earned the right to even the unjust judgments he makes of other writers. How earned them? He was constantly fighting through both the questions of craft and the deeper risks of imagination. He has won the right to make sweeping pronouncements on his peers. Of Sinclair Lewis, for example, he offers the most damning, most apt criticism: "Wanting to see beauty descend upon our lives like a rainstorm, he has become blind to the minor beauties our lives hold." Sherwood Anderson wants the same thing, but holds to the good sense which a poet can still have in a difficult time: he clings to the minor beauties which give tenderness to his longing, a hope of something else to his despair. For this reason Anderson's critique of America finally bites more deeply than the novels of the ferocious sentimental satirist who was his contemporary.

Of Henry James, Anderson wrote that he is a man who "never found anyone to love, who did not dare love. . . . Can it be that he is the novelist of the haters? Oh, the thing infinitely refined and carried far into the field of intellectuality, as skillful haters find out how to do." The Jamesian flight from direct fleshly feeling offended Anderson. James objectified, stipulated, laid bare, and then suffused his entire yearning personality over all his work, so that Isabel Archer and Hyacinth Robinson are, really are Henry James, in all his hopeless longing, and yet spiritualized, that is, without body, epicene as James seems to have made himself in real life. George Santayana believed that by withholding love from a specific object it could be given "in general" to the whole world. This is a curiously commercial, economical notion—the idea that there is a limited amount of love and that we have the choice of spending it on a few selfishly chosen objects or distributing it generally. "In general" we know that this is nonsense; our attachments to individuals are the models for our attachments to humanity as an ideal; but like many sorts of nonsense, it worked for Henry James to the extent that he really loved some spirit of Art which his "puppets," his "fables," as he called them, served.

Is Anderson, with all his mid-American distrust of intellectualized love, really so far from Henry James? He is strikingly the perpetual adolescent in love with love rather than with a specific girl with changing flesh. One can see him dreaming after his dreamgirl even as he approached old age. His romantic chivalry, his lust for the proletariat, his fantastic correspondence in which the letters seem to be written to himself, no matter how touching their apparent candor and earnest reaching out—is he perhaps the other side of the coin of his accusation against Henry James? To be the novelist of lovers who did not dare to hate—this too is a limitation. He seems obliged to love others as a function of his own faulty self-love, and therefore his love of others seems *voulu*, incomplete, and his moments of hatred a guilty self-indulgence. He presents an extreme case of the imperfections of an artist just because of the disparity between his intentions and his performance. He wanted to love, he wanted to sing of love. His failures help to make still more brilliant his achievements in certain of the stories of Winesburg, in "The Egg," and in scattered paragraphs, stories, and sections of novels.

For the fault of bookish derivations for his feelings, Anderson substituted at his worst the fault of self-indulgent derivation from gratifications and dreads never altered after boyhood. He carried his childhood like a hurt warm bird held to his middle-aged breast as he walked out of his factory into the life of art. The primitive emotions of childhood are the raw material of all poetry. Sometimes the indulgence of them to the exclusion of the mature perspectives of adult life prevents Anderson from equalling his aspiration and own best work.

But this is a vain quibble. Who can do his best work always? What counts is the achievement, not the failures, however exemplary they may seem to a critic. "I have a lot I want to tell you if I can," he wrote in a letter. "I am writing short stories." The faults of unevenness, egotism, lazy acceptance of ideals, and romantic self-glorification are as nothing against the realized works of art which force their way through. Sherwood Anderson "added to the confusion of men," as he said of the great financiers and industrialists, the Morgans, Goulds, Carnegies, Vanderbilts, "by taking on the air of a creator." He has helped to create the image we have of ourselves as Americans. Curtis Hartman, George Willard, Enoch Robinson, all of the people of Winesburg, haunt us as do our neighbors, our friends, our own secret selves which we first met one springtime in childhood.

# "The Simplicity of *Winesburg, Ohio*"

Walter B. Rideout*

It is probably impossible, except impressionistically, to isolate the essential quality of any work of art, but Hart Crane may have come close to isolating that of *Winesburg, Ohio* when in another context he wrote of Anderson himself that, "He has a humanity and simplicity that is quite baffling in depth and suggestiveness." Leaving the matter of "humanity" aside, one is indeed struck on first reading the book by its apparent simplicity of language and form. On second or subsequent readings, however, he sees that the hard, plain, concrete diction is much mixed with the abstract, that the sentence cadences come from George Moore and the King James Bible as well as from ordinary speech rhythms, that the seemingly artless, even careless, digressions are rarely artless, careless, or digressive. What had once seemed to have the clarity of water held in the hand begins to take on instead its elusiveness. If this is simplicity, it is simplicity—paradox or not—of a complicated kind. Since *Winesburg* constantly challenges one to define the complications, I should like to examine a few that perhaps lie closest beneath the surface of the book and the life it describes.

It has been often pointed out that the fictitious Winesburg closely resembles Clyde, Ohio, where Anderson lived from the age of seven to the age of nineteen and which became the home town of his memories. Even now the visitor to the two communities can see that Winesburg and Clyde are both "eighteen miles" south of Lake Erie; in both, the central street of the town is named Main, and Buckeye and Duane branch off from it; both have a Heffner Block and a Waterworks Pond; both lie "in the midst of open fields, but beyond the fields are pleasant patches of woodland." As recently as the summer of 1960, the wooden Gothic railroad station, from which Sherwood Anderson and George Willard took the train for the city and the great world, was still standing; and on the hill above Waterworks Pond, where George walked with Helen White on the darkened fair grounds, one can yet see, overgrown with turf, the banked-

*Originally published in *Shenandoah* 13 (Spring, 1962), 20–31, copyright © 1962 by Washington and Lee University. Reprinted by permission of the Editor and Walter B. Rideout.

up west end turns of the race track. Modern Clyde is perhaps half again as large as the town that the future author of *Winesburg* left in 1896, but the growth has shown itself principally in housing development on the periphery. The central village is basically unchanged, and even now to walk through the quiet old residence streets with their white frame or brick houses and wide lawns shaded by big elms and maples is to walk uncannily through a fictitious scene made suddenly real.

The more one learns of the town as it was in the 1890's, the more he sees the actual Clyde under the imagined Winesburg.[1] Anderson was a story teller, of course, not a historian, and the correspondence of the two communities does not have a one-to-one exactness. Nevertheless the correspondences become striking, particularly as one sees that in many instances Clyde names of persons and places appear only faintly disguised in the pages of *Winesburg*. Anderson wrote about Win Pawsey's shoe store, Surbeck's Pool Room, and Hern's Grocery; in the Clyde of the early 1890's there were Alfred Pawsey's Shoe Store, Surbeck's Cigar Store, and Hurd's Grocery, the last still very much in business. Wine Creek flows through Winesburg instead of the real Raccoon of Clyde, but the former follows the latter's course; and beyond the Wine rises the fictitious Gospel Hill in the same place as the actual Piety Hill, where the Anderson family lived for a time. Sometimes the disguise is somewhat less casual, though it may turn out to be merely a transfer of names. The owner of one of the two livery stables in Clyde was Frank Harvey, but there were Moyers in town, from whom Anderson borrowed half the name of Wesley Moyer for the livery stableman in Winesburg. Clyde personal names, it must be noted, are used almost exclusively for the minor characters, and except for one or two debatable possibilities no character, either major or minor, seems to be recognizably based on an actual resident of the town. The important matter, however, is that the "grotesques" of the several tales exist within a physical and social matrix furnished Anderson by his memories of Clyde.

That he should have visualized the locale of his tales so closely in terms of his home town is not surprising, and the reader may dismiss the matter as merely a frequent practice of realistic writers. Yet Anderson is not a realistic writer in the ordinary sense. With him realism is a means to something else, not an end in itself. To see the difference between his presentation of "reality" and the more traditional kind that gives a detailed picture of appearances, one needs only to compare the drug store on the Main Street of Sinclair Lewis's Gopher Prairie with that on the Main Street of Winesburg. Twice over, once as Carol Kennicott, once as Bea Sorenson sees them, Lewis catalogues the parts of Dave Dyer's soda fountain. Anderson, like his own Enoch Robinson preferring "the essence of things" to the "realities," merely names Sylvester West's Drug Store, letting each reader's imagination do as much or as little with it as he wishes. As with the drug store, so with many other landmarks of Clyde-Winesburg. As he repeats from tale to tale the names of stores and their owners or refers to such elements of town life as the post office, the bank, or the cemetery, there emerges, not a photograph, but at most the barest sketch of the external world of the town. Perhaps even "sketch" implies too great a precision of detail. What Anderson is after is less a representation of conventional "reality" than, to keep the metaphor drawn from art, an abstraction of it.

Realism is for Anderson a means rather than an end, and the highly abstract kind of reality found in Winesburg has its valuable uses. The first of these is best understood in relation to George Willard's occupation on the *Winesburg Eagle*. (Clyde's weekly newspaper was, and still is the *Clyde Enterprise*, but Sherwood Anderson was never its reporter.) It has been suggested that the author may have made his central figure a newspaper reporter in order that he could thus be put most readily in touch with the widest number of people in town and most logically become the recipient of many confidences; yet Anderson's point is that exactly insofar as George remains a newspaper reporter, he is committed to the surface of life, not to its depths. "Like an excited dog," Anderson says in "The Thinker," using a mildly contemptuous comparison, "George Willard ran here and there," writing down all day "little facts" about A. P. Wringlet's recent shipment of straw hats or Uncle Tom Sinnings' new barn on the Valley Road. As reporter, George is concerned with externals, with appearances, with the presumably solid, simple, everyday surface of life. For Anderson the surface is there, of course, as his recurring use of place and personal names indicates; yet conventional "reality" is for him relatively insignificant and is best presented in the form of sketch or abstraction. What is important is "to see beneath the surface of lives," to perceive the intricate mesh of impulses, desires, drives growing down in the dark, unrevealed parts of the personality like the complex mass of roots that, below the surface of the ground, feeds the common grass above in the light.

But if one function of Anderson's peculiar adaptation of realism is, as it were, to depreciate the value of surfaces, a corollary function is constantly to affirm that any surface has its depth. Were we, on the one hand, to observe such tormented people as Alice Hindman and Dr. Parcival and the Reverend Curtis Hartman as briefly and as much from the outside as we view Wesley Moyer or Bill Carter or Butch Wheeler, the lamplighter, they would appear as uncomplicated and commonplace as the latter. Conversely, were we to see the inwardness of Moyer and Carter and Wheeler, their essential lives would provide the basis for three more Winesburg tales. (The real lamplighter of Clyde in the early 1890's was a man named John Becker. It may well have given him the anguish of a "grotesque" that he had an epileptic son, who as a young man died during a seizure while assisting his father in his trade.)

Yet a third function of Anderson's abstract, or shorthand, kind of realism is to help him set the tone of various tales, often a tone of elegiac quietness. Just how this is done will be clearer if one realizes that the real

Clyde which underlies Winesburg is the town, not as Anderson left it in 1896, but the town as it was a few years earlier when, as he asserts in "An Awakening," "the time of factories had not yet come." In actual fact the "industrialization" of the small town of Clyde—which, it can be demonstrated, was strongly to condition Anderson's whole attitude toward machine civilization—came in a rush with the installation of electric lights in 1893—"Clyde is now the best lighted town in the state," boasted the *Enterprise* in its September 4th issue—with the paving of Main Street later that year, and with the establishment of a bicycle factory in the late summer of 1894. Subsequently Anderson was to give imaginative embodiment to this development in *Poor White*, but the Winesburg tales he conceived of as for the most part occurring in a pre-industrial setting, recalling nostalgically a town already lost before he had left it, giving this vanished era the permanence of pastoral. Here, as always, he avoids the realism of extensive detail and makes only suggestive references, one of the most memorable being the description in "The Thinker" of the lamplighter hurrying along the street before Seth Richmond and Helen White, lighting the lamp on each wooden post "so that their way was half lighted, half darkened, by the lamps and by the deepening shadows cast by the low-branched trees." By a touch like this, drawn from his memory of pre-industrial Clyde, Anderson turns the evening walk of his quite ordinary boy and girl into a tiny processional and invests the couple with that delicate splendor which can come to people, "even in Winesburg."

If Anderson's treatment of locale in his tales turns out to be more complex than it seems at first, the same can be said of his methods of giving sufficient unity to his book so that, while maintaining the "looseness" of life as he actually sensed it, the tales would still form a coherent whole. Some of these methods, those that I shall be concerned with, have a point in common: they all involve the use of repeated elements. One such device is that of setting the crisis scenes of all but five of the tales in the evening. In a very large majority of the stories, too, some kind of light partly, but only partly, relieves the darkness. In "Hands," "Mother," and "Loneliness," for example, the light is that of a single lamp; in "The Untold Lie" the concluding scene is faintly lit by the last of twilight; in "Sophistication" George Willard and Helen White look at each other "in the dim light" afforded, apparently, by "the lights of the town reflected against the sky," though at the other end of the fair grounds a few race track men have built a fire that provides a dot of illumination in the darkness. Finally, many of the tales end with the characters in total darkness. Such a device not only links the tales but in itself implies meaning. *Winesburg* is primarily a book about the "night world" of human personality. The dim light equates with, as well as literally illuminates, the limited glimpse into an individual soul that each crisis scene affords, and the briefness of the insight is emphasized by the shutting down of the dark.

Another kind of repeated element throughout the book is the recurrent word. Considering the sense of personal isolation one gets from the atomized lives of the "grotesques," one would expect a frequent use of some such word as "wall," standing for whatever it is that divides each person from all others. Surprisingly that particular word appears only a few times. The one that does occur frequently is "hand," either in the singular or the plural; and very often, as indeed would be expected, it suggests, even symbolizes, the potential or actual communication of one personality with another. The hands of Wing Biddlebaum and Dr. Reefy come immediately to mind; but, to name only a few other instances, George Willard takes hold of Louise Trunnion's "rough" but "delightfully small" hand in anticipation of his sexual initiation, Helen White keeps her hand in Seth Richmond's until Seth breaks the clasp through overconcern with self, in the field where they are working Hal Winters puts "his two hands" on Ray Pearson's shoulders and they "become all alive to each other," Kate Swift puts her hands on George Willard as though about to embrace him in her desire to make him understand what being a writer means. Obviously the physical contact may not produce mutual understanding. The hand may in fact express aggression. One of the men who run Wing Biddlebaum out of the Pennsylvania town at night "had a rope in his hands"; Elizabeth Willard, who as a girl had put her hand on the face of each lover after sexual release, imagines herself stealing toward her husband, "holding the long wicked scissors in her hand"; Elmer Cowley on the station platform strikes George Willard almost unconscious with his fists before leaping onto the departing train. Nevertheless, the possibility of physical touch between two human beings always implies, even if by negative counterpart, at least the possibility of a profounder moment of understanding between them. The intuitive awareness by George Willard and Helen White of each other's "sophistication" is expressed, not through their few kisses, but by Helen's taking George's arm and walking "beside him in dignified silence."

As for George himself, one can make too much of his role as a character designed to link the tales, unify them, and structure them into a loose sort of *bildungsroman*; on the other hand, one can make too little of it. Granted that Anderson tended to view his own life, and that of others, as a succession of moments rather than as a "figure in a carpet," that his imagination worked more successfully in terms of the flash of insight than of the large design, that his gift was, in short, for the story rather than the novel, still through his treatment of George Willard's development he supplies a pattern for *Winesburg, Ohio* that is as definite as it is unobtrusive. This development has three closely related aspects, and each aspect involves again the repetition of certain elements.

The first aspect is obvious. Whatever the outward difference between created character and creator, George's inward life clearly reflects the conflict Anderson himself had experienced between the world of practical affairs, with its emphasis on the activity of money-making and its definition of success in financial terms, and the world of dreams, with its emphasis on imaginative creativity and its definition of success in terms of the degree of penetration into the buried life of others. The conflict is thematically stated in the first of the tales, "Hands." Wing Biddlebaum's hands are famous in Winesburg for their berry-picking (hence money-making) skill, but the true story of the hands, as told by "a poet," is of course that they can communicate a desire to dream. Wing declares the absolute opposition of the two worlds by telling George that he is destroying himself because " 'you are afraid of dreams. You want to be like others in town here.' " The declaration indicates that George has not yet resolved the conflict, and his irresolution at this point is reinforced by his ambivalent attitude toward Wing's hands. Unlike the other townspeople he is curious to know what lies beneath their outward skill; yet his respect for Wing and his fear of the depths that might be revealed make him put curiosity aside. The conflict between practical affairs and dreams is again made explicit in the third story of the book, "Mother," where it is objectified in the hostility between Tom and Elizabeth Willard and the clash of their influences on their son. *Winesburg* is not a book of suspense, and thus early in the tales the conflict is in effect resolved when George implicitly accepts his mother's, and Wing's, way, the way of dreams. From this point on both the conflict and George's resolution of it are maintained in a formal sense by the opposition between the "daylight world" of the minor characters and the "night world" of the major ones, the grotesques. George continues to run about writing down surface facts for the newspaper, but his essential life consists in his efforts, some successful, some not, to understand the essential lives of others. From these efforts, from the death of his mother, from his achievement of "sophistication" with Helen White, he gains the will to leave Winesburg, committed, as the final paragraph of "Departure" asserts, to the world of dreams.

The second of these closely-related aspects of George's development is his growing desire to be a creative writer and his increasing awareness of the meaning of that vocation. George's interest in writing is not mentioned until the book is half over, when, in "The Thinker," it appears to have ben an interest that he had had for some time. He talks "continuously of the matter' to Seth Richmond, and the "idea that George Willard would some day become a writer had given him a place of distinction in Winesburg. . . ." At this point his conception of writing centers on externals, on the opportunities the writer's life offers for personal freedom and for public acclaim. In a remark that suggests a reading of Jack London, George explains to Seth that as a writer he will be his own boss: "Though you are in India or in the South Seas in a boat, you have but to write and there you are." Since writing for George is at this stage mainly a matter of fame and fun, it is not surprising to find him in "The Thinker" deliberately, and naively, planning to fall in love with Helen White in order to write a love story. The absurdity, Anderson suggests, is twofold: falling in love is not something one rationally plans to do, and one does not write thus directly and literally out of experience anyway.

Actually Kate Swift, in "The Teacher," has tried to tell George that the writer's is not "the easiest of all lives to live," but rather one of the most difficult. In one of those scenes where physical touch symbolizes an attempt to create the moment of awareness between two personalities, Kate has tried to explain the demanding principles by which the true writer must live. He must "know life," must "stop fooling with words," must "know what people are thinking about, not what they say"—all three being principles Anderson was to insist on himself as the code of the artist. That George is still immature both as person and as writer is signified at the end of "The Teacher" when he gropes drowsily about in the darkness with a hand and mutters that he has missed something Kate Swift was trying to tell him. This needed maturity comes to him only at the end of *Winesburg*. When, sitting beside the body of his dead mother, he decides to go to "some city" and perhaps "get a job on some newspaper," he is really marked already for the profession of writer, whatever job he may take to support himself, just as Anderson supported himself by composing advertising copy while experimenting with the Winesburg stories. In "Departure" the commitment of George Willard to writing unites with his final commitment to the world of dreams. For both George and his creator the two are indeed identical.

The third aspect of George's development provides another way of charting his inward voyage from innocence to experience, from ignorance to understanding, from apparent reality of the face of things to true reality behind or below. Three stories—"Nobody Knows," "An Awakening," and "Sophistication"—have a special relationship. They all center on George's dealing with a woman, a different one in each case; they contain very similar motifs; they are arranged in an ascending order of progression. The fact that one comes near the beginning of the book, one about two-thirds of the way through, and one at the end suggests that Anderson was not without his own subtle sense of design.

The first story, "Nobody Knows," is in all ways the simplest. In it George Willard enters traditional manhood by having with Louise Trunnion his first sex experience. In relation to the other two tales in the sequence, the most significant elements of the story, besides the fact of actual sexual conquest, are George's lack of self-assurance at the outset of the affair, his bursting forth with a "flood of words," his consequent aggressiveness and failure to sympathize with his partner, and his action at the end of the story when he stands "perfectly still in the darkness, attentive, listening as though for a voice calling his name." The sexual encounter with Louise has been simply that. It has brought him physical satisfaction and a feeling of entirely self-centered masculine pride. His expectation of hearing a voice, however, would seem to be a projection of guilt feeling at having violated the overt moral code of the community even though "nobody knows."

In the second and third stories these elements, or their opposites, appear in a more complex fashion. In both "An Awakening" and "Sophistication," George's relation with a woman is complicated by the involvement of another man, though, significantly, Ed Handby in the former story is laconic, direct, and highly physical, while the college instructor in the latter is voluble, devious, and pompously intellectual. In both, too, the final scene takes place on the hill leading up to the fair grounds, close, incidentally, to the place where Kate Swift tried to explain to George the difficulties that beset the dedicated writer. Yet the two stories have quite different, if supplementary, conclusions.

As George and Belle Carpenter walk up the hill in the final scene of "An Awakening," he feels no more sympathy for her, has no more understanding of her needs, than he had for Louise Trunnion; but before this last walk he has experienced an exaltation that keeps him from any fear of masculine incompetence. Earlier that January night a kind of mystical revelation has come to him when it seems as though "some voice outside of himself" announced the thoughts in his mind: "I must get myself into touch with something orderly and big that swings through the night like a star." Unlike the situation at the end of "Nobody Knows," George actually "hears" the external voice, and the voice is now the positive one of inspiration, which has replaced the negative one of conscience. Thereafter he talks volubly to Belle, as he had to Louise; but when in "An Awakening" his "mind runs off into words," be believes that Belle will recognize the new force in him and will at once surrender herself to his masculine power. Now, in actual fact an insistence on the necessity of universal order—" 'There is a law for armies and for men too'," George asserts—is a characteristic of Anderson's own thinking particularly as expressed in the novel, *Marching Men*, which preceded the Winesburg tales in composition, and in the poems, *Mid-American Chants*, which followed; yet George makes this concept ridiculous at the moment because of his intense self-centeredness about his inspiration. As Kate Swift would have said, he is still playing with words, a destructive procedure for the artistic personality as well as for the non-artistic one. Holding the quite uninterested Belle in his arms, he whispers large words into the darkness, until the passionate, non-verbalizing Ed Handby throws him aside, takes Belle by the arm, and marches off. George is left angered, humiliated, and disgustedly disillusioned with his moment of mystic insight when "the voice outside himself . . . had . . . put new courage into his heart."

Where "An Awakening" records a defeat, "Sophistication" records in all ways a triumph. Though Anderson presents the moment in essay rather than dramatic form, there comes to George, as to "every boy," a flash of insight when "he stops under a tree and waits as for a voice calling his name." But this time "the voices outside himself" do not speak of the possibilities of universal order, nor do they speak of guilt. Instead they "whisper a message concerning the limitations of life," the brief light of human existence between two darks. The insight emphasizes the unity of all human beings in their necessary submission to death and their need for communication one with another. It is an insight that produces self-awareness but not self-centeredness, that produces, in short, the mature, "sophisticated" person.

The mind of such a person does not "run off into words." Hence Helen White, who has had an intuition similar to George's, runs away from the empty talk of her college instructor and her mother, and finds George, whose first and last words to her in the story, pronounced as they first meet, are "Come on." Together in the dimly-lit fair grounds on the hill overlooking the town of Winesburg, George and Helen share a brief hour of absolute awareness. Whereas his relationship with Belle Carpenter had produced in George self-centeredness, misunderstanding, hate, frustration, humiliation, that with Helen produces quite the opposite feelings. The feeling of oneness spreads outward, furthermore. Through his communication with Helen he begins "to think of the people in the town where he had lived with something like reverence." When he has come to this point, when he loves and respects the inhabitants of Winesburg, the "daylight" people as well as the "night" ones, the way of the artist lies clear before him. George Willard is ready for his "Departure."

Like Hart Crane, other readers will find the simplicity of *Winesburg, Ohio* "baffling"; but it is very probably this paradoxical quality which has attracted and will continue to attract admirers to a book that Anderson himself, with a mixture of amusement, deprecation, defensiveness, and satisfaction, quite accurately termed "a kind of American classic."

Notes

1. I am grateful to be able to acknowledge publicly my great debt to Mr. Herman Hurd, Anderson's "closest friend" in his Clyde years, and to his son, Mr. Thaddeus Hurd, who have generously shared with me their memories of Sherwood Anderson and of Clyde.

# "Sherwood Anderson's Moments of Insight"

David D. Anderson*

In 1919 Sherwood Anderson published *Winesburg, Ohio*, a collection of short stories and sketches written between 1915 and 1917. During those years he had been under the influence of the Chicago Renaissance, a literary movement that was essentially romantic in nature, seeking liberation from the confines of the old literary forms and styles and emphasizing new subject matter, new techniques, and a new personal and artistic freedom from the machine-made culture that had come to dominate America. *Winesburg, Ohio* is perhaps the outstanding simple literary work that resulted from those years of rebellion, and its publication marked the emergence of Sherwood Anderson as a serious, native Midwestern literary artist. In it he had rejected the dissemination of propaganda and social protest that marred his earlier novels, *Windy McPherson's Son* and *Marching Men*; he went far beyond the liberating self-expression of his verse in *Mid-American Chants*; and he produced a mature work of literary art.

In the *Winesburg, Ohio* achievement, relationships to Anderson's earlier work are immediately apparent: in subject matter he returned to the small Midwestern town that had provided the background for the earlier parts of *Windy McPherson's Son*; in theme he was primarily concerned with the isolation of the individual as he had been to a lesser extent in the first two novels; and in technique he combined his natural Midwestern style with the short form that he had been experimenting with in the short stories published in *The Little Review*. But to say that Anderson merely combined all these factors and emerged with a major literary achievement is to over-simplify to an unacceptable degree; there is no intermediate work between his earlier unsuccessful attempts and *Winesburg, Ohio* that would show that Anderson was consciously striving for the literary effect that he achieved in the volume.

Anderson himself attempted to account for the abrupt shift from mediocre to substantial achievement several times, most recently and in detail in his *Memoirs*. According to him the first of the stories, "Hands",

*Originally published in David D. Anderson, *Critical Studies in American Literature* (Karachi, Pakistan: The University of Karachi, 1964), pp. 108–31.

was written in its entirety at one sitting as the result of a moment of intense emotional excitement. For days he had been sitting at the window of his room in his boarding house, watching people pass by. "Somehow it had seemed to me . . . that each person who passed along the street below . . . shouted his secret up to me. I was myself and still I felt out of myself. It seemed to me that I went into the others."

This must have been just before or shortly after he had completed the *Mid-American Chants* volume, in the writing of which he had consciously and deliberately released in himself a spontaneous lyricism produced by emotional release and the desire to probe deeply into the meanings of things as reflected in himself. At this time, as in the past, even in the years in Cleveland and Elyria, he found himself drawn strongly to the people with whom he felt so much sympathy. He was "Trying for something. To escape out of old minds, old thoughts put into my head by others, into my own thoughts, my own feelings." Thus far what he had been attempting was very much in keeping with the spirit of the Chicago Liberation, to look into his own heart and to understand others through himself, as he had emphasized in his essay "The New Note" a year or so before. Now he wanted to go farther:

> To at last go out of myself, truly into others, the others I met constantly in the streets of the city, in the office where I then worked, and still others, remembered out of my childhood in an American small town.

Suddenly it happened. He went to his table and wrote, finishing "Hands" at one sitting, knowing when he had finished that it was right, that he had captured the essence of ". . . a poor little man, beaten, pounded, frightened by the world in which he lived into something oddly beautiful." When he knew that it was right, he knew also that he had found both himself and his vocation, "getting for the first time belief in self". In the succeeding days and weeks he finished the rest of the stories, writing furiously in his room, at work, or wherever he could find a moment.

Whether this account is factually correct or not really doesn't matter. What had happened was that Anderson had attained artistic insight in a form eminently suited to his own peculiar talents for attaining empathy with other human beings. It is not a thing which can be sustained for long periods of time, certainly not throughout a novel, although flashes of it occur in almost all of his following novels, but in the short forms it is superb. He found, almost by accident, the form best suited for his ability, one in which he could fuse sympathy, insight, and lyrical excitement, and in the process lose consciousness of himself in the production of the work.

The last phrase contains the key to Anderson's achievement in the ensuing volume. In his earlier works Anderson had been dealing with himself, directly in the case of Sam McPherson in *Windy McPherson's Son* and vicariously in the figure of Beaut McGregor in *Marching Men*. Here he used the fruits of his personal experience as he had in the novels, but his experiment in *Mid-American Chants* had shown him that mere experience was not enough, that there was something beyond it. In *Winesburg, Ohio* he went beyond his own experience into an intuitive perception of the experiences of others.

Hence, in dealing with other human lives he has passed the surface appearance of each and caught it at a moment that reveals its essence. As he commented, it is as though each person had shouted his secret up to him. Each story is a moment in the life of the central figure, but in that moment Anderson reveals the secret that made that life what it was.

Incorporating these isolated moments of insight into an integrated whole presents a problem in categorizing the volume into one of the convenient pigeonholes of literary convention. It has been called both a novel and a collection of short stories, and Anderson himself always called each element a story, but in its entirety he considered it a novel in a form invented by himself rather than in the derivative form of his earlier works. In the *Memoirs* he recalls that

> I have even sometimes thought that the novel form does not fit an American writer, that it is a form which had been brought in. What is wanted is a new looseness; and in *Winesburg* I have made my own form. There were individual tales but all about lives in some way connected. By this method I did succeed, I think, in giving the feeling of the life of a boy growing into young manhood in a town. Life is a loose flowing thing. There are no plot stories in life. I had begun writing of the little lives I knew, the people I had lived, walked and talked with . . .

Again, whether this new form was a conscious contrivance at the time, as Anderson here indicates it was, or not makes very little difference. The form is, as he comments, a loose one, having elements that draw the stories together, but within the unity thus imposed, there is the diversity inherent in the dozens of lives portrayed, each of them different from the others, and all of them different from Anderson's own. The result is in a very real sense Anderson's first work that is undeniably fiction rather than autobiography.

The difficulty in ascribing a conventional category to the volume has resulted in a number of mistaken interpretations of the work, the most common being that Anderson is showing a cross section of a small town, revealing its secret sins in such detail that he is in effect "revolting from the village", as Carl Van Doren and Russell Blankenship have commented. Although this was an early attempt to categorize the book, the generality has endured, in spite of the fact that it is far from what Anderson had either intended or accomplished. Anderson was not writing about any particular social setting, nor was he attacking the social structure as he had in his earlier works. Rather he was writing about people, exploring deeply and in detail individual human lives in the attempt to set aside the barriers of human isolation and to discover them as individuals, at the same time discovering whatever it was that had erected those barriers. That the individuals he portrays are not unique products either of the small town or of the large city but common to both is demonstrated by his own statement that many of the characterizations came from ". . . everywhere about me, in towns in which I had lived, in the army, in factories and offices", and, as William Phillips' study shows, from Clyde and Elyria. The work is a composite, drawing for its substance on all of Anderson's experience; but it is not an attempt to describe or to explain any one. Anderson had left such attempts behind him as a result of what he had learned from writing the novels.

The book is in essence an exploration of the problem of human isolation; however, it does not approach the problem from the sweeping social-structure centered view of the earlier novels but from a much narrower point of view. Anderson had learned that isolation is not merely a product of modern materialism, as he had implied in *Marching Men*, but that it originates in a narrowness of human vision and an inability or in some cases an unwillingness to grapple with and attempt to understand the complexities of human life and experience. These shortcomings result in a self-centered world that precludes the understanding of others. His earlier protagonists, failing to realize this truth, had been unable to penetrate the barriers of isolation because they were attempting to approach others as extensions of themselves rather than as individuals; hence they became caricatures of the epic figures they might have been. In the short stories of this volume Anderson narrowed his field and determined to treat isolation as a phenomenon of the individual in an individual sense rather than as a manifestation of a social evil. That it cannot be cured by an all-embracing remedy, he learned from *Marching Men*, just as *Windy McPherson's Son* taught him that it cannot be understood by a direct, determined approach. In *Winesburg, Ohio*, Anderson approached the problem in its simplest individual terms, seeking understanding through intuitive perception of the essence of individuality.

In the first of the sketches, "The Book of the Grotesque", utilized as a statement of purpose, Anderson points out his approach in symbolic terms. As the title indicates, he shows that the individuals he is dealing with in the stories have each been twisted into psychological shapes having, in most cases, little to do with external appearance. This distortion results from both the narrowness of their own vision and that of others; in some cases the first is primarily at fault, while in others it is the latter. From this point the problem inherent in human isolation takes on two aspects: the first is, of course, the specific cause in individual cases; the second and more important is determining with exactness and hence understanding the nature of each grotesque. Thus, in the book he is approaching the understanding that Sam McPherson sought in a way that demands empathy, compassion, and intuition rather than fierce desire.

In this sketch, which characterizes an old writer who has attained understanding of his fellow men and has retired from life to observe men and to teach them understanding, Anderson defines his problem symbolically beause he has learned that there is no direct, obvious cause but that there are causes as diverse as the individuals who make up the world. In the sketch the old writer reveals his secret knowledge of the nature of mankind, noting

> That in the beginning when the world was young there were a great many thoughts but no such thing as a truth. Man made the truths himself and each truth was a composite of a great many vague thoughts. All about in the world were the truths and they were all beautiful.
> . . . There was the truth of virginity and the truth of wealth and of poverty, of thrift and of profligacy, of carelessness and abandon. Hundreds and hundreds . . . were the truths and they were all beautiful.
> And then the people came along. Each as he appeared snatched up one of the truths and some who were quite strong snatched up a dozen of them.
> It was the truths that made the people grotesques . . . the moment that one of the people took one of the truths to himself, called it his truth, and tried to live his life by it, he became a grotesque and the truth he embraced became a falsehood.

Using this symbolic interpretation as a basis, Anderson sets off to use intuitive perception to try to find in the lives of the people with whom he is dealing whatever it is in themselves that has prevented them from reaching their full potential as human beings and that has cut them off from their fellows. He shows, too, his realization that the cause is not something as easily perceived and denounced as modern industrialism but that it is as old as the human race. False ideas, false dreams, false hopes, and false goals have distorted man's vision almost from the beginning. Anderson is attempting in the stories to approach these people who have had such indignities inflicted upon them as to become spiritual grotesques, and most importantly, he is attempting to understand them as people rather than as curious specimens of spiritual deformity.

Anderson's use of the word grotesque is quite important in this context. In its usual sense in reference to human beings it connotes disgust or revulsion, but Anderson's use is quite different. To him a grotesque is, as he points out later, like the twisted apples that are left behind in the orchards because they are imperfect. These apples, he says, are the sweetest of all, perhaps even because of the imperfections that have caused them to be rejected. He approaches the people in his stories as he does the apples, secure in his knowledge that the sources or natures of their deformities are unimportant when compared to their intrinsic worth as human beings needing and deserving of understanding. This approach is based on intuition rather than objective knowledge, and it is the same sort of intuition with which one approaches the twisted apples; he believes that one dare not reject because of mere appearance, either physical or spiritual; that appearance may mask a significant experience made more intense and more worthwhile by the deformity itself.

In the body of the book proper, following this introductory sketch, Anderson has set up an organizational pattern that not only gives partial unity to the book but explores systematically the diverse origins of the isolation of his people, each of whom is in effect a social displaced person because he is cut off from human intercourse with his fellow human beings. In the first three stories Anderson deals with three aspects of the problem of human isolation. The first story, "Hands", deals with the inability to communicate feeling; the second, "Paper Pills", is devoted to the inability to communicate thought; and the third, "Mother", focuses on the inability to communicate love. This threephased examination of the basic problem of human isolation sets the tone for the rest of the book because these three shortcomings, resulting partially from the narrowness of the vision of each central figure but primarily from the lack of sympathy with which the contemporaries of each regard him, are the real creators of the grotesques in human nature. Each of the three characters has encountered one aspect of the problem: he has something that he feels is vital and real within himself that he wants desperately to reveal to others, but in each case he is rebuffed, and turning in upon himself, he becomes a bit more twisted and worn spiritually. But, like the apples left in the orchards, he is the sweeter, the more human for it. In each case the inner vision of the main character remains clear, and the thing that he wishes to communicate is in itself good, but his inability to break through the shell that prevents him from talking to others results in misunderstanding and spiritual tragedy.

The first of the stories, "Hands", immediately and symbolically approaches a problem that as a phase of the overall problem of human isolation recurs in Anderson's later work. The story begins by describing the remarkably active and expressive hands of an old recluse in the town. George Willard, a young reporter on the Winesburg *Eagle* and the unifying figure in the stories, is fascinated by the old man's hands, and in time Anderson as narrator tells his story: once, as a schoolmaster, he had been accused of homosexuality because in moments of excitement or affection he would tousle the hair of his students or touch them. Instead of being a means of expression, the old man's hands had become a source of shame to him, and he tried to keep them hidden. In the town he is a pitiful and fearful creature, always expecting the spontaneous actions of his hands to be misinterpreted.

The concept of hands as the basic tools of expression of the craftsman is very important in this story as it passes beyond the immediate and takes on overtones of the universal. As Anderson points out with increasing frequency during both this and the next periods of his career, man's efforts to communicate with his fellows have traditionally depended upon his hands because for many things words either do not exist or have been rendered meaningless. Hence, the hands of a craftsman, a painter, a surgeon, a writer, a lover communicate indirectly something of the truth and beauty that each of them feels inside. Although Anderson is fascinated by the idea, nevertheless he knows that the language of hands is as subject to misinterpretation as any other. In this story he points out that this is not only possible, but it is probable, that the widely-held truth in this case, the existence of homosexuality, has become a falsehood because appearance has been accepted in place of truth. Symbolically he shows how such widely-held truths become falsehoods have inhibited the forces in man that allow him to express himself intimately and creatively. Fortunately, however, he shows that the forces still exist, making their possessor the more human and the more deserving of compassion, because he has been deprived of the power to express his creativity.

In "Paper Pills" Anderson again writes of the relationship between a man's hands and his inner being, this time in the person of Doctor Reefy, a conventionally wise and perceptive country practitioner. Doctor Reefy is as cut off from effective communication with others as Wing Biddlebaum, but his problem is his inability to communicate his thoughts without being misunderstood. Because he recognizes this shortcoming, he writes his thoughts on bits of paper and puts the bits into his pockets, where they become twisted into hard little balls, which he throws playfully at his friend the nurseryman as he laughs.

Here Anderson carries further his introductory comment that there is no such thing as a truth, that there are only thoughts, and that man has made truths out of them through his own short sight. On the bits of paper Doctor Reefy knows that he is writing mere thoughts, but he knows that they would be misinterpreted if communicated directly, so to prevent them being reduced to the grim joke of misinterpretation he prefers that they become the means of a lesser joke in the form of paper pills. Cut off from attempts at direct communication through his knowledge of its inevitable misinterpretation, Doctor Reefy prefers that his paper pills be considered as bits of paper and no more; in effect, the hard shells of the pills represent the barriers of isolation that surround human minds, and Doctor Reefy, voluntarily isolating himself rather than trying to overcome those barriers, deliberately avoids inevitable misunderstanding.

Waldo Frank sees this story as representing the ineffectuality of human thought as it is isolated and fragmented on the bits of paper, but Anderson indicates no such shortcoming in the thoughts themselves. The difficulty, he points out, lies in the process of communication, which, as Reefy indicates, is something that cannot be carried out directly with any assurance of success. Rather than risk misinterpretation, he lets the paper pills be considered products of his hands rather than his mind. Yet, even while he throws them playfully at his friend, he hopes that his friend will see them in the light in which every craftsman hopes his work will be regarded—as a product that has taken shape through the work of his hands but that is expressive of his soul. Reefy knows that this intuitive understanding is as unlikely as direct understanding, and so he lets himself become a grotesque because he is unable to find a satisfactory means of communication. The shortcoming lies not in the thought but in the process of communication, and he prefers to convey his thoughts ironically in the form of a joke, even while he knows that faulty communication of the intimacies of human life is life's inherent tragedy.

The third story, "Mother", deals with the relationship between George Willard and his mother, Elizabeth Willard. In effect the story is the exploration of a theme that Anderson had adapted from his own experience and used in both *Windy McPherson's Son* and *Marching Men*: the inability to communicate love or understanding between mother and son. The relationship between the two is completely inarticulate, just as it was between mother and son in each of the novels and, more importantly, as Anderson's autobiographies show, as was the case between him and his own mother. As a result, although this phase is part of the overall problem of isolation, Anderson feels that understanding in this area is vital. As the theme unfolds in this story, Elizabeth has been forced, through the ineptness of her husband, to take over management of both the family hotel, a failing business, and the inner affairs of the family proper. She is resented by her husband as a usurper, and unable to love or respect him, she focuses her interest and love on her son, in whom she sees the potential for the individual fulfillment that her role as woman and as head of the household had denied her. Inwardly she was a mass of determination that violently defied anything that threatened her son; outwardly she was perfunctory, almost apologetic in his presence.

Consequently Elizabeth is continually afraid that her life, spent in opposing both the forces of conventional success and her husband, with her son as the stake, is indecisive and meaningless. She can only hope that somehow the boy understands. Finally he announces that he is going away: "I just want to go away and look at people and think." She is unable to reply, but she knows that she has won; "She wanted to cry out with joy . . . but the expression of joy had become impossible to her", and the story ends in perfunctory formality, the barriers still solid between them.

In these three stories Anderson sets forth the theme of the problem of human isolation in the three aspects that recur in most of the other stories. These three aspects, the inability to communicate one's feeling, one's thought, and one's love, are at the heart of the problem, and in the following stories he shows these shortcomings at work in other situations with other central characters but essentially as restatements of the same theme. In each of the characters something deep within him demands expression. In each case it is part of him that he wants desperately to share with others directly, and he is unable to do it, either through his own inability to break through the shell that surrounds him or else because society forbids it or distorts it. This inability makes him turn in upon himself, becoming a grotesque, a person deserving of understanding and wanting it desperately, but completely unable to find it except in occasional flashes, as in the embrace between Elizabeth and Doctor Reefy in "Death" and in the attempts made by many of them to seek understanding in George Willard. However, such moments merely serve to emphasize the intensity of their isolation as they are startled by a noise or as George misunderstands or fails to understand and leaves them behind in frustration.

As George Willard appears and reappears in about half of the stories as leading character, as an audience, or as a casual observer he lends a unity to the collection that makes it approach the novel form. Much more important, however, is his role in permitting full development of Anderson's theme. In two of the first three stories, "Hands" and "Mother", he plays the part that has been ascribed to him in more than half of the following stories. To each of the grotesques he appears to be what that individual wants him to be. To his mother he is an extension of herself through which her dreams may be fulfilled; to Wing Biddlebaum he is the symbol of the innocent love that had been denied him; to others he becomes, in turn, a symbol of a long-lost son, of father-confessor, of masculine strength and fertility, of innocent, undemanding human understanding. Each interprets George as he wishes, but to each he primarily serves the function of an ear into which can be poured the inner stirrings of fear, hope, love, and dreams of which each is made. Because he is part of the apparently integrated community in his job as reporter on the Winesburg *Eagle*, he represents to each of them the opportunity to restore communication with the world from which each feels excluded. These grotesques see in George the key that will release them from their personal prisons and enable them to resume normal human forms, either vicariously, as in the case of his mother and others, or directly, through understanding, acceptance, and love. Because George is innocent, unspoiled by the world that has rejected and isolated them, they see in him their only chance to return to the fellowship of men.

As a result, Wing Biddlebaum feels confident in his presence and is willing to walk freely with him through the town; his mother feels a sudden surge of strength in his presence; Doctor Parcival feels confident enough to reveal the secret behind his mask of hate—the overwhelming compassion that makes him declare that ". . . everyone in the world is Christ and they are all crucified"; Louise Trunnion in "Nobody Knows" seeks him out for a moment of love that manifests itself in sex. In following stories the role of George Willard parallels these. He is sought out, he receives confidences, he is receptive and sympathetic, and the grotesques for the most part go away momentarily satisfied, unaware that while they have found temporary release, they have not found freedom from the confines of their spiritual prisons.

Only in "Queer", the story of Elmer Cowley, does the grotesque resent the person of George Willard. Just as the others have seen Willard as the symbol of whatever will free them from their isolation, Elmer sees George as the manifestation of the society that rejects him. In this story Elmer resents George and yet attempts to establish satisfactory relations with him. Failing this, he assaults George, leaving him behind bewildered and half-conscious. As he hops a freight, Elmer voices his frustration by crying, "I guess I showed him. I ain't so queer. I guess I showed him I ain't so queer."

In this story Elmer Cowley points out the difficulty that the other grotesques thus far have failed to perceive: George Willard does not understand. All of the others had seen him as an extension of self that could not fail to understand and that could ease their passage into the intimacies of human life, and each believed that he did somehow understand, even as he left in sympathy but baffled or, as in the case of Louise Trunnion, completely misunderstanding. But Elmer sees him as society, as the symbol of rejection, and finding himself tongue-tied in George's presence, he can do nothing else but assault George and then run off, defiant but defeated. Elmer sees that George as society does not understand, while the others fail to see that as son, as lover, as mirrored self, he does not understand either.

As the grotesques reveal themselves to George, they do not arouse in him the conventional understanding that they seek, but without realizing it, each of them is contributing to the growth of a more important kind of understanding in him. This kind is based on compassion and on the sincere desire to understand what these people are trying to tell him, and it does not result from objective analysis but from intuitive perception of the nature and worth of the individual. As the stories unfold he is still too young and inexperienced to grasp much more than that, but his contacts with the grotesques are drawing him closer to eventual understanding through teaching him the compassion and the empathy that will permit him in time to know and understand others.

In the development of George Willard, Anderson indicates that one can learn to seek out moments of understanding, of acceptance, of communication without the use of words that can be twisted, distorted, or misunderstood. Early in the collection George had completely misinterpreted a lonely plea, mistaking it for an invitation to a sex adventure; later, with Kate Swift he almost makes the same mistake, finally realizing that "I must have missed something. I have missed something Kate Swift was trying to tell me;" and finally, in "Sophistication" his brief meeting with Helen White brought him to realize that sex and love are not synonymous but that they are often confused. This realization makes possible for him the eventual achievement of understanding. In the process he has learned something of the nature of the human heart, both of others and of his own, and he has learned to open his heart and to listen with it rather than with ears that have become too accustomed to the sound of the truths become falsehoods all around him.

The sketch "Departure" is for George anti-climax. In the microcosm of human nature that is Winesburg he had learned the fundamental secret of human society: that one must reach out and accept and love; he had ". . . for a moment taken hold of the thing that makes the mature life of men and women in the modern world possible"; and he is ready to take his place in that world, taking with him something of each of the grotesques who had sought him out. As long as he remembers that secret he can never become one of them; he knows that understanding comes only in moments of uncomplicated acceptance and love.

Willard's two-fold position in the volume goes well beyond the obvious factor of providing a unifying figure and becomes the means through which thematic development becomes apparent. Human isolation can be overcome and man can take his place in an understanding relationship with his fellows, but such understanding can only come about through intuitive perception of the others as human beings. The normal processes of direct communication are useless; what is needed are increasing and deliberate efforts to attain empathy with others through compassion, through love, and above all, through the process of one's own intuition. That this can be learned Anderson shows through the evolution of Willard's experience from complete misunderstanding through increasing awareness and finally into a state where understanding and fulfillment become possible, at least momentarily. For this, however, conditions of receptivity must be right; that is, the truths become falsehoods disseminated by society must have been driven from the consciousness.

In his progress from misunderstanding to intuitive insight George Willard's development parallels that of Anderson himself, and in this sense Willard is an autobiographical figure. In his own career Anderson had followed the same path. From misunderstanding and grasping at single truths and rendering them false as he pursued a business career, he had become increasingly aware of others and of the desire to understand them, while he let his business career go to pieces. Then, as shown in the pages of *Winesburg, Ohio*, he found the secret of intuitive communication with the inner lives of others. As he has pointed out in the *Memoirs* he had begun to write hoping to find understanding; after the false starts that he made in the novels when he had mistakenly focused on himself and on the world and had failed to find understanding, he turned away from self into others and had finally begun to find the understanding he had been seeking.

However, *Winesburg, Ohio* must not be interpreted as merely an exposition of the theme of human isolation, nor must it be seen primarily either in the light of a young man learning about life or as a symbolic representation of Anderson's acquisition of the powers of intuitive perception. The book's chief merit is that it is about people. Willard's role is secondary to the people about whom each individual story centres. Whereas the leading character in each of the novels was clearly Anderson himself, either as disillusioned seeker or as fulfilled hero, in this work his role is minor, and he has gone beyond himself and into the lives of others. Each character has elements in common with the others and with Willard, just as all men share the common bonds of humanity, but in each case the character is primarily an individual, differing from the others and, of course, from Anderson himself in all the idiosyncrasies that make up human character. For the first time Anderson was attempting to write fiction rather than disguised autobiography, and the breadth of individuality in the stories shows the success of the attempt.

Characterization in the stories is not fully developed, however. In the *Memoirs* Anderson points out that ". . . *Winesburg, Ohio* tried to tell the story of the defeated figures of an old American individualistic small town life . . ." and in this phrase he points out what he was trying to do and at the same time he sheds lights on both characterization and structural technique of the individual stories. The limitations in Anderson's statement account for the fact that although each character was an individual, each was primarily defined by one controlling characteristic that provided both the key to his character and to the nature of his grotesqueness.

More importantly, however, from the point of view of Anderson's narrative technique, each key characteristic was easily definable in a moment of the author's insight into the individuality of the person concerned. Thus, in the stories in which George Willard is absent or makes brief, unimportant appearances, Anderson utilizes not only theme and background to tie the stories into the unified collection, but he uses the same technique of a revealing moment to permit the reader to grasp both the nature of the individual's isolation and his controlling characteristic as an individual, at the same time effectively strengthening the unified structure of the whole. In "Godliness" he shows Jesse Bentley as a God-intoxicated man who sees in himself the reincarnation of an Old Testament patriarch; in "The Untold Lie" Ray Pearson is depicted as a man who has discovered the futility of judging an act absolutely; "Respectability" pictures a man who seeks love but finds it perverted into sex; "The Strength of God" shows a minister who renews his faith through an unconscious distortion of his own inner drives.

Each of the characters can be revealed in a phrase because each of them carries within himself the complicating factor that provides the framework for the story. But this does not mean that characterization in the stories is slight or simple; it does mean, however, that the characterizations are primarily based upon depth rather than breadth, and each is a narrow area deeply explored, with the emphasis placed upon the uniqueness of that basic trait.

This concept of characterization leads directly into the narrative technique that Anderson has employed in the stories. There are no carefully-constructed plots, sequences of significant incidents, or patterns of rising or falling action. Rather, the stories are character-plotted, and each consists of the revelation of the character core that is the essense of the central figure's being. Outside events in the stories are normally of little or no importance except as they provide opportunity for this revelation, and in effect Anderson has primarily been providing opportunity for his reader to peer deeply into a man's soul as he puts his stories together. In each, this is but the work of a moment, sometimes handled in a phrase, a sentence, or a paragraph, but in that brief moment Anderson has revealed, with his sincere compassion, the deepest secret of each character's being, the fear, the frustration, or the love or hope that he kept within himself, often afraid to reveal it.

In combining this method of characterization with an intuitive approach to its ultimate revelation Anderson has provided in the stories a series of moments of insight, each of them designed to provide a brief, intuitive, but true glimpse of the anguish of the human heart. Although his interest in psychoanalysis had been increasing during the Chicago years, he does not use the techniques of artificially induced self-revelation nor does he reveal for the sake of reaching objective conclusions. Rather the technique that he employs is intuitive perception accomplished not through analysis but through empathy, and his purpose is not to diagnose and to cure but simply to understand and to love. The stories are not literary psychiatrists' couches; they are vehicles by which Anderson as craftsman can express the insight into individual aspects of human nature as it has been revealed to him through the intuitive approach that he as artist feels is valid in artistic interpretation.

In attempting to measure the achievement of *Winesburg, Ohio* critics have evolved numerous conflicting theories. Some, such as Russell Blankenship, contemporary with the publication of the work, saw it as naturalistic or realistic; in the thirties Oscar Cargill called it primitivistic; and more recently James Schevill has seen in it an elaborate structure designed ". . . to replace the myth of the small town Christian virtues with the myth of the grotesque . . ." by showing ". . . the sexual and imaginative frustrations of the townspeople." This continued attention to the volume indicates the respect that critics have for it and their realization that Anderson has accomplished a substantial piece of work in writing it, but the resulting contradictions indicate the difficulty of ascribing satisfactory categories to or providing acceptable explanations for a complex literary work. The categories of realism or naturalism are unsatisfactory as an examination of Anderson's technique and theme shows clearly. Anderson is not expounding the theory of a universe of mechanistic forces operating on his people as the term naturalism would indicate, but he is showing the essense of their humanity. Neither does he depend for effect upon the constant and careful accumulation of sharply drawn detail in the tradition of realism, but rather he sketches, he implies, he insinuates, and he reveals insights in order to arrive at delineation of character and of situation that is inward rather than external. Both of these categories are unsatisfactory because the stories cannot be twisted or distorted to meet the demands even of loose application of the terms, while primitivism is a catch-all phrase that attempts to categorize by subject matter, ignoring what Anderson was trying to say.

The interpretation of the work as an attempt to construct an elaborate American myth is an unnecessary complication that never occured to Anderson in any of his published remarks on the book. Rather, as Anderson conceived and wrote the book and as the completed work shows, he was not writing about society in the aggregate, either realistically or in the symbolic structure of mythology. He was not writing about society at all; he was writing about people. Each of his people is conceived and presented as an individual rather than as merely another manifestation of society. That he is part of the social structure is important only insofar as every individual is part of that structure, and Anderson was not merely interested in treating the individual in terms of that relationship; he was interested in treating the individual as human being.

*Winesburg, Ohio* is the book that provides the solid foundation of Anderson's literary reputation in times of disfavor as well as of favor, and his accomplishment in the work is impressive. It is not a book of rebellion as were his earlier works of fiction; instead, it is an affirmation of Anderson's belief in the durability of the human spirit and of the compassion that he felt was needed at the heart of human relations. In it Anderson has examined the problem of human isolation, not in the hope of curing, but in the certainty of his belief that understanding of men is important because man himself is important individually as well as collectively. In doing so he points the way toward further understanding, hoping that barriers among men can be removed. However, understanding, he points out, must come first, not only because it may eliminate barriers, but more importantly because to know other human beings is to love them, and love is the essence of life.

In the process he examines many specific instances of human isolation, recognizing diversity in both kind and degree and showing understanding of the nature of the problem far greater than that he had shown in the two novels. This major shift in approach indicates that he was consciously avoiding the mistake of oversimplification as he became writer rather than propagandist or panacea seeker. His most important discovery, however, was his realization that human isolation stems primarily from entirely human shortcomings, those inherent in sex, in inarticulateness, in ". . . the old brutal ignorance that had in it also a kind of beautiful childlike innocence . . .", and even in deliberate cruelty. For its victims he had hope as well as compassion because, however seriously they might be distorted, nevertheless they were reaching out, aware that others existed and hoping that somehow they might be able to establish communication. Occasionally, however, when he perceived that the new materialism was making inroads among the people, as in "Godliness" and in "Queer", and the central figures were isolated by greed, flashes of the old Anderson shine through. For these people he had contempt, and compassion and hope are replaced by irony that rises at times, as in "Queer", to ludicrousness.

In an examination of *Winesburg, Ohio* in the light of Anderson's previous works a number of revealing factors come to light. In the first place, he has not shifted abruptly from the thematic focus of the previous works, but a gradual shifting of thematic focus has taken place. The theme of human isolation in *Winesburg, Ohio* is a direct and logical result of the shift that had evidently been taking place in Anderson's thinking. In both *Windy McPherson's Son* and *Marching Men* Anderson had started with the premise that the effect of industrialism on the individual was to isolate him. In the former Sam McPherson's acceptance of the concepts of materialism had completely cut him off from others, and half of the novel is devoted to his attempts to find his way back into human society. But his direct efforts are futile, and his final decision that it can only be done through love of others is vague and unsatisfactory and his concept of intimate relations with other human beings carries with it too much of the air of Madison Avenue togetherness. But in spite of its vagueness, the ending points out the direction that Anderson was to take in his efforts to find fulfillment through understanding his fellows.

In *Marching Men* Anderson attempted to reduce the vagueness of this ending to concrete terms. His villain was still industrialism and its destructive effects on the human qualities of individuals, but he attempted to break down the barriers of spiritual isolation among men by forging physical bonds among them, hoping that as a result the villain would be overcome and spiritual ties would grow also. Again, however, Anderson indicated in the end that he knew too little of the nature of the problem he was dealing with; such an easy solution, he realized, is primarily the result of wishful thinking and it is no solution at all; instead it raises other problems. Both of his early frontal assaults on the problem had proved futile, and a change of focus rather than problem became necessary.

*Mid-American Chants* represents this pause to re-examine both his own position and the validity of his original thesis. His own position had changed and he had found himself as writer; his point of view had been narrowed and deepened; and his realization grew that the problem of human isolation is not manifested in social movements but in individual circumstances in human lives. Combining these three factors he found that a new approach was necessary, that individuals cannot be categorized or manipulated as easily as he had thought. Using the symbol of the strong, fertile corn that does not seek to interpret, explain, or exploit its existence and its relationships but merely accepts them, he showed that man, too, can only be approached in the same intuitive, compassionate, and accepting manner. At this point, although his basic problem remained the same, his approach to that problem became an effort to understand rather than to generalize and cure.

*Winesburg, Ohio* was Anderson's attempt to incorporate this lesson in human terms. In a much looser form than that permitted by the conventional novel and yet unified by theme, by technique, and by the gradual emergence of intuitive understanding in George Willard, Anderson narrowed the range of human isolation from a manifestation of society to a characteristic of individuals. In the process he probed much more deeply than he had in the past, and he found that dehumanized materialism is only a symptom of a much older and much more serious human malady. Although he still condemned the isolation that results from the worship of things, he demonstrated many more basic isolating factors in human life: simple inarticulateness; the shortcomings of words as media of communication; the fallacies of class and of status; the misinterpretations which society makes, especially in the meaning behind sexual differences; and the confusion of spiritual seeking with sexual desire. All these, as he shows in the collection, can only be understood in individual rather than societal terms.

These factors, he points out, cannot be overcome by specific remedies; they can only be approached and penetrated through intuitive understanding and compassion. That this technique can be learned he demonstrates in the figure of George Willard. Anderson has not sought to erect a myth of the grotesque; he has sought to demonstrate that the grotesque is a human being, an individual who can be understood if one is willing to make the effort to learn the technique. The false gods, the isolated thoughts become truths become falsehoods, cannot be easily overcome; they can only be overthrown through intuitive perception of the worth of each individual, through understanding, and through mutual seeking.

*Winesburg, Ohio* is not an isolated work as some critics maintain, standing apart from Anderson's earlier works. Although as a work of literary art it is far superior to them, the thematic relationship, actually an intensification, is readily apparent. Equally apparent are stylistic and structural relationships. The rhetorical awkwardness that was so apparent in *Windy McPherson's Son* has almost disappeared, but it was becoming less conspicious in *Marching Men* and it received its final blows in *Mid-American Chants*. Conversely the experimentation with the natural rhythms of American speech that he had conducted in the previous work has in *Winesburg* become his major stylistic characteristic, pointing toward his later mastery of the reproduction of the oral story-telling tradition that halts, digresses, becomes seemingly irrelevant at times, and yet proceeds swiftly toward a carefully defined climax and impact. Conversations have become almost entirely natural, the flat Midwestern tones naturally reproduced replacing the earlier imitative and artificial rhetorical flourishes. Characterization has deepened in contrast to the earlier surface treatment, and the storytelling technique has become carefully controlled and orderly when compared to the formlessness of the earlier works. In the book as a whole and in most of the individual stories there is evidence of a plan. In *Winesburg, Ohio* Anderson knew where he was going, and he was consciously aware of the implications and ramifications of his theme. Each of the stories is a manifestation of that theme, and through the regular appearance of George Willard, the solution to the problem of human isolation becomes increasingly closer as George approaches eventual understanding.

In addition Anderson uses the technique of framing the collection by using sketches at the beginning and the end both to document this thesis and to further aid structural unity. "The Book of the Grotesque" sets up the problem of human isolation and presents its origins in symbolic terms; "Departure" shows that these shortcomings, made real in the stories, are not insurmountable, that there is hope if the individual seeks out the basis of understanding among men.

With the publication of *Winesburg, Ohio* Anderson had achieved full stature as a writer, but it was not a stature that could remain static. Rather the book marks both the close of the earliest period in his writing career and the beginning of the second. It represents the culmination of his discovery of his own particular talents and his own view of individual lives, and it points out the directions that his future works were to take, two directions that are diametrically opposed, one of them looking backward in time at the American past, and the other forward into the age of industrialism that formerly had been his prime interest.

In pointing to the past that Anderson was to become increasingly concerned with both in later works and in his own life, the volume is permeated with an air of nostalgia, a wished-for return to a state of human society that was uncomplicated, that was characterized not only as "brutal ignorance" but also and more importantly, ". . . a kind of beautiful childlike innocence [that] is gone forever." Coupled with this is, of course, the realization that the past is not perfect, nor did Anderson want it so. He realized, as did one of his people, ". . . the fact that many people must live and die alone, even in Winesburg". However, in a world less complicated, less dehumanized than the age of industrialism, he believed that understanding could be more easily achieved. As a whole, the book nostalgically evokes the memory of a way of life that is gone, and as George Willard looks back from the train he sees that ". . . the town of Winesburg had disappeared, and his life there had become but a background upon which to paint the dreams of his manhood".

# "Sherwood Anderson in Retrospect"

### David D. Anderson*

After an active literary career of nearly 30 years, Sherwood Anderson was in critical disfavor when he died, disfavor that has persisted in spite of its paradoxical nature. Critical opinion has generally relegated Anderson to a minor position in American literary history, and yet it has not only been unable to ignore him but has continued to give him more attention than many figures considered to be major. The reason for this is obvious. When he was at his best, he was very good, so good, in fact, that *Winesburg, Ohio* and some of the shorter works have become modern classics. On the other hand, when he was being most determinedly modern and artistic, as in *Many Marriages* and most of the later novels, he imposed a kind of dating on his work that made it old-fashioned almost as soon as it was written.

Behind this dichotomy in his work lies another reason for the continuation of critical examination in spite of the absolute pronouncements made by critics. Even while he was still alive, Anderson had become somewhat of a mythical figure, who, perhaps more than any other American, embodied the dream of almost every critic, academic or commercial, who has ever approached him. The myth has maintained that almost alone among people prominent in the history of twentieth-century American literature, Anderson had the courage to reject commercial success and to devote himself to his art. That this does not correspond exactly to the facts of his life has been pointed out by numerous academic critics, but such disagreement is unimportant because the Anderson myth is apparently embedded as firmly as the George Washington-cherry tree legend in American folklore.

The dichotomy in Anderson's work and the myth that has grown up around his life have resulted in two emotional stances that dominate Anderson criticism: a harshness, which stems from the difficulty in reconciling the two extremes of his work; and a sentimentality, which results from personal identification with the problem behind the myth of his life. These two emotional approaches have become so commonplace that they sometimes exist side by side in the same critical study, resulting in a

*Originally published in *Midwest Quarterly*, 3 (January, 1962), pp. 119–32.

stereotyped approach that hinders evaluation of Anderson's work, understanding of what he was attempting to do, and recognition of the importance of the close relationship between his work and the American experience through which he lived.

*Winesburg, Ohio* and a number of individual short stories, notably "I Want to Know Why," "I'm a Fool," "The Egg," and "The Man Who Became a Woman," have been frequently and justifiably pointed out as Anderson's permanent contributions to American literature; *Poor White* is often added to the list. These works, however, are the products of Anderson's earlier active career, when he still received wide critical acceptance, and their worth has never been seriously questioned. At the same time the list ignores the fact that the short stories have been lifted out of the context of the volumes in which they appeared and have lost much of their meaning and effectiveness in the process. This generally acknowledged list is accurate as far as it goes, but it is incomplete. To these products of his early period must be added all of *The Triumph of the Egg* and *Horses and Men*, not only because they include such other excellent stories as "Seeds," "Unlighted Lamps," "The Sad Horn Blowers," and "An Ohio Pagan," but because they are collections of comparatively even quality. These collections are unified by both structure and theme to comment on the nature of men's lives as effectively and as perceptively as does *Winesburg, Ohio*. Stories and sketches are included that are less satisfactory than the best, just as there are in *Winesburg*, but to ignore the subtlety with which Anderson brought unity out of apparent diversity is to ignore one of his greatest skills.

Because too many critics suggest that Anderson had lost his effectiveness at this point, worthwhile contributions of his later periods are unfortunately ignored. To the list of his permanent contributions must be added parts of *A Story Teller's Story*, especially Book One and a number of other sections. This volume does contain the same old stuff, as many critics are quick to point out, and the book as a whole is uneven in execution. Yet both structurally and stylistically Anderson is often at his best in it, reproducing the Midwestern rhythms and idioms almost flawlessly and incorporating them in the old oral storytelling tradition, thus elevating that same old subject matter to the realm of American mythology.

From the last 12 years of Anderson's career it is necessary to add parts of *Beyond Desire*, the complete volumes *Death in the Woods* and *Kit Brandon*, the incomplete *Memoirs*, and numerous essays from *Hello Towns!*, *Puzzled America*, and other sources. The first is not only his most consistently high level collection of stories, but it also contains two of his best, "Death in the Woods" and "Brother Death." *Death in the Woods* is an integrated and mature examination of Anderson's belief that reality must be separated from appearance if truth is to be recognized and understood. The collection as a whole is as good as anything he had done in the earlier years.

*Kit Brandon* is his most objective and most fully realized novel, suffering only from carelessness and inattention, neither of which is sufficiently serious to condemn it. In this novel Anderson comes close to understanding the nature of the American experience as a product of the peculiar circumstances inherent in the growth of the country, an achievement matched in his own work only by the incomplete *Memoirs*, his attempt at a definitive interpretation of the American experience as he had known it.

The best of the essays are parts of this interpretation. Each of them is an attempt to come closer to an understanding of a moment in space and time, whether it concerned an individual, a group, or a set of circumstances. Each one of these better essays is dominated by careful attention to craftsmanship as well as by penetrating, intuitive understanding of the essence of the material; in them Anderson focuses attention on the significance of the small, the seemingly unimportant, and the easily ignored in human life.

All of these cited works must be included in a convenient list of Anderson's permanent contributions to American literature, a list that, while it is not imposing, is substantial and significant. But in order to understand Anderson and what he was trying to do, it is not enough to limit attention to any list of his most successful works. Rather, as this study has attempted to show, Anderson's work can be regarded only as a whole composed of many parts, because the major theme to which he devoted his attention was the meaning of the American experience as he had known and lived it.

Anderson's work in its entirety is an attempt to penetrate appearance and to determine the nature of the reality beneath it. To Anderson, material manifestations were unimportant. He did not deny their existence; on the contrary, as in the case of the twisted apples left to rot in the orchards near Clyde, he knew that appearance was in some odd way often related to essential nature, but that the relationship was often ignored or misunderstood. This realization came early to him, certainly by the time he had established himself in business in Elyria. The literary career that followed resulted from the impact of that discovery on his mind—a mind essentially untrained and uneducated, a mind that found its way to a satisfactory resolution of the dilemma only through a long process of trial and error and of acceptance and rejection.

For Anderson the most obvious discrepancy between appearance and reality was the difference between the American ideal as he had learned it and its actuality as he had seen it put into practice during the years when America became dominated by material things at the cost of the values inherent in the ideal. The attempt to separate traditional values from a subverting materialistic ethic led him into literature by way of a back door because the words he had learned to use effectively in advertising were the only means he had by which to attack this distortion and confusion of values. In actuality Anderson began his literary career as a propagandist fighting against the corruption of the American ideal by materialism.

However, by the time he finished *Marching Men*, Anderson learned that there was no easy answer to the problem, and the discovery made him a writer instead of a propagandist. His goal had not changed, but he realized that the means by which he had sought to bring it to fruition were insufficient. Between 1915 and 1918 he began a tentative analysis that would lead him deeply into his subject matter, at the same time realizing the necessity of evolving a stylistic technique that would make his writing effective rather than merely functional.

With the writing of *Winesburg, Ohio* he had not forsaken his purpose to determine the relation between nature and experience and appearance and reality; he had merely intensified it by closely examining individuals who had been crippled spiritually by the confusion of values in a confused society. Encouraged by the success of his approach, he broadened it in following works, attempting to incorporate more of his experience into them. But he found that there still were no answers to his problem, a problem that became increasingly personal as he realized that he, too, had been confusing many things for a long time. Once again he shifted his direction and narrowed his scope in order to subject his experience to closer scrutiny. The introspection that followed enabled him to accept his inability to reconcile the apparent dichotomies in life, while penetration of his own life gave him a sense of identity and a sense of his role in life. These new insights pointed out the values that he had thus far been unable to define in his works.

Out of this crucial period Anderson formulated the concepts that dominated his later work and that remain as his final comments on the meaning of the American experience as it had been reflected in his own life. They were simple enough; so simple that they seem naive, even though their simplicity emphasizes their depth. The identity and the place he chose for his own were those he had misunderstood and rejected when he had accepted the appearance on which a material society is constructed. After re-establishing himself as an artist-craftsman who belonged in a town rather than to a center of materialism, he could go on to formulate his concepts of the nature of the reality behind experience. They were actually concepts that he had intuitively recognized when he first realized the existence of the discrepancy between appearance and reality, and they had been reflected in his work from the beginning. Through compassion and through empathetic understanding, man could break down the barriers that separated him from his fellows. In the process he would recognize the true values in human life, the understanding and love that, mutually achieved, would make life worth living.

This is the essence of Anderson's philosophy, a solution to the problems inherent in human experience that is both simple and complex. It was easy to say, as he had long known; but, he tentatively concluded, it was impossible to realize. Close as he was to naturalism and despair at this point, he finally acknowledged that the end itself was an ideal, and like all ideals, beyond the capabilities of human nature. Hence he reached the conclusion that the means rather than the end—life itself rather than an impossible perfection—was the only meaning man could know, but it was far from a petty or an ignoble meaning.

This is the concept that dominated both his life and works from 1929 to his death; man is his brother's keeper, he declared, whether or not he would acknowledge the fact. It was the realization of this truth that made human life meaningful, and its rejection, brought about by a preoccupation with things, had led to the inevitable dehumanization of American society. The American experience was therefore one that demanded a careful and continuous examination if one would find meaning inherent in it. Its nature, as he pointed out, had been such that from the beginning it demanded that man concern himself with the material appearance of life in spite of its great potential, and consequently only the individual himself could prevent the material from completely nullifying his own potential.

Anderson's works as a whole record his discovery of this truth, one that a more sophisticated man possessed of more education would have accepted as obvious and would then have promptly forgotten. However, Anderson, like his nineteenth-century predecessors Emerson, Thoreau, and Whitman, was not interested in discovering the physical laws that govern the universe; instead, he restricted his attention to the obvious problems of human life and tried to find a way to live with them. The entire range of his works from *Windy McPherson's Son* to *Memoirs* is the record of his attempt to make that possible by finding the meaning inherent in human experience as he had known it.

Anderson belongs properly in the main stream of American idealism which had its inception in the self-evident truths of natural rights, was nurtured in the transcendentalist realization that somewhere beyond physical appearance lay the ultimate truth of man's fate, and fell into confused disorder before the combined onslaught of Darwinism and economic determinism. The confusion endured in a world suddenly grown complex, but by the beginning of the twentieth century the disorder had been replaced by a counteroffensive determined to show the evils inherent in a world dominated by materialism. Anderson was temperamentally suited to become a member of this counteroffensive, and he was a member in spirit long before he became one in fact.

The literary movement and atmosphere with which he associated himself as a writer is clear indication of his membership in the idealistic counteroffensive. The keynote of the Chicago renaissance was liberation, and it was devoted to freeing the writer from confusion and from the concessions that idealism had made to genteelness. Liberation to Anderson meant honesty, and honesty meant that the major issues in American life could no longer be ignored. The movement had its superficial aspects, as Anderson learned; at times it seemed to be dominated by superficiality, but its core was a determination to right old wrongs at the same time that it established a new and honest American literary tradition.

Before Anderson joined the Chicago group, he had been primarily a propagandist, foscusing on issues rather than people. His reaction to materialism was instinctive and direct, so that the early novels, *Windy McPherson's Son* and *Marching Men*, are based on protest and rejection while they are expressed in the diction and style of late nineteenth-century popular literature. But the literary movement of which the Chicago group was a part taught him that what he was writing was not literature, and it pointed out his new direction.

In the context of the new literary tradition of protest and rejection, Anderson's relationship to his major literary contemporaries is evident in both his attitudes and his techniques. Although he often gave credit to Gertrude Stein for having made him aware of the potential inherent in words and style, nevertheless his affinity to others is much closer. He moved out of Miss Stein's orbit of experimentation after the initial impetus that it gave him and into a circle that was largely Midwestern—so much so that in its view of its birthplace it has been compared to the Russians by D. H. Lawrence.

The two major Midwestern novelists with whom Anderson can best be compared are Theodore Dreiser and Sinclair Lewis, while among the poets his closest relationship is with Vachel Lindsay and Edgar Lee Masters. Anderson has much in common with all of them although, at the same time, there are major differences. Like Dreiser and Lewis, Anderson protested against an environment that made people less than human; however, he was aware of a special kinship with Dreiser. But the protests of all three took difference directions. For Dreiser there was no way out of the deterministic environment that his people were caught in, while for Lewis, there was no need to wrestle with the imponderables as long as one could expose and at the same time secretly understand and sympathize with a society devoted to externals. Anderson could not accept the naturalistic helplessness of Dreiser's people even though the evidence overwhelmingly indicated that Dreiser was right, and Anderson's people exhibited the same symptoms. Not could he be satisfied with the indictment of a system as was Lewis. Instead he sought in his own way to find permanent answers, even after he accepted the impossibility of finding those answers and had to settle for the meaning inherent in the search and in love and compassion for his people.

In spirit Anderson is close to the poets Masters and Lindsay. Not only is the basic structural pattern of Masters' *Spoon River Anthology* close to *Winesburg, Ohio*, but both works penetrate below surface appearance to reveal the essence of repressed humanity; an approach that became

Anderson's most effective technique. Masters, however, is protesting against the system in the *Anthology*; in *Winesburg* and the other subsurface examinations, Anderson regrets the shortcomings inherent in human nature that prevent deep understanding.

The relationship between Lindsay and Anderson is closest of all because these two, more than any of the others, sought to go beyond protest and condemnation and to find new and enduring values upon which to build a humanized society. Both of them sought a faith that was essentially spiritual and idealistic, although Lindsay, especially in his early years, was primarily concerned with a faith firmly rooted in religion, while Anderson rejected such values in favor of a secular, although no less mystic, faith. Both of them moved beyond rejection and rebellion and into a final and positive affirmation.

In moving beyond rebellion Anderson became most clearly an idealist and a romantic. He believed firmly that a life based upon compassion, love, and understanding could be found somewhere; and he sought it in the past, and in the towns, where man could live communally and close to nature at the same time, finding strength and mutual fulfillment in the process of living.

This is the Sherwood Anderson who is little known and usually misunderstood, and this is the Anderson who did much misunderstanding himself. He was a seeker once he realized that there were no easy answers and put propaganda behind him. In his search for the almost perfect world (he rejected perfection because it is not human) he fused his work and his life, and in so doing moved across both literary and ideological lines so freely that he confused both his contemporaries and himself. Although he considered himself a "modern," he looked back in spirit to a romanticism that freed the individual from his environmental confines. As an artist he attempted to be advanced and experimental, but his most effective style grew out of an old oral tradition.

The confusion and misunderstanding inherent in these contradictions affected both Anderson and his contemporaries to the extent that the idealistic and romantic nature of his work passed almost unnoticed during his lifetime. Instead he was called a realist, a naturalist, a modern, a Freudian, and a Marxist, all of which he was not. To a great extent he must have accepted the titles because he did little or nothing to deny them, and the title of realist that he often applied to himself implies a close adherence to surface phenomena that is merely the point of departure for most of his work.

This misunderstanding has continued to the present. Generally Anderson is still grouped loosely with naturalism and occasionally to the post-World War I Decadents, especially Ezra Pound and T. S. Eliot. However, Anderson's links to these groups are tenuous at best. Not only did he go well beyond naturalism in his search for answers to problems that he saw as essentially spiritual rather than deterministic, but from the beginning of his literary career he rejected the decadence that eventually drove Eliot into the dogmatism of the past in religion and politics as well as literature and Pound into incomprehensibility and authoritarianism. The answers that Anderson sought were no less individual than mystic, and they resolved themselves into a compassion for people rather than theories or systems of any kind.

On the other hand Anderson's affinities to D. H. Lawrence and Ernest Hemingway are quite close. Like Lawrence, with whom Anderson identified himself in the twenties, Anderson was concerned with breaking down the artificial barriers isolating men so that mature and lasting love might become possible, and again like Lawrence, Anderson did not hesitate to use physical love as the outward manifestation of a deeper spiritual love. However, in spite of Anderson's reputation as a daring and shocking writer, he could never bring himself to treat the physical aspects of love with Lawrence's frankness.

The relationship between Anderson and Hemingway is even closer. Not only did Anderson's literary style inspire Hemingway and through Hemingway an entire generation of American writers, but also the thematic ties between them are quite close. Essentially both of them are idealistic romantics whose people, hurt spiritually by a hostile world, have embarked on a search for meaning in spite of the fact that apparently there is none. Eventually both of them point out in their works that the end of the search is not important; that what matters is the way in which the search is carried out. This is the position that Anderson approached as early as in *Horses and Men*, while Hemingway arrived there much later in *For Whom The Bell Tolls*. For each it came after a period of flirtation with despair.

After Anderson's idealism had rid itself of anger and indignation when he began his search for permanent values through his association with the Chicago renaissance, his search for the values that he could adopt and affirm led him to focus on people, on the individual human lives that make up the generality "America" that had been celebrated by others such as Carl Sandburg. In so doing Anderson found himself in the difficult position of trying to find abstract principles through examination of individual human lives. That he was never able to find those principles not only emphasizes the difficulty of the task, but more importantly, it provides the most enduring of his works—those in which he penetrates for a brief but revealing moment into the heart of another human being.

The durable qualities of Anderson's work lie in the closeness and persistence with which he came to grips with his purpose, and they lie in the subject matter, the techniques, and the spirit that he combined to give form to his theme. The experience that he chose for treatment in his work is the record of America as it moved from idealistic youth into cynical and selfish maturity. The loss of innocence concurrent with the rise of industrialism has had no more effective and conscientious chronicler. Furthermore, the people with whom he is always concerned are people who, still possessed of that innocence, find themselves lost in a society that no longer values either it or them. Anderson's portrayal, as he brings them alive, is honest, compassionate, and effective.

The durability of the style that Anderson made his own in *Winesburg, Ohio* and gave freely to the mainstream of American literature is unquestioned. As long as the American idioms are spoken in the easy rhythms radiating from the Midwestern heartland, Anderson's style will be recognized, understood, and appreciated by the people who gave rise to it, no matter what the current critical preference may be. In style more than anywhere else, Anderson has come close to reproducing and interpreting a vital part of the American experience.

The spirit of Anderson's work is the spirit of life, and this, too, will endure. The wonder of human life, a compassionate regard for it, and a compelling sense of discovering significance in the commonplace permeate his works, giving rise to a lyric beauty even in despair. Love, compassion, sympathy, and understanding are the human virtues that raise man above his animal origins and prevent him from being a machine, Anderson points out, while his faith in those virtues dominates his work. Life is not only the great adventure for Anderson; in the final analysis it is the universal value.

In an age that denies the values Anderson believed in even more emphatically than did his own, Anderson's place among the journalists and the sensationalists is smaller than it should be; and because of his shortcomings as a literary artist it will probably remain small in the over-all range of literary history. However, as a man who approached life with reverence, who spoke of it with love, and who provided some of the most eloquent expressions of both in his time, his place is secure.

# "Winesburg, Ohio
# As a Dance of Death"

David Stouck*

Sherwood Anderson's implied purpose in *Winesburg, Ohio* is "to express something" for his characters, to release them from their frustration and loneliness through his art. This motive is revealed in the prayer of Elizabeth Willard (mother of the nascent artist George Willard), who, sensing the approach of her death, says: "I will take any blow that may befall if but this my boy be allowed to express something for us both" (p. 40).[1] The view of art, however, in this book does not suggest the fulfillment of that prayer. Artists, like the old man in the introductory sketch and like Enoch Robinson in "Loneliness," are among those least capable of expressing themselves to others, either in their life gestures or in their art. The old man in "The Book of the Grotesque" is a pathetic figure preoccupied with fantasies about his failing health. He has a vision of people in a procession and a theory about the "truths" that make them grotesques; but he does not publish the book he is writing about these people, for he realizes it would represent only *his* truth about them, that it is not possible to express the truth for someone else. Enoch Robinson, the pathologically shy painter, tries to reach out to others through his work, but his paintings fail to make even his fellow artists experience what he has thought and felt.

The central insight in the book concerning human relationships is that each man lives according to his own "truth" and that no one can understand and express fully that truth for someone else. Or, put another way, every human being in this world is ultimately alone. In desperate reaction to this vision Elizabeth Willard, near the end of her life, seeks out death as her companion:

> The sick woman spent the last few months of her life hungering for death. Along the road of death she went, seeking, hungering. She personified the figure of death and made him now a strong black-haired youth running over hills, now a stern quiet man marked and scarred by the business of living.

*Originally published in *American Literature*, 48 (January, 1977), pp. 525–42. Copyright © 1977 by Duke University Press. Reprinted by permission of Duke University Press and David Stouck.

> In the darkness of her room she put out her hand, thrusting it from under the covers of her bed, and she thought that death like a living thing put out his hand to her. "Be patient, lover," she whispered. "Keep yourself young and beautiful and be patient." (p. 228)

In this one vivid paragraph are telescoped many of the book's central concerns: the suffering mother, frustration and loneliness, life as unending movement, the search for love, and the power of death. Describing death as Elizabeth Willard's lover, Anderson suggests not only a central theme but perhaps a principle of structure in his book—namely, the medieval concept of life as a Dance of Death.

# I

Anyone familiar with Anderson's writing is aware of the frequency of the word death in his titles. In *Winesburg, Ohio* "Death" is the title of a key sequence concerning Elizabeth Willard. "Death in the Woods" is the title of one of Anderson's most accomplished short stories and was made the title of a collection of stories published in 1933. One of the best stories in that collection is titled "Brother Death," a story of a boy who must die young but who, unlike his older brother, never has to part with his imagination. "Death" and "A Dying Poet" are two of the titles in *A New Testament* and "Death on a Winter Day" is a chapter title from *No Swank*. In the *Sherwood Anderson Reader* we find a magazine piece titled "A Dead Dog" and a sequence from the unedited memoirs published as "The Death of Bill Graves." The suggestion in these titles that Anderson was more than casually preoccupied with the theme of death is quickly borne out by an examination of his novels, stories, and memoirs.

In almost every book Anderson published the death of a beloved character is of crucial significance and casts the protagonist's life in a wholly different perspective. And on a more philosophical level Anderson saw modern man, alienated from creativity by mechanized factory work and by a repressive Puritan ethic, caught up in a form of living death. These two forms of death—the death of an individual and the death of a society—correspond to the distinction in late medieval art between a dance of Death and the dance of the dead. Holbein's *Dance of Death*, artistically the most sophisticated expression of this theme, depicts Death claiming various individuals and leading them away singly from this life. The more popular representations, such as the relief on the cemetery at Basel, depicted the dead either in a procession or dancing with the living. One of the popular beliefs associated with the Dance of Death was that the dead appeared to warn the living of their fate.[2] Such images and themes, as will be shown, were a part of Anderson's imagination throughout his career as a writer.

The death of Sherwood Anderson's mother when the author was

eighteen likely determined, more than any other experience, the persistent preoccupation with death in his fiction. The mother's death is recorded several times in Anderson's writings, in both semiautobiographical and fictional form. For some of Anderson's protagonists the death of the mother changes radically the course of their lives and initiates an unending quest to find a home and a place in the world. In *Windy McPherson's Son* Sam's mother dies when the hero is still a youth and he seeks in the motherly Mary Underwood someone to fill that role. His later attachments to women follow the same pattern. When he marries Sue Rainey he envisions a whole family of children, for he wants himself to be part of a family with Sue mother to them all. Because Sue cannot give birth to living children, the marriage fails for a long time, and Sam becomes an alcoholic, guilt-ridden over the deaths of motherly women he has known. Only after he has found three children to adopt does he go back and resume his life with Sue. In the more ideological novel *Marching Men*, the death of Beaut McGregor's mother has a similar profound effect on the course of the protagonist's life. The death of Beaut's mother is imaged as a Dance of Death in the manner of Holbein. Death personified comes unexpectedly one night up the stairs to the old woman's room, sits grim and expectant at the foot of the bed and carries the old woman away before morning. Grief stricken over the death of this humble and obscure figure, McGregor dedicates himself to a vision of mankind's purposeful march toward perfection, a march that will give the anonymous lives of people like his mother order and meaning.

In more directly autobiographical writings the mother's death initiates the youth into the world of experience and awakens him to his own mortality. In *A Story-Teller's Story* it is an experience of profound alienation for the boy; Anderson writes "for us there could be no home now that mother was not there."[3] Similarly in *Winesburg, Ohio* it occasions George Willard's departure from the town in which he has grown up. In *Tar: A Midwest Childhood* the mother's death spells the end of childhood and innocence. The day after his mother's funeral, Tar crawls inside a box car on a railroad siding and for the first time in his life thinks about his own death—what it would be like to be buried under a load of grain. When later he hurries up the street, forcing himself to take up his paper route again, we are told in the book's closing lines that although he did not know it he was "racing away out of his childhood."[4] In each instance the mother's death awakens the hero to the mortal view of existence and raises the difficult question of life's meaning and purpose.

Adult life in Anderson's fiction is repeatedly imaged as processional movement along a road. In *Marching Men* mankind is represented as shuffling in disorderly fashion toward death. Beaut McGregor's vision is that the procession will become orderly and dignified when men cease to serve the ambitions of individual leaders and march for the betterment of human kind. All of Anderson's writing is remarkable for its sensitivity to movement as a characteristic mark of American life. In *Poor White* it is the rapid change of America from a rural to an industrial nation; swarms of men, like the sky full of moving, agitated clouds, are seen moving from the prairies into the cities. The young, optimistic spirit of the country, we are told, made it "take hold of the hand of the giant, industrialism, and lead him laughing into the land."[5] But in *Many Marriages* those people working in factories, living side by side without communicating to each other, are represented collectively as a city of the living dead. When John Webster decides to leave his business and his timid, repressed wife, he feels he has come back from the dead. By contrast other people in the novel are imaged as moving steadily toward the throne of Death, who is also described as the god of denial. Death is personified as a general with an army made up not of the physical dead but of the living dead.

> Death had many strange tricks to play on people too. Sometimes he let their bodies live for a long time while he satisfied himself with merely clamping the lid down on the well within. It was as though he had said, "Well, there is no great hurry about physical death. That will come as an inevitable thing in its time. There is a much more ironic and subtle game to be played against my opponent Life. I will fill the cities with the damp fetid smell of death while the very dead think they are still alive . . . I am like a great general, having always at his command, ready to spring to arms at the least sign from himself, a vast army of men.[6]

Anderson sees America made up of lonely, frustrated individuals who cannot communicate with each other and who form a procession of the living dead. The same image occurs in *The Triumph of The Egg* in the long story "Out of Nowhere into Nothing." The heroine, Rosalind Wescott, returns from Chicago to her home town to find that her people "in spirit were dead, had accepted death, believed only in death" (p. 266).[7] The whole town, she feels, lies in the shadow of death: her mother, whose face appears death-like, sits like "a dead thing in the chair" (p. 248); and Rosalind feels she must herself run away "if she doesn't want death to overtake her and live within her while her body is still alive" (p. 185).

In *Dark Laughter*, Anderson's most Lawrentian novel, life is imaged as a dance. For the central character, Bruce Dudley, the image functions initially to suggest life's energy and potential rhythms ("Dance life . . . Pretty soon you'll be dead and then maybe there'll be no laughs"[8]), but the image acquires a darker dimension when Dudley thinks of his dead mother as having been "part of the movement of the grotesque dance of life" (p. 90).

As far as I know Anderson never referred to *Winesburg, Ohio* as incorporating the Dance of Death idea. The different images, however, fall together suggestively—life as a procession, life as a dance, life as a living form of death. He did frequently personify death in his writings, including in *A Story-Teller's Story* a traditional image of Death, the Grim Reaper, coming for the author (p. 404), and in the *Notebooks* an image of himself old and dying and listening to "the sound of the tramping of many feet."[9] Moreover, we do know that he conceived of the frustrated and defeated characters in his early stories as among the living dead. In a letter to M. D. Finley, December 2, 1916 (the period in which he was composing the Winesburg stories), he says:

> Men's fears are stories with which they build the wall of death. They die behind the wall and we do not know they are dead. With terrible labour I arouse myself and climb over my own wall. As far as I can see are the little walls and the men and women fallen on the ground, deformed and ill. Many are dying. The air is heavy with the stench of those who have already died.[10]

The same idea appears in *A New Testament* in "The Story Teller" where Anderson describes his tales as people dying from cold and hunger, while in his memoirs he says that dead people, such as his mother, would return to him in dreams and he concluded they wanted their stories told.[11]

Winesburg, Ohio may not have taken shape directly around the Dance of Death idea, but it was most certainly influenced by a book, Edgar Lee Master's *Spoon River Anthology*, of which the central theme is death. Master's poems were published in book form in the spring of 1915 (the year Anderson probably started writing the Winesburg stories), and we know that Anderson read the book shortly after its publication.[12] He professed a distaste for Masters's poems which critics have explained in the light of Masters's relationship with Anderson's second wife, but it may also reflect a literary debt that Anderson was reluctant to acknowledge.[13] However that may be, there is no denying some fundamental similarities between the two books. Both *Winesburg* and Spoon River depict in episodic fashion a cross-section of life in a small midwestern town. In both books at the deepest level there is an intransigent sense of despair. The Spoon River poems are vignettes of lives lived at cross-purposes, with recognitions after death that life has been wasted and is now forever irrecoverable. Masters's poems incorporate the medieval idea of the dead appearing to warn the living of their inevitable end. The voices of the dead, each one telling a story from the tomb, was a formal design which must surely have influenced Anderson considerably, for we have seen him speak of his Winesburg characters as each walled in by fears and already dead or dying. Anderson's characters are not presented as spirits returned from the dead, and yet in a very important sense that is what they are, for the characters in *Winesburg, Ohio* are people from the narrator's memory of his home town, and many of them, most significantly the mother, are in fact long dead.[14]

But what is particularly suggestive, given the fact that Anderson had seen Masters's book, is that several of Oliver Herford's illustrations for the first edition of *Spoon River Anthology* depicted the Dance of Death in various forms. Death swinging a lariat appears twice and, placed above the first of the poems, serves as a controlling visual motif throughout the collection. Death is also shown in the manner of Holbein leading away a child in one sketch and beckoning to a drunk in another. But two of the illustrations suggest actual situations in the Winesburg stories. One shows Death in bed as a lover and we are reminded of Elizabeth Willard's erotic personification of death in her last days. The other presents Death approaching an older man who has just taken a young wife, and we think of Doctor Reefy, whose young bride is snatched away from him by Death only a few months after the couple are married. Anderson may not have consciously conceived of his stories being arranged like a medieval Dance of Death, but it is hard to believe that the Masters's book with its death theme and design did not influence his imagination at some fundamental level.

## II

In *Winesburg, Ohio* the idea of death does not signify only the grave, but more tragically it denotes the loneliness and frustration of the unlived life. As in *Poor White* we are aware in *Winesburg, Ohio* of movement as characteristic of American life, but here it is the restlessness of the individual who grows increasingly oppressed by his loneliness and his inability to express himself to others. In each story when the character reaches an ultimate point of insupportable frustration or recognizes that he can never escape his isolation, he reacts by waving his hands and arms about, talking excitedly, and finally running away. In a very stylized pattern almost every story brings its character to such a moment of frenzy where he breaks into something like a dance.

The introductory sketch, "The Book of the Grotesque," is either ignored by critics or dismissed as a murky and confusing allegory. That Anderson intended it to carry significant weight in relation to the rest of the book is clear when we remember that "The Book of the Grotesque" was the publication title Anderson first gave to the whole collection of stories. In its oblique and terse fashion the sketch defines the relationship of the artist to his characters. The subject is an old man who is writing a book about all the people he has known. The first thing we notice is that the writer is preoccupied with fantasies about his failing health. When he goes to bed each night he thinks about his possible death, yet paradoxically that makes him feel more alive than at other times; thoughts of death heighten his awareness to things. In this state the old writer has a waking dream in which all the people he has known are being driven in a long procession before his eyes. They appear to the writer as "grotesques," for each of these characters has lived according to a personal truth which has cut him off from the others. These are the characters of Anderson's book. The procession they form is like a dance of the dead, for as mentioned above most of these people from Anderson's childhood are now dead. The youth in the coat of mail leading the people is the writer's imagination and also his death consciousness—his memory of the past and his awareness that loneliness and death are the essential "truths" of the human condition. We are told in this sketch that the old carpenter, who comes to adjust the height of the writer's bed and who instead weeps over a brother who dies of starvation in the Civil War, is one of the most lovable of all the grotesques in the writer's book. Just such a character apparently befriended Anderson's lonely mother in Clyde, Ohio;[15] this detail indicates both the personal and the elegiac nature of the book.

The first story, "Hands," tells about Wing Biddlebaum whose unfulfilled life typifies the other life stories recounted in the book. From his little house on the edge of town Wing can watch life pass by: ". . . he could see the public highway along which went a wagon filled with berry pickers returning from the fields. The berry pickers, youths and maidens, laughed and shouted boisterously. A boy clad in a blue shirt leaped from the wagon and attempted to drag after him one of the maidens, who screamed and protested shrilly. The feet of the boy in the road kicked up a cloud of dust that floated across the face of the departing sun" (p. 27). With its archetypal images of the public highway, youths and maidens, the berry harvest, and the cosmic image of the sun, the scene Anderson has created is a tableau depicting the dance of life. By contrast Wing Biddlebaum ventures only as far as the edge of the road, then hurries back again to his little house. He lives in the shadows of the town. Yet, like the berry pickers, his figure is always in motion, walking nervously up and down his half decayed verandah. His hands especially are always moving and are compared to the beating wings of an imprisoned bird. In *Tar* Anderson tells us that likely "the memory of his mother's hands made him think so much about other people's hands" (p. 276), again creating a link between his fictional characters and dead mother. Wing's story of being accused of perverted love for the boys he teaches ends in his flight from a small Ohio town. The newspaper reporter George Willard, persona for the young Anderson, listens sympathetically to Wing as he tries to describe his pastoral dream of living like the classical teacher Socrates; but his hands, caressing George Willard, betray him and he runs away to resume his endless pacing in the shadows of his old house.

Several of the stories follow the basic pattern of "Hands": a misfit in the town is telling George something of his story but cannot express himself completely; he begins to wave his hands about helplessly and breaks into a run. In "Drink" Tom Foster, a gentle, passive boy, is described as living "in the shadow of the wall of life." Like Wing Biddlebaum he watches the parade of life pass him by. But he conceives an affection for the banker's daughter Helen White, and one spring night he goes for a long walk and gets drunk on a bottle of whiskey. He becomes a grotesque figure moving along the road: "his head seemed to be flying about like a pinwheel and then projecting itself off into space and his arms and legs flopped helplessly about" (p. 218). He tries to tell George Willard that he has made love to Helen White, but the reporter won't listen because he too loves the banker's daughter. They take a long walk in the dark. Tom raises his voice to an excited pitch to explain that he wants to suffer because "everyone suffers," but George does not understand him.

In the story " 'Queer' " George does not get an opportunity to understand. Elmer Cowley, oppressed by his sense of being different from everyone else, resolves that he will be like other people. He goes on a long walk in the country where he encounters the half-wit named Mook. Walking up and down and waving his arms about, he tells Mook that he won't be queer any longer, and then goes on to tell of his resolution to George Willard, whom he sees as typifying the town and representing public opinion. They go on a walk together but Elmer cannot explain himself to the reporter: "He tried to talk and his arms began to pump up and down. His face worked spasmodically. He seemed about to shout" (p. 198). Having failed to communicate to anyone, he decides to run away from the town, but as he is leaving on the train he calls George Willard down to the station to try once again to explain. Still speechless he breaks into a grotesque dance: "Elmer Cowley danced with fury beside the groaning train. . . . With a snarl of rage he turned and his long arms began to flay the air. Like one struggling for release from hands that held him he struck out, hitting George Willard blow after blow on the breast, the neck, the mouth" (pp. 200–201).

George is similarly struck at by the school teacher, Kate Swift. Like so many of the characters in the book Kate takes long walks alone at night; one night she walks for six hours. In the eyes of the town she is a conventional old maid, but inside, her passionate nature yearns for companionship and for significant achievements. She half loves George Willard, her former pupil, and in her desire to see his genius flower, she goes to the office of the newspaper to talk to him. Like George's mother she wants him to be a serious writer and to express something for the people of the town. But confused by her love for the boy, she cannot express herself adequately and winds up beating him on the face with her fists, and then running out into the darkness. That same night the Reverend Curtis Hartman, who for weeks has paced the streets at night imploring God to keep him from his sinful habit of peeping into Kate Swift's bedroom window, bursts into the office of the Winesburg *Eagle* "shaking a bleeding fist into the air" as an emblem of his triumph. He has broken the church study window through which he had "peeped," so that now it will be repaired and he will no longer be able to indulge in his sin. Over and over inarticulate characters in a moment of passion wave their hands in the air and burst into a run.

Two of the stories present a macabre vision of life's "truth." In "The Philosopher" Doctor Parcival tells George Willard about his childhood, but when he reaches the point of telling about his father's death in an insane asylum, he breaks off and paces distractedly about the newspaper office. Doctor Parcival is another of the book's failed artists; he is writing a book and his sole vision is that life is a form of crucifixion, a long torture and dying as it was for Christ on the cross. "Respectability," the story of the cuckold Wash Williams, also involves a vision of living death. In reaction to his wife's faithlessness Williams holds the idea that all women are corrupt and dead.

Wash Williams is perhaps most remarkable for his hideous physical appearance. He is compared to "a huge, grotesque kind of monkey, a creature with ugly, sagging, hairless skin below his eyes and a bright purple underbody" (p. 121). Everything about Wash, including the whites of his eyes, looks unclean, everything except his hands which in striking contrast are well cared for. There is a medieval grotesqueness in the description of several of the characters; as in medieval art, the twisted inner nature of the people is manifested in imperfections and distortions of the physical body. Doctor Reefy in "Paper Pills" has a huge nose and hands; the knuckles of his hands are "like clusters of unpainted wooden balls as large as walnuts fastened together by steel rods" (p. 35). This stylized image of the doctor's physical body anticipates the description of his character as being like the sweetness of the gnarled apples left on the trees in autumn, and the image of the little balls of paper on which he has written a number of truths. Some of the characters are almost like gargoyles on medieval buildings. Doctor Parcival, who believes all men are crucified, has a yellowed mustache, black irregular teeth, and a left eye that twitches, snapping up and down like a window shade. Elmer Cowley's father has a large wen on his scrawny neck; he still wears his wedding coat which is brown with age and covered with grease spots. Elmer too is grotesque in appearance; extraordinarily tall, he has pale blond almost white hair, eyebrows, and beard, teeth that protrude, and eyes that are the colorless blue of marbles. Characteristically many of the physical portraits focus on hands. The hands of Tom Willy, the saloon keeper, are streaked with a flaming red birthmark, as if the hands had been dipped in blood and that dried and faded. Tom Foster's grandmother has hands all twisted out of shape from hard work. When she holds a mop or broom handle they look like "the dried stems of an old creeping vine clinging to a tree" (p. 211). There are two half-wits in Winesburg as well: Turk Smollet, the old wood-chopper, who talks and laughs to himself as he passes regularly through the village and Mook, the farm hand, who holds long involved conversations with the animals. Perhaps it is not accidental that George Willard thinks of the Middle Ages one night when he is walking through the town, and that the first word that comes to his lips when he looks up at the sky is "Death" (p. 184).

In some of the stories George Willard does not appear except of course as implied narrator; the characters nevertheless are pictured as breaking into a run or dance at peak moments of frustration or loneliness. Jesse Bentley in "Godliness," who has a vision of being a Biblical patriarch, runs through the night imploring God to send him a son; years later when he takes his grandson to sacrifice a lamb, hoping God will send him a visible sign of His blessing, the scene ends with the flight of the grandson from Winesburg. In "Adventure" Alice Hindman, who has been waiting for years for the return of her lover, one night runs out naked onto the lawn in the rain. In the story of the two farm hands, entitled "The Untold Lie," the moment of truth brings Ray Pearson to run across the field to save his friend, Hal Winters, from marriage.[16] Repeatedly the most vivid images in the book are those of characters in grotesque or violent motion: Louise Bentley, the estranged daughter of the Biblical patriarch, driving her horse and carriage at breakneck speed through the streets of Winesburg; Jesse Bentley's drunken brothers driving along the road and shouting at the stars; Enoch Robinson described as "an obscure, jerky little figure bobbing up and down the streets when the sun was going down" (p. 173); Hal Winter's father, Windpeter Winters, drunk and driving his team along the railroad tracks directly into the path of an onrushing locomotive. Such images seem to have coalesced to form a grotesque procession in the writer's memory.

The procession becomes a Dance of Death when the writer comes to recognize his own mortality. The death of his mother awakens George Willard to both the brevity and the loneliness of human existence. Elizabeth Willard, perhaps more than any of the other characters, seeks some kind of release from her perpetual loneliness. As a young woman she had been "stage-struck" and, wearing loud clothes, paraded the streets with traveling men from her father's hotel. Like the other grotesques her desire to escape loneliness is expressed in movement. Once she startled the townspeople by wearing men's clothes and riding a bicycle down the main street. After she married and still found no communion with another human being, she drove her horse and buggy at a terrible speed through the country until she met with an accident. (The image of a woman hurt in an accident or disfigured in some way recurs several times to the eyes of the artist figures in the book: one of Enoch Robinson's paintings depicts a woman who has been thrown from a horse and has been hurt [p. 170], while the old writer in the introduction is crying over "a woman all drawn out of shape" [p. 23].) Eventually when her long illness comes we are told that Elizabeth went along the road seeking for death: "She personified the figure of death and made him now a strong black-haired youth running over hills, now a stern quiet man marked and scarred by the business of living" (p. 228). As a young woman she had taken several lovers before she married; now her lover is Death.

"Sophistication," the penultimate chapter, is shaped around George's growing awareness of life as a procession or dance toward death. In the background is the Winesburg County Fair: people are moving up and down the streets and fiddlers sweat "to keep the feet of youth flying over a dance floor." But in spite of the crowds George Willard feels lonely; he wants someone to understand the feeling that has possessed him since his mother's death. Significantly we are told that "memories awoke in him" and that he is becoming conscious of life's limitations. The narrator, reflecting on youth, generalizes: "There is a time in the life of every boy when he for the first time takes the backward view of life. . . . If he be an imaginative boy a door is torn open and for the first time he looks out upon the world, seeing, as though they marched in procession before him, the countless figures of men who before his time have come out of nothingness into the world, lived their lives and again disappeared into nothingness" (p. 234). At this point George sees his own place "in the long march of humanity. Already he hears death calling" (pp. 234–235). And in the last chapter he joins the procession when he leaves on the train, and Winesburg becomes a "background on which to paint the dreams of his manhood."

## III

Twenty years after the Winesburg stories were written, Sherwood Anderson created a drama out of his famous collection of stories. *Winesburg, Ohio: A Play*[17] focuses more squarely on the figure of George Willard and the events, particularly the death of his mother, that precipitate his growth into manhood and nurture his desire to become a writer. The death theme running through the stories also stands out more boldly in the play. Nine scenes comprise the play and the first scene is set, like a Spoon River poem, in the Winesburg cemetery on the day of Windpeter Winters's funeral. The Winesburg people are seen formed in a procession and their conversation inevitably turns to the macabre. The young people, by contrast, create a dance of life; despite the sobriety of the occasion, they tease and jostle one another as the irrepressible life instinct demands expression. One of the sub-plots in the play involves Belle Carpenter, who has become pregnant and who goes to Doctor Reefy in Scene two to ask for an abortion. Reefy counsels against this request and says to Belle "there are always two roads—the road of life and the road of death" (p. 30). This image describes the two main narrative threads in the play: in the foreground is George's involvement with three different women in Winesburg and his sexual awakening, while in the background Elizabeth Willard makes elaborate preparations to die. Her death, as in the stories, precipitates George's departure from Winesburg, but the road of life he sets out on is also the road of death, for Elizabeth Willard, in prayer, has made her promise to come back from the dead if she sees her son becoming "a meaningless, drab figure." The fulfillment of that prayer eventually places George on the road back to Winesburg.

In his later books as well Sherwood Anderson continued to use the

Dance of Death motif as a measure of life's brevity and misdirection. When Red Oliver, the principal character in the novel *Beyond Desire*, is about to be killed for his peripheral involvement in a strike, a dancing death figure appears in the form of a limping stationer who exhorts the soldiers to shoot the communist leaders of the strike.

> The little stationer of Birchfield, the man with the bad feet had followed the soldiers to the bridge. He had come limping along the road. Red Oliver saw him. He was dancing in the road beyond the soldiers. He was excited, filled with hatred. He danced in the road, throwing his arms above his head. He clenched his fists. "Shoot. Shoot. Shoot. Shoot the son-of-a-bitch." The road sloped down sharply to the bridge. Red Oliver could see the little figure above the heads of the soldiers. It seemed dancing in the air over their heads.[18]

Just before the fatal shot is fired we are told that Red "saw the absurd little stationer dancing in the road beyond the soldier" and that he asked himself whether the little man "represented something" (p. 355). Anderson seems to be asking the reader at this point to give the figure thoughtful consideration. The image is reminiscent of such Winesburg figures as Elmer Cowley and Wing Biddlebaum who claw at the air with their hands and dance about in a hopeless effort to communicate with other people. The stationer in *Beyond Desire* is an emblem of countless repressed twentieth century men who find an outlet for their frustrations in violent mob action.

Anderson himself used the term "dance of death" when he was writing his *Memoirs*. In that posthumous volume he registered his horror at the spectacle of World War II in an entry entitled "The Dance Is On."[19] He begins, "It's a crazy dance of death now" referring to the war, but he quickly extends the image to include all the mechanical, dehumanizing forces of the modern industrial world. Anderson did not believe that modern industry was in itself negative. In *Beyond Desire* and his last novel, *Kit Brandon*, he describes the cotton mills as dancing with life, and in this entry from the *Memoirs* he points to a cloth mill and says "here is a gay dance, a purposeful dance. See the many colored cloth rolling out of the flying machines in the cloth mills." But he also saw a "monster" latent in the industrial process, an uncontrollable appetite for production and profit without reference to the needs of the human community. The monster's consuming, destructive power is imaged by Anderson in a sequence titled "Loom Dance" in *Perhaps Women* where a group of factory girls working at the loom are stricken with choreomania; they become mindless robots of production unable to stop their movements. The question Anderson puts in his *Memoirs* is "Can the dance be made, not a dance of death, but of joy and new life?" He equates the dance of life with man's ability to reach out and communicate with his fellow man: "Can men come out of their selves to others?" Although Anderson despairs at the world around him, he believes that "men never intended it to be the dance of death," rather "dreamed of making it a great new dance of life." Similarly Anderson in his epitaph insisted that "Life not Death is the great adventure."

But the question still to be asked is what is gained by viewing *Winesburg, Ohio* in the light of the recurrent death imagery in Anderson's writing. Most obviously it directs us to something dark and pessimistic in the book that recent critics, unlikely the early reviewers, have either ignored or explained away.[20] In a period of rapid economic growth and expansion, Anderson was drawing attention to the tragedy of those people, like his own parents, who did not succeed, and who were alienated from each other by economic failure and by the repressive American Puritan ethic. Seeing the lives of such people as a form of living death underscores the social tragedy that the book presents, and also suggests a continuity between Anderson's early writing and those later books and stories such as *Many Marriages* and "Out of Nowhere into Nothing" where he envisions America as a land of the dead. As a Dance of Death *Winesburg, Ohio* functions as social satire to warn the living of what is happening to their lives.

The Dance of Death idea is most closely associated with the mother figure and directs us to a personal tragedy implicit in the book—the narrator's sense of filial guilt. While she lived, Elizabeth Willard and her son seldom spoke to each other; before her death Elizabeth prayed that her son would some day "express something" for them both. But the artist's central insight in the book is that all truth is relative to the individual, so that he cannot really express anything for his characters—he can only hint at their secret, repressed lives. Ironically, in attempting to give dignity to the lives of his people, the narrator has made them grotesques, and like the old writer in the introduction must be left to whimper like a small dog at the "woman drawn all out of shape" (p. 23). At best the narrator, like the author of the *Spoon River Anthology*, has erected out of love a series of tombstones for the people he once knew. The Dance of Death perspective functions then as a framework around the book reminding us that these characters are now gone, and that they were never released from the agony of their loneliness while they lived. This tragic personal emotion is described by the narrator in "Sophistication" when he says: "One shudders at the thought of the meaninglessness of life while at the same instance, and if the people of his town are his people, one loves life so intensely that tears come into the eyes" (p. 241).

The narrator's sympathy and love for his people makes more poignant the failure of art to expiate his filial guilt. Anderson had dedicated the book as an expression of love to his mother; we cannot help feeling that it has come too late. But this of course does not mean that *Winesburg, Ohio* fails as a work of art. On the contrary, seeing the book as a Dance of Death further testifies to its richness of pattern and form. The medieval Dance of Death was a highly ritualized art and it is that quality of stylized repetition which is most striking formally in Anderson's book. To see *Winesburg, Ohio* as a Dance of Death is not only to underscore rightly its essentially tragic nature, but also to recognize its considerable artistry and to recognize that this modernist work does belong to an ancient and venerable tradition.

## Notes

1. This and subsequent page references to *Winesburg, Ohio* are to the "Compass Book" edition (New York, 1960).

2. For a comprehensive treatment of the historical origins of the Dance of Death see James M. Clark, *The Dance of Death in the Middle Ages and the Renaissance* (Glasgow, 1950).

3. *A Story-Teller's Story* (New York, 1924), p. 127.

4. *Tar: A Midwest Childhood* (New York, 1930), p. 346. All references are to the same text.

5. *Poor White* in *The Portable Sherwood Anderson*, ed. Horace Gregory (New York, 1949), p. 162.

6. *Many Marriages* (New York, 1923), p. 217.

7. *The Triumph of the Egg* (New York, 1921). All references are to this text.

8. *Dark Laughter* (New York, 1925), p. 68. All references are to this text.

9. *Sherwood Anderson's Notebooks* (New York, 1926), p. 22.

10. See William A. Sutton, *The Road to Winesburg* (Metuchen, N.J., 1972), pp. 446–447.

11. See *Sherwood Anderson's Memoirs: A Critical Edition*, edited by Ray Lewis White (Chapel Hill, 1969), pp. 524–526.

12. See William L. Phillips's article "How Sherwood Anderson Wrote *Winesburg, Ohio*" in *The Achievement of Sherwood Anderson: Essays in Criticism*, ed. Ray Lewis White (Chapel Hill, 1966), pp. 71–72.

13. See Sutton, pp. 299–300. Anderson's second wife, Tennessee Mitchell, had been the poet's mistress and this may have prompted Anderson's dislike of the book. But Anderson seems to have encouraged the myth that his stories were appearing in print before Masters's poems. This is demonstrably untrue and suggests Anderson was concerned about the question of originality.

14. Typically Anderson gave two different accounts about the source of his Winesburg characters. At one point in his memoirs he says that the tales came "out of some memory or impression got from boyhood in a small town," but only a couple of pages further he claims that the characters were portraits done of his fellow boarders in a cheap Chicago rooming house on Cass Street. See *Sherwood Anderson's Memoirs: A Critical Edition*, pp. 346–348. Probably both accounts are true, but certainly figures like the mother, Doctor Reefy and the old carpenter are from Clyde, Ohio. See also William L. Phillips, "How Sherwood Anderson Wrote *Winesburg, Ohio*," pp. 69–74.

15. See *Tar: A Midwest Childhood*, pp. 71, 85.

16. Anderson told his son in a letter that "The Untold Lie" was inspired by the memory of sitting on a train once and seeing a man run across a field. *Letters of Sherwood Anderson*, selected and edited with an introduction and notes by Howard Mumford Jones and Walter B. Rideout (Boston, 1953), p. 357.

17. *Plays: Winesburg and Others* (New York, 1937). All references are to this text.

18. *Beyond Desire* (New York, 1961), p. 354. All references are to this text.

19. "The Dance Is On," *Sherwood Anderson's Memoirs: A Critical Edition*, pp. 552–553.

20. For example, in his introduction to the 1960 "Compass Book" edition Malcolm Cowley concludes that "*Winesburg, Ohio* is far from the pessimistic or destructive or morbidly sexual work it was once attacked for being. Instead it is a work of love, an attempt to break down the walls that divide one person from another, and also in its own fashion, a celebration of small-town life in the lost days of good will and innocence." And in his article "*Winesburg, Ohio*: Art and Isolation." *Modern Fiction Studies*, VI (Summer, 1960), 106–114, Edwin Fussell sees the loneliness and frustration of the characters being dissolved by the future art of George Willard, who will give these people a voice.

# "Earth-Mothers, Succubi, and Other Ectoplasmic Spirits: The Women in Sherwood Anderson's Short Stories"

William V. Miller*

Herbert Gold was not the first to note the limitations of Sherwood Anderson's characterization of women, but his statement offers a starting point for more definitive observations about women in his short fiction: "Except for the poetic school teacher and a few others, women are not women in Anderson's stories. . . . For Anderson women have a strange holy power; they are earthmothers, ectoplasmic spirits, sometimes succubi, rarely individual living creatures."[1] Lionel Trilling contended that *all* of Anderson's characters tend to "vanish into the vast limbo of meaningless life" because, unlike D. H. Lawrence whose themes fed Anderson's imagination in the early 1920s, Anderson failed to provide for his characters the kind of palpable milieu which is necessary for full character realization.[2] Indeed, there are no characters in Anderson's fiction who attain the kind of realization that transcends particular stories, but many of his characters impress us as being real because we accept their psychological reality. However, Anderson's women are peculiarly circumscribed in their development, and the patterns of their characterization reflect both the expressive basis of Anderson's art and his narrow vision of womanhood.

Because the novels (excluding the hybrid *Winesburg, Ohio*) are considered only indirectly in this study, there may be dimensions of Anderson's characterization that are neglected. However, the short stories are universally regarded as Anderson's most durable artistic achievements; the body of tales considered here includes seventy-one published stories in addition to the twenty-five in *Winesburg*; and while the broader canvas of the novel encouraged Anderson to dramatize his cultural interests more concretely than those ideas appear in the tales, it would seem that his characterization of women is substantially the same in the two genres.

*Originally published in *MidAmerica I* (East Lansing, Mich.: The Midwestern Press, 1974), pp. 64–81. Reprinted by permission of the Society for the Study of Midwestern Literature and William V. Miller.

The biography of a writer is always important in fully understanding his work. One of the first tasks in approaching Poe is to sweep away the cobwebs and dust of spurious biography in order to confront specific stories and poems; one of the important *later* tasks is to consider that in Poe's life and thought which illuminates his art. Of course, the problem is to discern what biographical evidence is pertinent and how the writer's experience is transmuted into art—in works of fiction as apparently diverse in this respect as those of Flaubert and Thomas Wolfe. Sherwood Anderson's characterization of women reflects persistently and with a minimum of artistic distancing the doubts and frustrations of his own relationships with women, especially with his mother Emma Anderson and his four wives.

Before examining some of those relationships, we need to consider those aspects of Anderson's aesthetic views and practices which bear on his characterization. One useful approach to his aesthetic views is through a comparison of them with certain views of James Joyce, as they are expressed through Stephen Daedelus in *Stephen Hero* and *A Portrait of the Artist as a Young Man*. The narratives of these two masters come in contact directly and indirectly in a number of instances: *Winesburg, Ohio*, like *Portrait*, is an important achievement in the *Kunstlerroman*, an important fictive genre in the late 19th and the early 20th centuries, and like *Dubliners* it is a group of short stories unified in setting and theme; Anderson acknowledged his indebtedness to Joyce, whom he met in Paris in the 1920s, for the stream-of-consciousness technique Anderson employed in *Dark Laughter* (with disastrous results); and many have noted that what Joyce called the "epiphany" technique is very similar to a structural principle which is central in Anderson's story creation.[3]

These parallels invite comparison, but here the concern is only for somewhat isolated aspects of Joyce's art which may help illuminate Anderson's fiction—especially that central crux of *Portrait* criticism—what Joyce's attitude is toward Stephen Daedelus—which bears on Anderson's characterization in a contrasting way. Obviously, Stephen is, in many particulars, James Joyce as a young man; but how does Stephen's creator regard him? The consensus view seems to be that Stephen is treated ironically with disagreement about the target of the irony ranging among critics from those who believe that the irony is aimed at youthful naivete to those like Hugh Kenner and other "Stephen Haters" who argue that Stephen is not an artist but an "egocentric rebel."[4] If, then, Stephen Daedelus tends to be removed by ironic distancing from virtual identity with his creator, whatever the target of the irony might be, it would appear that in the characterization of Stephen, Joyce achieved the kind of dramatic form he sought as an artist.

In *Portrait* Joyce expresses his classification of forms through Stephen's exposition in colloquy with Lynch (which is usually read unironically).

The image, it is clear, must be set between the mind or senses of the artist himself and the mind or senses of others. If you bear this in memory you will see that art necessarily divides itself into three forms progressing from one to the next. These forms are: the lyrical form, the form wherein the artist presents his image in immediate relation to himself; the epical form, the form wherein he presents his image in mediate relation to himself and to others; the dramatic form, the form wherein he presents his image in immediate relation to others. . . .

The personality of the artist, at first a cry or a cadence or a mood and then a fluid and lambent narrative, finally refines itself out of existence, impersonalises itself, so to speak. The esthetic image in the dramatic form is life purified in and reprojected from the human imagination. The mystery of esthetic like that of material creation is accomplished. The artist, like the God of the creation, remains within or behind or beyond or above his handiwork, invisible, refined out of existence, indifferent, paring his fingernails.[5]

There are obviously many more ramifications of these aesthetic statements than we can pursue here; but we can observe now, as James B. Baker has pointed out, that the classification of forms is presented as a series moving from the lyric to the epic to the dramatic and that the variable is the degree of detachment.[6] Furthermore, Joyce considered the achievement of dramatic form to be the highest level of art. As the following account demonstrates, in theory and in technique Anderson's stories depend not upon detachment, but upon the artist's personality. His aesthetic images can be placed, perhaps, somewhere between the lyric and the epic in Joyce's scale of detachment.

Lacking Joyce's penetrating, trained intelligence, Anderson never thought systematically. Alfred Kazin observed accurately that Hemingway went beyond Anderson in creating a conscious sense of design.[7] In three major autobiographical books (A Story-Teller's Story, Tar, and Memoirs), in many essays and lectures and in thousands of letters, Anderson talked about his craft; but, again, one finds no "conscious sense of design." However, Anderson's statements about his art are consistent and form a body of views which can be described as expressive, focusing on the poet and his creative act rather than on such matters as the nature of his "imitation" or the psychology of his audience. He had a sense of form, but his notion of it tended to be very subjective and intuitive, concerned less with meters than "the meter-making argument."

Anderson had much to say about the "poison plot" which he felt was corrupting American short stories. What was needed was the kind of story written by Chekhov or Turgenev in which human life was not sacrificed to the trickery and juggling of clever plotting. For Anderson the form of a story should depend neither on plot nor on any Poe-like, mathematical design. Instead, in his theory of form, the personality of the writer was central. To a friend he wrote, "You see, Pearson, I have the belief that, in this matter of form, it is largely a matter of depth of feeling. How deeply do you feel it? Feel it deeply enough and you will be torn inside and driven on until form comes."[8] In this same letter and elsewhere Anderson also stressed the morality of the struggle to achieve form: "I suppose I think that the author who doesn't struggle all his life to achieve this form, let it be form, betrays the morality."[9]

We can understand his moral concern better when we consider what he said about his imagination and the creative process. Many readers of Anderson have noted his remarkable commitment to his imaginative life, which often served him as a therapeutic retreat from too harsh reality. He once wrote, "The life of reality is confused, disorderly, almost without apparent purpose, whereas in the artist's imaginative life there is purpose."[10] Within his imagination lived characters for whom he had an extraordinary sense of obligation. A letter written to a young writer is a fair statement of his moral regard for these characters: "As though I, a writer, had a right to do as I pleased with people carried into an imagined life. The thing never understood was the sacredness of that life, too. The obligation to that life, to my mind is greater than to the characters in what we call real life. . . . [When one betrays a character], it is display of immorality."[11]

Two more aspects of Anderson's theory of the creative process should be stressed here. First, and here he emphasizes a point made with greater precision by T. S. Eliot and by Henry James as well as by Joyce in *Portrait*, Anderson insisted that art comes from the imagination, not life, though the imagination must feed on life; or, to use another of his metaphors, fleeting "seeds" of experience are planted in the imagination where they germinate.[12] A second consideration is that while Anderson highly valued character creation and was intensely loyal to these children of his imagination, fundamentally his characterization was subservient to his themes—not that Anderson sought to illustrate a philosophical idea but that a single idea like Hawthorne's "iron rod" seems to determine the nature of all aspects of a particular short story. He once wrote of the artist's "determination to give the tale, the song, the painting, form—to make it true and real to the theme, not to life."[13] Typically, "theme" meant for Anderson that essential quality of a character or of a relationship.

In light of his theoretical views it is not surprising that for Anderson a short story was "The result of a sudden passion. It is an idea grasped whole as one would pick an apple in an orchard."[14] In a narrow sense this concept and the other theoretical views are not precisely predictive of the techniques of his stories: we find less of Kazin's "sense of design" than we discern in the relationship between Stephen Daedelus' classification of forms and the pattern of Joyce's developing fiction as some Joycean students have seen it. Nevertheless, the techniques and recurring patterns in Anderson's stories are not incongruous with his theory.

Three closely related facets of Anderson's short stories deserve special attention here. The first is the characteristic tone of the stories. What Irving Howe in describing the prevailing tone of *Winesburg, Ohio* called "accents of love" accurately describes Anderson's attitude toward his characters.[15] Whether it is the frustrated father in "The Egg," one of the grotesques in *Winesburg*, or the old couple in "The Corn Planting," nearly all of his characters are regarded compassionately. Even the portraits of venal, life destroying businessmen are not without sympathetic touches—the fat, garrulous advertiser in "Two Lovers" who speaks wistfully of living on a farm is a good example.

The narrative voice in Anderson's stories is the chief means of conveying tone. Whether in first person or third person, Anderson's narrator frequently introduces a character by sketching in the contours of his personality. The following quotation is the narrator's description of David (actually William Faulkner thinly veiled) in "A Meeting South": "He told me the story of his ill fortune—a crack-up in an airplane—with a very gentle manly little smile on his very sensitive, rather thin lips. Such things happened. He might well have been speaking of another. I like his tone and I like him."[16] The narrator is providing necessary information, establishing an evaluation of the character supported by the full narrative and revealing the deeply sympathetic feelings of his own character. We may find the narrative voice—a somewhat groping storyteller in an oral tradition—obtrusive at times or even a convention which untenably shatters the epistemological basis of the narrative (how could he know that?); but in the best stories it is an essential instrument in achieving the vital tone.

Finally, the chief character in Anderson's stories tends to be Anderson himself. The most important character type in the stories is the artist. Not only are the stories filled with painters and writers; but also many of his characters are potential artists, storytellers like May Edgely in "Unused" and the doctor in "A Midnight Walk"; and what may be called the "artistic impulse" is shared by an even larger group of characters. In addition to this repetitive dramatization of his adult role, Anderson drew heavily on his specific adolescent experience in Clyde, Ohio, in some of his best stories. Furthermore, to the presence of Anderson through the narrative voice and chief character types as indicated above, should be added another pattern of autobiographical characterization which appears in the stories. Anderson simply could not achieve what Joyce called dramatic form. Lincoln and Twain were two of his heroes, but in characterizing them he could only recreate them in his own image, restyling the careers of both of these complex men to suggest his own struggles against Philistia. This is not to say that we can precisely equate Anderson even with his sympathetic narrators. But Anderson's informing vision, while often incisive, confines his characterization. Anderson is not the "God of creation . . . invisible, refined out of existence, indifferent, paring his fingernails." His role and art are better described by Stephen Daedelus' comments about epical form: "The simplest epical form is seen emerging out of lyrical literature when the artist prolongs and broods upon himself as the centre of an epical event and this form progresses till the centre of emotional gravity is equidistant from the artist himself and from others. The narrative is no longer personal. The personality of the artist passes into the narration itself, flowing round and round the persons and the actions like a vital sea."[17] Anderson's personality so enfolds his characters: they live momentarily but not out of *his* vital sea.

Such extraordinary women as Gertrude Stein, Margaret Anderson, Mary Emmett, and Laura Lou Copenhaver (Eleanor's mother) all contributed to Anderson's view of women. But closer to Anderson were his mother, Emma, and his four wives: Cornelia Lane, Tennessee Mitchell, Elizabeth Prall, and Eleanor Copenhaver. Of course, we can but name here some of those with whom he had conventional, recorded relationships. Many more, often oblique experiences with women are suggested as well as mentioned directly in his writings.

Anderson's image of his mother expressed both in his fiction and in apparently factual statements is best described as idealized and guilt-ridden. In *A Story Teller's Story* Anderson's description of his mother is a mixture of truth and romance. "Mother was tall and slender and once had been beautiful. She had been a bound girl in a farmer's family when she married father, the improvident young dandy. There was Italian blood in her veins and her origin was something of a mystery. Perhaps we never cared to solve it—wanted it to remain a mystery. It is so wonderfully comforting to think of one's mother as a dark, beautiful and somewhat mysterious woman."[18] We have further his dedication of *Winesburg, Ohio*: "To the memory of my mother, Emma Smith Anderson, whose keen observations on the life about her first awoke in me the hunger to see beneath the surface of lives, the book is dedicated." The most thorough and dependable biographer of Anderson's early life, William Sutton, offers contrasting and qualifying evidence. Emma's mother was German, not Italian and there were apparently no Italian ancestors; the concept of a "bound girl" that Anderson described, for example, in "Death in the Woods," inaccurately describes the affectionate "working-ward" relationship Emma held with the family who kept her from the age of nine until she married; and the incisive wisdom attributed to her in the dedication appears to be incongruous with other glimpses of her personality and the severe limitations of her experiences in her brief life.[19] She was perhaps attractive and stoically patient in shouldering the heavy burdens of work, bearing children and worrying about the family's financial problems; but she was apparently very taciturn; and, other than

Anderson's statement, no evidence has appeared to suggest that Emma had any remarkable insight or interest beyond her domestic duties. Irving Howe plausibly suggested why Anderson tended to idealize her: "He had not loved her enough as a boy, he had taken her long silences as tokens of distance, he had failed to see her suffering and endurance—and now he would recompense her even if she could no longer receive his gifts."[20] Her death in 1895, apparently from tuberculosis and overwork, when she was forty-three and Sherwood only eighteen, served to fix his youthful impressions of his mother.

In his analysis of Anderson's four marriages, Howe found the oedipal pattern as the basis for Anderson's marital problems. "Consider the evidence: repeated expressions of aggression toward his father, an intense and guilt-burdened love for his mother, numerous references in his books to unfulfilled sexuality, three marriages to mother-wives and then rebellions against them, strong spiritual attachments to male friends—are not these the traits of the psychic configuration classically described as oedipal?[21] Howe's assessment of the marriages is subject to important qualifications. In building his theory that Anderson was drawn toward "mother-managers" but left them because of his "adult wish for an exciting mate," Howe tended to stereotype the wives as "possessive" and "stark" in appearance and to consider inadequately Anderson's valid assertion that the artist's preoccupation with the world of the imagination and his inattention to material demands can make him a difficult mate. In Anderson's case these preoccupations are to be underscored, for his art demanded a high degree of self-absorption and his career was styled by the gesture of turning his back to material pursuits. More to our point here, Cornelia, his first wife, had a literary education; held according to a friend, radical views about literature; and claimed (in context, reliably) that "the spirit of adventure was strong in both of us."[22] Howe, himself, spoke of Tennessee Mitchell's being to Anderson "the epitome of independence and rebelliousness," hardly essential attributes of a mother figure, and acquaintances of Tennessee found her physically attractive.[23] Indeed, none of the four wives should be described as "stark."

Nevertheless, these qualifications do not negate Howe's theory. His analysis aids us both in understanding Anderson's stated views of women and his women characters and in helping to explain why Anderson's last marriage was apparently successful, for Eleanor appears to have been for Anderson both a capable but discreet manager and one who approached the demands of his ideal in a lover.

It would seem from some of his statements that Anderson thought women superior to men. "One does so hate to admit that the average woman is kinder, finer, more quick of sympathy and on the whole so much more first class than the average man."[24] "The women are a hundred times as good as we men. They are more moral, finer."[25] But closer to his true persuasion is the view that women are distinctly different and lower in his esteem than men. By the very act of idealizing women Anderson denies their essential humanity. In 1935 he wrote to Dreiser:

> You see definitely my idea has been, for a long time, that all this talk of men and women being the same, except for a slight physical difference is the purest nonsense. You are never in a room with a woman but that you feel the impulse TO BE. They want beauty of person and I do not think any man, at all male, ever thinks of that. Man does want the thing outside self. I want it in this book [probably *Kit Brandon*], in the building I am making, in a stone wall. I want always to do something to materials in nature. Any such impulse in a woman, who is really feminine, has been put into her by man or to try to compensate for lack of maleness in men.[26]

This view is consistent with that in *Perhaps Women*. He claimed that man's uniqueness was his imagination; women rule in a factual world. Most revealing is a statement made in an unpublished memoir titled "Brother Earl": "I would have gone all on some fool's track with her for I have seldom been a whole-hearted lover of women. I could never really believe in women artists and cannot to this day. Perhaps in some essential part of me—never in the flesh—I have, all of my life, loved men more than I have ever loved women."[27]

Whatever these data might mean to a psychoanalyst, they do reinforce a classification of the salient characteristics of the women in his short fiction. For the most part, his female characters are managers, defenders of the home who entrap men, wholehearted givers to men, frustrated gropers after a higher life, or characters in whom these qualities are combined.

There is awe before the wonders of how women manage men in "Another Wife." In this story a forty-seven-year-old widower doctor is confused about his relationship with a woman of thirty-seven he has met in the hill country. He thinks he may be in love with the woman, but he is unsure and overly impressed with her culture and her "modernity." Finally, they seemingly blunder into an understanding that they will marry. But the confusion is all male: she is understanding, patient, and sure of what she wants.

Other "managers" include Aunt Sally in "A Meeting South"; the doctor's wife in "Pastoral"; Gretchen, the nurse in "The Rabbit-Pen"; the mother in "The Egg"; and the girl in "Nice Girl." The latter three characters can serve here to illustrate the managing pattern. In "The Rabbit-Pen," Anderson's first published short story, Gretchen epitomizes all that Joe Harkness, his wife, Ruth and the writer Fordyce are not. Joe hides behind riches and romantic love, Ruth cannot handle her children, and Fordyce can neither understand nor come close to women. But Gretchen manages the entire household with super efficiency and aplomb.

The mother in "The Egg" and the girl in "Nice Girl" are contrasting types of capable, ambitious women. The former suggests Anderson's image of his mother. "She was a tall silent woman with a long nose and troubled gray eyes. For herself she wanted nothing. For father and myself she was incurably ambitious" (21). First she induced the father to become an independent chicken farmer. Then she got the idea of having a restaurant business, rented a store building, "decided that our restaurant should remain open at night," and tended the restaurant during the day. The father is willing enough, but the mother determines the family moves. Her competence serves as a foil for his poignant frustration in the story's climax.

"Nice Girl," which appeared in 1936, is noteworthy for a potential new direction for Anderson's stories which was never fully exploited: the new note is the objectivity, the irony, and the narrator's lack of sympathy. Agnes Wilson, the unscrupulous protagonist of the story, is unobtrusive and apparently diffident, but behind the scenes she is cunning and manipulating. She secretly arranges for her brother's bootlegger to be arrested and in the course of the story schemes to get her sister's husband.

In one of his typically powerful images, Anderson described the feelings of a young man at the moment he confronts the necessity of getting married. "Some shadowy, lovely thing seemed fleeing out of him and out of her. He felt like a beast who is playing about at night in a forest (and) has suddenly put his foot into a trap. . . . He was held fast, bound down to the earth, not by desire now, but by a strange hesitating sympathy with the thing that bound her to earth."[28] In other stories, too, sex is the bait in the trap of marriage. In this story, "The Contract," and in "Not Sixteen," Anderson could be sympathetic with the necessity of marriage in our culture and with a woman's needs, for he recognized that behind the "trembling figure" of the girl in "The Contract" stands "the whole fact of organized life." The frustrated would-be lover of Lillian in "Not Sixteen" comes to admire the iron will of Lillian, who is a giving woman but insistent that she will give herself to no one until she is sixteen.

But Anderson could also be very forceful in depicting the trap of marriage. Bill in "His Chest of Drawers" is torn between his sexual needs and the needs of self-respect, beauty, and freedom. The small, slender copywriter is left only a chest of drawers in his own house by his wife and four daughters. When most of that space is taken, he gets drunk to regain the illusion of self-respect. " 'After all,' he said, 'they do bestow their favors upon us' " (281). For Hugh Walker, the protagonist in "The Door of the Trap," marriage is a prison. We are led to believe that Walker frees Mary, a young girl in the story, from the jeopardy of being emotionally imprisoned when Walker kisses her and sends her off. At a time when Anderson's own marriage to Tennessee Mitchell was distintegrating, he published "Brothers" (1921), which includes a bitter description of the murderer's marriage: "His wife in particular was like some strange unlovely growth that had attached itself to his body" (35).

The best presentation of the marriage dilemma is also one of the best tales in *Winesburg*, "The Untold Lie." The focus is not on the wife who wants Ray Pearson to "hustle" more but on Ray and what he should tell young Hal Winters about marriage. When the devilish Hal asks him if he should marry Nell Gunther, who is pregnant, there is "only one thing that all his own training and all the beliefs of the people he knew would approve" of his saying.[29] But he cannot tell this "lie."

> As he ran he shouted a protest against his life, against all life, against everything that makes life ugly. "There was no promise made," he cried into the empty spaces that lay about him. "I don't promise my Minnie anything and Hal hasn't made any promise to Nell. I know he hasn't. She went into the woods with him because she wanted to go. What he wanted she wanted. Why should I pay? Why should Hal pay? Why should anyone pay? I don't want Hal to become old and worn out. I'll tell him. I won't let it go on. I'll catch Hal before he gets to town and I'll tell him." (207)

But he remembers also the moments of joy with his thin-legged children as well as the nagging wife and does not tell him; he realizes that "whatever I told him would have been a lie" (209).

The guilt Anderson felt about the exploitation of women by himself and other men is expressed in the characterization of some of the women in the stories as "feeders." He loved the women who freely gave of themselves like, to name a few, Lillian in "Not Sixteen" (though she postpones giving physically), Kate in "Daughters," Alice in "Like a Queen," the woman in "White Spot," the wife in "Brother Earl," Kate Swift in "The Teacher," and the woman in "A Man's Story." He wrote in *A Story Teller's Story*: "I had always been drawn toward . . . women who gave themselves to physical experiences with grave and fine abandon. . . ."[30]

However, this love is mixed with guilt and the memory of his over-burdened mother. He stated the theme of "Death in the Woods" in observations dated 1937: "It seems to me that the theme of the story is the persistent animal hunger of men. There are these women who spend their whole lives, rather dumbly, feeding this hunger. For years I wanted to write this story."[31] The word *feed* and its different forms reverberate through the story. This paragraph illustrates the point: "Then she settled down to *feed* [all italics mine] stock. That was her job. At the German's place she had cooked the food for the German and his wife. . . . She *fed* them and *fed* the cows in the barn, *fed* the pigs, the horses and the chickens. Every moment of every day, as a young girl, was spent *feeding* something" (123). She also fed her husband sexually, but "that hadn't lasted long after their marriage and after the babies came" (124).

Anderson's artist-writers particularly need a woman to feed on, to give them the constant, selfless love that helps sustain their art. Kate Swift and Elizabeth Willard seek passionately to nurture the incipient artist in

George. In "The Yellow Gown" Mildred is as absorbed in Harold the painter as he comes to be in his masterpiece. Most directly, the woman in "A Man's Story" gives her total life to Edgar Wilson, a poet. She leaves her husband; supports Wilson with love and money; and even though mortally wounded, her dying act is to light a fire in the small apartment she shares with him.

Rex Burbank has noted accurately that some of Anderson's best "adult" tales are "similar to the stories of Alice Hindman, Kate Swift, and Louise Bentley in *Winesburg*, tales which portray young women who are defeated by the coarseness, the insensitivity, or the moral cowardice of man and by the hypocrisy behind conventional Puritan moral codes."[32] What his statement omits is the positive qualities of these women. They are intensely alive, more aware and sensitive than those about them, seekers after a higher degree of self-fulfillment. Once again Anderson appears to dramatize in them his concepts of the buried life of his mother. In doing so, he creates his most successful women. Only Alice in "Like a Queen" and Aunt Sally in "A Meeting South," who are unique and seem to draw directly on specific biographical material, have the character dimensions of Elizabeth Willard, Kate Swift, Elsie Leander in "The New Englander," May Edgely in "Unused," Mary Cochran in "Unlighted Lamps," and Rosalind Westcott in the long story "Out of Nowhere into Nothing."

Kate Swift is characterized through contrasts. With her poor complexion, she was not regarded as a pretty woman in Winesburg. But "alone in the night in the winter streets she was lovely" (160), with a straight back and the "features of a tiny goddess" (160). Her usual attitude in the classroom was one of silent, cold sternness. But like many other Anderson characters, when she tells stories, she becomes animated and virtually hypnotizes her students. "Behind a cold exterior the most extraordinary events transpired in her mind" (162). Although people thought of her as an old maid lacking in human feeling, "in reality she was the most eagerly passionate soul among them" (162). When she thinks George may have a spark of genius in his writing, Kate Swift wants "to blow on the spark" (163). She tells him "to know what people are thinking about, not what they say" (173); and on another occasion "a passionate desire to have him understand the import of life, to learn to interpret it truly and honestly, swept over her" (163–4). But her passion becomes physical, both she and George feel the confusion of her intense hopes for him and sexual passion, and she breaks away from George, hitting him in her frustration. Kate Swift is brought to life in but a few pages, but she is one of Anderson's most memorable creations.

Kate Swift is lonely, too; but some of the other questing women we are considering here more keenly seek fulfillment in sex. Before her marriage Elizabeth Willard expressed her restless nature by dreaming of being on the stage, "of joining some company and wandering over the world, seeing always new faces and giving something out of herself to all people" (46). The second expression of her restlessness was giving herself physically to some man. In these ways and others "there was something she sought blindly, passionately, some hidden wonder in life" (224). But this poor woman, who desperately needed to be loved, found release "but twice in her life, in the moments when her lovers Death and Doctor Reefy held her in their arms" (232).

May Edgely in "Unused" wants to be used, to be connected with the stream of life.[33] Her two sisters are promiscuous, and the males in the family are rough but self-reliant. But May alone competes with the establishment in Bidwell (another Clyde, Ohio). She is an excellent student and berry picker, and she dresses neatly and cares for her mother. However, the year she graduates second in her class, her mother dies; and soon afterwards, in a blatant gesture, she goes into the woods with Jerome Hadley. The town view is that May "who had been treated almost as an equal by the others had wanted to throw something ugly right in their faces:"[34] But they do not know her: she wants only to answer some strong impulse in her personality. The rest of the sad tale is the steady decline and final death of May, victimized by the community.

Rosalind Westcott is warned against men by her taciturn mother; but at the end of "Out of Nowhere into Nothing," she runs toward experience, back to life in a Chicago love affair with a married man which is anything but promising. Elsie Leander, the frustrated title character in "The New Englander," longs for release that is generally sexual in the cornfields of Iowa. And Mary Cochran is the victim of town gossip and her father's inability to communicate. She rejects the young man who misunderstood her actions and determines too late to express her love for her father. The pattern of light imagery in this fine story is epitomized by the image of the title, "Unlighted Lamps." Mary poignantly needed some glimpse of her widower father's buried life to illuminate her own identity, but in critical moments he is unable to light the needed lamp.

All of these women—some of his most successful creations (as Gold noted)—have Elizabeth Willard's need: "Like all the women in the world, she wanted a real lover" (224). That Anderson's women never find the sustained, patient love they need is only one dimension of the limitations of their characterization. Rare, indeed, is the character in all of Anderson's fiction who finds such love.

Love is a vital force which permits the men and women of his fiction to escape, if only for the moment, the barrier of conventions and neuroses and find a kind of fulfillment and wholeness lacking in his grotesques and other gropers; but for Anderson "love" differs importantly between the sexes. He could stress the biological role of women with genuine respect: he seemed awed by the capacity of women to create out of their own bodies. Despite the surfacing of deeply felt antagonistic feelings about women in, for example, the story "Respectibility," Anderson was not a misogynist. And it is extraordinary that all three of his divorced wives continued long after the divorces to regard him with affection. But as has been noted earlier, Anderson denied to feminine sensibility the realm of the creative imagination. In this realm the artist man, who is not different in kind from other craftsmen, can rise to impersonal love and thus combat what he called the "disease of self." He insisted that this kind of love gives power to art: "Few enough people realize that all art that has vitality must have its basis in love.[35] In a letter to his son dated 1927 he spoke of impersonal love and made a rare reference to religion. "In art there is the possibility of an impersonal love. For modern man it is, I think, the only road to God."[36]

At this point one must exercise great care in generalizing. On the one hand, we have these stated views about women; on the other, the created characters. The personal fulfillment of an individual character is not tantamount to successful characterization. Kate Swift, for example, may be successfully realized and still be terribly frustrated. Furthermore, the "extraordinary events" which "transpired in her mind" suggest an imaginative capacity which Anderson would not allow real women.

Personal fulfillment and "rounded" characterization come together in a few of Anderson's artist men—notably but still not definitely in George Willard, who contrasts with the grotesques in his capacity to get outside himself. However, Anderson's women are circumscribed in their development, fixed in repetitive roles, essentially as they have been described here—managers, defenders of the home, feeders of men, and frustrated gropers after a higher life. These characters reflect both Anderson's bewildered understanding of women and the expressive basis of his art of characterization.

## Notes

1. Herbert Gold, "*Winesburg, Ohio*: the Purity and Cunning of Sherwood Anderson," *Hudson Review*, 10 (Winter 1957-8), 554-5.

2. Lionel Trilling, "Sherwood Anderson," *The Liberal Imagination* (New York: Viking Press, 1950); reprinted, Anchor Books, 1953, pp. 28-9.

3. The structuring of stories around epiphanies appears to be a very significant parallel between their stories; however, Anderson's reading of Chekhov and Turgenev, his attacks on "poison plot," his lyrical rather than epical gifts, and his view of life as a series of luminous but infrequent moments would also have to be considered were a more definite line of influence from Joyce established.

4. Chester G. Anderson, "The Question of Esthetic Distance," *James Joyce, A Portrait of the Artist as a Young Man: Text, Criticism, and Notes*, ed. Chester G. Anderson (New York: The Viking Press, 1968), pp. 446-454.

5. James Joyce, *A Portrait of the Artist as a Young Man* (New York: Viking Press, 1964), pp. 213-5.

6. James R. Baker, "James Joyce: Esthetic Freedom and Dramatic Art," *Western Humanities Review*, 5 (Winter 1950-1), 30-1. Baker actually is immediately concerned with *Stephen Hero*, but his generalizations noted here hold true in the later work.

7. Alfred Kazin, *On Native Grounds* (New York: Reynal and Hitchcock, 1942), p. 215.

8. Letter to Norman Holmes Pearson, September 13, 1937, in *Letters of Sherwood Anderson*, ed. and with an introduction, Howard Mumford Jones and Walter B. Rideout (Boston: Little, Brown, 1953), p. 387.

9. *Ibid.*, p. 388.

10. Anderson, "Man and His Imagination," in *The Intent of the Artist*, ed. Augusto Centeno (Princeton: Princeton U. Press, 1941), p. 70.

11. Letter to Carrow De Vries, August 9, 1939, *Letters*, p. 446.

12. Anderson, "A Note on Realism," *Sherwood Anderson's Notebook* (New York: Boni and Liveright, 1926), p. 72.

13. Anderson, "Man and His Imagination," p. 70.

14. Anderson, *Sherwood Anderson's Memoirs* (New York: Harcourt, Brace, 1942), p. 341.

15. Irving Howe, *Sherwood Anderson* (New York, William Sloan, 1951); reissued, Stanford U. Press, 1966, p. 109.

16. Anderson, "A Meeting South," in *Sherwood Anderson's Short Stories*, ed. Maxwell Geismar (New York: Hill and Wang, 1962), p. 170. Unless indicated otherwise, subsequent page references to Anderson's stories are to this edition.

17. Joyce, *Portrait*, pp. 214–5.

18. Anderson, *A Story Teller's Story* (New York, B. W. Huebsch, 1924), p. 7.

19. William A. Sutton, "Sherwood Anderson's Formative Years," Diss. Ohio State University, 1943, p. 23. Sutton treats Emma's life before her marriage (1852–1873) on pp. 22–24. An account of the remainder of her life is found on pp. 56–63.

20. Howe, p. 20.

21. *Ibid.*, p. 212.

22. Sutton, *Exit to Elsinore*, Ball State Monograph Number Eleven (Muncie: Ball State U. Press, 1967), pp. 39 and 19.

23. Sutton, "Sherwood Anderson's Second Wife," *Ball State University Forum*, 7 (Spring 1966), 39.

24. Anderson, *A Story Teller's Story*, p. 216.

25. Letter to K. K. (apparently Dwight MacDonald), ? April, 1929, *Letters*, p. 193.

26. Letter to Theodore Dreiser, December 22, 1935, *Letters*, pp. 339–40.

27. Unpublished memoir (not the short story with the same title), Newberry Library, Chicago, Illinois.

28. Anderson, "The Contract," *Broom*, 1 (December 1921), 148–153, in *The Portable Sherwood Anderson*, ed. and with an introduction, Horace Gregory (New York: Viking, 1949), p. 447.

29. Anderson, *Winesburg, Ohio*, ed. Malcolm Cowley (New York: Viking, 1960), pp. 205–6. Subsequent references to *Winesburg* are to this edition.

30. Anderson, *A Story Teller's Story*, p. 269.

31. Anderson, statement included with the "Death in the Woods" MSS, the Newberry Library.

32. Rex Burbank, *Sherwood Anderson* (New York: Twayne, 1964), p. 88.

33. Anderson, "Unused," *Horses and Men* (New York: Huebsch, 1924), p. 65.

34. *Ibid.*, p. 47.

35. Anderson, "After Seeing George Bellows' Mr. and Mrs. Wase," *Sherwood Anderson's Notebook* (New York: Boni and Liveright, 1926), p. 83.

36. Letter to John Anderson, ? April, 1927, *Letters*, p. 168.

# "Myth and the Midwestern Landscape: Sherwood Anderson's *Mid-American Chants*"

The dichotomy between nature and civilization has existed throughout American literature. Cooper's forests and garrisons, Hawthorne's forests and scaffold, and Twain's Mississippi River and riverbank society exemplify the romantic impulse to contrast idealized natural landscapes with despoiled man-created environments.

This recurrent dichotomy gains new and terrible associations with the rise of Midwestern industrial cities. America's westward expansion occurs in and through the Middle West. The resulting Mid-American industrial cities, like Chicago, possess all the failings of Cooper's garrisons along with many that author never imagined.

Despite the cities' promise of bright lights and excitement, early twentieth century Midwesterners often respond with shocked rejection. Several elements combine to foster this reaction. Even from a distance, turn-of-the-century cities come as a shock. Skyscrapers begin to thrust into the air, disturbing the hypnotically somnolent horizontal of Midwestern landscape. From a closer perspective, the cities are ugly. They are a response to the needs of commerce and industry, not those of beauty. Furthermore, industry, experiencing unprecedented expansion, beckons rural Midwesterners to the cities and then exploits them ruthlessly. As rural people join the ranks of the urban proletariat, "robber baron" capitalism, the industrial milieu, and the vastness of the cities undercut Midwestern identity with the land, the community, and Christianity.

But what are Midwesteners to do? By the early twentieth century it was clear that America's future was in the nightmarish industrial cities. Like many Midwestern writers, Sherwood Anderson was horrified by American industrialism. But in *Mid-American Chants* Anderson confronted his fears and moved beyond romantic rejection of the present. Using Mid-American land- and city-scapes as the focus of his vision, he forged an optimistic myth for twentieth century urban-industrial man.

*Originally published in *MidAmerica VI* (East Lansing, Mich.: The Midwestern Press, 1979), pp. 79–87. Reprinted by permission of the Society for the Study of Midwestern Literature and Philip Greasley.

Anderson's quest for the future begins with emphasis on traditional American landscapes themselves. References like, "the long fields and standing corn . . . the west winds . . . the vast prairies . . . (and) the black swampy land" abound. Indeed, whole poems are given over to nostalgic reminiscences of rural Middle America, as these lines from "Evening Song" illustrate:

> Back of Chicago the open fields—were you ever there?
> Trains coming toward you out of the West—
> Streaks of light on the long gray plains?—
>
> Back of Chicago the open fields—were you ever there?
> Trains going from you into the West—
> Clouds of dust on the long gray plains.
> Long trains go West, too. . . .

Anderson joyfully affirms traditional American experience. He expresses wonder and awe at the immensity, fertility, and power of the land. Thus, the poet announces himself as one of the people, saying,

> I am of the West, the long West of the sunsets. I am of
>     the deep fields where the corn grows. The sweat of
>     apples is in me. I am the beginning of things and the
>     end of things.

Next, Anderson presents ecstatic Whitmanesque catalogues proclaiming America's unique greatness. He begins with "Keokuk, Tennessee, Michigan, Chicago, Kalamazoo—don't the names in this place make you fairly drunk?" Later, he adds, "I am one with the old gods—an American from Dakota—from the deep valley of the Mississippi—from Illinois—from Iowa—from Ohio." Sharing Whitman's enthusiasm at America's burgeoning numbers and power, Anderson concludes, ". . . Wait! Try to believe./ Stronger, deeper, stronger . . . over the land—wide—wide—over the land. . . . / Ninety, a thousand, a million, a nation. . . . See my young strength how it grows."

Yet beyond simple love for the land, Anderson—like earlier authors—uses landscape to affirm certain values. His desire for fixed values, personal and national identity, and closeness to the divine order produces an almost pantheistic reverence for the land and traditional agrarian pursuits. Thus, long straight rows of corn and dark, rich soil take on associations of fertility, permanency, and fulfillment. In this same way, Anderson maintains, "Out of the land of my fathers, from Huron to Keokuk, beauty shall come—out of the black ground, out of the deep black ground." This beauty, he believes, will go far beyond the physical. It will attach itself to all aspects of American life.

If the American rural past offers security, identity, and fulfillment, the urban-industrial future seems at first to threaten just the reverse. Both emotions are present as Anderson's persona asserts,

> I am mature, a man child, in America, in the West, in the
> great valley of the Mississippi. My head arises above the
> cornfields. I stand up among the new corn.

> I am a child, a confused child in a confused world. There are
> no clothes made that fit me.

The second half of this quotation expresses his unpreparedness for the experiences and values of the twentieth century. The old philosophical garments no longer seem to fit.

The city initially means more than confusion. It is frustration and degradation. The city means "factories and marts and the roar of machines—horrible, terrible, ugly and brutal. It crush(es) . . . things down and down. The urban-industrial order seems filthy and spiritually contaminating. Dust and the roar of mankilling machines symbolize Anderson's early response to the city. The persona tells us,

> . . . in the streets of my city I stood. My clothes were foul.
> In the woven cloth that covered my body the dust of my
> city had lodged. The dust of my civilization was in my
> soul.

Anderson initially believes people in the cities are smothered. They need the beauty, the communion with the land, and the values fostered by agrarian life.

Increasingly, however, Anderson moves beyond idealization of the past and rejection of the present. Here, as before, natural and urban-industrial environments carry the theme. Though the city still remains threatening, Anderson begins to find some basis for hope. He starts negatively, with

> . . . there are the broken things—myself and the others. . . .
> We are all that, here in the West, here in Chicago. . . .
> There's nothing but shrill screams and a rattle.

But then he adds the assertion of divine plan, saying,

> That had to be—it's a part of the scheme.
> Now, faint little voices do lift up.
> Little faint beginnings of things— . . . a
> life lived in Chicago—in the West—in the
> whirl of industrial America.

The poet begins to see purpose in the hitherto apparently meaningless brutality. He comes to accept that, "In denser shadows by the factory walls, /In my old cornfields, broken where the cattle roam/ The shadow of the face of God falls downs."

At this point Anderson is able to integrate images of traditional

American landscapes with those of the twentieth century city and show the possibilities for positive new values and modes of living. He finds that even urban-industrial life can become fulfilling. The negative portrayals of the city—which Anderson had previously viewed as man's ironic response to the natural landscape—give way to an understanding that the city is the environment of the present and future. Within it man *will* be able to work out his destiny.

> We're just a lot of muddy things caught up by the stream.
> You can't fool us. Don't we know ourselves?
>
> Here we are, out here in Chicago. . . . We are like the sewerage of our town, swept up stream by a kind of mechanical triumph—that's what we are.
>
> By God, we'll love each other or die trying. We'll get to understanding too. In some grim way our own song shall work through.
>
> We'll stay down in the muddy depths of our stream—we will. There can't any poet come out here and sit on the shaky rail of our ugly bridges and sing us into paradise.
>
> We're finding out—that's what I want to say. We'll get at our own thing out here or die for it. We're going down numberless thousands of us, into ugly oblivion. We know that.
>
> But say, bards, you keep off our bridges. Keep out of our dreams, dreamers. We want to give this democracy thing they talk so big about a whirl. We want to see if we are any good out here, we Americans from all over hell. That's what we want.

The traditional American rural landscapes and the contemporary urban-industrial milieu have then become synonymous with the values, opportunities, and restrictions of past and present. Systematic presentation of nature and industrial society has developed and clarified these. These symbolic landscape references become even more important because the Chants are a collection of impressionistic, sometimes surrealistic, topical poems. They lack a logical statement of theme and even a consistent unifying, clarifying voice. Each poem records the emotional intensity at a specific moment without a direct statement of theme. The totality of these emotional responses is at first a nightmarish stream of consciousness. Only the consistent recurrence and juxtaposition of landscapes make clear Anderson's moods, themes, and changes of perspective. Without references to "oil on their boots" and "the roar of machines," poems like "The Beam" would be simply incoherent screams of pain. With these references, however, the sacrifice of human lives and hopes to the industrial order becomes clear.

> Eighteen men stood by me in my fall—long men—strong men—see the oil on their boots.

> I was a guest in the house of my people. Through the years I clung, taking hold of their hands in the darkness. It rained and the roar of machines was incessant. Into the house of my people quiet would not come.

> Eighteen men stood by me in my fall. Through their breasts bars were driven. With wailing and with weeping I ran back and forth. Then I died. Out of the door of the house of my people I ran. But the eighteen men stood by me in my fall.

With Sherwood Anderson's recognition of the importance of the role of landscape to his message and an understanding that the city can offer man a viable future, he moves toward the creation of new song—a new set of values, a spirit, again based on man's relation to the land. In the "Foreword" to *Mid-American Chants* Anderson maintains that

> Song begins with and has its birth in the memory of older things than we know. . . . In the beaten paths of life, when many generations of men have walked the streets of a city or wandered at night in the hills of an old land. . . . But in our towns and fields there are few memory haunted places. Here we stand in roaring city streets, on steaming coal heaps, in the shadow of factories from which come only the grinding roar of machines. We do not sing but mutter in the darkness. Our lips are cracked with dust and with the heat of furnaces. We but mutter and feel our way toward the promise of song.

*Mid-American Chants* ultimately asserts the possibility of song, but here again, the chants start negatively. They ask, "Can a singer arise and sing in this smoke and grime? Can he keep his throat clear? Can his courage survive? Soon after, the poet refers to the urban landscape, exclaiming, "We have to sing . . . in the darkness." By the middle of the chants, symbols associated with the urban-industrial environment show that a commitment has been made. The city will be man's new home:

> It is day and I stand raw and new by the coal-heaps. I go into the place of darkness at the beginning of the new house. . . . New song is tearing the cords of my throat. I am become a man covered with dust. I have kissed the black hands of new brothers and cannot return to bury my beloved at the door of the long house.

Later, landscapes again mirror the progress toward Anderson's dream of new song. He calls the workers to song, saying,

> In denser shadows by the factory walls,
> In my old cornfields, broken where the cattle roam,
> The shadow of the face of God falls down.
>
> From all of Mid-America a prayer,
> To newer, braver gods, to dawns and days,
> To truth and cleaner, braver life we come.
>
> Lift up a song,
> My sweaty men,
> Lift up a song.

Finally, the chants end, reaffirming that the industrial environment will not destroy man. The last poem concludes in a call to song:

> I look far into the future beyond the noise and the clatter.
> I will not be crushed by the iron machine.
> Sing.
> Dare to sing.
> Kiss the mouth of song with your lips.
> In the morning and in the evening
> Trust to the terrible strength of indomitable song.

Landscapes express, then, the poet's growing willingness to work out his destiny in the industrial city. His growing faith in the industrial future is mirrored in the increasing emphasis on song. Anderson sees the problems, but he moves forward, knowing the values of the Midwestern past, those of the long straight rows of corn and the black swampy earth, will guide man as he moves into a newer world. The old world will bring forth the new, and the cornfields will become sacred,

> . . . our cornfields, the old dreams and prayers and thoughts
> . . . sweetening our broad land and getting even into our
>   shops and into the shadows that lurk by our factory doors.
> It is the time of the opening of doors.
> No talk of what we can do for the old world.
> Talk and dream now of what the old world can bring to us—
>   the true sense of real suffering out of which may come the
>   sweeter brotherhood.
> God, lead us to the fields now. . . .
> May our fields become our sacred places.

Yet Sherwood Anderson is not content to simply express the joy and faith in the American landscape or to invest the landscape with meanings and values. Having accomplished these in *Mid-American Chants*, he attempts to build support for the values he favors. Anderson chooses myth

as his tool. As such American landscapes and cities acquire mythic overtones. These descriptions consistently use the language and symbols of
Christian and classical mythology. Christian myth contributes "the
flood," "fires which do not burn," "the beginning of things and the end of
things," and "the upper room (and) . . . down below the others . . .
waiting—Judas and Peter and John—He was crucified for them."

Classical mythology suggests references to "Ulysses," to "soldiers
emerging from the corn and killing each other in battle," and to a "hoarse
and terrible singer, half man, half bird, floating in cold bleak
winds. . . ., wings burned by the fires of furnaces."

Anderson heightens the intensity by employing repeated mythic
references to sexuality and to the annual fertility cycle. Mid-American
cornfields become shrines, and the American growth cycle assumes
mythic stature commensurate with the Eleusian mysteries. Often, Anderson links his fertility myths in *Mid-American Chants* with sexuality. For
example, in "Spring Song" comes the declaration,

> In the spring I press your body down on wet cold new-
> plowed ground. . . .
> I would have my sacred way with you.

Thus, Anderson closes the circle. He joins land and air, body and
spirit, life and death in support of his vision of fulfillment. This combination of mythic appeals lends an air of importance, inevitability, and
divine sanction to Anderson's program for America. The myths encompass the major theologies of western civilization, the central fertility myth
of birth and death, and the most primal human urge—sexuality.
Together they assert the possibility for fruitful life in the present and
future based on Mid-American land and the traditional values derived
from it.

Thus, Anderson's *Mid-American Chants* offers a new myth for
urban-industrial man, building the future on the bedrock of the
Midwestern past. The poems themselves become the Holy Book, the Song
which men will carry with them into the future.

# "Sherwood Anderson's *Death in the Woods*: Toward a New Realism"

Mary Anne Ferguson*

Though recent critics stress the importance of Sherwood Anderson's later works and most critics admire "Death in the Woods" as one of his best short stories, if not his masterpiece, the volume *Death in the Woods and Other Stories* (1933) has not been studied. Yet Anderson, always concerned with the "baffling question of form achieved or not achieved,"[1] took special pains with the book. When he was reading proof, he perceived unevenness in the quality of the stories and "threw out two or three"; he wrote a new story to complete the volume, "Brother Death," a story which in his opinion would "make the book"; "It is, I'm pretty sure, one of the finest stories I've ever done, and I even dare say one of the finest and most significant anyone has ever done." Anderson was especially pleased with these changes because, as he explained to Ferdinand Schevill, "I did want the book, dedicated to our friendship and my esteem for you and your mind, to have real integrity."[2] Anderson "sounds cocky," he admits; but as Schevill would have realized, such self-assurance with respect to a collection of short stories was a new note for Anderson. In his dedication to Dreiser of *The Triumph of the Egg* (1921) he wrote of his sense of inadequacy: "Many tales are dying in the street before the house of my mind"; and in the first selection in the volume, "The Dumb Man," the persona reiterates this despair: "I have no words. . . . I cannot tell the story." In the Foreword to the collection *Horses and Men* (1923) Anderson says that he may be deaf, blind, and unable "with these nervous and uncertain hands . . . [to] feel for the form of things. . . ." In the Introduction to a collection of sketches, *Perhaps Women* (1931), he apologizes for his failure to have found a suitable form: "The whole thing is nothing but an impression, a sketch. I know that. I have kept it by me for a year now. I have tried to give it better form but that now seems impossible to me." Anderson's cockiness about having achieved his goal of "real integrity" in *Death in the Woods* suggests that the volume may

*Originally published in *MidAmerica VII* (East Lansing, Mich.: The Midwestern Press, 1980), pp. 73–95. Reprinted by permission of the Society for the Study of Midwestern Literature and Mary Anne Ferguson.

217

represent a new departure for him. I find in the volume a movement away from a persona seeking the meaning of life in "the preternatural or archetypal,"[3] a passive observer upon whom reality impinges itself, toward a persona who shares the life he observes and locates the center of reality outside himself. The change in the persona is associated in the volume with a change in attitude toward women and toward death.

The story "Death in the Woods" is the first in the volume; "Brother Death" is the last, and Anderson indicates that this arrangement was his intention.[4] Obviously the volume is unified by the theme of death; but it is not death alone. As he had elsewhere,[5] Anderson links the topics death and woman. Of the sixteen stories in the volume, five deal with the death of a woman and its effect upon a male character. In "Death in the Woods" the male narrator is a stranger to the woman whose death is an episode in his development. In three stories—"The Return," "Another Wife," and "The Flood"—the focus is on a widower trying to find a substitute for his dead wife. The narrator of "In a Strange Town" flees his wife and home in order to recover from the depression he felt upon upon the death of a young woman student; he consoles himself by meditating upon the meaning of life for a widow he sees at a railroad station in a funeral party. These stories reflect the conviction which led Anderson to publish *Perhaps Women* in spite of his dissatisfaction with its form, his sense "that modern man is losing his ability to retain his manhood in the face of the modern way of utilizing the machine and that what hope there is for him lies in women."[6] Other stories illustrate ways in which women may save men and make explicit the faults from which men need to be saved. Their need for wordly success is the primary life-denying fault, whether it be in a mountaineer moving to the city for work, a young man seeking sophistication among expatriates, or a writer abandoning family and human values for the sake of his craft. In one powerful story, "The Flight," Anderson shows male rivalry as ruinous; in another, he shows jealous possessiveness as absurd. Through their interaction with other characters the males in these stories either ironically reveal their illusions about themselves or gain self-knowledge. In a few stories Anderson focuses on the positive qualities of the women characters—their wisdom and their ability to deal with the realities of life—which enable them not only to survive in a hostile world but to help men. Finally, in "Brother Death," he uses a female central consciousness to show that in the midst of death one can live fully.

The stories in *Death in the Woods* were written over a period of years—some were published as early as 1925—when Anderson was also writing the avowedly autobiographical works *A Story Teller's Story* (1924) and *Tar: A Midwest Childhood* (1926). But from these and the many letters and passages in the *Memoirs* (1941) which tell about this period in Anderson's life, one cannot get a trustworthy chronology. The tantalizingly frequent parallels between his biography and his fiction cannot be made into a study of development.[7] But the changes I perceive in Anderson's male personae in the volume *Death in the Woods* are paralleled by changes in six versions of the title story which have survived.

Anderson considered "Death in the Woods" one of his best short stories but, he added, it "was one of the stories I wrote, threw away, and rewrote many times." Recognizable versions of the story appear in three works unpublished during Anderson's lifetime: "Paris Notebook" (1921); "Father Abraham: A Lincoln Fragment"; and the recently discovered fragment "A Death in the Forest." Three published versions exist: as part of *Tar: A Midwest Childhood* (1926); as a separate short story in *American Mercury*, (September 1926); and finally in 1933 in the volume *Death in the Woods*.[8] In a passage in which he compares the gestation of a story to pregnancy, "the telling of the tale . . . [to] the cutting of the natal cord," Anderson remarked that out of his private world of fancy, he would like to introduce and tell the story of, among others, "the old woman accompanied by the gigantic dogs who died alone in a wood on a winter day."[9] In "Death in the Woods" Anderson does tell the story of such a woman, using as narrator a grown man looking back to a memorable incident in his boyhood twenty years earlier. The narrator mentions that he did not understand the significance of the woman's story until later in life when he "had a half-uncanny mystical adventure with dogs in an Illinois forest on a clear moon-lit Winter night." In his *Memoirs*, Anderson describes such an experience when he was living in Chicago and spending weekends in the country nearby in order to write. The troop of dogs which accompanied him on a walk one snowy night "seemed excited"; they "ran in circles," and when Anderson stopped to doze, lying half-way up the slanting trunk of a fallen tree, they made a circular path in the snow beneath him, running head to tail; one by one they dropped out of the circle to run up the tree trunk and gaze into Anderson's face. Anderson felt "something of the mystery of the night," of the "strangeness" of the animals' reversion to a primitive state, but he thought that part of their ritual, their stopping to run to him, indicated their tie to civilization.[10]

Anderson ascribes a similar feeling of awe to Abraham Lincoln in "Father Abraham: A Lincoln Fragment." The narrator projects himself into the mind of Lincoln whom he imagines as the defense attorney for a woman accused of killing her employer. Like Anderson's mother a bound girl, the woman had no defense but violence when her master attacked her. Lincoln is able to imagine her feelings as well as those of the man who sees her as his rightful conquest; he knows that the man's wife tacitly condoned the rape as a way of keeping the girl bound to their service for life. With great insight Lincoln perceives the farmer as a misguided human being, not a brute; but his sympathy is for the the victim. Earlier in "Father Abraham," Anderson wrote about Lincoln's passion for Ann Rutledge and his mourning for her at her grave in the snow on a winter night; Anderson presents Lincoln's love and loss as the experience which liberated him from the merely personal and allowed him to extend his sympathy and influence to strangers. In "Death in the Woods," Mrs. Grimes' early life as a bound girl parallels that of the woman on trial; the death scene bears many resemblances to that of Lincoln at Ann Rutledge's grave.[11]

The version of the old woman's story in "Father Abraham" is close to that of the sketch in the "Paris Notebook"; in both the emphasis is on the brutalized life of the old woman, told with compassion for all participants. In the "Notebook" the old woman, who has not attempted to murder the farmer, relives in dreams her youthful experience. The woman whom she served, habitually "silent & sullen," "did not mean to be unkind"; the farmer is not evil but amoral, perceiving the girl as his rightful prey. The man she married, "filled with wrath that was bottled up inside him" and which he did not understand, had in his youth expressed "a kind of love" in the only way he could, drinking and fighting. "Ma Winters" now dreams of herself as "frightened, a young girl in a torn dress," trying desperately to care for the animals which love her. In one of her dreams, trying to rescue herself and trapped animals from an airless barn, she cannot reach the bar which would open the door. "The bar she could not reach was as cold as death. It was death. One raised death out of its sockets on the great door and then joy and light came in." Without raising death, she awakes. This version focuses on the meaning of death to the girl who is the central consciousness; her dream vision seems associated with Anderson's dreamlike experience in the Illinois forest.

But the bound girl's story, Lincoln-like compassion, and the dreamlike incident of the dogs were not always linked. In a recently published holograph version of the story entitled "A Death in the Forest" Anderson treats the old woman's death almost entirely as it concerns the narrator as a young boy. Anderson focuses on the boy's encounter with death and the nakedness of woman not as a rite of passage, made mysterious and "mystical" by the ritualistic circling of the dogs, but as the occasion for his finding a role model. At the death scene he meets Ben Lewis, a young man of the town who for five years has been a newspaper reporter in Chicago. His success and its importance to the narrator are symbolized by Ben's "grand overcoat . . . (all silk lined and everything)"; to the boy the most significant aspect of the death scene was Ben Lewis' giving his overcoat to him to hold:

> . . . the charge lay upon me with a delicious weight. Could men, actual flesh and blood men, who had been raised in our town, wear such gorgeous garments? Did such unbelievable things happen to young fellows who left our town and become reporters on city newspapers?

The coat was of broad yellow and green plaid and to my fingers the touch of it was delicious. And it was lined with silk. How reverently I carried it home to our house and how good and kind I thought my mother when she laughingly permitted me to have the coat hanging in my own room overnight.

I slept but little that night and often crept out of bed to touch the coat again. How deliciously soft the fabric. The death of Ma Marvin in the snow in the wood was forgotten. . . . Would I, could I, sometime, grow up, go away to a city, get a job on a newspaper and like Ben Lewis wear a coat like a king? The thought thrilled me beyond words. . . .

As to the actual story of Ma Marvin's death, I found all about it in a rather queer way nearly twenty years later. Now I will tell you of that.

The manuscript ends here, but even if it had been continued, the story would not have been that of the old woman; the narrator has already dismissed that possibility in a few short paragraphs of narrative summary beginning "It was a poor little story after all." Obviously at this stage Anderson did not perceive a significant relationship between the woman's life and her death; the narrator dismisses the death as something beyond a boy's capacity to understand and immediately shifts his attention to the death as the cause for a gathering of the townsmen and the opportunity for him to hold Ben Lewis' coat. For the narrator, following in Ben Lewis' footsteps would lead to his heart's desire: success enough to buy luxury that would be visible to the townspeople.

Even for the adults in "A Death in the Forest," the old woman's death is not deeply significant. It occurs as an interruption to the town's happy preparation for Christmas and enjoyment of winter, "crowds of boys. . . . shouting and laughing" as they jump on and are thrown from bobsleds on Main Street. The first sentence of the story announces the death bluntly: "It was December and snowing when Mrs. Ike Marvin—we knew her as Ma Marvin—died in the little hollow in the center of Grimes' woods, about two miles south of our Ohio town." The next two paragraphs personify the town: the return home of a few girls rich enough to have been away at boarding school and of Ben Lewis makes the narrator feel "one's town putting its nose up in the air like a fine pointer dog" on "a day to remember." The day is memorable because of the effect on the townsmen of the news of Mrs. Marvin's death: all activity in the town ceases, and the narrator recalls in detail what many of the townsmen were doing as "things went bang then, like putting a light out in a room." He recalls the bustle as the news is shouted by two young hunters who run down Main Street, figures remembered as "not quite human. . . . more like Gods." The sudden cessation of activity is accompanied by a change in the weather as the townspeople, including "even women who had no babies to look after," went in a group to the scene. The old woman's life and the manner of her death, "just as plain as though there had been an eyewitness to her death there to tell the tale," are very briefly summarized. The narrator remembers the "white, half frozen little old figure, pitched a little forward," and the "pack of big ugly dogs,"; he imagines "the stillness of death coming softly, night and the cold," but comments "My boy's mind couldn't grasp it then" and goes on to give details of Ben Lewis's participation in moving the body and handing him the coat to hold. In this version it is the boy as part of the town, indeed, the town itself which is the center of the story.[12]

In the three published versions of the story the old woman's death and her life become the central memory of the adult narrator and the story becomes his attempt to perceive its true significance. The final version published in 1933 intensifies the mystical and mythical nature of the experience and its effect upon the narrator as a boy. All three of these versions omit any reference to Ben Lewis and his coat. The immediate impact of the death scene on the narrator and his brother is its function as sexual initiation for them: "She did not look old, lying there in that light, frozen and still. One of the men turned her over in the snow and I saw everything. My body trembled . . . and so did my brother's. It might have been the cold. Neither of us had ever seen a woman's body before." (20).

But before this scene the story of the old woman's life as a bound girl, as brutalized wife and mother, as a person totally isolated from human contact, has been amply told; the boy's previous impressions of her during a summer when he had observed her when he was idled by sickness, make his interest in her believable; his final view of her as a "feeder of animals" is made convincing when he presents it as arrived at "slowly, long afterward" (22).

Anderson gains credibility for the narrator in the published versions by carefully detailing his relationship to the old woman. An omniscient narrator first describes the old woman's trip to town on the fatal day as one of many such trips viewed "one summer and fall" by the boy. Her actions are presented as those habitual to "such old women" often seen by "all country and small-town people" but seldom understood by anyone. The use of the present tense to describe habitual action and of the conditional in verbs like "may own" and "might spend" is interrupted in the second paragraph by a specific statement about the boy's distaste for liver; now he becomes the central consciousness but the use of the habitual present continues. "The old farm woman got some liver. . . ." is inconspicuous in the midst of the habitual present; it prepares the reader to believe the narrator's assertion that he had often observed the old woman. Continued shifts between the habitual present and the specific preterite are reinforced by apparently casual explanations of the narrator's knowledge both of the woman's past and of the day of her death. Such observations as "she got into my thoughts," "I remembered afterwards," "I later knew all about it. It must have stuck in my mind from small town tales, heard when I loitered about where men talked," augmented by conversational tags like "You see," "Well," "Maybe," and rhetorical questions like "then what would she do?", subtly establish the tone of oral narration, of a tale being told. This tone not only achieves suspension of disbelief but imparts to the old woman's story the aura of myth. The detailed narrative of her death becomes part of a larger story; the sense of strangeness Anderson felt in the Illinois forest is communicated through dwelling on the dogs' return to their primordial origin as wolves, their memory of civilization and perhaps their fear of death expressed in their interrupting their circling to come close to the old woman, who had stopped to rest against a tree trunk beside a clearing. Further details about the dogs' tearing into the old woman's bag of supplies and tearing off her dress "clear to the hips" prepare for the denouement when the narrator and his brother "saw everything" and perceived the body of the old woman as that of a slender young girl.

Even such a minor change from "A Death in the Forest" as omitting any women from the group of townspeople who went to the clearing, prepares for the climax as ritual: the old woman is completely alone among men who are reduced to silence by being in the presence of death and who treat her body with ritualistic reverence. Later the townspeople make her part of the community as she had never been in life, by banishing her husband and son, scapegoats for the townspeople's communal guilt for excluding her in life. The young brothers experience the scene as sexual initiation and as a story to be told; the inability of the older brother to tell the story properly increases the sense of its strange effect, which the narrator only later could understand as awe. He remembers the scene as if he had been a spectator of himself, seeing himself among "the men standing about, the naked girlish-looking figure, . . . the circle made by the running dogs, and the clear cold winter sky above," his angle of vision like that which Anderson had in the Illinois forest suspended on the tree trunk above the clearing. This distanced perspective of the adult narrator—like that of the tall Abraham Lincoln standing at Ann Rutledge's grave—along with new experience gained over time, enables him to see the woman's life and death as a cycle of feeding animal life, a cycle matching the dogs' ritualistic circle and representing a return to primordial origins. Mrs. Grimes becomes the archetype of female experience; the telling of her story brings her out of isolation into the reader's world. The substitution of the title "Death in the Woods" for "A Death in the Forest" underlines the mythical dimension.

That such a focus was deliberate is even more apparent when we examine other comparatively small but important changes among the three published versions. The version included in *Tar*, told in the third person, is quite different from the version published in the *American Mercury* in the same year as *Tar*; the shift to a first-person narrator, division into five parts, and many small changes in wording resulted in a story Anderson changed little for the 1933 volume. All the changes for the final version emphasize the mythical dimension. The words "lovely" and "charming" are added to the description of the body; the effect on the narrator is emphasized when "with some strange mystical feeling" is added to the sentence "his body trembled," and the words *the mind and* are inserted in the predicate of the sentence "something creepy steals over the body." Significant changes occur in the final paragraphs of the story summarizing what the narrator had gradually come to perceive as the meaning of the story, which became to him "like music heard from far off." In the sentence "The woman who died was one destined to feed animal life," the phrase "destined to feed" has replaced "who fed"; "animal life" has replaced "animals," preparing for the subsequent addition of the idea that "She was feeding animal life before she was born," a completion of the cycle which ends with her feeding animal life at her death. Such additional statements by the narrator as "I wonder how I know all this," "I remember now," "I have just suddenly now, after all these years, remembered her," and "It all comes back to me now" distance the adult narrator; dredging up the details from his memory, telling the story, is like perceiving the archetype. The narrator's "It is a story" near the beginning and "A thing so complete has its own beauty" near the end frame Mrs. Grimes' story, which has become also the story of the artist's creation of the "thing so complete." This story is "a story teller's story," an exemplum of the process by which the artist crystallizes experience into art.[13]

The other stories in *Death in the Woods* continue to reveal the creative process; the narrator-persona becomes confident and unapologetic, increasingly involved in the life a described. One story, "The Flight," shows the necessity of putting aside childish views if one is to be taken seriously; another, "The Return," shows the futility of returning to childhood scenes and conditions—of going home again—in order to find a sense of adult identity. In twelve stories first-person narrators are adult males able to understand the meaning of events as they learn about or experience them in a specific environment, whether it be New York, Paris, the Virginia mountains, or the New Orleans of "A Meeting South." The locales are neither typical nor mythical; the narrators are at home in them. They are also more rational in putting two and two together in order to find a pattern than is the adult narrator of "Death in the Woods," and they rely on others than themselves for help in the process; they are very good at listening.

Many of the first-person narrators furnish an authoritative framework for their stories. Anderson had always taken ideas for stories from what he called "feeders," people who could tell him their stories but could not see their significance or write them.[14] In earlier collections "feeders" lack reinforcement as authoritative sources; they are casual acquaintances or unreliable characters: a "woman met on a train" ("War"), "a man" ("The Other Woman"), "my friend—his name is Leroy" ("Seeds"), a college professor unable to communicate with his own wife ("The Man in the Brown Coat"). "Feeders" in *Death in the Woods* are much more reliable. In the three stories about Virginia mountaineers, the narrators discourage disbelief by not demanding total belief. One has lived "for some time" among "These Mountaineers," but does not pretend to understand them when they reject his pity. Another has been told the story of "A Sentimental Journey" by a scholar who has become the friend of "a mountain man, named Joe, a man much older . . ."; the scholar tells the narrator Joe's story after first admitting to his earlier belief in "Romantic tales." In "A Jury Case" the narrator has most of his information from a mountaineer who participated in the crime and who is "something of a dramatist"; the narrator disarms disbelief by stating flatly, "His version is, to be sure, all a matter of fancy," and by not insisting on the truth of any version.[15] In "Like a Queen" a friend tells his story to the narrator after experience of thirty years has corroborated it; the story gains verisimilitude when Alice, who is the focus of the story, tells her own life history. In "A Meeting South" a young poet tells the narrator the "story of his ill fortune" as if he were "speaking of another"; his command of words wins the narrator's—and the reader's—belief. Being able to use language appropriate to the subject is a test for other narrators and "feeders." In "There She Is—She is Taking Her Bath," the first-person narrator calls attention to his own use of clichés, a step which increases the verisimilitude of his self-revelation; and in "That Sophistication" the hostess's repetition of the word *corked* each time she pours out a new bottle of wine for her guests reveals her absurdity. The narrator of "In a Strange Town" creates a story for us as an illustration of his techniques; because we know that the widow's life he has imagined is fiction, we tend to believe as fact the narrator's concluding story about his own experience. Unlike the persona of "The Dumb Man," this narrator has found a way to go beyond his first reaction of sitting "dumbly" upon learning of his student's death. Credibility for the narrator's perception of hidden truths about people is gained by repetition, at the beginning and end of the story, of examples of his amazing ability to hear sounds unheard by those familiar with them.

"In a Strange Town" more directly than "Death in the Woods" epitomizes the process behind this assured narrative voice. In his *Memoirs* Anderson recorded the centrality of this story to his concept of himself as a writer.[16] He tells us that his habit of wandering in strange towns, immersing himself in a "bath of new impressions, of people seen," often results in mystical self-loathing which brings him to the point of suicide—"and then something happens." This "something" makes "the person called Sherwood Anderson" disappear. But he does not commit suicide; he is able by writing to get "entirely rid of self," to project the "darkness," the "corrupt mass of self." Even as a child, he had felt the "selfishness and slickness in me," the tendency to "control and use men and women," had felt the need for salvation, to which others suggested religion as an answer. Anderson says that such an answer was not possible to him because he could not make the total commitment to art that imitating God as the supreme artist would entail; such a decision is impossible for him because he is not willing to let "everything else go." The creative process described in "In a Strange Town" allows the writer to make stories without controlling lives; the narrator need not feel self-loathing but through his art may achieve a catharsis of despair and self-centeredness.

The narrator of "In a Strange Town" is a professor of philosophy, "no longer young"; he has fled the familiar in order to renew his creativity by making up stories of the lives of strangers he encounters. He demonstrates this renewal by gradually imagining the story behind a group of people in the railroad station: he sees them as "people of no importance" who in becoming mourners have "suddenly become important . . . [as] symbols of death. Death is an important, a majestic thing, eh?" (145) says the narrator, who has already shown the townspeople's sense of awe as they make a "little path of silence" for the group. He "reconstructs" the life of the widow to illustrate his perception that all lives are similar but that "the little circumstances of no two lives anywhere in the world are just alike." From perceiving the "little odd fragmentary ends of things" he is able to perceive the mystery of life in general which he represents in his reconstruction of the widow's life. This process of relating the particular and the general is, of course, appropriate for a professor of philosophy. Also appropriate to the mature professor is the fact that when he wanders in strange places he is an observer, not a participant in life: he no longer picks up women but tries to escape involvement. "It may be that I am a bit dirty with life and have come here, to this strange place, to bathe myself in strange life and get clean and fresh again" (150). Now, he tells us, he is refreshed. This could be the end of the story if it were meant like "Death in the Woods" to exemplify the process by which the artist goes beyond self or if the focus were on the imagined characters as symbols of death. But the narrator goes on to reveal that the immediate cause of his wandering to a strange town was the sudden death of a young woman, his student, whose attention had flattered him and whose experience had often caused him to re-experience his youth. Her death has caused him to take this trip in order to become "more aware," "more alive": as in "Death in the Woods," a woman and her death have been the inspiration for a narrator; but his learning process here is the result of active imagination, of purposefully weaving observed particulars into a pattern of meaning.

The changes in the narrative voice in *Death in the Woods* are paralleled by changes in the attitudes towards women revealed in the stories. All of them go beyond the suggestion in "A Lincoln Fragment" and in "A Death in the Forest" that a woman's death was more significant than her life because it freed a man from provincial limitations, though "Death in the Woods" itself comes close to this egocentric attitude. Mrs. Grimes's nobility in suffering exalts her almost to the dimensions of the mythical suffering servant who can redeem mankind, but this exaltation is essentially demeaning to the character's humanity. However much the reader is inclined to sympathize with Mrs. Grimes's stoicism, it is difficult to overlook its inadvertence. Her suffering is that of a victim, not of an autonomous human being. In other stories about women who are helpful to men because of their greater generosity and nobility, Anderson creates more nearly autonomous characters. Alice in "Like a Queen" arouses in the narrator a "great surge of love" when she obtains a gift of a thousand dollars to support him in his work, which she tries to convince him is a source of power. As a young beauty she had given her lovers something; as an old woman she is still a nurturer, acting as go-between for rich parents and their alienated children. Aunt Sally of "A Meeting South" is like a mother; she saves their nest-eggs for men who had patronized her gambling and drinking establishments, more than re-paying them for what they had paid her for her services. Significantly, Alice and Aunt Sally, though now old and ugly like Mrs. Grimes, are perceived as beautiful by the narrator, who dissociates them from any preconception of beauty.

Anderson's exaltation of women is distilled in *Perhaps Women,* a small volume he wrote after months of wandering to observe the impact of industrialization at the beginning of the Great Depression. The woodcut Anderson commissioned for the frontispiece of the volume shows a strong woman on an impressive steed leading a small man on a nag; Anderson felt that his friend Lankes caught exactly the meaning expressed in the volume.[17] But the repetition of "Perhaps Women" as the title of three separate sections within the book emphasizes the *perhaps*; Anderson sees women as potentially strong leaders of men but is not sure that they will actually become saviors. In fact, he feared that women, especially as consumers, might contribute to industrial man's castration; and he recognized that women too might stand in need of salvation. In the concluding section, "A Cry in the Night," he suggests that the factory women's calls to men may become only parts of a game, greeted by "an outburst of laughter from many women, ironic laughter." In spite of such doubts, the narrator persists in suggesting that women, because of their biologically-caused tenderness, may be able to bring back to life men deadened by their roles in industrial society.

Other stories in *Death in the Woods* show men's weakness and consequent need for the saving grace of women. Males who view women primarily as sex objects are shown to be foolish, if not vicious. The absurdly jealous narrator of "There She Is—She is Taking her Bath" ironically reveals his foolishness while defending his suspicions that his wife is committing adultery; the reader easily perceives the innocence of the wife who is merely taking a bath—symbolically renewing herself. The narrator in "The Lost Novel," shocked by the injustice of a novelist's perception of his wife as an object to be abused and used for literary purposes, perceives the novelist's self-deception. The narrator in "The Return" realizes that casual sex is no longer significant or even possible for him and that his marriage for the sake of professional advancement has been sterile. The difficulty men have in learning such lessons is wryly shown in "The Flood," in which a professor of philosophy intent upon finishing his life-work on values succumbs for the second time to marrying a frivolous woman. Although the woman in the story is not admirable, she is a tie to life more important than professional achievement. In these stories the women are more than objects; they have lives of their own and men must accept them as they are. In them Anderson moves away from exaltation of woman as a mythical creature to a realistic view of women sharing men's lives.

Two stories go further to show women as actively initiating involvements that will benefit men. "Why They Got Married" is a playful story in which a married couple tell the story of their courtship to an interested observer; both acknowledge the woman's skill in winning the man's love and his parents' approval, and credit her with their present happiness. As co-narrator as well as wife, the female character is on a par with the man; both relish the story of the wife's manipulation of her in-laws so that "marriage sure seemed like salvation to them" (268). In "Another Wife" a widowed doctor is happy to marry a woman who has, without regard to local mores, pursued him. The doctor realizes that his view of her as surrounded by admirers and therefore too good for him has been a stereotype, and he sees her as a person with her own specific life history, a unique identity. She is admirable, worthy of his love, and able to renew his self-confidence and vitality, but she is not above him on a pedestal. Through his new insight about her the doctor is able to end his own brooding introspection. In this last story the change in attitude toward women is accompanied by a significant change in the male character's view of himself.

In "Brother Death" Anderson went beyond perception of women as sharers of experience with males upon whom the stories focus; he uses a creative and wise female as the central consciousness.[18] No narrator intrudes between the reader and the characters. An assured but unidentified voice paints the scene and describes the characters before focusing on Mary Grey. Unlike the young boy in "Death in the Woods," Mary is already mature at fourteen. At the time the incidents of the story begin " . . . she was both a child and a grown woman. The woman side of her kept popping out at unexpected moments" (273), and she and her younger brother Ted understand life better than their elders. Like the narrator of

"Death in the Woods," Mary does perceive the events of her childhood more completely when she grows up, but she never shares his naiveté. So sure is she of the validity of her own perceptions that she guards Ted, who has a heart ailment which they all know will soon kill him, from the over-protectiveness of the rest of the family, and stands up to her mother who spoils Ted's joy in life with her warnings. Mary and Ted both perceive that the very imminence of his death warrants his risking all for joy; embracing "Brother Death" is the only way for Ted to live. Later Mary realizes that living Ted's way, risking all for joy, is the only way to avoid "the more subtle and terrible death" in life that is the choice of their older brother who sacrifices his independence to share in the materialism and success of his parents.

In making his mature voice a female, Anderson has blended his perceptions of the artist and of woman. It is not only the male free to roam—often freed by woman's sacrifice—who has "glimpses" that can become stories; woman living her life can have and fight for creative insights. Mary's wisdom coincides with the motto Anderson ascribes to Socrates as the ultimate wisdom: "Not life but the good life" and to Anderson's choice for the inscription on his grave: "Life not death is the great adventure."[19] *Death in the Woods* moves from a mythic view of woman and of the artist's quest to a definition of the good life, of the kind of success Americans need to substitute for the materialism that has blighted the fulfillment of their heroic quest for meaning.

In "Brother Death" Anderson goes beyond the kind of realism in which abstractions reveal meaning,[20] beyond myth which evokes "a connotative style approaching the idiom of poetry."[21] It is significant that Professor Tony Tanner, who found Anderson not only incapable of but opposed to rational analysis, focuses on *Winesburg, Ohio* for his examples.[22] Tanner epitomizes what he considers Anderson's childlike refusal to discriminate among random details in order to find the general behind the particular—his refusal to reason—by citing from *Tar* the child's concept of God as juxtaposed with his sensation of straw tickling his belly and the statement "There's a lot to think about you can never really think about." "Brother Death" opens with a statement that two oak tree stumps were to two children "objects of wonder." But their wonder is no passive awe, no mystical feeling. Soon after seeing the trees cut, the two children start "wondering" about them, attempting to understand the event, to find reasons for it, to integrate it with their previous knowledge. They suggest that perhaps the stumps had bled, as they imagined the stump of an armless man they had seen must have; they argue over this idea, the girl insisting that a woman could have had an armless stump, so that the trees' experience could be compared with that of a woman just as well as with that of a war hero. Mary's "Why not? I'd like to know why not?" sets the keynote of the entire story in which the tree stumps become a rich symbol. She would like to have verified the hypothesis by touching the tree stumps to see if they were warm, but it is too late for that experiment, since she and her brother ran away "just as the trees fell." In the rest of the story they do not run away from experience; they escape into reality. Their escape is based upon the fact, the sure knowledge that Ted must soon die. The special bond between them because they accept the implication of their knowledge is verified by everyone who knows them; they are perceived as being "too serious" for childhood and they do not fit the romantic stereotype of the innocent, the ignorant child. It is the adults whose "recognition wasn't very definite"; Mary's sense of "something concerning her brother Ted" is not the result of an intuitive glimpse but stems from a reason, her knowledge of his condition and her rational facing up to its implications.

It is significant that Mary is not merely a passive observer of her brother's life and death; she participates in them, initiates action, though Ted too "was imaginative and could think of plenty of risky things to do." The children's actions are connected, purposive. Far from being passive, they create and re-create their own world daily; "being in their own created world, feeling a new security there, they could suddenly look out at the outside world and see, in a new way, what was going on out there in the world that belonged also to others" (282). They do not perceive the world as isolated details; they do not intuit some mythic world behind the perceived details. They create their own reality and use it to perceive the objective reality of others. The two children are reasoning; they are Man Thinking, inducing and deducing. The narration goes on to give the facts about the cutting down of the trees, about the irrationality and tyranny of the father who has ordered them cut, the ineffectiveness of the wife in trying to get him to change his mind, about the submission of the older son Dan after a brief rebellion against his father's will. The stumps can be taken to stand for the sterile lives of the father and son who make material success their goal, a living death far worse than the real death Ted experiences. They can be perceived just as physical facts without either the anthropomorphic meaning the two children suggest or the symbolic meanings of the struggle between father and sons or between the two sons, one literally dead and one metaphorically so. The stumps are a true symbol, open-ended in their meaning; Anderson has resisted the imposition of his own view of the world or that of characters in the story. Each reader must create his own reality. In going beyond the authoritative voice of other narrators in *Death in the Woods*, Anderson anticipates the modern critical view of the need for readers to participate in the creation of a text.

Even a partial analysis of the style of "Brother Death" shows Anderson's change from the paratactic style Professor Tanner considers his hallmark. Compared with the first two hundred words of "Death in the Woods," the opening of "Brother Death" is clearly in a hypostatic style. It contains almost twice as many subordinate clauses, one-third as many simple sentences; the average number of words per sentence is 15.4 compared with 11.8 for "Death in the Woods," a significant difference when linked to the preponderance in the latter of compound predicates joined by the paratactic *and* and in the former of participial embedding. One-line paragraphs found in "Death in the Woods"—there are nine—as portentous statements of simple narrative facts are used in "Brother Death" only for dialog; just a glance at the story establishes the paragraph length as much greater than that of any other story in *Death in the Woods*, the main reason being for continuous narrative. The style is also different in that it lacks the vagueness of "Death in the Woods" about the old woman as "one of those," "such a," one seen by all but unknown by any. "Brother Death" opens with the fact "There were the two oak stumps" (Anderson added *oak* in revising an earlier version) and within four sentences begins direct discourse between the two children who exchange ideas, even argue about the stumps.

The continuity of action in the story belies Anderson's fictional view of the writer's technique as the piecing together of isolated incidents, of understanding the general through erratic glimpses into the lives of others. The narrator of "Brother Death" knows the history of the land and the people in the story; he gives us details of the cutting down of the trees and the children's death-defying activities, but neither the trees nor the death of the younger brother becomes the focus of the story. Like "Death in the Woods," the story is beautiful because of its completeness. But it is not a completeness imagined by an observer of someone else's life; it is a completeness experienced by the characters. Their concept that death is the accompaniment, the fulfiller of life has the authority of direct truth, not of myth. The narrator of this story is no naive observer of life; he has gone beyond wonder to understanding.

"Death in the Woods" is probably Anderson's greatest story in the style of his early writing, his greatest achievement in mythopoesis. In it he resolved the dichotomy between the observer and the observed by absorbing the external world into the mind of the observer. In the volume *Death in the Woods* he undercuts the authority of an observer as creator of the observed world by showing the absurdity of egocentricity, by increasing the credibility of other observers (his "feeders"), and finally, in "Brother Death," by allowing the meticulously reported details observed by the narrative voice to constitute the story, a story not about writing a story but about living a life. Perhaps this shift is the effect of Anderson's fully releasing the woman within himself. The old writer of "The Book of the Grotesque" felt that his creative force was a young woman within him, "wearing a coat of mail like a knight"—ready to go out and seek adventure. In "Brother Death" a young woman wise beyond her years creates the meaning of her brother's life; she leads him not because of superior strength and nobility like the woman of Lankes's woodcut for *Perhaps Women* but because of sympathetic sharing of his life. In Mary Grey the voice of Sherwood Anderson expresses the wisdom learned by living; "Brother Death" is a fitting climax to *Death in the Woods*.

## Notes

1. Sherwood Anderson, *The Modern Writer* (San Francisco, 1925), p. 43. For a summary of critical attitudes toward Anderson, see Walter B. Rideout in *Sixteen American Authors: A Survey of Research and Criticism*, ed. Jackson R. Bryer, 2d. ed (New York 1973). Michael Geismar was one of the first critics to see the importance of *Death in the Woods*; he saw as the unifying theme of the volume a deepening of Anderson's commitment to "the realm of ordinary human relationships . . . the mysteries of the commonplace" (pp. xix, xx, Introduction to Geismar's edition *Sherwood Anderson: Short Stories* [New York, 1962]). A more recent assessment is that of David D. Anderson who considers *Death in the Woods* Anderson's "most consistently high-level collection. . . . an integrated and mature examination of Anderson's belief that reality must be separated from appearance. . . ." See his "Sherwood Anderson after Twenty Years," pp. 246–56 in *The Achievement of Sherwood Anderson: Essays in Criticism*, ed. Ray Lewis White (Chapel Hill, 1966). See also his "Anderson and Myth," pp. 118–44 in *Sherwood Anderson: Dimensions of His Literary Art, A Collection of Critical Essays*, ed. David D. Anderson [East Lansing, Michican], 1976. Interestingly, the imputation of form to *Winesburg, Ohio* and its designation as a "novel" instead of a collection of stories is a post-facto critical phenomenon; as John H. Ferres points out, early critics saw no form in it at all (see his Introduction to *Winesburg, Ohio: Text and Critical Edition* [New York, 1966]). William L. Phillips has shown, however, that Anderson conceived the stories of the "Book of the Grotesque" as complementary parts of a whole, unified by setting and the character George Willard; see his "How Sherwood Anderson wrote *Winesburg, Ohio*," in *The Achievement of Sherwood Anderson*, pp. 62–85.

2. Letter to Schevill, March 2, 1933, in *Letters of Sherwood Anderson*, ed. Howard Mumford Jones and Walter B. Rideout (Boston, 1953), pp. 277–78. In July, 1933, Anderson reiterated his high opinion of "Brother Death" to Paul Rosenfeld, saying that the story was "written last winter after the rest of the book was in press" (p. 292). That this was only partially true is apparent from a study of a collection of notes and six versions of the story; see Earl Hilton, "The Evolution of Sherwood Anderson's 'Brother Death,' " *Northwest Ohio Quarterly*, XXIV (Summer, 1952), 125–30.

3. Benjamin T. Spencer, "Sherwood Anderson: American Mythopoeist," *American Literature*, XLI (March 1969), p. 3 (rpt. in *Sherwood Anderson: A Collection of Critical Essays*, ed. Walter B. Rideout [Englewood Cliffs, N.J., 1947] pp. 150–65.) Professor Spencer has brilliantly shown that Anderson's prevailing style up to and including "Death in the Woods" involved the process of turning into myth his observations about American life; and that his attempts, like those of Whitman, "to project the democratic beyond concept into myth," contrast with the techniques of "such contemporary naturalists or realists as Dreiser or Lewis."

4. See the letter to Paul Rosenfeld referred to above, *Letters*, p. 292.

5. One of the main foci in *Winesburg, Ohio* is the death of George Willard's mother; in fact, David Stouck considers death "a persistent preoccupation" in Anderson's work, though he does not discuss *Death in the Woods* per se; see his "*Winesburg, Ohio* as a Dance of Death," *American Literature*, XLVIII (January 1977), 525–42. In the first selection in *The Triumph of the Egg*, the tale the "dumb man" could not tell was that of the relationship of a woman to four men, one of whom "may have been Death;/The waiting eager woman may have been Life." The long story "Unused" from *Horses and Men* is about a young boy's first view of death; he sees the bloated distorted body of a woman who had committed suicide because she could find no man who could accept her proffered love.

6. Introduction, *Perhaps Women* (New York, 1931, rpt. Mamaroneck, N.Y., 1970). For Anderson male impotence was not just a sexual but a total failure, essentially a failure to

be an individual. To him women represented not just sex but the sense of life. For more detailed considerations of Anderson's view of women as a civilizing force, his debt to Henry Adams and rejection of Freudian formulas, see Rex Burbank, "The Artist as Prophet," pp. 107–23 of his *Sherwood Anderson* (New York, 1964), and Frederick J. Hoffman, ["Anderson and Freud"], rpt. in the Ferres edition of *Winesburg, Ohio*, pp. 309–20. In a study limited to Anderson's short stories, William V. Miller links Anderson's life experiences with women to his artistic view of them as idealized but limited to their biological roles. Miller points out as a "new note . . . the objectivity, the irony, and the narrator's [comparative objectivity]" in a story of 1936 but fails to find the evidence for this new note that I believe exists in *Death in the Woods*. See Miller's "Earth-Mothers, Succubi, and Other Ectoplasmic Spirits: The Women in Sherwood Anderson's Short Stories," *MidAmerica* I (Fall, 1973), 64–81.

7. For dates of publication of the stories, see *Sherwood Anderson: A Bibliography*, ed. Eugene P. Sheehy and Kenneth A. Lohf (Los Gatos, Cal., 1960). Of the sixteen stories in the volume, four were published for the first time in *Death in the Woods*: "Like a Queen," "That Sophistication," "The Flood," and "Brother Death." For all the stories but "Death in the Woods" and "Brother Death," Anderson seems to have used the writing habits described by Phillips for *Winesburg*: he frequently changed single words but seldom whole paragraphs or the original narrative order. The stories with previous magazine publication, except for "Death in the Woods," were almost unaltered for the volume. Anderson's shaping of the volume depended largely on the arrangement of the stories and the final writing of "Brother Death." None of the stories can be specifically linked to incidents which must have deeply influenced his ideas about women and about death, such as the death by suicide of his second wife, Tennessee Mitchell, in 1929, her body discovered in her apartment several days afterwards; and the lonely life and death (1927) of his youngest brother Earl who never found a woman to rescue him. But Anderson does explicitly credit his fourth wife, Eleanor Copenhaver, whom he married shortly after *Death in the Woods* was published and with whom he was traveling when he put the volume together, with "awakening in me again the desire to participate in life at any cost." See his letter to Paul Rosenfeld, *Letters*, p. 292.

8. See Michael Fanning, *France and Sherwood Anderson: Paris Notebook, 1921* (Baton Rouge, La., 1976), pp. 62–65, for what Fanning thinks may be Anderson's first attempt at "Death in the Woods." "Father Abraham: A Lincoln Fragment" appeared in *The Sherwood Anderson Reader*, ed. Paul Rosenfeld (Boston, 1947), pp. 530–602; Rosenfeld thinks the piece may have been alluded to in a letter of 1925, and there is a reference to "working on Lincoln" in a letter of April [1924] to Jerome and Lucille Blum (see *Sherwood Anderson: Centennial Studies*, ed. Hilbert H. Campbell and Charles E. Modlin [Troy, N.Y., 1976], p. 9.) "A Death in the Forest" was edited by William V. Miller as an appendix to *Tar: A Midwest Childhood*, ed. Ray Lewis White (Cleveland, 1969). The first and only edition of *Death in the Woods* was published by Horace Liveright in New York; the volume appeared on April 8, 1933, in the depth of the depression, and Liveright went out of business a month later. This fact may account for the scarcity of reviews elicited by the volume—there were only seven—and the scarcity of subsequent attention, though preoccupation with *Winesburg, Ohio* as Anderson's most important if not only significant work was also a cause of neglect of the volume. All quotations from the story are from the 1933 final version in *Death in the Woods* except when specific reference is made to one of the earlier versions.

9. *A Story Teller's Story* (New York, 1924), pp. 122, 121.

10. *Memoirs*, ed. Ray Lewis White (Chapel Hill, N.Y., 1969), pp. 425–26. In the first edition of the *Memoirs* (New York, 1942), the incident appears as part of Book IV, The Literary Life, entitled "Old Mary, the Dogs, and Theda Bara," pp. 306–12. The specificity of the title makes the incident seem biographically credible; if it occurred, it would have had to be between 1920–22, according to Professor Walter Rideout, who kindly gave me this information in a letter dated February 3, 1978.

11. Anderson had long been fascinated by Lincoln and identified himself with him. See David D. Anderson, "Sherwood Anderson's Use of the Lincoln Theme," *Lincoln Herald*, LX-IV (Spring 1961), 28–32. Lincoln's mysticism Sherwood Anderson associates with his "being

alone in the forest on still summer afternoons" ("A Lincoln Fragment," p. 567). The fact that Anderson added a comment about the cruelty encountered by bound children to the 1933 version of "Death in the Woods" indicates that the Lincoln story may have been in his thoughts at the time, though his own fictionalization of his mother's life as a bound girl may have been uppermost in his mind: see *A Story Teller's Story*, p. 7.

12. The town as Anderson's mythopoetic creation is discussed by Professor Spencer in part three of the article cited in n. 3 above.

13. Many critics have seen the focus on the artist as the center of the story; see Jon S. Lawry, " 'Death in the Woods' and the Artist's Self in Sherwood Anderson," *PMLA*, LXXIV (1959), 306–11; and Sister Mary Joslyn, "Some Artistic Dimensions of Sherwood Anderson's 'Death in the Woods,' " *Studies in Short Fiction*, IV (Spring 1967), 252–59. Professor Mary Rohrberger has explored the story as the narrator's retrieval of myth from the subconscious, suggesting that underlying the image of Mrs. Grimes are those of the goddesses worshipped in the Eleusinian mysteries, Demeter, Proserpine, and Hecate; see her "The Man, the Boy, and the Myth: Sherwood Anderson's 'Death in the Woods,' " *Midcontinent American Studies Journal*, III (Fall 1962), 48–54.

14. See *Memoirs*, ed. White, pp. 376–81, for Anderson's account of his friend George Daugherty as a "feeder."

15. Anderson's objectivity in these stories was apparently deliberate; in a letter dated October 29, 1929, he wrote to friends that "These Mountaineers" was "just a description of some people, all my own feeling left out. I think it was good." (*Letters*, p. 196). In the Introduction to *No Swank* (c. 1934; rpt. Mamaroneck, N.Y., 1970), Anderson comments that his "glimpses" are not "a complete or even a just picture" of his friends.

16. Pp. 435–37.

17. See Welford D. Taylor, "Two Dismounted Men: Sherwood Anderson and J. J. Lankes," in *Sherwood Anderson: Centennial Studies* pp. 224–34. See also Sherwood Anderson, "Mr. J. J. Lankes and His Woodcuts," *No Swank*, pp. 25–29.

18. In his article on "Brother Death" cited in n. 2 above, Earl Hilton points out that the use of Mary as central consciousness occurs in Anderson's notes as well as in all six versions of the story; and that one of the main effects of Anderson's changes is to give more of the story through Mary. Hilton's view that the evolving central theme is "success" as a living death is borne out by Anderson's comments in a letter written in the spring of 1933 (to Roger Sergel; quoted by William V. Miller, "In Defense of Mountaineers: Sherwood Anderson's Hill Stories," *Ball State University Forum*, XV [Spring 1974], p. 57). In the context of *Death in the Woods*, the major theme seems to be a definition of life lived fully, the life lived *with* "Brother Death."

19. *Memoirs*, pp. 558–560.

20. Walter B. Rideout ("The Simplicity of *Winesburg, Ohio*," rpt. in Ferres' edition, pp. 287–300) considers Anderson's realism in the early work as "a means to something else, not an end in itself" as it was for more traditional writers such as Sinclair Lewis; the result was that Anderson produced a "highly abstract kind of reality," one effect of which was to "depreciate the values of surfaces."

21. Spencer, p. 3.

22. Professor Tanner's view of Anderson as expressing in appropriately static paratactical style his passively glimpsed fragments of life is found in "Sherwood Anderson's Little Things," pp. 205–27 in *The Reign of Wonder: Naivety and Reality in American Literature* (New York, 1965).

# " 'An Aching, Hurting Thing':
# The Aesthetic of
# Ritualistic Reenactment"

Roger J. Bresnahan*

> O Youth! It is the great fertile time for the taking in and the
> sorting out of impressions. There are these towns, fields, hills,
> cities, days and nights, men and women, seen and felt when
> seeing and feeling, often dumbly, an aching, hurting thing.
> How passionately the youth wants an outlet for all his pent up
> feelings and how difficult it is to find the outlet.[1]

A sense of the inarticulate suffering of humanity runs through much
of Sherwood Anderson's writing. His characters exist in a world where
their own significance is least apparent to themselves. George Willard,
the young reporter for the *Winesburg Eagle*, enables the essentially
grotesque characters of Anderson's novel *Winesburg, Ohio* to make some
sense of themselves. Only with George is Wing Biddlebaum, the pathetic
character of "Hands," able to "put into words the ideas that had been accumulated by his mind during long years of silence."[2] As a newspaper
reporter, George assumes a position in the life of the town analogous to
that of the writer, and so the citizens of Winesburg seek him out to confide their secrets. George was not a little confused by these manifestations
of truth. Wing Biddlebaum's half-coherent revelations left him "perplexed and frightened," and beside the manic Wash Williams he felt "ill
and weak . . . old and shapeless."[3] To his mother, George seemed to be
"groping about, trying to find himself."[4] Of course, none of those who
confide in George expect to see their stories in the newspaper, but the
stories of these grotesque figures do achieve meaning in their ritualistic
reenactment within the novel. In that respect, George becomes a kind of
innocent narrator who gives significance to his own existence as well as to
the lives he observes.

This is a paradox. Such persons as George Willard and the neurotic
Alice Hindman are not real people in a real midwestern town in the early
years of the twentieth century. The only reality they can have is the
reality experienced by the reader of *Winesburg, Ohio*. What makes this

*This original essay was written for this volume and is published by permission of Roger J.
Bresnahan.

act of reading important, therefore, is not only the verisimilitude of Anderson's characters, but especially the author's ability to convey a sense of urgency. It is a sense that without the novel such persons as Winesburg contains can only face lives of quiet desperation. Without the novel to give expression to the urgency of her despair, such a person as Alice Hindman—who discovered herself naked on the street one rainy night— might have no recourse but to "force herself to face bravely the fact that many people must live and die alone, even in Winesburg."[5] Indeed, all of Sherwood Anderson's characters are in some measure reducible to the reader. As readers, we are reminded how precarious is our grasp on our own significance. We seek the ritualistic reenactment of the desperate lives that the author provides so that we may save ourselves from final meaninglessness.

Sherwood Anderson's apostrophe to youth, with which this essay begins, commemorates an urgency to find significance in life while warning how difficult that will be to achieve. His wry comments on the differences between hack writers and literary artists indicate that Anderson believed the proper activity for the latter was to enable the reader to achieve just such a perception of self-worth. The "unforgiveable sin" for the hack is "to actually touch people's lives." He considered his own practice as a writer as growing "naturally out of the lives and the hopes, joys and sufferings" of real people. It was just such advice that Kate Swift gave to George Willard, the aspiring literary artist: to "stop fooling with words" and know life.[6] We may recall Anderson's observations on the "little children of the arts" with whom he lived on Chicago's North Side. They were delicate people in a closed world. Like so many of his characters, they were not "equipped to wrestle with life."[7] He felt he had become their instrument for getting their stories out to the world: through the medium of his art their lives could take on meaning. For us readers, as well, the ritualistic recital of the narrative converts undifferentiated reality into significant experience.

The model for such a recital derives from Anderson's father, an impoverished harness-maker who was a born story-teller. For a time Irwin Anderson worked as an itinerant book-peddlar who advertised his wares by reading passages to prospective customers. One of his titles was *The Personal Memoirs of General Grant*. By reading passages from this book and embellishing them with personal recollections, he was able to exaggerate his own importance in the Civil War and to establish for his auditors a personal intimacy with Grant which never existed. Reincarnated as Dick Moorhead in the autobiographical novel, *Tar*, Irwin goes from house to house reading aloud and telling his tales, thus escaping the drab circumstances of his own life. For the reader aware of Grant's ignominious death in poverty, this refashioning of the actual past effects a change in the storyteller's own destiny and in the reader's, as well. An alternate version in *A Story Teller's Story* depicts Irwin Anderson as part of a traveling magic-lantern show. There he tells his stories to secure room and board for himself and his partner and to bask in the adulation of the simple folk who listened. Sherwood allows Tar to wittily observe of Dick Moorhead: "It was fun to hear him if you weren't depending on him for a living."[8]

Sherwood Anderson follows in his father's footsteps as a storyteller. By reenacting the miserable events of people's lives, by retelling their tales of loneliness and frustration, by rehearsing the contests they won and those they lost, he is able to control life, to give it a structure it did not have when considered as one event running into another. By relating experiences which he did not have but plausibly might have had, Irwin Anderson was not saved from failure. But he saved himself from confronting failure. In Sherwood's stories, the plausible events which may be relived by the reader, and thus form that outlet which youth seeks to find, are often embedded in a contest. Sometimes the contest is a plausible duel of wits or force with another, as in the unrelenting animosity which sprung up between the Moorhead boys and Hog Hawkins over the price of a newspaper. Hog had the brittle satisfaction of cheating Tar of a few pennies, and Tar had the satisfaction of having the townsfolk on his side. Late one night, however, Tar stumbled on the old man in the cemetery praying over his wife's grave. After that, Tar let Hog Hawkins have the little victory occasionally out of pity for the greater battle which Hog had clearly lost.

More often, the contest is with the self. Left to pine away in Winesburg by a lover who never returned, Alice Hindman becomes desperate over the years. On the night of her "adventure" Alice is suddenly impelled to run naked in the rain, "to find some other lonely human and embrace him." She believes the rain will have "some creative and wonderful effect on her body."[9] Only when she encounters a half-deaf old man at her gate does she return to her senses. The comic attempt at self-assertion ends with Alice retreating to her bedroom where she bolts the door and shores it up with her dressing table.

Sherwood's sister, Stella, in her loneliness as guardian of the young family after her mother's death, asks Sherwood to walk out with her as if he were her beau. This is perhaps the most extraordinary of Sherwood Anderson's private revelations. It is matched by Stella's pathetically comic self-perception related in Sherwood's *Memoirs* as "My Sister Stella: The Story of a Christian Life."[10] As they listen to the preacher's eulogy at Stella's funeral, Sherwood and his brothers discover a sister they never knew. The preacher derived the story from a pamphlet Stella had authored. In her struggle with life she had transformed her image into that of a girl who had sacrificed self-fulfillment to educate her brothers. Though he feigns offense at the distortion, Sherwood uses the story to demonstrate that the storyteller can create meaning even where none apparently exists. Like Dick Moorhead, Stella mythologized her life and then retold the myth. Although the ritualistic reenactment which the retelling constituted did not change the reality, it insured that reality would keep its distance.

The Hog Hawkins tale depicts a contest between Hog and the Moorhead boys at one level and between Hog and the imponderable forces at another. While Hog could stave off the effect of one aspect of reality with another and Stella could substitute an imagined reality, Alice Hindman has no outlet. Like Wing Biddlebaum, she has only the most tenuous rein on her urge to flout those social conventions which protect her from her own enthusiasm. Anderson relates a similar contest in the grim narrative of soldiers training for the Spanish-American War who amuse themselves on a quiet Sunday afternoon by raping an old woman. The contest which occupies Anderson is that between the narrator who observes the sordid episode and his own self-image. A "small man . . . a clerk in a store at home," he was invited to take his turn. He bolted into the woods, and from there he watched: "I was ashamed but I wanted to see."[11] Like Alice and Wing, he is one of those not "equipped to wrestle with life" because, unlike Hog Hawkins and Stella Anderson, he hasn't the storyteller's ability to tame life by transforming it into a more livable reality. He gives himself over to the human compulsion to tell the uncomplimentary tale, but like the "little children of the arts" he requires a storyteller to finally get his story out.

In these contests with life which his characters win and lose, Sherwood Anderson is an observer. This is so even when he relates an event in which he was an actor. Describing Ring Lardner, he deliberately places himself in the role of the observer: ". . . I was like a man standing in the dressing room of a theater and watching an actor at work on his make-up."[12] A Story Teller's Story portrays Anderson's childhood not in the expected manner of autobiography but as boyhood fantasies out of The Last of the Mohicans. Carl Sandburg told Anderson about his public appearances—"I give 'em a good show." Reflecting on Sandburg and on the showman in his father, Sherwood decides that is what he does, too. Oversimplifying, he posits two courses in life, the life of the fancy where "even the most base man's actions sometimes take on the form of beauty" and the life of the "mere smart-aleck" who "without humbleness before the possibilities of life . . . may remain to the end, blind, deaf and dumb, feeling and seeing nothing."[13] George Willard in Winesburg, Ohio has these two courses dangling before him and, to the extent of identification with George, so does the reader. At the same time, the reader is more perceptive than George who wishes to live the life of fancy but has not yet recognized that he is becoming the smart-aleck.

From the contests which he observed or pretended to observe Anderson creates an artistic model to interact with the reader so that both narrator and reader are saved from an action's normal consequences by this ritualistic reenactment in narrative. Because this model impels us as readers to identify with Anderson's characters, we may often catch ourselves imagining that this reenactment of their stories in narrative will save them from meaninglessness, as if they existed in the same way we do. "My Sister Stella: The Story of a Christian Life" portrays just such a projection. Stella's imagined autobiography metamorphosed her life. Having received a vision from Jesus who got into bed with the lonely woman to caress and comfort her, Stella remodelled her past so that it would be consonant with the future she projected for herself.

The story is suspect. It seems, as Anderson says of *A Story Teller's Story*, "more or less, if not entirely, authentic . . . the true authenticity of a thing felt."[14] But despite our suspicions concerning his literal veracity, Anderson's telling of Stella's tale elevates her reality to a controlled and mythic level, just as the narrative reenactment of the clerk's tale of cowardly voyeurism enables us, as readers, first to identify with the clerk and then to separate ourselves from him, call him a "small man," and believe we would do differently.

The rubric of ritualistic reenactment is especially useful because it is not required that the narrator understand why the tale must be retold, but only that it must be. Certainly George Willard is confused and often terrified by the scenes around him. Dr. Parcival believes that he will himself be sacrificed before he finishes his own book, and so he begins to instruct George. Joe Welling, Winesburg's coal-oil seller, believes George is ill-cast as a writer:

> "It's what I should be doing, there's no doubt of that," he declared, stopping George Willard on the sidewalk before Daugherty's Feed Store. His eyes began to glisten and his forefinger to tremble. . . . "I'm only telling you," he added. "I've got nothing against you but I should have your place. I could do the work at odd moments. Here and there I would run finding out things you'll never see."[15]

George's friend, Seth Richmond, thinks him a "profound fool" because he aims to fall in love with Helen White in order to compose a love story. George Willard is neither the narrator of *Winesburg, Ohio* nor a stand-in for Sherwood Anderson. But the reader is made to feel that if only George can follow Kate Swift's advice to observe the real dramas being played out all around him he will become the narrator of such a book as *Winesburg, Ohio* just as the reader is becoming the narrator by ritualistically reenacting in imagination the dramas of Anderson's novel.

As the observer of the contests he narrates, Anderson deprecates his own role. His method is akin to the policy of the country newspaper for which George Willard worked. George would rush about gathering details about each inhabitant's doings so that as many subscribers as possible could be mentioned by name. But where George thought the vocation of the writer entailed creating a reality of which he could be in complete

control, Anderson seeks to tame the actual by recounting it sympathetically. Because he deprecates his own importance in this process, and
because he seldom steps out of the storyteller's role, it is difficult to assess
how deliberately he assumed the role of the innocent narrator. In one of
the many passages of the *Memoirs* where he puzzles over his own creativity he observes: "My own imagination . . . is constantly superimposing
something on others, on my own eyes, on my ears. I am always building
and rebuilding." He adds, as a droll afterthought, that this process "is one
of the things that makes any straight view of life, as we all live it, so difficult to get."[16] His practice as a teller of tales denies the value of "any
straight view of life."

Critical approaches to Sherwood Anderson's work stand or fall as
they deal with his endings. One writer has wittily observed that if Anderson had "started his novels at the point where most end, chaos would per-
vade the entire book, not merely the ending."[17] Anderson consistently rejected the "splashy" denouement typical of Hollywood and the yarns of
his father. It is in his endings, which are full of hope yet conscious that
even this hope lies in a "fog of illusory optimism,"[18] that the proper role of
the reader is discovered. For it is at the end of the author's narration that
the reader projects the story in his own imagination and continues the
ritualistic reenactment initiated by the author. Anderson wished to en-
dow his characters with a separate existence so that they could "live on
and on in the fanciful life of others."[19] The only salvation for such
characters as he creates is that their stories get out through ritualistic reenactment in the imagination of the reader. It is in Anderson's
remarkably sensitive portrait of Theodore Dreiser that we can best
understand the shared role of the reader and the writer in rebuilding lives
through ritualistic reenactment. Dreiser, Anderson writes, "does not
know what to do with life, so he tells about it as he sees it, simply and
honestly. The tears run down his face and he folds and refolds the pocket-
handkerchief and shakes his head."[20]

## Notes

1. *Sherwood Anderson's Memoirs: A Critical Edition*, ed. Ray Lewis White (Chapel
Hill: Univ. of North Carolina Press), p. 237.

2. Sherwood Anderson, *Winesburg, Ohio: Text and Criticism*, ed. John H. Ferres
(New York: Viking, 1966), p. 28.

3. *Winesburg*, pp. 31, 127.

4. *Winesburg*, p. 43.

5. *Winesburg*, p. 120.

6. Sherwood Anderson, *The Modern Writer* (San Francisco: Lantern Press, 1925), pp.
21, 24; *Winesburg*, p. 163.

7. *Memoirs*, pp. 347–348.

8. Sherwood Anderson, *Tar: A Midwest Childhood*, ed. Ray Lewis White (Cleveland:
Case Western Reserve Univ. Press, 1969), p. 206; see also Sherwood Anderson, *A Story*

*Teller's Story: A Critical Text*, ed. Ray Lewis White (Cleveland: Case Western Reserve Univ. Press, 1968), pp. 23–56.

9. *Winesburg*, p. 119.

10. *Memoirs*, pp. 135–141.

11. *Memoirs*, p. 189.

12. Sherwood Anderson, *No Swank* (Philadelphia: Centaur Press, 1934), p. 7.

13. *A Story Teller's Story*, p. 59.

14. *Memoirs*, p. 238.

15. *Winesburg*, p. 106.

16. *Memoirs*, p. 159.

17. Nancy L. Bunge, "The Ambiguous Endings of Sherwood Anderson's Novels," *Sherwood Anderson: Centennial Studies*, ed. Hilbert H. Campbell and Charles E. Modlin (Troy, N.Y.: Whitson, 1976), p. 261.

18. Bunge, p. 249; concerning "splashy" endings see *A Story Teller's Story*, p. 51.

19. *A Story Teller's Story*, p. 93.

20. Anderson, "Dreiser," *Horses and Men: Tales Long and Short from American Life* (New York: B. W. Huebsch, 1923), p. xii.

# "Women in Sherwood Anderson's Fiction"

Nancy Bunge*

Sherwood Anderson believes that once upon a time everyone lived happily ever after. Men practiced crafts and their ability to reach beyond the limits of egotism and shape the environment gave them the self-esteem necessary to risk themselves in relationships with women. The women returned and perpetuated the men's love by having their children. Then machines imprisoned the men. The humiliated men no longer had the strength to love the women; they could only ignore or abuse them. Although the women's love changed to frustration and hurt, they continued to have babies; but these children, like their parents, knew more about humiliation, hurt and frustration than love. Anderson concludes that since all that remains of that happier, earlier time is that women give birth, the responsibility for re-establishing harmonious relationships between the sexes rests with women.

Childbirth ties women to instincts men have lost touch with; consequently, old women "attain a beauty that seldom comes to old men. Such an old woman may carry about a wornout body, may walk with difficulty, her body may be wracked with pain, but a beautiful aliveness still shines out of her old eyes and it may be because women are less defeated by modern life . . . They have been creators. Children have been born out of their bodies."[1] Men who want to restore their lost wholeness must abandon themselves to the healing powers women have retained: "To me, women are as a flowing stream in which I bathe and clothe myself. They are rich wine drunk, fruit eaten. They have washed me as summer rains wash me."[2] The solution seems simple enough, but Anderson acknowledges many obstacles. The decline of craftsmanship reduces the number of men capable of enjoying women: "The outward signs of that impotence that is the natural result of a long illness are all about us in America. It is to be seen in our architecture, in the cowboy plays in our moving picture theaters and in our childish liking of the type of statesman who boasts of walking softly and carrying a big stick. True maleness does not boast of its maleness."[3] Men cannot lose their instinctual wholeness

*This original essay was written for this volume and is published by permission of Nancy L. Bunge.

without also losing touch with women. Women react to the limited supply of responsive men by withdrawing from their instinctual needs, by having fewer children: "Women who choose childlessness for themselves, choose also impotence—perhaps to be the better companions for the men of a factory, in a standardization age."[4] Anderson urges women to reverence the nurturing impulses they retain rather than capitulate to the way of life which has already injured so many men; accordingly, his fiction is filled with passionate heroines who continue to reach out to others despite a history of bruising disappointments.

Anderson's fiction recognizes that most women have already replaced their yearning to love men with a determination to dominate them; thus, women too have learned to protect their egos at the cost of their relationships, and their manipulation of men accelerates the destruction of healthy relationships between the sexes. Trusting men still exist, but their idealism makes them especially vulnerable to these women; accordingly, his wife's betrayal converts Wash Williams of *Winesburg, Ohio* from a romantic idealist to a bitter cynic. Not only are these relationships unfair to men, they disappoint the women. In *Beyond Desire*, Blanche Long maneuveres herself into marriage with a wealthy older man; when it produces emotional starvation as well as financial security, she brutalizes him and slips into a pattern of slovenly living death. The title character of *Kit Brandon* quickly learns from her girl-friends in the mills and shops that she can get the luxury and power she associates with happiness by manipulating men.

> A mountain girl, ex-mill girl, getting keen. Get always a little keener. Why should the daughters of mill owners, store-keepers, daughters of professional men, novel writers, etc., etc., have anything on you, cotton-mill girls, overall-factory girls, shoe-factory girls, big department-store girls . . . when it comes to handling men? You've got to learn it, haven't you girls? They sure try to get away with it with you too, don't they?
>
> Sharpen your wits. Life's a game. Women know. Working women, particularly the ones that have the looks, the ones that have what it takes, have opportunities. They should learn to know a lot.[5]

She carefully frustrates Gordon Halsey, the son of a wealthy rum-runner, into marrying her, but discovers that despite her new comfort, she is still unhappy. The imitation of male behavior implicit in her pursuit of Gordon becomes explicit when she attempts to find satisfaction in the exhilaration of rum-running. She temporarily succeeds, but loneliness pursues her until she is finally overwhelmed by a need to give herself so profound that she considers sacrificing her own life in order to kill Tom Halsey, Gordon's brutal father. As the novel ends, she decides it would be more productive to find a man who will accept her love: "There was in her mind an almost definite notion of a new kind of adventure she might begin. She felt warm and alive. Young Hanaford had done that for her. She had been carried out of herself and her own problems and into the life of another puzzled human being. There were people to be found. She would get into some kind of work that did not so separate her from others. There might be someone other puzzled and baffled young one with whom she could make a real partnership in living."[6] Women try to accommodate to the alienation of their men by adopting the same values, but they cannot find peace; they only exacerbate the conditions producing their original frustration.

All hope rests with instinctually whole women who continue to reach out to men; and Anderson insists that they keep trying even though their attempts bring them pain and humiliation more frequently than love. Many women in *Winesburg, Ohio* spend their lives in futile attempts to touch unresponsive men. Louise Bentley and Elizabeth Willard try sex and then marriage, but neither satisfies them. Like Alice Hindman and Kate Swift, they also attempt to hide in fantasy; but the insistent demands made by their instincts drive all four women out of doors where they attain some peace through contact with nature. In *Dark Laughter*, Aline Grey must exorcise her unhappiness with her emotionally vacuous marriage by assuming ridiculous poses in the garden:

> It was a dramatization, childish, meaningless, and full of a comforting satisfaction to one who in the actuality of life remains unfulfilled. Sometimes when she stood thus in the garden, her husband within the house reading his paper or asleep in his chair, minutes passed when she did no thinking, felt nothing. She had become a part of the sky, of the ground, of passing winds. When it rained, she was the rain. When thunder rolled down the Ohio River Valley, her body trembled slightly. As a small, lovely, stone figure, she had achieved Nirvana. Now was the time for her lover to come—to spring out of the ground—to drop from the branches of a tree—to take her, laughing at the very notion of asking consent.[7]

Nor can these women expect much sympathy from those women who have renounced their instincts. These more conventional women attack them with the rage reserved for those who seriously challenge the terms on which one has been confronting life. In *Windy McPherson's Son* those women who have renounced passion assail with gossip any woman they suspect of living vitally; the gentle Mary Underwood becomes their special target: "Having fallen upon a side light in the life of a Mary Underwood they return to it again and again as a dog to its offal. Something touching the lives of such as walk in the clean air, dream dreams, and have the audacity to be beautiful beyond the beauty of animal youth, maddens them, and they cry out, running from kitchen door to kitchen door and tearing at the prize like a starved beast who has found a carcass . . . In them is all of femininity—and none of it."[8] Although Anderson recommends that women keep trying to make contact with men, he offers them little motivation. They can expect to find disappointment and even malice.

Yet some good usually comes of their attempts. Although most of these women fail to find appropriate men, they impress and influence the youngsters who have not yet been completely molded by social norms. All of George Willard's healthy capacities derive from his contact with those Winesburg women who spend their evenings taking wild rides in the country or energetic walks through the streets. Before he hears what they have to tell him, he adulates himself and power. He exults over his first sexual conquest; he dismissed the girl, but worries briefly about his reputation until he remembers that nobody knows. He turns to Belle Carpenter theoretically because he has something important to say to her, but in fact because he wants an audience for his new-found ability to declaim pompous words. Kate Swift nurtures his craft, by warning him against his egocentric fascination with words and urging him to emerse himself in life before trying to write of it. He initially sees her speech as a testimony to his charms, but puts aside his self-congratulation long enough to consider that he might have missed something she was trying to tell him. His mother's death finally pushes him out of selfish isolation. While alive his mother could only repeat inarticulate phrases to him, yet George apparently learned something from her stunted declarations; for he has assimilated her fascination with dreams and contempt for conventional success. At her death, he repeats the same exclamations used by Dr. Reefy, the one human being to whom Elizabeth has unburdened her longing; for a moment George understands his mother's stooped figure contained a lovely person: "The body under the sheets was long and in death looked young and graceful. To the boy, held by some strange fancy, it was unspeakably lovely. The feeling that the body before him was alive, that in another moment the lovely woman would spring out of the bed and confront him, became so overpowering that he could not bear the suspense . . . 'The dear, the dear, oh the lovely dear,' the boy, urged by some impulse outside himself, muttered aloud."[9] The realization that he loved someone who is now dead makes him feel authentic sadness.

George's new experience of empathy modifies his grandiosity, replacing it with a humble sense of shared human frailty: "With a little gasp he sees himself as merely a leaf blown by the wind, through the streets of the village. He knows that in spite of all the stout talk of his fellows he must live and die in uncertainty, a thing blown by the wind, a thing destined like corn to wilt in the sun." Only companionship can assuage George's new lonely vulnerability; for the first time he wants to talk to a woman, not use her: "Already he hears death calling. With all his heart he wants to come close to some other human, touch someone with his hands, be touched by the hand of another. If he prefers that the other be a woman, that is because he believes that a woman will be gentle, that she will understand. He wants most of all, understanding."[10] He received the sympathy he wants from Helen White who in turn connects him with everyone he has ever known: "The presence of Helen renewed and refreshed him. It was as though her woman's hand was assisting him to make some minute readjustment of the machinery of life. He began to think of the people in the town where he had always lived with something like reverence."[11] Whether George cultivates his newly acquired gentleness or becomes a "dull clod" as his mother fears, depends on whether he obeys his father's injunctions to be "smart and successful" or listens to the more intangible emotional lessons of the Winesburg women who struggle against the norms his father embraces.

Like George Willard, the adult males in Anderson's fiction who show any capacity for vital relationships were influenced by loving women in their youth. Although passionate women may fail to establish satisfactory relationships, they leave a fruitful legacy. In *Dark Laughter*, Bruce Dudley leaves a conventional job and wife to recapture the intense emotional experiences of his youth. The memory of a day when he sensed a special attachment between his mother and an unknown man particularly haunts him:

> His body rocked. The body of the slender young man on the boat, who was trying to keep up a conversation with his companion, the broad-shouldered man, was rocking almost imperceptibly. The body of the woman who was Bruce's mother was rocking.
>
> To the boy on the boat that evening the whole world, the sky, the boat, the shore running away into the gathering darkness seemed rocking with the voices of the singing niggers.[12]

He returns to the town where the experience occurred and stirred once more by the same feelings, he rescues Alice from her garden.

While young, Sam McPherson of *Windy McPherson's Son* receives motherly love from Mary Underwood and learns about brotherly love from John Telfer. The social shame of poverty quickly overshadows these nurturing episodes, and Sam grows up to be a ruthless businessman. Fortunately, encounters with sensitive women recall Sam to his kinder self. Janet Eberley alters Sam both sexually and intellectually: she "was the first woman who ever got hold of and stirred his manhood, and she awoke something in him that made it possible for him to later see life with a broadness and scope of vision that was no part of the pushing, energetic young man of dollars and industry who sat beside her wheeled chair during the evenings on Wabash Avenue."[13] After Janet's death, Sam marries Susan Rainey who continues his education: "For six weeks they led a wandering, nomadic life in that half wild land. For Sue six weeks of tender lovemaking and of the expression of every thought and impulse of her fine nature, for Sam six weeks of readjustment and freedom, during which he learned to sail a boat, to shoot and to get a fine taste of that life into his being."[14] Still, his compulsion for money making grows until his marriage collapses. Finally forced to face the hollowness of his life, Sam sets out to find truth, only to return to Sue with three strange children. The child in Sam, his buried instinctual self, led him back to Sue: "The boy of Caxton was still alive within him. With a boyish lift of the head he went boldly to her."[15] He knows Sue has more to teach him, if he can keep from running away; the strong maternal instinct reflected in her ready acceptance of the three children should help her fight to keep him there.

Sarah Shepard, a flinty woman from New England, raises Hugh McVey of *Poor White*. She anxiously urges him to discipline his tendency to dream; this apparently destructive advice reflects strong love which she sometimes expresses more directly: "The scolding of the New England woman, that had but accentuated his awkwardness and stupidity, came to an end and life in his adopted home became so quiet and peaceful that the boy thought of himself as one who had come into a kind of paradise."[16] He returns her love the only way he knows how, by trying not to dream. He uses his work as an inventor to channel his wayward imagination and shut out his loneliness; both his dreams and his compassion lead him to invent a machine which will make farming more comfortable. Clara Butterworth recognizes Sam as a man who has the creativity and earthiness she lacks and concludes he is best capable of completing her: "There was but one man of them all who was not a schemer. Hugh was what she wanted to be. He was a creative force. In his hands dead, inanimate things became creative forces."[17] Although they marry, they remain distant from each other for the first three years. Only when forced to defend Hugh does Clara realize she needs to give to him rather than take from him: "At that moment, the woman who had been a thinker stopped thinking. Within her arose the mother, fierce, indomitable, strong with the strength of the roots of a tree. To her then and forever Hugh was no hero, remaking the world, but a perplexed boy, hurt by life. He never again escaped out of boyhood in her consciousness of him."[18] Hugh completes her in a way she never imagined. The novel closes with Hugh and Clara happily anticipating the birth of their child; Hugh is confused by doubts about the value of industrialism, but Clara's abandonment of intellectualism and absorption in her pregnancy shows that she has settled into the role Anderson would have her play, and that in which she can be most helpful to Hugh.

The generative power of courageous commitment permeates *Many Marriages*. John Webster's sudden acknowledgement of his instincts makes him abandon his deadly conventional life for what promises to be a more vital existence with his secretary Natalie. He now comprehends his attachment to his maid Katherine. She had had the courage to run away with a younger man: " 'She had lived and sinned and suffered,' he thought. There was about the woman's person a kind of strong quiet dignity and it was reflected in her physical being."[19] His reawakening reminds virtually everyone about him of something in themselves. His daughter joyfully accepts the new awareness he shares with her. His wife also understands, but it makes her sad with the knowledge that she has missed something:

> She had heard the cry of love for a man come out of her daughter's throat and the cry had stirred something within her so deeply that she had come back into the room where her husband and daughter sat together on the bed. Once there had been the same cry within another woman, but for some reason it had never got itself out, past her lips. At the moment when it might have come from her, at that moment long ago when she lay naked on a bed and looked into the eyes of a young naked man, something, a thing people called shame, had come between her and the getting of that glad cry past her lips.[20]

His wife kills herself, but Katherine comforts his daughter; for she "had become, by her quick impulsiveness, sister to something that was her own real self too."[21] *Many Marriages* suggests that despite the powerful influence of destructive social norms, healthy instincts lie sleeping in virtually everyone; it takes only one vital person to awaken many. Consistent with Anderson's general attitude, all those who cause and learn from John Webster's awakening are women.

Anderson believes his contemporaries woefully alienated from their better impulses, yet he hopes they can be healed. Since more women than men retain the instincts that can redeem everyone, responsibility falls to them. He sympathetically portrays the obstacles which will obstruct and even injure them, but his writings also reflect the optimistic faith that their efforts must move someone; if not their husbands, then their sons and friends. He asks much of women, but in his value scheme voluntary kindness is not humiliating but fulfilling. It is this ability to risk themselves that many men have tragically lost, and Anderson asks women not to ignore what remains of it in themselves; for only by comforting men can women comfort themselves.

## Notes

1. *Sherwood Anderson's Memoirs*, ed. Ray Lewis White (Chapel Hill, North Carolina: University of North Carolina Press, 1969), p. 58.

2. *Sherwood Anderson's Memoirs*, p. 554.

3. *Sherwood Anderson's Notebook* (Mamaronek, New York: Paul P. Appel, 1953), p. 153.

4. *A Story Teller's Story* (New York: The Viking Press, 1969), p. 195.

5. *Kit Brandon* (New York: Scribner's, 1936), p. 173.

6. *Kit Brandon*, p. 373.

7. *Dark Laughter* (New York: Liveright, 1970), pp. 207–08.

8. *Windy McPherson's Son* (Chicago: The University of Chicago Press, 1965), p. 103.

9. *Winesburg, Ohio* (New York: Modern Library, 1947), pp. 231–32.

10. *Winesburg, Ohio*, pp. 234–35.

11. *Winesburg, Ohio*, p. 241.

12. *Winesburg, Ohio*, p. 110.

13. *Windy McPherson's Son*, p. 150.

14. *Windy McPherson's Son*, p. 187.

15. *Windy McPherson's Son*, p. 329.

16. *Poor White* (New York: Viking Press, 1966), p. 9.

17. *Poor White*, p. 247.

18. *Poor White*, p. 360.

19. *Many Marriages* (New York: B. W. Huebsch, Inc., 1923), p. 31.

20. *Many Marriages*, p. 157.

21. *Many Marriages*, p. 246.

# "Sherwood Anderson and the Women of Winesburg"

Marilyn Judith Atlas*

*Winesburg, Ohio* has been studied biographically, geographically, historically, thematically, structurally, mystically, and mythically.[1] However one enters the novel, attention is given to its characters. Edwin Fussel and Carlos Baker have seen the novel within the tradition of the Bildungsroman and have found George Willard's journey toward self and subsequent escape from Winesburg to be its center;[2] David D. Anderson has demonstrated that George Willard's role is secondary to the people about whom each story centers and that one must understand the individual characters and their human experience in order to fully comprehend the novel.[3] But serious critical attention has not been paid to all of the individuals in Winesburg. The women, although they appear in almost every story, have not been studied collectively. Such a study can illuminate *Winesburg, Ohio* as well as Sherwood Anderson's understanding of and relationship to women. One scholar, Chris Browning, has attempted to understand Anderson's relationship to women by exploring one character, Kate Swift, the teacher of Winesburg. In her essay, "Kate Swift: Sherwood Anderson's Creative Eros," she discusses Anderson's relationship to this character, establishing that Anderson's portrait of Kate Swift is an embodiment of his ideal woman.[4] And if we accept that Kate Swift is Anderson's ideal, is this kind of idealization enough? Why does Anderson leave her isolated and weeping in Winesburg? How typical is this pattern in the novel?

As empathetic as Sherwood Anderson was toward the women he created in *Winesburg, Ohio*, he allowed neither Kate Swift nor any of the other women in Winesburg the escape that he hinted was possible for George Willard. While for George, Winesburg might become a background on which to paint his dreams of manhood, for even the most promising women of the town—for Kate Swift, Elizabeth Willard, Louise Bentley, Alice Hindman, and Helen White—Winesburg remained the foreground, if not the entire canvas of their lives. Even when Sherwood Anderson made George Willard and Helen White momentary equals and allowed them to find understanding and acceptance in one another, he

*This original essay was written for this volume and is published by permission of Marilyn Judith Atlas.

ended his novel treating them in vastly different ways. The last image the reader has of George is one of ascension. He is boarding a train that will take him away from his home town and ideally toward further understanding of himself; the last image that the reader has of Helen is one of misdirected energy. Helen chases the very same train on which George departs, hoping to have a parting word with him, herself having no thought of permanently leaving town. While Helen chases George, he is seated on the train preoccupied with himself and his future. Granted, it is George Willard, not Helen White, who is the main character of these stories, and it is his growth and escape which is central to *Winesburg, Ohio*, but since Anderson clearly portrayed that there was no salvation for those who remained in town and since he did allow a few other male characters—David Bentley, Seth Richmond, and Elmer Crowley—the possibility of beginning a new life elsewhere, one wonders why no woman leaves Winesburg.

Perhaps one of the reasons Anderson allowed no woman to leave Winesburg was because he created out of his own experiences, and his early experiences with women were with those who may have been sensitive but who were also clearly trapped. His mother, Emma Smith Anderson, followed the pattern of the sacrificing woman, dying in her forties worn out from having to maintain a family of six children with insufficient financial and emotional support from her husband. Anderson was very much affected by his mother's drudgery and as an adult confessed that he never looked at a working woman without recalling his mother's life.[5] Not only did he perceive his mother's hard life, but he also perceived her yearning for something past the surface of her experience. He acknowledged her influence on him in his dedication to *Winesburg, Ohio*, where he gave her credit for his hunger to see beneath the surface of lives.

The other major female figure of his youth, his older sister Stella, led an equally self-effacing life. If Anderson inherited his mother's sensitivity, Stella inherited both that sensitivity and a sense of obligation to be the family's nurturer. Before her mother's death she wrote verse, graduated as valedictorian from her high school class, and taught for two years, but after her mother died her personal ambitions were frustrated. She became the caretaker of her five brothers and found few outlets for her own creative energy. In his memoirs, Anderson recalled that one evening she asked him to walk with her and pretend he was some other man. On their walk her fantasy burgeoned. She caressed her brother's hair and asked him " 'Do you love me, James?' " In recreating this scene, Anderson touched delicately yet powerfully on the extent of his sister's desperation. Eventually, Anderson's older brother, Karl, and he responded to their sister's need for her own life, and Stella was able to attend the University of Chicago. But she stayed for over six years, and Sherwood and Karl decided that was too long. Sherwood Anderson was chosen to tell her that she would have to quit school and work. In his memoirs he recalled his sister's initial anger at his request and verbalized that he found her response to be both inappropriate and selfish. While he empathized with Stella's need to make her own life, he was displeased when her independence exceeded the boundaries he and his older brother had established for her. Soon after Sherwood's request Stella quit school, found a teaching job, and had an overpowering religious experience which caused her to repent her "selfishness." She apologized to Sherwood. Later she married, but felt that her life should have been dedicated to God. In 1917, forty-two years old, she died. A tract she wrote, "The Story of a Christian Life," was read at her funeral: in it she portrayed her life as one of self-sacrifice and obligation.[6]

Anderson's mother and sister both had starved lives and their lives understandably left a strong impression on Anderson. Many of the frustrated lives in *Winesburg, Ohio* are very likely patterned on these women. But there were other women in Anderson's life who were strong and confident.

His first wife, Cornelia Platt Lane, was a graduate of Western Reserve University, a literary editor of the school Annual, and an avid fan of the theater. After her marriage to Anderson she remained active in literary clubs and discussion groups, and after their separation she turned her attention to getting work in order to support herself and her three children. She taught from 1915–1917, clearly trying to see her options and to make the most life-giving choices she could.[7]

The woman Anderson was involved with during the creation of *Winesburg, Ohio*, Tenessee Claflin Mitchell, was an intelligent, creative woman who was making untraditional choices. She left a small town, Jackson, Michigan, to move to Chicago where she danced, sang, sculpted, and wrote, supporting herself by teaching music and dance, and by tuning pianos.[8]

There were many other independent, expansive women in Anderson's life by the time he began writing Winesburg in the fall of 1915. Margaret Anderson, editor of *The Little Review*, was one of Anderson's first connections to the literary world of Chicago.[9] Edna Kenton, Harriet Monroe, and Agnes Tietjens were all part of Chicago's artistic community, the community which nurtured Anderson's own exploration and intellectual growth during that period of his life.

One of the writers who was to most strongly influence his work was Gertrude Stein. Irving Howe suggests that his response to Stein and her innovative art was not simply positive as Anderson recollected in his memoirs. Howe presents the evidence:

> Anderson has recalled that he "had come to Gertrude Stein's book about which everyone laughed but about which I did not laugh. It excited me as one might grow excited in going into a new and wonderful country where everything is strange. . . ." The truth, however, was somewhat more complex than Ander-

son's memory. His first reactions to Stein were antagonistic: at a Chicago party in 1915 he told Edna Kenton that he thought it merely funny that anyone should take *Tender Buttons* seriously, and shortly afterwards he even composed a parody of Stein for his advertising cronies.[10]

Regardless of how Anderson actually responded to Stein, he was aware of her impact on experimental writing, of her power, independence, and individuality.

It is clear that while Anderson was writing *Winesburg, Ohio*, he was aware that women, even some from small towns, were escaping from their repressive environments and trying to live creative, self-directed lives. He even mentioned in "Adventure" that there was a "growing modern idea of a woman's owning herself and giving and taking for her own end in life."[11] But Anderson was not interested in making any woman of Winesburg a carefully delineated, fully developed "modern woman." He began to make a number of his women strong but each one eventually catches herself in a traditional trap: Elizabeth Willard needs love first as does Louise Bentley. Alice Hindman can go as far as accepting economic independence, but she too prefers to live through her lover, even after he has obviously deserted her; Helen White shows potential: she is intelligent and seems capable of making choices, but Anderson finally chose not to develop her individuality, and presented her only through her relationships with others. At the end he was more comfortable leaving her safely at home.

While Anderson could be sympathetic to women, he could also unrealistically limit not only his presentation of them, but his understanding of what they needed. Too often he was comfortable assuming that what women wanted most was to give themselves away to an ideal lover. His belief that women wanted men and men wanted to create is depicted in the love relationships of Winesburg. Alice Hindman's relationship with Ned Currie and Helen White's relationship with George Willard are examples of this belief. What he portrayed in *Winesburg, Ohio*, he stated in his later essay, "The Modern Writer."[11] "It is true as there is a sun in the sky that men cannot live in the end without love of craft. It is to the man what love of children is to the woman."[12] Anderson did not let his experiences with women get in the way of his idealizations: contact with intelligent, creative, ambitious women did not liberalize him. Rather as he grew older these stereotypes crystalized. Even while accepting that his memoirs were never edited by him, it is still impossible not to take seriously the implications of his statements about women. For example, in his memoirs, he began one discussion about modern women by analyzing the difficulties his wives had living with an artist, who, like all artists, emotionally withdrew when in the process of creating. While he willingly took blame for his unsatisfactory marriages, he managed to define women and men at the expense of women's creative and independent natures. He wrote not only about himself, but about all artists, male artists, that is:

> When one of us makes a failure of marriage it is, almost in-
> evitably, his own fault. He is what he is. He should not blame
> the woman.
>
> The modern woman will not be kicked aside so. She wants
> children. She wants a certain security, for herself and for her
> children, but we fellows do not understand the impulse toward
> security. When we are secure we are dead. There is nothing
> secure in our world, out there, and as for the matter of
> children we are always having children of our own.[13]

Anderson needed to make women simpler than they are and when angry,
or frustrated, or afraid, he easily moved into traditional, and safe,
categories. When angry at critical responses to his work he could write
that success was overrated and amounted to nothing more than "silly
women mouthing over you."[14] But he knew in the midst of his statements
that women wanted men and men wanted to create, that women needed
more security than men, that women were somehow more stupid than
men, that he was frightened of women. Most of all, he was frightened of
needing them, losing his independence, of somehow being seduced by sexuality into being corporeal rather than creative. Whether emotionally or
artistically, Anderson was convinced that "One of the things a man has to
learn is to fight most bitterly the influence of those who love him."[15] It
was easier for him to create what he did not fear and what he did not
need.

When Anderson wrote "Impotence," a story concerning the life of
Marietta Finley, a woman with whom he corresponded from 1916 to
1931, rather than trying to portray her strength, he consciously limited it.
He wrote to her, willing to share his creation, but afraid of insulting her.
He warned her that "Impotence" was not an accurate presentation of her
life or her strength:

> Now let me explain. If you want to see the story I shall have to
> have an understanding with you first. There is something gone
> out of my Marie that is not gone out of you. You have a thou-
> sand things she has not. I could not bear to have this story
> taken as an interpretation of your life. That will have to be
> understood or I will tear it up and throw it to the winds.[16]

Anderson was not totally unconscious of his fear of strong women. In
"Loneliness," one of the Winesburg stories, he reduced the main
character, Enoch Robinson, to a complaining child because Enoch is so
afraid of strong women that he makes his life devoid of love. In
love, Enoch Robinson runs from a woman to whom he is attracted
because he is convinced that she is too "large" for his room and will sub-
sume him. He treats her cruelly, forcing her out of his life. Overcome by
the implications of his actions he whimpers: " 'I'm alone, all alone. . . . It
was warm and friendly in my room but now I'm all alone.' "[17] Although

Anderson's depiction of Robinson is not sympathetic, his involvement with this story was very strong; he was very anxious that it be accepted by his friend and editor, Waldo Frank, for publication in *Seven Arts*. Anderson, by recreating the horrors of isolating oneself because of fear of strong women, was making a statement which he found important and for which he needed outside support. When Waldo Frank rejected the story in December 1916, Anderson responded strongly:

> Damn it, I wanted you to like the story about Enoch Robinson and the woman who came into his room and was too big for the room.
>
> There is a story every critic is bound to dislike. I can remember reading it to Floyd Dell, and it made him hopping mad. "It's damn rot," says Floyd. "it does not get anywhere."
>
> "It gets there, but you are not at the station," I replied to Floyd, and I think I was right.
>
> Why do I try to convince you of this story? Well, I want it in print in *Seven Arts*. A writer knows when a story is good, and that story is good.
>
> Sometimes when I am in New York, I'll bring that story in, and I'll make you see it.[18]

Anderson was himself confused over the strength of his response, but if one remembers that this exchange took place six months after his marriage to Tenessee Claflin Mitchell, a marriage that according to his memoirs "did not take," a marriage to a woman who was trying to be creative, who may at times have felt too "large" for his room, his passionate response makes psychological sense. He might condemn his character for forcing the strong woman out of his life, but he understood the impulse and the fear of being subsumed.

Anderson also knew that if he were large enough, an independent woman would not function as a threat whom he needed to perceive in limited terms. Rather, she could be a friend with whom he could share both sensuality and art. In a larger mood he wrote to Waldo Frank:

> The world has a wart on its nose.
> In the night the winds come down out of Medicine Hat.
> They play in dead cornfields.
> In the cold and the night the gods burrow deep in the ground.
>
> There is a stretch of land in the West over which a man may walk 30 days seeing nothing but cornfields. I have a picture. In the midst of that vast open space, exposed to the winds that tramp the world, Edna Kenton and Harrison Grey Fiske are talking of art.
>
> See the moon. Isn't the night delightful?[19]

In Anderson's ideal world two Chicago artists, a man and a woman, serve as allegorical figures. They are connected to nature and art and they walk without fear. But in his own life, and in his creation of women in *Winesburg, Ohio*, he felt that he must settle for less.

The women that Anderson created most sensitively in *Winesburg, Ohio* were those who posed no threat for either him or his male protagonists. Helen White is a potential threat to George Willard's freedom and she is a possible competitor: leaving her behind with no solid aspirations of her own and only George Willard's wish that she not become like all the other women in Winesburg, was as much strength as Anderson was willing to allow her. Anderson created no overt power struggle between these two characters and he in no way dealt with the fact that he sacrificed Helen's potential in order to simplify George's exit.

But Anderson's unwillingness to allow his female characters the same amount of mobility as he allowed his male characters did not blind him to the fact that men's attitudes toward women can and do damage them irreparably. In "Godliness," Anderson created a protagonist who succeeds in killing his wife, not out of cruelty but by watching her take on a role for which she is not sufficiently strong, and who succeeds in emotionally crippling his daughter because she was not the son who would help him " 'pluck at last all of these lands out of the hands of the Philistines.' "[20] In *Winesburg, Ohio* Anderson questioned some of the traditional myths; but he embraced others. Women, in Anderson's understanding, did not long to be worked to death, they did not long to be rejected because they were female, but they did long to be subsumed in a man.

If one journeys through *Winesburg, Ohio* looking carefully at the female characters that Anderson created, one senses that even if Anderson was not accurately or openly exploring all the various aspects of women in a small Midwestern city, he was seriously exploring them. The stories reflect both a deep sensitivity to female traps and an unwillingness to allow women the same choices, needs, and strengths that it allowed men. The first woman in Winesburg that Anderson presented in detail appeared in "Paper Pills." She remained nameless throughout the story, hardly more than a sacrifice. The force of her powerlessness and of her accepting silence colored not only this tale, but all of *Winesburg, Ohio*. The reader is told little about her other than that her parents are dead and have left her a large fertile farm, and that this inheritance, coupled with the fact that she is dark, mysteriously attractive, and alone, interests suitors. One young man, the jeweler's son, talks constantly of virginity and another, a silent, black-haired boy, impregnates her. She is, in the context of Winesburg, a twisted apple, sweetest of all those in the orchard, and she sees herself in just such passive terms:

> At times it seemed to her that as he talked he was holding her
> body in his hands. She imagined him turning it slowly about in

the white hands and staring at it. At night she dreamed that he had bitten into her body and that his jaws were dripping.[21]

When the silent, dark-haired suitor seduces her, it is not without violence. In his moment of passion, he bites her. Shortly after this barbarous but brief encounter she realizes that she is pregnant and goes to see Doctor Reefy. In his office, she watches a woman whose tooth is being removed bleed. The woman's husband is also watching, and at the moment of extraction both the woman and her spouse simultaneously scream. The main female character does not react. She accepts the pain around her as simply as she accepts her own. The story quickly progresses and we are told that she falls in love with Doctor Reefy, and passively accepts the truths he shares. After a vague illness in which she loses her unborn child, she marries Doctor Reefy, and in the spring of that year, she quietly dies.

From this silent, bloody, dreamlike tale, the reader is introduced to Elizabeth Willard, George Willard's mother. She, unlike the woman in "Paper Pills," has the hunger to express herself, but she is no less silent and no more free. Elizabeth prays that her son be allowed to express something for them both. Desperate for this, her prayer becomes violent and the violence is willingly directed against herself:

> "Even though I die, I will in some way keep defeat from you," she cried, and so deep was her determination that her whole body shook. Her eyes glowed and she clenched her fists. "If I am dead and see him becoming a meaningless drab figure like myself, I will come back," she declared. "I ask God now to give me that privilege. I demand it. I will pay for it. God may beat men with his fists. I will take any blow that may befall if but this my boy be allowed to express something for us both."[22]

When we are introduced to her, she is forty-five and broken. Her death hovers over the length of the novel and her wish for George Willard's creativity increases our own investment in it. In "Death," one of the last stories in *Winesburg, Ohio*, we are told of her love relationship with Doctor Reefy and of her youthful aspiration to be an actress. As a young woman, her need of love stood in the way of her need of self. This, the narrator explains, is the way of women. But Elizabeth is less sure of this. She takes some responsibility for her defeat and states that she "let" the dream within her be killed.[23] But more frequently she feels that she has been a victim. Anderson has her put down her head and weep when the Winesburg baker throws sticks and bits of broken glass at the druggist's cat who crouched behind barrels in an attempt to escape the abuse. Elizabeth eventually stops looking at the grey cat. The relationship between the cat and the baker seems too much like "a rehearsal of her own life, terrible in its vividness."[24]

In "The Philosopher" we are again introduced to women as victims.

Doctor Parcival describes his mother quietly working without complaint: " 'My mother, who was small and had red, sad-looking eyes, would come into the house from a little shed at the back. That's where she spent her time over the washtub scrubbing people's dirty clothes.' "[25] This story ends with another bloody image of women's lives and women's lot: a female child is defenselessly thrown from a buggy and killed.

Louise Trunnion, one of the two central characters in the next sketch, "Nobody Knows," is a return to the Elizabeth Willard type: a female character who hungers but does not get what she wants. Louise Trunnion is a confused young girl living in her father's house who wants something for herself but she is neither sure what she wants nor how to get it. First, she sends George Willard a note offering herself: " 'I'm yours if you want me,' " but she is not comfortable being the chooser and when Willard appears she sulkily says, " 'How do you know I want to go out with you. What makes you so sure? ' " George's encounter with her is coldly insensitive. After it, he is simply impressed that his pleasure is free: " 'She hasn't got anything on me. Nobody knows,' he muttered doggedly and went on his way."[26]

The next story, "Godliness," is written in four parts. Through the development of Louise Bentley, the central female character, Anderson again explores how women are victimized by the society they live in and the people with whom they associate. When Anderson presents Louise Bentley's frustrated life and her inability to find the love she needs he has his narrator intrude with a statement indicting society and calling the writers of the period to action: "Before such women as Louise can be understood and their lives made livable, much will have to be done. Thoughtful books will have to be written and thoughtful lives lived by people about them."[27] Ironically, it is also in "Godliness" that Anderson states his theory that what women want most is to be possessed: "Sometimes it seemed to her that to be held tightly and kissed was the whole secret of life, and then a new impulse came and she was terribly afraid. The age-old woman's desire to be possessed had taken possession of her. . . ."[28] But in developing his character, Anderson shows that Louise Bentley wants more than someone to possess her: she wants spiritual communication with another human being.

All through her life Louise longs for love. Her father had rejected her because she was not the son with whom he could build God's kingdom on earth; Mary and Harriet Hardy, the daughters of Albert Hardy, the man whose house Louise lives in while she attends Winesburg's high school, view her negatively because she receives their father's praise for being academically successful. Wanting control, Louise decides that if she were only braver, she could get the love for which she longs. Anderson carefully depicts that bravery is not the issue: the issue is communication and the channels are not yet open between either men and women or women and women.

In creating Louise Bentley and giving her a need for love which over-powers all her talents, Anderson is dooming her to an unhappy life. Wanting a friend, she takes John Hardy to be her lover, but sexuality does not satisfy her. John cannot understand what she wants and her frustration turns to bitterness. Her unhappiness does not cause her to reconsider the practicality of love as life's central solution. Instead it leads her to be an angry, ineffectual woman, and a hater of men. Interestingly, she does not reject women; for her they remain fellow victims, but she rejects all men and this anger negatively affects her relationship with her son whom she treats ambivalently. When her husband reproaches her for being a cruel mother she laughs: " 'It is a man child and will 'get what it wants anyway,' she said sharply. 'Had it been a woman child there is nothing in the world I would not have done for it.' "[29] But Louise Bentley does not have a woman child and she is given no opportunity to satisfy either her need to love or her need to be loved. She is clearly one of the female victims of Winesburg whose strength and creativity lead nowhere.

In the next story, "A Man of Ideas," Anderson creates a strong female character, but he fails to develop her. Sarah King is an outcast of the town; she is neither beautiful nor a member of a socially acceptable family. While the story suggests that a meaningful relationship exists between her and Joe Welling, another outcast, and that this relationship is mutually fulfilling, he fails to support this. While the two characters nurture one another, the relationship seems to lack honesty. Joe Welling may tell her that she is intelligent, and Sarah King may allow him to talk to her about his ideas, but she is frightened when he decides to share these ideas with George Willard for she is convinced that Joe and George will quarrel over their worth. Her response implies that she finds Joe's ideas less intelligent than she privately encourages him to believe. Anderson, through the narrative tone, implies that Sarah is lucky that she is not more isolated being neither of fine breeding nor fine beauty, and certainly the town's people laugh at Joe's protestations of love, but the reader must question the degree of her luck, her happiness, and her strength.

Anderson is not allowing women many options. In his next story, "Adventure," we are introduced to Alice Hindman who has good standing in her society, is strong and creative as well as beautiful. But he has her use that strength to repress herself rather than to love or create. In her youth, she impulsively and passionately loved Ned Currie, a reporter, who goes to Cleveland promising to return when he has found work. He clearly deserts her and the remainder of the story explores her unwillingness to let him go and to find some other route toward her own happiness and fulfillment. Alice Hindman is willing to support herself economically, but she is unwilling to make realistic life plans for herself. She waits for Ned Currie to return, at first actively rejecting other suitable men, and then, in desperation, passively accepting the attention of a middle-aged drug clerk. After a few years of his tedious visits she can no longer bear his company and only then will she send him away. She represses her passionate nature as long as she can and only when she is beyond reason does she allow herself to act. If she is going to betray her lover by being sexual, she can only do so unintentionally:

> For a moment she stood by the window hearing the rain beat against the glass and then a strange desire took possession of her. Without stopping to think of what she intended to do, she ran downstairs through the dark house and out into the rain. As she stood on the little grass plot before the house and felt the cold rain on her body a mad desire to run naked through the streets took possession of her.
> She thought the rain would have some creative and wonderful effect on her body. Not for years had she felt so full of youth and courage. She wanted to leap and run, to cry out, to find some other lonely human and embrace him. On the brick sidewalk before the house a man stumbled homeward. Alice started to run. A wild, desperate mood took possession of her. "What do I care who it is. He is alone, and I will go to him," she thought; and then without stopping to consider the possible result of her madness, called softly. "Wait!" she cried. "Don't go away. Whoever you are, you must wait."[30]

The scene ends in irony. The man to whom she calls is old and somewhat deaf. He does not comprehend her, and she, realizing what she had done, drops to the ground, waits for him to go, and then crawls home.

Alice Hindman tries to force herself to accept that many individuals live without love. She at no time considers finding a healthy outlet for her needs, but rather she demands that instinct be controlled; she does not consider being larger and learning to own the various parts of her nature, but rather demands that she be smaller and survive that smallness.

Instead of moving forward, creating a woman who is attempting to define new, more life-giving categories for herself, in Anderson's next story, "Respectability," he depicts two female characters who are destructively passive at best, evil at worst. The central character of "Respectability," is Wash Williams, a woman-hater who once idealized a woman, and because she disappointed him has decided that all women are "bitches." He tells George about his days of innocent happiness with the woman who wronged him:

> "In the garden back of our house we planted vegetables, . . . you know, peas and corn and such things. We went to Columbus in early March and as soon as the days became warm I went to work in the garden. With a spade I turned up the black ground while she ran about laughing and pretending to be afraid of the worms I uncovered. Late in April came the planting. In the little paths among the seed beds she stood holding a paper bag in her hand. The bag was filled with seeds. A few at a time she handed me the seeds that I might thrust them into the warm, soft ground."[31]

Wash Williams' relationship with his wife seemed ideal; their gardening is a metaphor of interdependent fertility. But as we watch each character play his or her respective role we realize that they are exactly that, characters, to each other: Wash does not know his wife, nor is there any evidence that he cares to know her. When she takes lovers he is surprised and feels betrayed. He sends her back to her mother who, in an attempt to reconcile the couple, invites Wash to her home, sits him in the parlor and then sends her daughter to him naked. When she enters the parlor she stands passively awaiting Wash's acceptance or rejection of her. Wash responds with violence, striking the mother, but fails to kill her. As he finishes his tale he tells George that his only regret is that the mother died a few months after this incident and therefore removed all possibility that he might take his revenge later. George Willard empathizes only with Wash Williams. In this tale Anderson is indirectly portraying the empty lives of women, but he has his narrator identify only with the man who suffers because women's lives *are* empty. Wash is portrayed as loving his wife even if he does not attempt to understand her, and Anderson's sympathy for him implies that love, without any attempt to understand, is enough. The fact that a dream cannot be actualized if it is not built on solid ground, the fact that women should be accountable to themselves before they are accountable to either husband or mother, are not explored or in any way discussed. Wash Williams is angry and hurt, and Anderson, through George Willard, simply accepts that anger as righteous. There is no hint that George will ever consider Wash Williams' story from the point of view of either woman and there is no hint that Anderson sees the danger of so limited a focus.

Kate Swift, the teacher, stern and cold toward her students, unable to communicate though passionate and sensitive, fares no better than her less intelligent, or less good, sisters. At thirty, she is considered a spinster, and has no outlet other than aborted attempts to communicate, and late night walks. Her mother, Elizabeth Swift, is angry when she stays out late. She reinforces her daughter to repress all instinct. During one quarrel she tells Kate:

> "I am glad you're not a man. . . . More than once I've waited
> for your father to come home, not knowing what new mess he
> had got into. I've had my share of uncertainty and you cannot
> blame me if I do not want to see the worst side of him
> reproduced in you."[32]

Kate Swift stays in Winesburg frustrated, unwilling to be sexual, unable to communicate, watching herself grow old. Once she was adventurous and travelled, but five years have passed since then, and there is no hint that she will search her fortune elsewhere.

Helen White, the woman with the most potential in *Winesburg, Ohio*, first appears in "The Thinker." She is still young, a high school student, and, according to George Willard, has more "get up" than any other girl in Winesburg. She is attracted to George Willard, and to any young man, it seems, who has the least potential for leaving Winesburg and directing his own life. In "The Thinker," Seth Richmond and George Willard compete for her attention. Rather than being shown her spiritual or intellectual complexity, we are shown her hunger for a worthy suitor. When Seth Richmond tells her that he is going to leave Winesburg and get some work, she is immediately impressed: " 'This is as it should be,' she thought. 'This boy is not a boy at all, but a strong, purposeful man.' "[33] She does not think of her own freedom, but rather is overcome by the sadness of losing the possibility to relate with Seth.

We meet Helen White again later, but we never see her actively working out her own goals. She is always caught between men, watching other characters define themselves and strike out new paths or she is simply the object of admiration and fantasy. In "Drink" Helen White appears as Tom Foster's fantasy. Tom works for her father, the town banker, and falls in love with her, but is afraid of sexuality and wants only to get drunk and verbalize his dreams of her. He tries to tell George Willard about these fantasies, but succeeds only in aggravating him. Helen White appears as a fantasy in "Death," the story that centers on the death of Elizabeth Willard. When George's mother dies, he thinks of Helen and how he would have to postpone being with her. George's vision of her, young, alive, sexual, becomes intermingled with his thoughts about his mother. He longs to lift the sheet covering Elizabeth and imagines that somehow she is not underneath the sheet at all, but another woman is there who can spring up from the bed and comfort him. George's vision almost overpowers him. When his Aunt Elizabeth comes into the room, George is shaken by sobs. First he tells his aunt that his mother is dead and then half turning from Aunt Elizabeth says, " 'The dear, the dear, oh the lovely dear.' " The impulse that urges him to verbalize this is outside himself. He weeps for his mother's lost youth. Again, the story turns toward Helen White. She will serve as the place where he can momentarily rest his heart:

> With all his heart he wants to come close to some other human, touch someone with his hands, be touched by the hand of another. If he prefers that the other be a woman that is because he believes that a woman will be gentle, that she will understand. He wants, most of all, understanding.[34]

George looks to Helen White for comfort less as an individual than as a nurturing woman. However, while he thinks of her, she is entertaining a young instructor whom her mother, the town organizer for poetry study groups, has invited down from college. Helen is also thinking of him. The main difference between George and Helen lies in the fact that George is caught between his thoughts of her and his thoughts of his own future, while she is much more involved in comparing two men than in seriously considering her independent existence.

When George and Helen next meet, George is more interested in tell-

ing her what he needs her to be than in listening to what she herself feels
she needs:

> "I want you to do something, I don't know what. Perhaps it is
> none of my business. I want you to try to be different from
> other women. You see the point. It's none of my business I tell
> you. I want you to be a beautiful woman. You see what I
> want."[35]

Helen is neither offended nor satisfied. They part before either one of
them is ready and they both want to somehow reestablish contact.
George's solution is to go over to her house. Helen is less comfortable
being so calculating and simply runs to her garden and calls his name. He
is within hearing by then and they walk, successfully establishing mutual
feelings of unity. But it is George Willard's feelings, the narrator tells us,
which are reflected in Helen White. He is renewed and refreshed by her
presence. While the narrator feels comfortable dealing with George's
thoughts, at this point of the novel, the narrator refuses to deal with
Helen's. He tells us: "There is no way of knowing what woman's thoughts
went through her mind but, when the bottom of the hill was reached and
she came up to the boy, she took his arm and walked beside him in
dignified silence."[36]

Helen White is thus reduced to an abstract figure whom we cannot
know. She is the shadow of a strong woman and her major role at the end
of *Winesburg, Ohio* is one of reflection rather than independent action.
Here is Anderson's chance to develop a character who might try to break
old patterns, find more life-giving categories, use her impulses and intelligence to form a balanced, self-directed life, but Anderson does not
take it. We are given no evidence that Helen White will ever leave
Winesburg or that she will ever transcend traditional roles. We have
never seen her do so, and there is no suggestion that she can.

One might apologize for Anderson by simply accepting that George
Willard's exit is what he is concentrating on at the end of *Winesburg,
Ohio*, or, as Nancy Bunge points out in her article, "The Ambiguous
Endings of Sherwood Anderson's Novels," we might say that the ending of
this novel reflects his general difficulty finding satisfactory endings.
Bunge feels the inadequancy of his endings reflects his need to be
optimistic:

> Anderson would rather write novels with indcterminate end-
> ings than reinforce the despair he sees around him. The gener-
> ous wish that Americans can be cured rather than a faulty
> aesthetic sense makes him stop in mid-air rather than follow
> the lives of his characters through to their logical conclusion.[37]

I do not believe that the ending of *Winesburg, Ohio* portrays Anderson's
lack of an aesthetic sense; nor do I believe that the ending portrays Anderson's generous wish that Americans be cured. Perhaps he does wish

American men to be cured, for through George Willard he grants them mobility, but he cannot wish American women to be cured if he leaves them, like Helen White, at the platform speaking to the wind.

While Anderson is harsh in his final depiction of Helen White, this harshness seems to come from his discomfort in viewing her as anything more than a fulfillment of George Willard's momentary need for warmth. He is more comfortable with Tandy Hard who embraces her role as reflection. Only a child, she wants nothing more than to be " 'brave enough to dare to be loved.' "[38] The grief to which she gives herself over at the end of her story is never explained. She sobs with abandon "as though her young strength were not enough to bear the vision the words of the drunkard had brought to her."[39] The story is presented without irony for Tandy Hard's solution is one whose legitimacy Anderson does not question. Anderson is also more comfortable when he presents Nell Gunther in "The Untold Lie," because she is a threat to no male protagonist. She has been impregnated by Hal Winters who after some thinking decides to willingly do the honorable thing and marry her. Hal Winters is fond of her because she is strong and because she makes no demands. His older friend, Ray Pearson, trapped into marriage by his pregnant lover and now overwhelmed with pale, thin children, runs to discourage his friend from making the same mistake, but after Hal tells Ray of his intentions, Ray realizes that whatever advice he would have given Hal would have been dishonest. There are losses and gains for men whichever way they choose. In *Winesburg, Ohio* men are given the privilege of the decision and women are often rewarded for being silent and making no demands.

For all the sensitive attention Anderson can pay to his female characters, for all the sympathy he uses to present the story of Louise Bentley, Alice Hindman, and Kate Swift, for all his tenderness toward Elizabeth Willard, he does not, even when the opportunity naturally presents itself, create a female character who wants, and is able, to form her own life. It is interesting that between 1915 and 1917 when *Winesburg, Ohio* was being created, Anderson was attempting to form an I-Thou[40] relationship with a woman; he did not succeed. It may be that through the Helen White–George Willard relationship Anderson is also attempting to form this type of relationship, but again he does not succeed. He is not yet ready, even fictionally, to create a liberated woman with whom his protagonist must relate on equal terms. But Sherwood Anderson is aware that attitudes toward women must change, for the lives women are forced to live are unnecessarily cruel and destructive. If Anderson does prefer women to be reflections of men, he does not want them to be tortured or destroyed. *Winesburg, Ohio* does not satisfactorily portray the possibility of an active, independent, and creative woman who is also a survivor, but at least it portrays the women whose lives are limited because they live within a system which was never created for their benefit. By exploring the lives of the women in Winesburg we explore the biases of a period, the biases of a town, and the biases of an author, but we also experience moments of insight from which we may explore our own biases, our own potential, and our own alternatives.

## Notes

1. Douglas G. Rogers, *Sherwood Anderson: A Selective, Annotated Bibliography* (Metuchen, N.J.: The Scarecrow Press, Inc., 1976), pp. 111–28.

2. Edwin Fussell, "*Winesburg, Ohio*: Art and Isolation," *Modern Fiction Studies*, 6 (Summer 1960), p. 106; Carlos Baker, "Sherwood Anderson's *Winesburg*: A Reprise," *Virginia Quarterly Review*, 48 (Autumn 1972), p. 578.

3. David D. Anderson, "Sherwood Anderson's Moments of Insight," *Critical Studies in American Literature: A Collection of Essays* (Karachi, Pakistan: University of Karachi, 1964), p. 123.

4. Chris Browning, "Kate Swift: Sherwood Anderson's Creative Eros," *Tennessee Studies in Literature*, 13 (1968), p. 141.

5. William A. Sutton, *The Road to Winesburg: A Mosaic of the Imaginative Life of Sherwood Anderson* (Metuchen, N.J.: The Scarecrow Press, Inc., 1972), p. 503.

6. Ray Lewis White, ed. *Sherwood Anderson's Memoirs: A Critical Edition* (Chapel Hill: The University of North Carolina Press, 1969), pp. 105–09; 135–41.

7. Sutton, pp. 162; 181; 237.

8. Sutton, p. 244.

9. Sherwood Anderson to Oscar H. Fidell, January 9, 1933, Howard Munford Jones and Walter B. Rideout, eds., *Letters of Sherwood Anderson* (Boston: Little, Brown and Company, 1953), pp. 274–75.

10. Irving Howe, "The Book of the Grotesque," *The Achievement of Sherwood Anderson: Essays in Criticism*, Ray Lewis White, ed. (Chapel Hill: The University of North Carolina Press, 1966), p. 93.

11. Sherwood Anderson, *Winesburg, Ohio* (New York: The Viking Press, 1965), p. 115.

12. Sherwood Anderson, *The Modern Writer* (San Francisco, Edwin and Robert Grabhorn, 1925), p. 29 as quoted in Bernard Duffey, *Chicago Renaissance in American Letters* (East Lansing: The Michigan State College Press, 1954), p. 203.

13. *Memoirs*, p. 9.

14. Sherwood Anderson to Waldo Frank, after? November 18, 1917, *Letters*, p. 26.

15. Sherwood Anderson to Waldo Frank, ? May, 1917, *Letters*, p. 14.

16. Sherwood Anderson to Marietta D. Finley, December 21, 1916, Sutton, p. 328.

17. *Winesburg, Ohio*, p. 178.

18. Sherwood Anderson to Waldo Frank, December 14, 1916, *Letters*, p. 5.

19. Sherwood Anderson to Waldo Frank, December 7, 1917, *Letters*, p. 28.

20. *Winesburg, Ohio*, p. 73.

21. Ibid., pp. 37–8.

22. Ibid., p. 40.

23. Ibid., p. 43.

24. Ibid., p. 41.

25. Ibid., p. 53.

26. Ibid., p. 62.

27. Ibid., p. 87.

28. Ibid., p. 94.

29. Ibid., p. 96.

30. Ibid., p. 119.

31. Ibid., pp. 125–6.

32. Ibid., p. 162.

33. Ibid., p. 141.

34. Ibid., p. 235.

35. Ibid., pp. 236–7.

36. Ibid., pp. 242–43.

37. Nancy L. Bunge, "The Ambiguous Endings of Sherwood Anderson's Novels," *Sherwood Anderson: Centennial Studies*, Hilbert H. Campbell and Charles E. Modlin, eds. (Troy, New York: Whitston Publishing Co., 1976), p. 261.

38. *Winesburg, Ohio*, p. 145.

39. Ibid., p. 146.

40. Martin Buber, *I and Thou*, trans. Walter Kaufman (New York: Charles Scribner's Sons, 1970), p. 30. An I-Thou relationship as Buber defines it is a relationship in which two individuals confirm and accept one another, not in terms of what each wishes the other to be, but in terms of what each individual is.

# "Anderson and Myth"

David D. Anderson*

## I

In August 1924 Sherwood Anderson had just finished reading the proofs of *A Story Teller's Story* and, writing to his brother Karl about that volume of what was for him autobiography, he said, "Don't know about *A Story Teller's Story*, whether I got what I went after or not. I didn't try to set down obvious facts, only tried to get the spirit of something."[1]

The statement was not only curiously prophetic of much of the adverse criticism directed at the work when it appeared and since—the common core of that criticism is that the work is formless and that it treats facts casually—when, indeed, it recognizes them at all—but at the same time it was as close as Anderson ever came, in any of the many statements he made on the nature of fiction and the process of writing, to indicating what it was that he had attempted in each of his works. From the early, destroyed "Why I Am A Socialist"[2] to *Home Town* (1940), the last work he published in his lifetime, and the posthumous, twice-edited *Memoirs* (1942, 1969), Anderson was concerned not with facts or with things but with whatever it was, often only vaguely defined, that gave them purpose and meaning.

That brief comment to his brother, significant in a time of Anderson's life when, as he approached fifty, he was attempting desperately, almost feverishly, to understand himself, his life, his time, his relationships with his past, his father, his place and his craft, in many ways describes the search, both literary and personal, that he had begun more than a decade before and was to carry on until his death nearly twenty years later. Anderson's search, as he had suddenly realized at that vital point in his career, was for "the spirit of something," for the beauty of the reality that lies beyond the facts; consequently, "I have perhaps lied now and then. . . ," he wrote in *A Story Teller's Story*, "but have not lied about the essence. . . . In the world of fancy . . . no man is ugly. Man is ugly in fact only. . . . It is my aim to be true to the essence of things . . ."[3]

*Originally published in David D. Anderson, ed., *Sherwood Anderson: Dimensions of His Literary Art* (East Lansing, Mich.: Michigan State University Press, 1976), pp. 118–41.

The tangible result of Anderson's search of more than thirty years is the body of his work: some of the finest short stories in English or any other language, and an impressive array of other works that are less than his best but, much contemporary and recent criticism notwithstanding, none of them a failure. That body of work, that impressive documentary record of Anderson's search for the essence of things, for the beauty that lies beyond human experience, is expressed in what Northrop Frye calls "the only possible language of concern,"[4] a language that, for Frye, is called *myth*; for Anderson, "the spirit of something." In neither case are facts important; just as Anderson admitted frankly and guiltlessly that he lied, Frye, on a more sophisticated level, described myth as having "more to do with vision and with an imaginative response than with the kind of belief that is based on evidence and sense experience."[5]

Whatever distinctions may be drawn between the admission of the artist and the definition of the critic are far less consequential than the shortsightedness of so many of Anderson's critics, then and more recently, who failed to see the unity and beauty that lie beyond what has been called garbled history or garbled autobiography. The first is an early definition of myth,[6] and the latter is the essence of Irving Howe's insistence that *A Story Teller's Story* was "neither record nor fiction, loyal neither to fact nor to imagination,"[7] a statement that unfortunately misled too many of Howe's contemporaries and followers and caused them to ignore a book central to Anderson's work, his craft, and his life.

Howe also points out that Anderson was not one of America's "willful mythmakers,"[8] and it is certainly obvious that he was not one of those who constructed or perpetuated the images of America popular with the followers of Horatio Alger, Jr., or Russell Conwell. Anderson had spent too many of his days "in the writing of advertisements for somebody's canned tomatoes"[9] to become, consciously or not, a booster, one who would "pile up words to confuse"[10] or to mislead. For Anderson, essence, not appearance, was reality; nevertheless, in attempting to define that essence, clearly and in detail, he became, consistently and eloquently, one of the compelling seekers of the American reality, one of its most dedicated interpreters, and one of the most dedicated and reverent makers of the American—indeed, the human—myth.

The recognition that Anderson was a mythmaker is not new; James Schevill wrestled tentatively with the idea in his biography in 1951,[11] as I did, more reluctantly, in my own study sixteen years later,[12] and more recently Benjamin Spencer has examined Anderson as "American Mythopoeist" in a moving essay in *American Literature*.[13] What is new, and what I intend to explore here, are the dimensions of his mythmaking and the deliberateness with which he defined and observed those dimensions, two vital aspects of the attempt to understand a literary artist, the goal of whose art and craft was the delineation of what he called the essence of things.

Central to this consideration of Anderson the delineator of the essence of things and Anderson the mythmaker is his own concept of the complex relationships among Sherwood Anderson, average American male, "a rather heavy-looking individual going along wearing a suit of clothes, socks, shoes, any amount of gent's furnishings";[14] Sherwood Anderson, storyteller, who "spends most of his time trying to get out of his system certain stories";[15] Sherwood Anderson, romantic wanderer, seeking to tap the roots of the American experience—his own, that of his father, and that of "that strange, grotesque, sweet man,"[16] Abraham Lincoln; Sherwood Anderson, townsman, possessed of the conviction that "we Ohio men have taken as lovely a land as ever lay outdoors and that we have, in our towns and cities, put the old stamp of ourselves on it for keeps";[17] and Sherwood Anderson, writer and former businessman, fascinated with his own escape from business, motivated by a belief that beyond escape one may find fulfillment, and convinced that his own story, his experience, reduced to its essence and then disseminated widely in whatever form that essence demands, might yet become the American story and ultimately the essence of the American experience.

Anderson the craftsman and Anderson the storyteller share with Walt Whitman a peculiar self-identity: that of the average man who, like Emerson's poet, is one with his fellows but whose eye is keener and intuition more sensitive and who consequently, at whatever cost, permits those of us who are not so gifted to see with his eyes beyond the immediate to whatever lies beyond. Thus, Anderson, with confidence in the face of increasing adverse criticism, proclaimed as early as the winter of 1923–24 that he was writing, in A Story Teller's Story and, by implication, in the canon of his works, "an autobiography of a man's fanciful life. In that," he insisted, "I have been more interested than in any account of facts."[18]

In Anderson's search for the "spirit of something," "the essence," the central incident in both his factual and his fanciful life was his decision, at age thirty-six, to leave his moderately successful business career, to earn his living in whatever undemanding way he could, and to pursue a career as a writer of fiction. These incidents, taking place over several months during the winter of 1912–13, have been recounted a number of times by Anderson's biographers as a series of confusing and intriguing but relatively uncomplicated events; they have also been used as the basis of much of Anderson's fiction, most notably Windy McPherson's Son, his first published novel; Poor White, his best novel; and the two novels that follow, Many Marriages and Dark Laughter. They are also the first manifestation of the fundamental myth that Anderson created, the myth of escape and fulfillment, a myth that dominated much of his work over nearly all of his literary career.

This myth as Anderson created it appears in three forms: that in the early fiction, roughly to 1923; that which appears in his accounts of "a man's fanciful life" in the autobiographical volumes written in the mid-1920s; and that which dominates both fiction and nonfiction during the last fifteen years of his life. The earlier form is both simpler and easier for his critics to understand or accept; the second has been almost uniformly overlooked; and the latter, in several forms, has become the most profound and most durable.

In *Windy McPherson's Son* the myth appears for the first time. In four phases, it carries the protagonist, Sam McPherson, through ambition, rejection, search, and fulfillment, a formula much more closely related to that developed by the great romantic poets of the nineteenth century than to the work of Anderson's contemporaries. It is also closely related to the faith that took generations of people from Europe to America, from the East to the West, and finally from the country to the city, a migration in which Anderson himself had participated.

The parallels between Sam's life and Anderson's own—the central image of the father, the role of the mother, the preoccupation with success, the nature of the town and the city—are more significant in many ways than the plot, but that plot was Anderson's first attempt to define the essence of what he believed had happened to him and to America as the pursuit of happiness became corrupted by the promise of material success. At the same time the plot suggests the ease with which he apparently hoped or perhaps even believed that a new, spiritual, and humane fulfillment might be found, a suggestion that, in the last Elyria and early Chicago years, those in which he wrote the novel, Anderson must have known was misleading if not downright fraudulent when accepted literally.

In spite of the fact that he recognized the weakness of the novel's optimistic conclusion—he rewrote the ending, with no more conclusiveness for the second, 1922 edition—he continued to permit the myth of rejection, of escape to fulfillment, to dominate his fiction. In *Marching Men* he depicts a bitter, headlong assault on the same perverted values that had misled Sam McPherson. The assault is both literal and metaphorical and, like Sam's rise to success, it is ultimately unsatisfactory. At the end Anderson took refuge in ambiguous oversimplification as the novel's protagonist, Beaut McGregor, and his wife deliberately chose the path composed of continued resistance, a threatened ultimate failure, and a promised personal fulfillment together.

Even *Winesburg, Ohio*, a major stylistic and structural advance over the first two novels, contains suggestions, however muted, of the same ambiguous promise: as George Willard, in the final sketch, "Departure," leaves the town, his apprenticeship served and his goal a vague success in the city, he goes West, not, however, to follow the setting sun, but to conquer Chicago; Winesburg (or Clyde or Elyria) had become for George not a source of satisfaction or fulfillment, frustration or oppression, but "a background upon which to paint the dreams of his manhood."[19] In its ambiguity the ending approaches a Twain-like purity, but at the same time it adds a further dimension to the myth, the dimension that had led George Willard, Sherwood Anderson, and hundreds of thousands of others to Chicago, among them Sister Carrie and Theodore Dreiser, Felix Foy and Floyd Dell, all from small Midwestern towns; later, it took Upton Sinclair's Jurgis from Lithuania; and still later, Bigger Thomas and Richard Wright from the black South. Each, whether creator or created, went confidently to a success that ultimately proved elusive or nonexistent.

Yet recognition, search, and success continued to be the fictional reality for Anderson, most notably in *Poor White*, *Many Marriages*, and *Dark Laughter*, the latter the last of his novels of escape. But in each of them Anderson's honesty and grasp of reality prevail; in each, a note of mockery is directed at those who find an easy fulfillment or, perhaps more accurately, believe that they have found it and move confidently to accept it. At the end of *Poor White*, as Hugh McVey and his wife move toward each other in acceptance and understanding, the factories whistle triumphantly, and what is left is ambiguous at best; at the conclusion of *Many Marriages*, John Webster remains trapped, his long explanation misunderstood (as it has been by Anderson's critics) and the woman at his side a stranger; and in *Dark Laughter*, as Bruce Dudley, the refugee from artistic liberation, elopes with his new-found love, the blacks laugh mockingly and wisely as they recognize the futility of escape.

## II

This, then, was the early nature of the myth Anderson created, a myth essentially romantic and yet real, based upon his own concept of what had happened to him and what might yet happen to America and Americans; this is also the myth that he gave widespread dissemination for the first time under the prosaic title "When I Left Business For Literature" in *Century* for August 1924, and a short time later, in identical words, in *A Story Teller's Story*;[20] at the same time it is the story of the beginning of his search for "the spirit of something," for the meaning of his own life and for his own identity in the context of the time and place that had given him purpose and direction.

As Anderson's biographers and critics have pointed out on many occasions and for many reasons, his accounts of his departure from his business career are pure fiction, accounts that are at once rational and mystic, contrived and intuitive. In terms reminiscent of the long explanation that occupies much of *Many Marriages*, Anderson describes the incident first of all as a moment of insight into himself and his father simultaneously:

> It came with a rush, the feeling that I must quit buying and selling, the overwhelming feeling of uncleanliness. It was in my whole nature a tale-teller. My father had been one, and his

not knowing had destroyed him. The tale-teller cannot bother with buying and selling. To do so will destroy him . . ."[21]

From this moment came the first impulse to escape:

There was a door leading out from my office to the street. How many steps to the door? I counted them, "five, six, seven." "Suppose," I asked myself, "I could take those five, six, seven steps to the door, pass out at the door, go along that railroad track out there, disappear into the far horizon beyond. Where was I to go? . . . I was still respected in the town, my word was still good at the bank. I was a respectable man.[22]

To Anderson, in retrospect a decade later, this moment was no less than a microcosm of the American experience:

The American is still a wanderer. . . . All of our cities are built temporarily. . . . We are on the way—toward what? . . . the American man has only gone in for moneymaking on a large scale to quiet his own restlessness . . . there is no time for unquiet thoughts.
On that day in the office at my factory I looked at myself and laughed. The whole struggle I am trying to describe, and that I am confident will be closer to the understanding of most Americans than anything else I have written, was accompanied by a kind of mocking laughter at myself and my own seriousness about it all . . .
. . . Any American will understand that.[23]

After his moment of insight, of his discovery of his own identity as a craftsman and as his father's son, of his recognition that his experience, in microcosm, was the American experience of his time, the rest of the account of the incident, that about which so much has been made in Anderson biography and criticism, that which became the foundation of what has been called the Anderson myth, is actually anticlimax in spite of its dramatic quality. First, Anderson records what is ostensibly an awareness that he must make a rational explanation to his secretary, to whom he had stopped dictating in the middle of a typical business-English sentence:

. . . Could I explain it all to her? The words of a fancied explanation marched through my mind.
"My dear young woman, it is all very silly, but I have decided no longer to concern myself with this buying and selling. It may be all right for others, but for me it is poison. There is this factory. You may have it, if it pleases you. It is of little value, I dare say. Perhaps it is money ahead, and then again it may well be it is money behind. I am uncertain about it all and now I am going away. Now, at this moment, with the letter I have been dictating, with the very sentence you have been

writing left unfinished, I am going out that door and never come back. What am I going to do? Well, now, that I don't know. I am going to wander about. I am going to sit with people, listen to words, tell tales of people, what they are thinking, what they are feeling. The devil! it may even be I am going forth in search of myself."[24]

So thoroughly imbued with the enchantment of that vision of his own personal escape did Anderson remain that five years after having left Elyria and the paint factory—five years of writing advertisements in Chicago as well as publishing two novels, a book of verse, and many of the stories that were to become *Winesburg, Ohio*—he still envisioned a future that was free, as he made clear in a letter to Van Wyck Brooks:

> God damn it, Brooks, I wish my books would sell for one reason. I want to quit working for a living and go wander for five years in our towns . . .[25]

A short time later, just before the success of *Winesburg, Ohio*, he wrote to Trigant Burrow in the same vein:

> . . . I hate to see the years and the days go by in the writing of advertisements for somebody's canned tomatoes or in long days of consulting with some fellow as to how he can sell his make of ready-made clothes instead of the other fellow. I want to go up and down the great valley here seeing the towns and the people and writing of [them] as I do not believe they have been written of.[26]

In spite of his remembered account of the event, the reality for Anderson in his office in Elyria, Ohio, in the late Fall of 1912 was not the promise of an escape into fulfillment, but it was the predicament of a middle-class family man, father of three children, the youngest only a year old, and it was the prospect—a prospect soon realized—of exchanging necessary enslavement in a business office in Elyria for necessary enslavement in an advertising office in Chicago. It was a prospect Anderson must have anticipated at the time, but as he recounted the escape a decade later, realization of another kind came to him at that moment:

> . . . There was wanted a justification of myself not to myself, but to the òthers. A crafty thought came. Was the thought crafty, or was I at the moment a little insane, a "nut," as every American so loves to say of every man who does something a little out of the groove . . .
> . . . What I did was to step very close to the woman and looking directly into her eyes, I laughed gaily. Others beside herself would, I knew, hear the words I was now speaking. I looked at my feet.
> "I have been wading in a long river, and my feet are wet," I said.

> Again I laughed as I walked lightly toward the door and out
> of a long and tangled phase of my life, out of the door of buy-
> ing and selling, out of the door of affairs . . .
>     . . . "My feet are cold, wet and heavy from long wading in a
> river. Now I shall go walk on dry land," I said, and as I passed
> out at the door a delicious thought came. "Oh, you tricky little
> words, you are my brothers. It is you, not myself, have lifted
> me over this threshold. It is you who have dared give me a
> hand. For the rest of my life I will be a servant to you," I
> whispered to myself, as I went along a spur of railroad track,
> over a bridge, out of a town, and out of that phase of my life.[27]

Nowhere in either account does Anderson suggest the series of incidents that followed—his disappearance and hospitalization in Cleveland, the inane accounts that appeared in the Elyria *Evening Telegram*
and the Elyria *Democrat*,[28] as well as those in the Cleveland *Press* and the
*Leader*[29] of his breakdown and his return to Elyria, the care with which
he wound up his affairs, and the deliberateness of his determination to
return to Chicago—once more to an advertising office as well as to a
liberation movement and a writing career. His break with business was
certainly not a literal break, although he implied clearly that it was.

But to Anderson the physical continuity was meaningless. The reality
of the move, that which he had tried to make clear in his fiction as well as
this allegedly factual account, had nothing to do with what he actually
did. The real break was spiritual and allegorical; not only did he never
again give a lasting allegiance to anything except his art and his craft, but
at the same time his experience became for him the archetypical experience of the artist, of the American, of the human being in the twentieth century, who must consciously reject materialism if he is to survive
and pursue his vision of happiness.

Although Anderson proclaimed to the end that he was a simple
townsman, an observer and teller of tales—just before the final trip in
March 1941, which ended with his death in a hospital in Panama, he explained that what he would like to do on that journey was to "get up into
some South American town, say of five to ten thousand people. . . . as far
as possible getting to understand a little their way of thinking and feeling,
and trying to pick up the little comedies and tragedies of their
lives . . .,"[30]—it is evident that from his departure from Elyria to the end
of his life his concern was for the spirit rather than the facts of what he
learned in his search, that through his art and his craft the facts would
then be transmitted into something a great deal more meaningful than
they were in their natural, limited settings.

### III

For the next seventeen years after publishing *A Story Teller's Story*—
to the end of his life in the midst of that fateful journey—Anderson sought

to define that essence, that spirit distilled from mere facts, and the result is a curious but significant unity in his work, a unity that he had intuitively pursued earlier but by 1924 had begun consciously to seek. During these years Anderson's attempt to define the myth underlying his own life and his country's experience takes on a new emphasis, not upon escape and an easy fulfullment, but upon the reality of a search that may never end.

That search, a continuation of the search that had begun with his acceptance of the necessity for rejecting materialism, for revolting from modern industrial America, more than a decade before, takes, from the time he wrote *A Story Teller's Story*, a distinctly different turn. No longer the attempt to portray a symbolic escape, it is, simultaneously, the search for the meaning of his own experience, that of Sherwood Anderson, his father's son, literary craftsman and teller of stories, and the meaning of American experience in his time. An attempt at fusion, at defining a microcosmic relationship between himself and his America, it was, in essence, the attempt to find a truth higher and more profound than that of mere fact and to find and define the spirit beyond fact. He had indeed defined his purpose in writing his spiritual autobiography, but at the same time, it became clear to him that that purpose was also to be the substance of his work from that point on. It was evident to him that the ultimate truth was not the act of rebellion but the search that followed, and that search became for him the substance of the ultimate meaning and myth of America.

The first attempts to define that essence were a curious pair of works: *Dark Laughter*, the ambitious novel that was as close to a best-selling commercial success as Anderson ever wrote, and *The Modern Writer* (1925), a brief, limited edition statement of faith. *Dark Laughter*, a work which came easily for Anderson, a book which "flows like a real river,"[31] as he wrote to Paul Rosenfeld while writing it during "days [which] have joy in them,"[32] has stylistic shortcomings that result from his shortlived search for a modern idiom, but it is an important book—important in Anderson's work and important to Anderson himself. Equally important in a different dimension is *The Modern Writer*, Anderson's first attempt to define the nature of his craft.

A transitional work between Anderson's early visions of escape and his definitions of the essence of his experience, *Dark Laughter*, is Anderson's fictional interpretation of the meaning—for him as well as for his time and place—of the Chicago Liberation, the movement that promised a fulfillment that it not only could not deliver but instead substituted for the old material enslavement a new kind of submission, a conformity as destructive of the individual as was the old materialism. To Anderson it had become clear that the revolution proclaimed by the Liberation was neither the answer to conformity nor the fulfillment sought; rebellion was but a beginning, an opportunity to construct a new, uncomplicated life, not among the sophisticates, those who seek freedom in a demeaning submission to values that, like those they protest, are extraneous and artificial, but among an uncomplicated, unpretentious people. The laughter of blacks in the background of the novel, the "dark laughter" of a natural freedom, stands in stark contrast to the factory whistles that echo throughout *Poor White*; while both are mocking, the whistles mark a mechanical superiority, but the laughter of the blacks is human, uncomplicated, simple, and close to the natural origins of life itself.

In effect, *Dark Laughter* is the rejection of rejection, the rejection of an easy answer to a complex search that had begun for Sherwood Anderson on the dusty main street of Clyde, Ohio, in the 1890s; for his father, Irwin, in his first visit South as an Ohio cavalryman thirty years before; and for Americans in general in the restless movement westward that carried them across an ocean and distributed them across a continent. For Anderson, for the first time, it was evident that rejection and rebellion were symptoms of a vision, a vision as subject to corruption as any other human endeavor, unless one was wary, and, with a clear idea of his origins, his identity, and his purpose, he was determined to be as wary in his work as the townsman on the midway at the county fair.

All this is evident in *The Modern Writer*, another microcosmic work. The "modern writer" he attempts to define is surely Sherwood Anderson, but it is also the archetypical American, now, for the first time, sure of himself. Echoes of Walt Whitman abound in his assertion that the writer is but another workman, differing only in that he is a workman "whose materials are human lives";[33] his goals must be honesty, must be "control over the tools . . . and materials of his craft."[34] Of most importance, it is evident that Anderson had learned the nature of fulfillment, an ideal and a reality not fixed but in constant flux, the fulfillment of the craftsman who rejects the mass-produced for a demanding, organic work that is in itself both fulfillment and reward: "You are undertaking a task," he asserts, "that can never be finished. The longest life will be too short to ever really get you anywhere near what you want."[35]

To Anderson at this point, work, identity, and purpose had become one, a mosaic, all of the pieces of which, however, he had not yet identified individually. But the totality of that mosaic was not merely his own life and work; it was clearly that of all the people of his time. For Anderson, as for Whitman and Emerson nearly a century before, it was evident that not only was life itself a continuous whole, but that beyond it lay truth. To Anderson, the writer's responsibility was to define that truth in work that laid bare, in increasing detail, the essence of experience. That essence, that "spirit of something," might never become entirely clear, even in several lifetimes, but the pursuit and partial delineation of it gave meaning and direction to life. Consequently, to Anderson, the craftsman, literary or other, shared, in perhaps a minor but never an insignificant way, in the creative process that has gone on from the beginning.

The fifteen years remaining in Anderson's life were years devoted to searching, examining, and attempting to gain understanding of himself, his time, and his experience as they reflected and were reflected in the world around him. His decision to locate himself permanently in western Virginia, to build the stone house at Ripshin Farm, to purchase and edit the town newspapers in Marion, are all reflected in the work that he produced during the rest of that decade.

In those writings between 1926 and 1930, he defines, in essence and in spirit, the experiences that had led him to self-discovery and to the discovery of the meaning of the American experience in his time. These works—*Tar: A Midwest Childhood* (1926), *Sherwood Anderson's Notebook* (1926), *A New Testament* (1927), *Hello Towns!* (1929), *Nearer the Grass Roots* (1929), *Alice and the Lost Novel* (1929), and *The American County Fair* (1930), the list a curious mixture of substantial, intense work and brief, limited, personal statements—are clear definitions of the spirit of the things that had affected him, shaped him, and directed him, the Americans of his generation and place in the Midwest, and those of a later generation in the South. In these works, clearly and for the first time, Anderson uses his own experience as the basis for an examination of the universal American experience of his time and our own.

The work of those years is rooted in simplicity—the simplicity of a Midwestern childhood and of small-town maturity—and in the conscious search for the spirit that gives that simplicity the dimensions of complexity and profundity. Of the works, *Tar* is the most important, the most effective, and the most durable, for at the same time that it explores the origins of the American experience, it creates a new dimension of the American myth and a myth of its own, that of the American childhood and the childhood of America, that of innocence and brutality combined and of the beginning of a search for a security and love that one knows in childhood and loses and tries forever to regain.

There is something of Freud in Anderson's delineation of the spirit of childhood, or perhaps, more properly, one may read something of Freud into it, but there is more of Emerson and even more of Whitman, who, like Anderson, saw in clearer detail and with deeper insight than most of their contemporaries. The attempt to recreate the growth of a boy "from the ages of consciousness and until adolescence begins,"[36] as Anderson comments on the jacket, *Tar* is also the record of the growth of human consciousness; it is, as he continues, "of course, autobiographical, as such a book would be bound to be, but it is not written as an autobiography."[37] As critics pointed out then and since, it defies an easy categorization.

As in *A Story Teller's Story*, Anderson is searching for the "spirit of something" that he had been seeking for so long. Consequently, some critics then and later insisted that he had lost whatever creative impulse he once had and was once again covering the same old ground, an unfortunate observation that has prevailed for too long, particularly because in a number of important ways *Tar* goes far beyond anything Anderson had attempted before in the search for origins of a myth that had misled him and his American contemporaries since the end of the Civil War.

In the book this myth is portrayed in ways quite different from those that influenced Sam McPherson in Anderson's first novel. McPherson was motivated by shame and by envy—shame for a father who was a failure in an age that worshipped success and envy for those who had learned to ride the crest of the times. As Sam's instinctive perceptions were focused by John Telfer, his vision was narrowed so that only success, a visible material success, had any significance. Nothing had any meaning except as an obstacle to be overcome or a tool to use in constructing a successful material reality.

However, *Tar* is neither a real nor an idealized portrait of a Midwest childhood, an America, or an era itself neither real nor idealized; it is an attempt to define the essence of simplicity, of innocence, and even of brutality, much as Anderson had defined these qualities in *Winesburg, Ohio*. However, at the end, Tar, the Midwestern child, is not moving out of that simplicity into an idealized, successful future, as was George Willard; instead he is hurrying into a twentieth century dedicated to hustling, to moneymaking, to the pursuit of a material ideal. The unthinking innocence, the omnipresent brutality, the simplicity itself are the very elements that not only permit the people of Winesburg, of the Midwestern childhood, to move into the new age, but they make it inevitable that the people of that childhood do so. As Anderson concludes the book, he defined clearly what has been the foundation of the myth that had, in three hundred years, led America from East to West and from innocence to corruption, the myth that he had devoted his life and work to refuting and replacing:

> A boy, if he is any good, has to be tending up to his job. He has to get up and hustle. . . . What he had to do was to bring into the family all the money he could. Heaven knows, they would need it all. He has got to tend up to his job.
>
> These the thoughts in Tar Moorhead's head as he grabbed his bundle of newspapers and, wiping his eyes on the back of his hand, raced away up the street.
>
> Although he did not know it Tar was, at that very moment perhaps, racing away out of his childhood.[38]

At the end of *Winesburg, Ohio*, when George Willard boarded the train to move westward with the setting sun, westward to Chicago, the Mecca for thousands of Midwestern farm boys, he neither noticed that the train had moved on, and "the town of Winesburg had disappeared and his life there had become but a background on which to paint the dreams of his manhood,"[39] nor felt the impetus that motivated Tar—the specter of hunger and the glitter of success. Neither Tar nor George represent for Anderson either reality or idealization; they represent instead competing myths, those of the craftsman-artist and the successful moneymaker, myths that had come to a stormy confrontation in his own life, a conflict that he had finally, in middle age, been able to resolve.

That resolution is celebrated in *A New Testament*, enthusiastic if

technically deficient verse prose, and in *Hello Towns!*, the product of his
venture into rural journalism. In both, Anderson celebrates his newly accepted identity as artist-craftsman-townsman-editor, as well as one who
had learned that his experience and the American experience had been
one and would become so again. In *A New Testament*, he writes,

> I double my fists and strike the ground a sharp blow.
> Ridges of land squirt out through my fingers.
> I have remade the land of my fathers. I have come out
> of my house to remake the land.
> I have made a flat place with the palms of my hands.[40]

In *Hello Towns!*, designed to portray the life of the town as it passes
through the year's cycle, the pulse of its life recorded in the pages of his
papers, he writes again,

> Yesterday I drove my car down a street of our town I had
> never been on before. I did not know the street was there. Men
> hailed me. Women and children were sitting on doorsteps. "It
> is our editor."
> "Well, you have been a long time getting down here."
> When I drive on a country road in this county farmers or
> their wives call to me. "Come in and get some cider, a basket of
> grapes, some sweet corn for dinner." The women of the town
> and county keep the print shop fragrant with flowers.
> I have a place in this community. How difficult to feel that
> in the city.[41]

With the complexities of his own identity and those of his time and
place firmly behind him, Anderson devoted his life to his work: the search
for the "spirit of something" in works that define the continuing conflict
that he had resolved but that America had not yet learned to understand.
Thus his works alternate between exercises in celebration and myth-
making at their purest—*The American County Fair, Alice and the Lost
Novel, Nearer the Grass Roots, Death in the Woods* (1933), *No Swank*
(1934), and, at the end of his life, *Home Town*, and the *Memoirs*, unfinished and twice edited since his death—and the works that grew out of
his recognition that materialism and industrialism had failed—*Perhaps
Women* (1931), *Beyond Desire* (1932), *Puzzled America* (1935), *Kit Brandon* (1936), all mythmaking of another sort, statements of regret but at
the same time of the human potential for a rediscovery of origins and
renewal of values. At the heart of them is a new image, a new mythical
hero or heroine who, Anderson was certain, would one day lead America
out of its confused present and forward into its living past, the past of
values still surviving, still strong in spite of the industrial-material complex whose weak foundations and inadequate framework had led to
economic collapse.

This myth-image is a fusion of Anderson's past and his present; it is made of the mother who had dreamed her dreams for George Willard and had rubbed the chapped hands of Tar Moorhead, and of the women whose innocence, like that of Helen White, whose earthiness, like that of Louise Trunnion, and whose wisdom, like that of Clara Butterworth, fuse with the girls from the southern hills, the mill girls, the country girls, those who seek to use rather than to be used by the values and machinery that had already corrupted American men.

Anderson's first visions of this new myth-image—certainly not an earth-mother but a person of innate wisdom, strength, grace, and inner beauty—are in "Alice," the story of an East Tennessee mountain girl grown into a woman of the world, and in "Elizabethton, An Account of a Journey." In the former he defines the true beauty of a woman—that inner strength and love that permits her to give generously of herself and yet remain herself, and in the latter, after a tour of the mills, he observes the town's shoddy monument in the square and comments, "How I would have liked to see one of those delicately-featured, hard-bodied little mountain girls, done in stone by some real artist standing up there."[42]

The image recurs, expanded and fully fleshed, as Doris Hoffman in *Beyond Desire*, as the central figure in *Kit Brandon*, as the old woman of the title story that opens the collection *Death in the Woods* and in the young girl in "Brother Death," the story that closes it. She is the composite of the women of whom Anderson might have been thinking, as he wrote, in one of the last letters he wrote before embarking for South America and death,

> . . . I have been very fortunate. A surprising number of very great people I have known have been women, not young, inexperienced women, but women who have been ground by life and fate into something very shining and beautiful.[43]

The chaos of materialism out of control, as vividly portrayed in *Beyond Desire* as in *Puzzled America*, has nevertheless the potential to become something different, something old and yet new, into which the innate strength that Anderson sees still existing in America—in women, but in men, too—might yet take us. This is the world that he portrays in *Home Town* and in portions of the *Memoirs*, a world symbolically rather than literally that of the small town, a world that prefers a simple, close—although far from perfect—way of life to that dominated by impersonality and greed.

This way of life was certainly that of the past, Anderson knew, and it was threatened in the towns where it could still be found. But at the same time it continued to survive, and, as Anderson made clear in his last major effort at defining the "spirit of something" in his *Memoirs* (much of which he wrote and thought of as "Rudolph's Book of Days," a far less prosaic title), it could be discovered, in space and time but also, most importantly, in one's self, if he were willing to pay the price of wandering, searching, and suffering, even of public ridicule, that that discovery demanded.

## IV

Shortly after Anderson's death on March 8, 1941, Burgess Meredith introduced a radio drama presented by the Free Company, founded by Anderson and others earlier that year. The drama, "Above Suspicion," was to have been written by Sherwood Anderson, but it was unfinished at his death. In his introductory comments, Meredith said,

> . . . For thirty years Sherwood Anderson represented a vital part of the United States, the America of the small town. He was never fooled about our small town life; he saw its ugliness and pettiness and limitations, but he was never fooled about its good side either. He saw its beauty too; its courage and its never ending struggle for a freer life. Not only in his work did Anderson stand for freedom, he stood for it in his life. He was kind and gentle, he was the easy-going friendly American with everybody he met. But there was nothing soft about this friendliness. When it came to justice for the oppressed, to freedom for all in equal measure, nothing could move him. He was poor, he was not always well, but he was always ready to give himself for a juster, a fairer, a more honest world.[44]

Meredith might have added, and we surely must, that the essence of Anderson's dedication to human freedom, the goal of his personal search and that of the people about whom he wrote with wisdom and compassion, was that freedom about which Meredith spoke. And he might have added, as we surely must, that the "spirit of something" that Anderson defined so clearly, that which emerged from his own history and that of his time, is, as myth must be, the substance of concern—for himself, for the people in his life, and for those about whom he wrote. Anderson's mythical world, complex and yet simple, clear and yet profound, is the story, to paraphrase Northrop Frye, of the origin, the situation, and the destiny of the America of which Anderson was so intrinsically a part. And, if we continue to muddle through, to avoid a self-destruction either nuclear or narcotic, we may yet discover, as did Sherwood Anderson, the "spirit of something," that is, the reality that we have sought for the two hundred years since America became a nation and throughout the century in which Anderson lived and the continuing life of his work. And as long as that search goes on, the search, as Anderson well knew, that is the substance of human life, Anderson's works will be read and their meaning and significance will be clear and relevant. Myth and reality, fused and clearly defined, the essence of meaning in human life and the substance of Anderson's works, are the substance, too, of a literary reputation more secure than ever before as we observe the passage of a century since his birth.

## Notes

1. Anderson, *Letters*, edited by Jones and Rideout, p. 129.

2. Knowledge of this book depends on Anderson's testimony and Cornelia Anderson's memory. See Sherwood Anderson, *Memoirs* (New York: Harcourt, Brace, 1942), p. 186, and Sutton, *The Road to Winesburg*, p. 373.

3. Sherwood Anderson, *A Story Teller's Story* (New York: B. W. Huebsch, Inc., 1924), pp. 383, 78, 100.

4. Northrop Frye, "Literature and Myth," in James Thorpe, ed., *Relations of Literary Study* (New York: Modern Language Association of America, 1967), p. 40.

5. Ibid.

6. Lord Raglan, "Myth and Ritual," in Thomas A. Sebeok, ed., *Myth: A Symposium* (Bloomington: Indiana University Press, 1974), p. 122.

7. Irving Howe, *Sherwood Anderson* (London: Methuen & Co. Ltd., 1951), p. 143.

8. Ibid., p. 250.

9. *Letters*, p. 45.

10. Sherwood Anderson, "My Word to You," in United Factories Company catalogue for Oct. 1906, p. 5.

11. See James Schevill, *Sherwood Anderson: His Life and Work* (Denver: University of Denver Press, 1951), pp. 101–08, 348–51.

12. See David D. Anderson, *Sherwood Anderson*, pp. 163–73.

13. Benjamin Spencer, "Sherwood Anderson: American Mythopoeist," *American Literature* 41 (Mar. 1969): 1–18.

14. Sherwood Anderson in "Among Our Contributors," *The Century Magazine* 108 (Aug. 1924): n.p.

15. Ibid.

16. *Letters*, p. 121.

17. *Sherwood Anderson's Notebook*, p. 91.

18. "Among Our Contributors," n.p.

19. Sherwood Anderson, *Winesburg, Ohio* (New York: B. W. Huebsch, 1919), p. 303.

20. The account appears on pp. 489–96 in *The Century* CVIII, and on pp. 298–313 in *A Story Teller's Story*.

21. *A Story Teller's Story*, p. 308; *The Century*, p. 494.

22. *A Story Teller's Story*, p. 304; *The Century*, p. 494.

23. *A Story Teller's Story*, pp. 309–10; *The Century*, pp. 494–95.

24. *A Story Teller's Story*, p. 311; *The Century*, p. 465.

25. *Letters*, p. 31.

26. Ibid., p. 45.

27. *A Story Teller's Story*, pp. 312–13; *The Century*, pp. 495–96.

28. The Elyria *Evening Telegram*, Dec. 2, 1912, p. 1; Ibid., Dec. 3, 1912, p. 1; the Elyria *Democrat*, Dec. 26, 1912, p. 5; ibid. Feb. 6, 1913, p. 5; Ibid., Feb. 13, 1913, p. 8.

29. The Cleveland *Press*, Dec. 2, 1912, p. 2; the Cleveland *Leader*, undated (Dec. 3, 1912?) clipping in the Sherwood Anderson Collection, Newberry Library.

30. *Letters*, p. 465.

31. Ibid., p. 130.

32. Ibid.

33. Sherwood Anderson, *The Modern Writer* (San Francisco: Gelber, Lilienthal, Inc., 1925), p. 29.

34. Ibid., pp. 31–32.

35. Ibid., p. 44.

36. On the jacket of the Bonibooks edition.

37. Ibid.

38. Sherwood Anderson, *Tar: A Midwest Childhood* (New York: Boni and Liveright, 1926), pp. 345–46.

39. *Winesburg, Ohio*, p. 303

40. Sherwood Anderson, *A New Testament* (New York: Boni and Liveright, 1927), p. 39.

41. Sherwood Anderson, *Hello Towns!* (New York: Horace Liveright, 1929), pp. 335–36.

42. Sherwood Anderson, *Nearer the Grass Roots* (San Francisco: The Westgate Press, 1929), p. 35.

43. *Letters*, p. 467.

44. In *The Free Company presents*, James Boyd, compiler and chairman (New York: Dodd, Mead & Company, 1941), p. 270. Meredith served as narrator in each of the plays in the series.

# MANUSCRIPT FACSIMILES

Buckeye Blues

The newspaper man called it the Buckeye Blues but it wasn't just

Ohio. It was something large loose and curiously alive in the air

of the middlewest,crowds in the streets in the cities,the big farms,

the great stretches of farm land...this put against what I had for a *through Indiana,*

long time been seeing in the East and South. Coming up from Ohio and

into Chicago on the grey fall days I had seen a combine at work in a

grain field. *man in the fields making things tight against the winter. You had the sense of full barns, real wealth and you*

Before that the flat fields,miles of them. You began thinking of *in other places you had been in. For example in the upper and lower South*

men trying to farm for profit against in the hill country. *There were the*

*(over)*

It is true that,in some of the Ohio and Indiana towns,I had seen,too

many empty silent factories. *over in fancy* I was back home,in the middlewest I had

known so well,fifteen,eighteen years ago. "There must be thousands of

people who have gone broke here." After all a man wants people to have

things,big houses,if they want them,warm rich clothes,the comforts of *the factories can make*

life." You get the feeling,traveling about America,and this particu-

larly in the middlewest...it is so rich,so big,the farms are so easiky

worked...If you are an old Ohioan you remember back to other times of *and other*

depressions.

Then you remember also the quick sharp recovery,the coming of the boom

years in Ohio,Indiana and Illinois,oil and gas being discovered,the

factories when they came crowding in. Your mind goes away back...why

it isn't so long ago,*that* the towns were such isolated places. To go

from one town to another,a matter of ten miles,was a great event.

Then suddenly everything began to open up. The bicycle came,quickly

followed by the automobile. You also,as a boy saved your *money* and

got an automobile byoicle. You joined a club known as the Century

Club. To get in you had to travel,on a bidle,a hundred miles in twen-

ty-four hours. You did it,not once but again and again,pushing your

safety bicycle

From the Sherwood Anderson Papers, The Newberry Library, Chicago, Ill. Published by permission of Eleanor Anderson.

grimly along through the deep sand of dirt roads, up hills...you rested
as you coasted down. They gave you a chain to wear, a link added for
everytime you accomplished the heroic feat. "There, I've done it again." You
had to keep going, sometimes, all day and into the night, but how proudly
you wore the chain. I remember a boy who faked it. He began wearing
a chain of fifteen links, we all knew he hadn't earned, and with what contempt we looked upon him. It wasn't just that he was selling out the
rest of us. He was selling out a whole civilization.

For, in the middlewest, we did so believe. "See, we are marching on."
In my town there was a photographer who was great fellow for books and
he got Bellamy's Looking Backward and took some four or five of us, boys
of the town, into an arbor in his back yard. He read to us from the
book. "There it is. That's what we are going toward."

There was this faith in the physical development of life, first the bicycle, then the automobile, the the airplane. The towns grew so rapidly.
Some did and some didn't. There began that great movement that went on
for so long, the going away from the land.

And why hadn't it all turned out better?

"Oh," said the Ohio newspaper man, "you've got 'em. You've got the Buckeye
Blues." He thought it was because, in coming back to Ohio, and to other
middlewestern states, loafing about in them for a time, I had raked up old
dreams, got as a boy from the men about me. "There's no use your coming
back here to preach a funeral service over us."

The Ohio man, the newspaper man, had been taking me about. He ~~spoke of
things to me,~~ introduced me to men, to politicians, merchants, labor leaders and workers. I don't know why I had got into the blue mood but he xxx
shook me out of it a little and I was grateful to him. Again he made
me feel a thing I am always forgetting and always trying to remember.

It is just I think that man isn't defeated in America. You get out
of the cities and into the towns again. It's good. There was a dream of
~~that he is always defeat-~~ ~~ed. xxx~~ what the machine, the factories could mean when they
came. It's a good deal busted. The

3

dreams was
dreams were such splendid things and I have this sharp impression of
boyhood and young manhood in the Middlewest, that the Middlewesterners
xxxxxxxxxxxx were then...the newspaper man thought they were yet....
great dreamers.

It is only, at best, a broken fragmentary impression you get by going
about in this way, talking to individuals. I went with the newspaper reporter
fellow to meet a lot of other men but after a time we gave that up. We
sat in a place where beer was sold. xxxxxxxxx
        We spoke of
Of the New Deal of course. He was a man whose work took him into
all kinds of places. He said that he thought that what everyone wanted was some kind of belief. "They are determined to believe that
                                              now
Roosefelt is all right", he said.    The strength of the man, with all
kinds of people, lay in the fact that he never gave the impression of
thinking himself infalible. Was there much real radicalism? He didn't
think there was but there was a growing curiosity, an eagerness. He had
been a newspaper man in Ohio during the Harding & Coolridge administra-
tion. "There wasn't any interest in government at all. It was dead.
Now everywhere it had come to life again."  "Formerly, when I first became a newspaper man in Ohio, and if I had met you....when I was a young
reporter you were already well known in Ohio as a tale teller...
                                                     writer

He pointed out that he, like most newspaper reporters, had tried to
write a novel. "I tackled a play too," he said. "Now, I swear,
I'm not interested."

"If we had met at any time before the depression hit us we would
have talked of nothing but writing. Now you writers have got it too.
You can't let politicts alone."

He was glad that I was doing what I was doing, going about, trying
to look and listen. I thought him a pretty keen fellow as I think most
newspaper men keen and after we had a beer or two and he tried to get

4

at what he himself believed I found that he was, as I ~~believe~~ think most Americans still are, esswentially a democrat. "This idea that you can solve
anything as big and complex as government by a definate formula is pretty absurd,"he said. He began telling me about Ohio, the new Senator, who
had ~~been~~ defeated the republic Fess, Donehy, who had been three times gov-
enor of Ohio. He told me the baked potato story, of how Donehy, when he
was state auditor had fouhd, in the expense account of a state official
an item of seventy-five cents for a potato and had made that baked potato famous. As for Donehy he was a shrewd man and had caught the fancy
of the voters because they thought he was honest. He hadn't been strong
for Roosevelt but ~~xxx~~ during the campaign he had pretty much stayed at
home, not making many speeches while the men running for congress and
the speekers going through the country all did put it up to the voters'
that they were voting for or against Roosevelt.

"There was," the Ohio newspaper man thought, a something, not very definate they were voting for. It wasn't just an individual.

"Well then, what was it,"that what I want to know?"I demanded and he
thought that by their votes the people of Ohio and of all the Middlewestern states were voting a willingness to experiment.

"That's just it,"he said,"a willingness to experiment, not too fast.

"Don't think,"he said that Roosevelt's pull with the people is all
in his smile or in the charm of person they talk about. And it isn't
in his voice, although they have all heard it over the radio. It is just
that they think he is willing to go about as far as they are willing to
go and not much futher.

"And that's what democracy is, isn't it,"the newspaper man said. He
thought that the average man, of the middlewest was pretty far from wanting to give up democracy.

.............................

I had got in with a man, met casually on ~~thxxxtxxxt~~ a street of a certain Ohio Town. There was a long freight train grinding slowly across the road at a place where there was no grade crossing and ~~hxx~~ his car pulled up close beside mine. We both leaned out at our car windpws and a conversation began.

It was the Virginia liscence on my car. "I've been down there," he said and began telling me of a grandfather who lived near Lynchburg Virginia.

The conversation begun this continued after the train passed

**RiPSHiN FARM** TROUTDALE, VA.

May 19, 1939

Mr. Sidney Hook
48 Grove Street
New York, New York

Dear Sidney Hook:

I sincerely hope the New York
Times publishes the letter from you, a
copy of which was sent to me today. When
I signed the paper you sent me, I took it
to be merely a sort of declaration in favor
of Cultural Freedom, and I was amazed to
find it had been given another twist.

Personally I have been unable to keep
up with the exact purpose of all the groups
now working, I am sure sincerely, for intellectual freedom. I think of myself as
primarily a story teller and a man not very
politically minded. And for that reason,
certainly not competent to attack the intent of any of these groups.

Sincerely yours,

Sherwood Anderson

From the David D. Anderson Collection. Published by permission of
Eleanor Anderson

# RiPShiN FARM TROUTDALE, VA.

Monday

Dear Sidney Hook

I was pleased to get your letter. Of course
I knew that the newspaper thing was distorted.
Just the same I think I won't go on the com-
mittee. I am leaving for the country in a few days
now. In the past I have gone on too many committees
and then have done nothing. Controversies start. People keep calling me up, wanting me to sign this and
that.

Truth is my own absorption is in just people. The
political slant only confuses me. When I feel there
is real danger of a dictatorship here I'll get in.
I want to avoid more and more this half getting
into things.

I'm really fed up on being a stuffed shirt, Hook.

Most sincerely

Sherwood Anderson

# INDEX

(All references to Sherwood Anderson's works will be found under his name)